SCALE OF KILOMETRES

*Heights are given in Metres and Feet*
*Points triangulated by Survey of India, thus*
*Camera Stations, thus*          *Intersected points, thus*
*Route and Camps in Red*

from the photographic
India, on the Mount Everest
Hari Singh on the Expedition
ree expeditions. ¶ Reproduced
Royal Geographical Society
nce Survey, 1925.

# THE FIGHT FOR
# EVEREST
## 1924

# THE FIGHT FOR
# EVEREST
## 1924

BY LIEUTENANT COLONEL
E.F. NORTON, D.S.O.
AND OTHER MEMBERS
OF THE EXPEDITION

NEW EDITION
WITH FOREWORD BY DOUG SCOTT CBE

Published by Vertebrate Publishing, Sheffield.
www.v-publishing.co.uk

# THE FIGHT FOR
# EVEREST
## 1924

The Fight for Everest: 1924 first published in 1925 by Edward Arnold & Co.

This edition first published in 2015 by Vertebrate Publishing.

 Vertebrate Publishing
Crescent House, 228 Psalter Lane, Sheffield S11 8UT.
**www.v-publishing.co.uk**

Cover illustration: Everest from the north-east, showing the east face of the mountain.
Painted by Norton from near Jikkyop, about sixty miles away.

A CIP catalogue record for this book is available from the British Library.

Front endpaper: Mount Everest and the Group of Chomo Lungma map from the original 1925 edition.
Rear endpaper: The route from Darjeeling to Everest and The Everest Region: The Rest Period Itineraries.
Maps on rear endpaper and page XIV copyright © Christopher Norton 2015.

ISBN: 978-1-910240-39-7 (Hardback)
ISBN: 978-1-910240-40-3 (Ebook)

Every effort has been made to obtain the necessary permissions
with reference to copyright material, both illustrative and quoted.
We apologise for any omissions in this respect and will be pleased
to make the appropriate acknowledgements in any future edition.

 Design and production by Jane Beagley.
Vertebrate Graphics Limited.
**www.v-graphics.co.uk**

Vertebrate Publishing is committed to printing on paper from sustainable sources.

MIX
Paper from
responsible sources
FSC® C013056
FSC
www.fsc.org

Printed and bound in the UK by T.J. International Ltd, Padstow, Cornwall.

# CONTENTS

# PREFACE TO THE
# 2015 EDITION

This definitive account of the 1924 Everest expedition by Edward Norton and others was published the following year. It has never previously had a reprint in this country. We feel that the time is right to correct this state of affairs. There is still a surprising amount of interest in those pioneering expeditions of the early 1920s, fanned in part by the sixty-year celebration in 2013 of the mountain's first ascent. This interest is perhaps focused especially on the 1924 expedition, partly because of the enduring mystery of what happened to George Mallory and Andrew Irvine in their ill-fated summit attempt; partly, also, because on this expedition Edward Norton, who has been described as the greatest of the pre-war Everest expedition leaders, personally achieved – with Howard Somervell in close support – a world altitude record without oxygen that was not to be exceeded for fifty-four years.

Hitherto, those wishing to read the story of this expedition have largely had recourse to later accounts, since copies of the original volume are now very hard to come by. Excellent though some of those later accounts are – with Wade Davis's *Into the Silence* deserving special mention – we should like the original version of the story to be available to readers as well. The idea of a new edition has been enthusiastically endorsed by the families of all the other contributors to the book whom we were able to contact.

As a special feature of this edition we are privileged that one of Britain's greatest living mountaineers, Doug Scott – who famously made the first ascent of Everest by its very hard south-west face with Dougal Haston in 1975, when they became the first Britons to stand on the summit – has contributed a new foreword, in which he sets the achievements of 1924 in a wider context.

The text of the first edition is reproduced in its entirety, as are all the original illustrations, though in a new arrangement which corresponds more closely to the text. Some extra illustrations have been added from material which was kept by Edward Norton himself and which has been preserved by the family. These include some original letters and other documents, such as Mallory's note to Norton sent down from Camp V announcing the failure of his first summit attempt with Geoffrey Bruce. There is also a selection of Norton's watercolours and pencil sketches from the 1924 expedition.

The full set of his sketches and his diaries from both the 1922 and 1924 Everest expeditions have recently appeared in another volume: *Everest Revealed – The Private Diaries and Sketches of Edward Norton, 1922–24*, edited by Christopher Norton and published in 2014 by The History Press. This forms in a sense a companion volume to the present book.

Finally, we should like to record that any royalties from the present volume are to go to the Mount Everest Foundation, for its work in supporting mountain exploration and science.

*Dick Norton*
*Bill Norton*
*Hugh Norton*
*Christopher Norton*

# FOREWORD

## BY DOUG SCOTT, CBE

It is wonderfully satisfying to read a ninety-year-old account of a mountain climb and to completely identify with all that the authors have written. Here in this reprint of *The Fight for Everest: 1924* is the sum total of knowledge gained from the first three attempts to reach the highest place on the planet, in 1921, 1922 and 1924.

This was the last of the most extreme environments left for man to explore – later termed 'the third pole': where the oxygen level near the summit is two-thirds less than that at sea level, so high as to be well into the westerly jet stream for most of the year, where the depleted oxygen and the chill factor mean that only the strongest men can bear the cold of the altitude, where you must be always alert to the dangers of frostbite and hypothermia as fingers of cold sap the strength from the body's core.

Every day moving above Base Camp the climbers suffered from the UV light reflected off the snows that blistered skin, cracked lips and caused the unwary painful snow blindness. The cold, dry air frequently caused hacking coughs, sore throats and laryngitis, especially at extreme altitude. One terrible strain on the bodies of these men was dehydration on a scale never before experienced, due to the extreme height, the constant panting for oxygen and the cold, dry air which drew liquid from each breath. Food is often discussed, as is loss of appetite, but the vital importance of re-hydration is rarely mentioned – Norton's otherwise excellent summary of the climb does not discuss it and Hingston's chapter on physiology only does so in passing. The importance of liquid intake was not fully realised until Griffith Pugh convinced the Everest expedition of 1953 to make re-hydration a priority.

In other respects a great deal of new information was gathered and disseminated for the benefit of future attempts on Everest and all other Himalayan peaks. The big and intriguing question was that of acclimatisation. Even before the first attempt on Everest, experiments had been conducted from balloons. On one occasion in 1875, of the three men involved, one passed out and two others died on reaching 28,000 feet. Other experiments were later carried out by the RAF from biplanes and on the ground by the Aberdonian chemist and most experienced Himalayan climber of his day, Alexander Kellas. He made many useful observations, including the fact that the slower the acclimatisation, the longer deterioration is delayed. Somervell in 1922 was a good example of this, and none was more so than Odell in 1924 when, after a very slow acclimatisation at the beginning of the expedition, he went on to spend over two weeks above 23,000 feet, going twice up to Camp VI in support of Mallory and Irvine. On the last occasion he used oxygen, 'but the effect seemed almost negligible: perhaps it just allayed a trifle the tire in one's legs ... I switched the oxygen off and experienced none of those feelings of collapse and panting that one had been led to believe ought to result.'

It was also observed that those men who had been high on Everest before acclimatised more rapidly than those at high altitude for the first time. In 1924 all the old timers were unanimous in finding that they slept better, their minds were clearer, they had more of an appetite and they were generally fitter than the fresh recruits. This was to be subsequently borne out by later Everest expeditions.

The question of using oxygen was not, in 1924, such an ethical consideration as it had been in 1922, but was more a matter of whether it would be of practical help or not. Would the weight of the bottles, not to mention the time and organisation involved in their transport and use, outweigh the benefits of their contents? Despite the practical help experienced by Finch and Bruce using oxygen in 1922, there were still doubts over its usefulness at the beginning of the 1924 expedition and even more so at the end, since Norton had reached over 28,000 feet without oxygen. The debate continues on this one, except among those who have experienced high altitude with and also without canned oxygen. In my opinion, given time to properly acclimatise, those that are reasonably adaptable will find it wonderful to be up high with just a 'butty bag' on their backs, free of the encumbrance of oxygen bottles and fittings.

It would be some time before climbers improved on clothing and equipment, could borrow from the experience of the polar explorers, and gain from the invention of nylon and energy-efficient stoves. In many other respects lessons were learned and recommendations made for the future, neatly summed up in Colonel Norton's chapter 'Future Possibilities'. The way was now known and tested up to within 1,000 feet of the summit. Norton's recommended route which he and Somervell followed was more or less that taken by Reinhold Messner in 1980, albeit during the monsoon and solo. With all the experience gained on these first three expeditions, the effective use of porters, the siting of camps and the best way to acclimatise were now understood. With only a little refinement all these discoveries have withstood the test of time. The only unknown for which the Everest pioneers had no satisfactory answer was how to predict the weather.

In those days, before satellite phone contact with meteorological experts and weather stations, the early Everest expeditions had very little idea of what to expect. Every day the outcome was uncertain, which is why perhaps we can identify with these men pushing the limits of endurance on the virgin flanks of Everest. Our ancestors for thousands of generations had faced up to uncertainty on a daily basis, which is why it has a familiar taste for all of us; even if everyone can't climb Everest, we can understand a little of why men climb high, or push out across hot deserts and polar wastes. This is why the majority of people who go to lectures on climbing Everest or who will read this book are not themselves mountaineers.

So this book reveals how it was thought best to climb Everest next time. Younghusband in his excellent introduction states that the loss of Mallory and Irvine did not deter efforts to climb Everest, since even before the team returned home it recorded 'the unanimous wish … that the attempt should be renewed'. The public too was enthused at the prospect of trying Everest again. The outcome 'has roused the spirit of men and women in every country … and Mallory and Irvine will for ever live among the great who have helped to raise this spirit of man.'

How do such men as Mallory stay motivated and focused despite all the hardships listed in this book? What drives men to forever look around the next corner, to go where no one has gone before, embarking on such noble and heroic deeds? Is it of intrinsic interest at the time or is it a quest to be immortalised, talked of and written about for years after – in a way, to have cheated death, since the names of such people live on for eternity? The reader will know better for having read *The Fight for Everest: 1924*.

*Doug Scott*
*Cumbria, April 2013*

# PUBLISHER'S NOTE – 2015

In preparing this new edition of Colonel Norton's book it became quite clear that to edit the work so as to match our current – and modern – house style would not be appropriate. This work, a ninety-year-old text – the record of the third expedition to Everest – is a snapshot of a particular moment in time and it is entirely sensible to preserve much of the original formatting and language which contributes in no small way to the content and appeal of the book. A handful of factual corrections which Norton pencilled into the margins of his own copy of the book have been incorporated into the text. Otherwise, we have sought to faithfully reproduce the original 1925 text – inconsistencies, unusual and outdated spellings, limited typographical errors, and so on – with the minimum of editing. The book is richer for it and we hope it will help transport readers back to a time before the highest mountain on Earth – indeed, any of the fourteen 8,000-metre peaks – had been climbed.

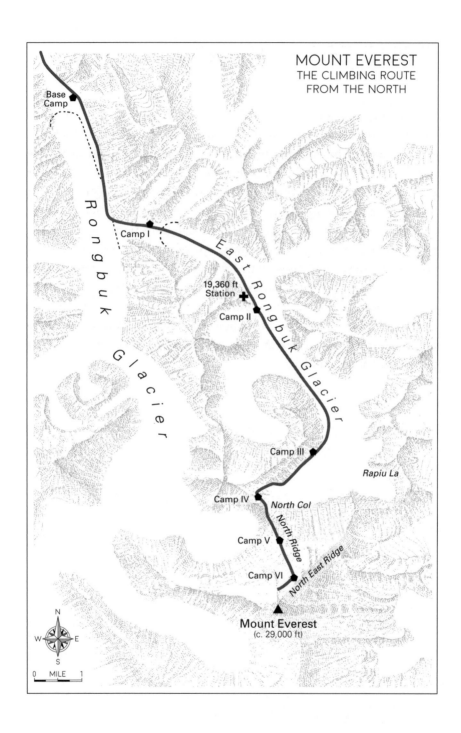

Mount Everest, the climbing route from the north. The 1922 expedition established Base Camp and Camps I–V; Camp VI was established by Norton and Somervell during the 1924 summit attempt.

# THE FIGHT FOR
# EVEREST
## 1924

## ACKNOWLEDGMENT FROM THE 1925 EDITION

Since their return from Mount Everest the members of the Expedition have had many calls upon their leisure, but they have willingly responded to the request of the Mount Everest Committee that they should describe the part that they severally took in the great adventure; and the Committee desires cordially to thank them for the sacrifices they have made in order that a full account may be offered to the public.

*June, 1925.*

# INTRODUCTION TO THE 1925 EDITION

## BY SIR FRANCIS YOUNGHUSBAND, KCSI, KCIE

This book is the record of a repulse. Mallory and Irvine may possibly have reached the summit; but they have not lived to tell us. And besides these two English lives, one Scottish and nine Indian lives have also been lost in assaulting Mount Everest. The repulse has been cruel. Yet the pain has not diminished the determination of man to conquer the mountain: it has increased it. And the men who are most determined are not we who stay at home and watch the struggle from afar; they are the assailants themselves: they are the men who have reached nearest the summit and have stood the hardest buffetings and faced the gravest dangers. Long before they knew what was in the minds of people at home, Colonel Norton had recorded in a dispatch in *The Times* the unanimous wish of the whole Expedition that the attempt should be renewed. And among the public generally there is a distinctly firmer determination to prosecute the project than there was when the idea was first mooted. At that time the public took very little interest in it. Douglas Freshfield, Bruce, Collie, Longstaff, and a few others who had actually climbed in the Himalaya, had for long dreamed of climbing Everest whenever political conditions made it possible to get at the mountain. But beyond the Alpine Club, and in a lesser degree the Royal Geographical Society, little interest was taken in the project, and a combined appeal from the Presidents of the two bodies to the general public produced only £10.

Very different is the feeling now. There are of course still many – very many – who do not care a rap whether Everest is climbed or not. There are others who think the expenditure of thousands of pounds on these expeditions is a great waste of money. And there are a few who think it positively wicked to throw away human life on so useless an enterprise. Still, the number of those who do see some value in these efforts has greatly increased. And in the hope that it may still further increase we may once more review what we expect to get from these efforts.

And first we must sum up what we have already gained.

When these expeditions to Mount Everest were first started it was still very problematical whether man could sustain himself at extreme altitudes, and, if he could just sustain himself, whether he could survive the exertion of climbing. With great difficulty man had attained a height of 24,600 feet in another part of the Himalaya, a few years previously; but between that and the summit of Everest there was a difference of 4,400 feet. Could man overcome that great difference in height? To do this he would have to sleep at a height of approximately 27,000 feet, for it would not do to leave more than 2,000 feet to climb on the final day. Would he be able to sleep at 27,000 feet? And could even the lightest camp be carried for him to that height? Many thought that both these questions would be answered in the negative – that it would be impossible to get a camp carried to so great a height, and that even if it were man could not sleep there and would therefore be dead beat before he started for the final effort.

The present Expedition has proved, however, that a camp can be carried to 27,000 feet, that man can sleep even at that tremendous altitude, and that without any artificial aid he can reach 28,000 feet. Colonel Norton and Dr Somervell accomplished this last feat in an exceptionally bad year and when they were in a thoroughly exhausted state. For a whole month previously they had been severely strained in establishing the high camps on the glacier, and on the North Col, battling with blizzards and experiencing extreme cold. Yet in spite of these drawbacks Colonel Norton reached a point only 900 feet below the summit. And it cannot be doubted that, if climbers could be put on the mountain in a less exhausted condition than Norton and Somervell were in, the summit could be reached. Norton was able to see enough of the last portion to be sure that there were no physical obstacles to prevent this; and if he in his condition could have reached so near we may be certain that at his best he could have attained the summit. The problem is now merely a matter of putting men on the mountain in a fit condition. What was before a mere probability is now anyhow a possibility, and some consider a certainty. Where originally all was doubt and speculation there is now conviction. We feel convinced that sooner or later man will stand on the summit of the highest mountain. And these climbs to higher heights have added to man's knowledge of himself. Once again he has found that by exercising his capacity he increases it. By forcing himself to live at higher and higher altitudes, he finds that his body adjusts itself to the new conditions. The amount of oxygen in the air near the summit of Mount Everest is only a third of the amount in the air at sea-level, and unless the body made some adjustment to these altered conditions man could not survive them. And this last Expedition has shown that the human body does make this adjustment if it has the requisite time for the purpose. Major Hingston, in part 3, gives full details. Ascending suddenly in a balloon to a height of 28,000 feet in 1875, one man fainted and two men died. But on Mount Everest last year the same altitude was attained by Norton and Somervell and because the ascent had been gradual their bodies had been able to adjust themselves; they showed no signs of fainting and were able to make the effort of climbing.

The experience gained on last year's Expedition further showed that men who have once experienced high altitudes will acclimatise very much more rapidly than those ascending to them for the first time. Climbers who had been on two expeditions suffered less on the second than they did on the first; and the new members of last year's Expedition were distinctly more affected than the members who had been on a previous Expedition.

Thus it has been found that not only does man's body adapt itself to high altitude conditions, but adapts itself more rapidly on successive occasions. And the members of this expedition are of opinion that climbers can be so acclimatised to altitudes of between 24,000 and 26,000 feet that they would be able to climb to 29,000 feet without the use of oxygen. The summit of Mount Everest will not be attained without the climbers, somewhere or other on the seven stages between the base camp and the summit, suffering from hardships of extreme cold, furious winds, uncomfortable accommodation, and the poor food and indifferent cooking incidental to life in such regions. And these sufferings and discomforts must sap into the vitality. But this much we now do know which we did not know before, that the body does find better means than the normal of taking in what little oxygen there remains in the air, and that therefore the climbing of the highest mountain on the earth is a feasible proposition.

So much for the body; and with the spirit also it has once more been found that as it exerts itself so does it grow in capacity. And it not merely adapts itself to new conditions: it masters them. When man first started out to assault the mountain he was full of doubt and hesitation and not a little fear. Everest was formidable enough in herself, but she had with her terrible allies in the wind and the cold and the snow; and man might well have quailed before her. But he faced her squarely, and now he knows the worst about her, and knows that he himself has further resources within him which he can bring up against the mountain and he is confident of victory. He knows the limit of what Everest can do. She may have frost and snow and wind on her side, but she cannot loose off poison-gas or belch forth volcanic fire or shake man off in an earthquake. Whereas man can use his intelligence and profit by the experience he has gained; can equip himself better against the weather; and having once nearly reached the summit the way is known to him and he can march forward with confidence.

His increasing confidence is indeed very remarkable. The members of the 1924 Expedition, marching across Tibet, took it as a certainty that they would reach the summit; and that they got so near as they did after their terrible experiences during the months on the glacier before they could even make the attempt, must have been due to this confidence that was in them; they would never have reached so high if they had not had confidence born of their experiences in 1922. And Colonel Norton speaks of the stimulating effect there was in passing the highest point they had reached in 1922. Anything then seemed possible. And the want of success on this occasion did not diminish the feeling of confidence. They were as confident on the way back as they were on the way out, that the summit would be reached.

Everest cannot add to her height; but the spirit of man heightens even under repulse.

And what is the value of this heightened spirit is well exemplified in the contrast between Mallory and the Sherpas. These men are born and bred in the mountains below Everest, and as Captain Geoffrey Bruce tells us, they are sure-footed and owing to the rigorous climate of their homes can withstand more than average exposure and fatigue. In ordinary life they are quite accustomed to carrying loads across a 19,000-foot pass. And on this expedition they actually carried small loads to a height of 27,000 feet. So there, right on the spot, must be dozens of men who could, as far as bodily fitness goes, reach the summit of Everest any year they liked. Yet the fact remains that they don't. They have not even the desire to. They have not the spirit.

Compare these people with Mallory. He undoubtedly was fine in body. But in fitness to endure the cold and wind of Everest and in adaptation to high altitudes, he naturally could not compare with the men whose homes were at over 12,000 feet and who, all their lives, were used to carrying loads to still greater altitudes. They must obviously have excelled him in bodily fitness to climb Mount Everest. But where he excelled was in spirit. As Norton describes in his book, his spirit drove his body to the utmost limit. He was not *asked* to make that last climb. And there was no call for him to make it, for he had already done more than his share in the whole great adventure. He had taken part in all three Expeditions; on the first, it was he who at the last moment discovered the only possible way up the mountain; on the second, he climbed to a height of nearly 27,000 feet; and on the third he had had most of the hardest work in making a way up the dangerous

North Col and had already taken part in one attempt to reach the summit. He might well have now left others to take up the burden. But his spirit would not allow him; he must make one last desperate effort.

Many of the Sherpas with the expedition also showed magnificent spirit. But the point is that these people, living under the very shadow of Mount Everest and having, as is now known, all the bodily capacity to enable them to climb it, had never had the spirit to make the attempt, while Mallory, though he was an inhabitant of a distant island with not a snow mountain on it, had the spirit to travel thousands of miles and to risk his life in climbing this mountain, and this spirit did enable him almost to reach the summit.

Mallory's spirit did indeed force his body to his death. But the manner of his and Irvine's death was such as to kindle the spirit in thousands of others. Their lives were not thrown uselessly away, for it is a fact, just as real as any 'scientific' fact, that the story of their death has roused the spirit of men and women in every country. Few can be Everest climbers, but all can be inspirited by a deed like Mallory's and Irvine's last climb. And many there are who, on hearing of it, have felt themselves helped in battling with their own stern difficulties. And Mallory and Irvine will for ever live among the great who have helped to raise this spirit of man.

Another fact which must also be put to the credit of these Everest Expeditions is that the story of their attack on the mountain has aroused interest throughout the world. And the value of this interest can, in this case, be measured in box-office receipts; thus giving us tangible evidence. For the telegrams relating that story, newspapers were ready to give substantial sums of money. And to hear the lectures and to see the wonderful cinematographic record which Captain Noel brought back, hundreds of thousands of men and women and children all over the world have been ready to pay. In this practical manner they have shown that they do attach value to what these expeditions have done.

Those scientific results which have, as it were, incidentally accrued, are also of no mean value. Odell, a geologist by profession, was able, while he was on Mount Everest, to gather information which has enabled us to determine the character of this highest portion of the earth's surface. And Major Hingston, the medical officer and naturalist of the Expedition, has made valuable observations on both human and animal life at the highest altitudes. Besides which he has collected some 10,000 specimens. Additions to the map have also been made.

These are the more immediate results of the Expedition. But further results in the future, we may also anticipate. Norton and Somervell reached an altitude practically equal to the height of Kanchenjunga. So when visitors to Darjeeling look up at that wonderful mountain they will take pride in reflecting that man has, without any adventitious aids, ascended even as high as that. They may further reflect that as far as the effects of altitude have anything to do with it, man could climb any of that magnificent array of peaks there stretched out before them. Visitors to Kashmir may feel the same when they look at Nanga Parbat, which, unattainably high as it appears, is fifteen hundred feet below the height which Norton reached on Everest. And reflections such as these cannot but inspire men to climb, if not these, yet other Himalayan peaks. The spirit will drive the body on, and the body, we now know, will respond to the calls of the spirit.

So far it has been in the Himalaya as it was in the Alps till a century ago. Man dreaded and shrank from the great mountain. But as man began to climb the Swiss peaks and became more familiar with the mountains, he gradually overcame his fears and prepared to assert himself, till now he has conquered every peak, and not only climbed the mountains but built habitations high up on them and driven roads and railways through them.

So also may we anticipate that man will master the mountains in the Himalaya. Having climbed about them and come to feel more at home among them, he will want to build more roads and then more railways, till he has established his supremacy, and this not for the barren purpose of saying he is master, but, as in the Alps, for the sake of enjoying their beauty.

For here in the Himalaya is a source of human enjoyment more valuable far than any gold mine or any oil spring, for it cannot be exhausted. What is its exact value, we cannot say; but we can form some estimate, for we have Switzerland to go by. There hundreds of millions of pounds have been spent for no other purpose than to enable people to enjoy the beauty of the mountains. That is to say, people are ready to pay these millions of pounds in order that they may be able to see the mountains. To places like Chamonix, for instance, roads and railways have been constructed at a cost which must necessarily be very high on account of the mountainous character of the country traversed. And numbers of hotels – some of them of the most fashionable description – have been built. And from here funicular railways have been made to points from which the best view of Mont Blanc can be obtained. Moreover, the very snow has been made use of to get enjoyment from the mountains, and besides those who come there in the summer, numbers flock there in the winter for the winter sports. And if in Switzerland men think it worthwhile to spend so much money simply to get enjoyment from the Alps, it may be assumed that, in course of time, they will be no less anxious to get similar enjoyment from the Himalaya.

It is not necessary to compare the beauty of the Alps with the beauty of the Himalaya, and to say that the one is greater than the other. It is sufficient to say that the one is different from the other. Each has its own peculiar beauty. And there can be found in the Himalaya beauty of a type which does not exist in the Alps, and for that very reason – in order to find variety – men may be drawn to the Himalaya. Neither the combination of tropical vegetation with snowy peaks thousands of feet higher than Mont Blanc, nor glacier regions like the Baltoro, can be found in the Alps. And these must always have an attraction even to lovers of the Alps.

It is indeed to men who have acquired their love of mountain beauty in the Alps that the discovery of the Himalaya as a source of beauty is mainly due. It is to the expeditions of Conway, Freshfield, the Duke of the Abruzzi, Longstaff, the Bullock Workmans and de Fillippi, that the enjoyment to be found in the Himalaya has become known. And the Everest Expeditions are only the climax of these more modest assaults. We may anticipate then that more will follow – that as the glories of the Himalaya become more widely known many others will make their way from the Alps to the Himalaya.

And now the way is shown it is not necessary that men should always proceed by the Alps. The Himalaya mountains are on the edge of a country with three hundred million inhabitants. They too have always been attracted to the Himalaya, and have formed holy places there to which thousands of pilgrims yearly resort. Increasing numbers go there also for health and to enjoy the beauty, and more still will follow as the mountains are made more accessible.

This is the prospect before us, and many will shudder at it. To have Kashmir, Sikkim and Kulu covered with hotels and funicular railways will fill many with horror. But the Himalaya is a larger playground than Switzerland, and there will be room for all for many centuries to come. And accessibility to the beauty of the Himalaya will bring enjoyment to thousands and thousands from all over the world as well as from India. The Himalayan peoples too will have their manhood stirred, and, like the Sherpa porters on Mount Everest, be shown of what they are capable.

These are some of the far-off results which we may anticipate may come of these efforts to scale the Himalayan peaks of which the Everest Expeditions are only the climax. In their final result they will open up a whole new realm of beauty. And the men who have pioneered the way deserve in full measure the gratitude of their kind for the sacrifices they have made.

# PART 1
# NARRATIVE

# 1 THE START

BY BRIG. GENERAL HON. C.G. BRUCE, CB, MVO

March 1, and once again, and for the third time, the members of the Mount Everest Expedition are collecting in Darjeeling.

This in itself is a sufficiently stimulating idea. The first Expedition, which left to reconnoitre an, until that time, almost unknown part of the Himalaya, may seem to have removed some of the mystery and, so to speak, to have skimmed the cream from the exploratory milk. But this is really but a superficial impression.

To begin with, part of their way led over country which had been reached before by European travellers, and about which a great deal was known.

It was only when they turned south from Shekar that they came into the real thrills. And although the subsequent expeditions, following on their lines, could never quite reproduce the extraordinarily satisfactory feeling which was granted to the first Expedition – the first Europeans to get to the Rongbuk Valley, and to view that vast Himāl – that desperate, desolate country, from the north – still, both the First and the Second Expeditions, quite apart from their efforts on the mountain, added to our geographical knowledge, and probably still more to our appreciation of the people of that country.

It is rather strange to find, in the light of subsequent efforts, that the account of our work in the second Expedition is called 'The Assault on Mount Everest.'

That no doubt it was. But one of the most experienced and wise of mountaineering authorities said a long time ago, 'It may take a dozen assaults, but final success is certain.' And that adequately summarises the position.

Anyhow, here we are, collecting again!

I must, however, spare a few words as to how some of us managed to get here.

Norton and myself came out by the mail steamer arriving in Bombay February 16, reaching Delhi on the 18th. There we were able to discuss certain details with H.E. Lord Rawlinson, the Commander-in-Chief, and also with the political authorities.

H.E. the late Lord Rawlinson, from the outset, had been a very keen supporter of our enterprise, and his sympathy and assistance were always to be counted on.

At Delhi Norton and I parted, to meet again by arrangement in Calcutta on February 27. My road first of all taking me to the Frontier and Abbottabad, where I was to join Captain Geoffrey Bruce, and to see the four Gurkha non-commissioned officers, who, by the kindness of H.E. Lord Rawlinson, were again to accompany the Expedition, and also to pick up certain stores best supplied from Abbottabad and its district – notably putties – a small item, but an important one. I do not wish to make a dissertation on putties, and will merely state that anyone who has worn a properly woven pair of putties, from their own original home – that is the mountains surrounding Kashmir – will never wish to wear any other type, and for high climbing it is a fact that improper pressure round the calf and ankles gives extra work to the heart, and may be actually an assistant cause of frostbite of the feet.

From the North-west Frontier, we journeyed down to Calcutta: Geoffrey Bruce, myself, and five Gurkha soldiers, one being my own orderly.

Again, in Calcutta, we met Norton. All the arrangements for meeting our stores, which had been dispatched from London by sea to Calcutta, were settled with the Army and Navy Stores, and the manager took over the whole onus of forwarding them, together with our oxygen apparatus, up to the station of Kalimpong Road, the terminus of the Darjeeling Hill Railway in Sikkim.

Alas, we missed our old ally who had been of such great assistance to us on previous occasions. I refer to Mr Brown, of the Army and Navy Stores, and regret to say that he had died about six months before we arrived in India. We owe an immense debt of gratitude to the Army and Navy Stores for the way they have always forwarded our interests.

Thence, from Calcutta, with as little delay as possible, to Darjeeling. I confess that the journey from Siliguri to Darjeeling, often as I have made it, never palls. Partly, no doubt, because of the complete change from the plains of India to the mountains; the great forests one passes through, and the wholly different type of peoples one meets. And then the wonderful vistas of ever-deepening blue as the railway climbs higher and higher, and the brilliant coral blossoms of the cotton tress, which in the early months of the year strike such a bold note of colour against the blue depths of the valleys. And again, as soon as the Ghoom ridge is passed, the exciting views of the Himalayas. All these attractions only add to my own pleasure and to the delightful memories which these journeys leave in my mind, and to which each successive journey contributes. The funny fussy little Hill Railway, and its clever engineering; even the scrubby little bazaars one passes through, and the many little races and short cuts I have taken with the train – all these pictures are a vivid remembrance.

On this last occasion we found Narbu Yishé, called by us in '22 the 'purana miles,' or old soldier – a real stalwart – who again was to hugely distinguish himself. And then, in typical March weather, came the last and always exhilarating stage, the short run from Ghoom into the Darjeeling Railway Station.

Here we were promptly met by one of our new members, Shebbeare. Shebbeare belongs to the Indian Forest Department, and it was a great bit of luck being able to acquire his services. Naturally, from his profession, he was brought much in contact with local conditions, and with the type of men that we employ as our porters, and who form the *personnel* of our Expeditions. Of course anybody may be brought into close contact with people, but it by no means follows that they will understand them or have the sympathetic temperament required to get the best out of them. We knew, however, that Shebbeare possessed all these qualities, hence our jubilation at getting him as one of our party. He was our Official Transport Officer, failing Captain C.J. Morris, who had been unable to get the necessary leave to join us again. Shebbeare had no previous training in the technique of high mountaineering, but that was not his business. He was, is, and ever will be, a glutton for work, and with him discomforts count not.

Our excellent Agent, Mr Weatherall, also met us, and gave us a most encouraging account of the number of Sherpas, Bhotias, and hill-men generally, who had come in hoping to be chosen as porters for the Expedition. This news was most cheering, as it shewed that our reputation was still good, and that the sacrifice of the seven porters in 1922 had had no deterring effect on the supply of volunteers.

Our Interpreter, Karma Paul, was to the fore once more, and also his assistant, Gyaljen, both as keen as ever. And even the melancholy Moti, the cobbler, once more rolled up, bringing an ill-fated brother with him. Also the deprecatory and mild Rhombu, the Lepcha naturalist, crept in from the back, so to speak, and intimated with his hat in his hand, in complete silence, that he was ready again. We ear-marked him as Hingston's assistant, as soon as the latter should arrive.

Then we were joined by Somervell, hailing from Travancore, followed by Odell from the Persian oil-fields, while Hingston arrived from his RAF hospital in Bagdad. All were set to work at once, according to their several qualifications. But Norton and Shebbeare promptly rushed off to Kalimpong to receive and forward our heavy baggage as it arrived. Odell was our

Oxygen Expert, and the oxygen apparatus was placed in his charge from now on.

We had been warned in the most solemn fashion by the India Office of the terrible penalties which would be incurred by the Tibetans if any more interest was displayed in the geological formations of the mountains, or if any stones were removed from their sides. But murder will out, and it was discovered that Odell was a geologist by profession. This dreadful news had immediately to be counteracted. Odell was taking a complete holiday from his profession. He was now following his infinitely greater calling, that of a mountaineer, and though he was obliged by orders of the Expeditionary Headquarters Staff to take upon himself other scientific duties, still his own profession was in abeyance. Telegrams of reassurance flew from every direction over the Himāl, and confidence was re-established. No epidemics and no disturbing of the local demons should occur if it was possible to avoid this terrible risk.

Hingston had arrived as fit as possible after a Mesopotamian winter, which is not to be despised. In addition to being the Official Doctor and Surgeon of the Expedition, he was also its Naturalist. In his first capacity he came bursting with energy and enthusiasm to test every member of the Expedition with every terror known to the RAF authorities. In his second capacity, as Naturalist, we knew that he would have his work cut out, and we hoped that but little of his time would be required for looking after the humans. In the actual event, as will be seen, he had his hands full, both with his Natural History collections, and in dealing with the many troubles of the Expedition: one of the most annoying of these troubles being the one I myself occasioned. To his great attainments, both as Doctor and Naturalist, are added a complete placidity of temperament, and an unfailing humorous outlook. I shall be intensely obliged if anyone can point out a better make-up for the trying duties which he was asked to carry out. All our thanks are due to him. Hingston was not a mountaineer. Oh, no! But read to the end of this book, and then make a comment on this statement!

Somervell had arrived from Southern India, looking fit and well as usual. A Medical Missionary now, and full of his opportunities, medical, sportive, and other, which he had enjoyed while ministering to his enormous panel. I think, though, that the soft and enervating climate of Travancore had begun to tell on even his wonderful constitution to a certain extent, and Somervell has a very tough physique. The cassowary, however, had spared him, and he joined us just the same T.H.S. as of old. My last meeting with him had been at Zermatt in 1923, during that astounding campaign he made in the Alps, having Bentley Beetham with him most of the time, when they bagged something like thirty-five peaks in six weeks' climbing.

We had, as usual, a very amusing time picking our *personnel*. There were several old followers – notably old Pu – coming with us for the third time, and among them turned up my former porter and henchman, Llakpa Chédé, who in 1922 had done his best to come, but was at that time very ill with malaria. This year he was in first-rate condition, and, as will be seen in later accounts, a very great success. A native born of Darjeeling, he had never been to the hub of the Sherpa universe, the large Sola-Khombu settlements at the head of the Dudh Kosi in Nepal, although his father hailed from that place. We took with us a larger outfit of porters than in 1922, but, on the whole, an equally satisfactory lot.

All was ready for the march: stores packed and forwarded from Darjeeling by the time our last contingent arrived, Mallory and Irvine, Bentley Beetham and Hazard. This our last, and almost most important, contingent, Hazard, who had previously served in India as a sapper, and who had a great mountaineering record. Bentley Beetham, a born mountaineer, and – how shall I describe him? – a mountaineering *Ghazi*, and Somervell's climbing companion, and also a skilled photographer, to whom was deputed by Noel much of the still-picture work. Then Mallory, the Bayard of the Mountains – '*sans peur et sans reproche*' – the only member of the Expedition who was making his third journey. And finally, our splendid 'experiment,' Irvine, bringing with him magnificent recommendations from Longstaff and Odell after Spitzbergen experiences, and, further, bringing his own great personality. He rapidly ceased to be an experiment, for we soon found that with a young body he possessed a mature judgment, combined with a very remarkable handiness and adaptability as a practical working engineer. All these valuable qualities, combined with infinite stamina and infinite unselfishness, made Irvine a very great asset to our party.

I really don't think that I ought to say anything about Geoffrey Bruce! He was confidential Staff Officer, dealing with all branches – GSO and Q in all its ramifications. During the whole of my service in the Army I have been singularly dependent upon a *Fidus Achates*, on whom I could always put the nasty work I didn't like myself, and whom I could always blame for anything I did myself if it was wrong. I think that is a good enough recommendation for anybody. Possibly, just as an aside, I might add that he is a really very remarkable performer on the hillside. One of those untrained mountaineers who is always 'all there.' At any rate, if I never did anything else to help Colonel Norton, I at least passed Geoffrey Bruce on to him.

On March 25 we left Darjeeling, everybody, with the exception of myself, riding or walking: the members of the Expedition, the Interpreter, the Sirdars, porters, personal servants, cooks, and Gurkha non-commissioned officers. I went like a lord, in a motor-car put at my disposal by Mr Wrangham-Hardy of Darjeeling, and driven by his chauffeur, a man whom, curiously enough, I had myself enlisted into the Kashmir Army twenty-five years ago. He drove me round *via* Siliguri, and thence up the Teesta Valley to Kalimpong Road, from which place we mounted 3,800 feet to Kalimpong. This last about the steepest drive, and with the narrowest turns, that I have ever been over in a motor-car, the excitement of the drive being hugely enhanced by the fact that we were overtaken by a furious thunderstorm just as it was getting dark. However, that night the whole Expedition was collected, and had a cheerful evening together.

Captain Noel, who was the Official Photographer in the 1922 Expedition, was again with us, although his arrangements were different from those of 1922. He was very keen to take again a complete cinema record of all that the Expedition hoped to do. But so difficult had it been in 1922 to develop the films in Tibet, owing to the continual winds, the amount of dust raised by them, and its character, and also the low temperatures at night, that it was considered to be far more efficacious to establish a regular laboratory in Darjeeling, and to send back his films from Tibet to be developed there under these much better conditions. We were luckily able to make postal arrangements which, under the circumstances, worked very well.

In 1922 I had the privilege of being the bearer of a message from Sir Robert Baden-Powell to the Scouts of Dr Graham's magnificent 'Homes' in Kalimpong. And I was happy in 1924 to be entrusted with another message. Again we had a most interesting ceremony, and, to my special interest, I found that the large and very flourishing troop of Nepali Scouts, looked after by Dr Graham, were in charge of a young Welshman who hailed from very near my own home in Glamorgan.

Again, they all saw us on our way, after a most interesting function.

And so to Pedong. After all this is the real start for Tibet. We travelled in two parties as usual: the second in charge of Norton; the first with me.

I have an affection for Pedong. It is charmingly situated, and looks well over the Sikkim Valleys. But this year the air seemed full of smoke: possibly unusually thick haze, possibly actual smoke driven up from the forest fires in the plains.

Pedong is on the frontier between British Sikkim and the Sikkim State, and while I was sitting in comfort in the bungalow I was visited by a young Sikkim military policeman who wished to see our passes, and also brought books to be signed. Having complied with these requests, I had relapsed into comfort when I was startled by a yell of 'Attention!' from the young Gurkha policeman, followed by 'Right-hand salute – Left turn – Quick march!' at the top of his voice. Thus having given himself orders he departed satisfied on his way.

The road through Sikkim is always a joy, warm though the deep valleys are. But their warmth, and the heat engendered by running down the very steep short cuts, through the gorgeous Sikkim forests, were partly compensated for by the luscious pineapples of Rhenok.

And so to Rongli-Chu, 2,700 feet above sea-level. Here a typical Sherpa incident occurred. Take it all round our Sherpas had been very good. Of course when leaving Darjeeling it was up to them, for luck's sake, to take as many drinks of their chang as they could before setting out for Tibet. But this mild sacrifice to the god of Luck only added to their intense friend-liness for everybody and everything.

But at Rongli-Chu two of them really did burst out much more than was necessary, and I am afraid, on this occasion, they did not confine themselves to the mild chang, but added to it much of the rough spirit of the country. A furious fight between two of them was the result. They were finally brought into camp, and Somervell was woken up to treat them. They were dreadfully smashed about, and much sewing up of wounds and bandaging of heads and hands had to be done.

The following morning, when they were coming up for a second dressing I thought I would add a little dressing down on my own account. They were very sorrowful, but also much *hurt*, and carefully explained to me that they hadn't quarrelled, and that they were bosom friends. That it was not they, but the *drink* that had quarrelled! This naive way of putting things was typical of the Sherpa character. Unfortunately, neither of these two Sherpas turned out among the best. That, however, is another story.

From Rongli began the great ascent, *via* Sedongchen, Gnatong, and over the Jelap La, always an interesting journey.

Again, as in 1922, we stopped for our wayside refreshment at Ling Tham. There was the same little lady and her children, the latter much grown, and again she refreshed us with excellent tea and her 'shéli' bread. However, on this occasion we were lucky, as we had had some rain on the way up, and the atmosphere had cleared.

Crossing the open ground over the Minor Kapup Pass we had the most inspiring view of the whole Kanchenjunga massif. One of those strange mysterious atmospheric effects, when the great mountains appear to be floating in mid-air, their lower slopes swallowed up in the blue depths of the valleys, and their outlines obliterated, while all above the snow-line seemed detached from an earthly base and floating in space. It was a truly wonderful picture.

On this occasion we marched direct from Gnatong, and without halting at Kapup, crossed the pass to the Tibetan rest-house, which is six miles from the top. Naturally this rest-house has not the conveniences of a Dak bungalow, but for all that it is no mean shelter, and is well built with heavy timbers.

More than ever was it borne in on me during this journey, the differences between the Eastern and Western Himalaya.

Here we were on April 1, high up, having crossed a pass of 14,400 feet, and yet had never been really inconvenienced by the snow, nor had the night temperatures been particularly low.

The descent from the summit was certainly over snow for a time, and the path below unpleasantly iced, and dreadfully slippery for animals. How those heavily laden Chumbi mules managed to get over it was a wonder.

Compare these conditions to those which prevail on April 1 on the other great trade route, that from Kashmir to Ladakh or Little Tibet. On that route only one pass, the Zoji La, an insignificant 11,700 feet, and yet I am not exaggerating when I say that there would have been ten feet of snow on it at that date, and, almost certainly, it would have been impassable for a train of laden animals.

And further, our pass, the Jelap La, remains open, nearly always, for the whole winter, for it is down over this track that the great mule trains, with their bales of wool, pass annually.

We waited on the top of the Jelap La for some little time, but it was a wild rough morning and not very attractive.

Still, we managed to take one or two photographs, including one of the Sherpa, Angtarké, who was one of the two men rescued in the disaster of 1922. I don't think poor Angtarké has ever really recovered from that terrific experience, for he was dug out unconscious, firmly fixed in the snow, standing on his head, having fallen some sixty feet. We felt bound to take him on again, but he soon broke down, and returned with me.

The next day brought us to Chumbi, or more correctly speaking, Shashima.

David Macdonald, the Trade Agent, was up in Tibet, but his son, John Macdonald, looked after us in place of his father.

We had a little business to transact here, which did not take very long, and the following day we were joined by the second party, all fit and well. We were all bidden that afternoon to a Tibetan dance and a performance by professional Tibetan players and acrobats.

The entertainment took place on the lawn of the Macdonalds' garden, and was really most fascinating, not only from its own spectacular merits, but from the picturesqueness of the crowd, and also from the intense personal enjoyment of not only the entertained, but also of the entertainers themselves.

The whole of the inhabitants of the Chumbi Valley – men, women, and children – were present; many Nepalese traders, settlers, and the like, and also the men of the detachment of the Panjabi Regiment stationed in Chumbi.

One of the actors, dressed up as a Mahomedan, with a long beard, was excruciatingly like an old Mahomedan friend of mine up in the Kaghan Valley, which tickled me immensely.

We did not, however, stay long in Chumbi, but left, again in two parties, on April 5. Always an interesting journey, I think, that route through the Gautsa Defile.

In the wooded parts of the Himalaya one often meets with beautiful scenery, magnificent scenery, indeed, combined with real wildness, but the upper parts of the Gautsa Defile, in contrast to the lower parts, impress one with a sense of *savage* wildness.

We reached Phari on April 6. But it was not the Phari we anticipated, neither was it the Phari of 1922.

I don't think Phari could have possibly behaved better than it did in 1924. It was, in fact, almost a mild climate, and Phari is over 14,000 feet.

We found, as we had expected, all our stores collected here, and our very efficient 'Tindel,' who was in charge, had pitched the whole of our tents for inspection.

No time was lost in getting into touch with the Dzong Pen. Knowing, however, the character of the Phari civil authorities of old, we were prepared for a battle over prices. In fact, we had previously taken certain steps, communicating our doubts of the attitude likely to be expected from the Phari headmen, and so forth, to General Tza-za Laden La, who was on a mission to Lhasa.

It was lucky for us that we had done this, for we found that the prices in Phari Dzong had risen altogether out of proportion to the cost of living, so to speak.

Our battle with the Dzong Pen went on for two days.

As before we had travelled to Phari in two parties, and so were again assembled there on April 7. Again it was my birthday, and once more we opened a bottle of the old family rum specially sent by my brother from England for the occasion. Many compliments have been paid to this old rum, but never more hearty ones, and never has it done its duty better than on these two occasions, for really old mellow rum is a generous fluid.

We had one day of complete rest for all, and that day was largely occupied in submitting ourselves individually to Major Hingston's innumerable physiological tests.

I was hugely elated by finding that I passed a better examination in Phari Dzong than I had in London. I think the little devil who deals in disappointments must have sat on the mantelpiece and chuckled.

Between times, and while the tests were going on, we continued our battles with the Dzong Pen.

The Dzong Pen himself, a grasping, avaricious, but feeble, albeit well-mannered individual, was really in the hands of his subordinates, the Gyembus, a truculent, but determined, crowd of cheerful rascals, who had quite clearly not taken on their duties for health's sake alone.

However, we discovered that a telegram had arrived from Lhasa, instructing the Dzong Pen to give us every assistance, and to see that we were not overcharged. Without letting it be known that we were in possession of this information, an ultimatum was issued, and before all, in open Durbar, a telegram was written out to the Tibetan Prime Minister, complaining of our treatment at the hands of the Phari authorities.

This bluff had its desired effect, and very shortly an agreement was drawn out and signed, and, after much bowing and ceremonial kow-towing, by general request the telegram was torn up in full sight of the Durbar.

A dramatic and very amusing finale to the situation. There remained but to get off! And the departure from Phari, as is always the case, and probably always will be the case in the East for a first day, was a prolonged scramble.

But on the following day, after the agreement had been signed, and during the day, we did actually get off and again in two parties. Hingston, myself, and John Macdonald had elected to travel by the more lengthy Tuna-Do-chen-Tat-sang route, up to then new to me; the Do-chen lake and its innumerable wild fowl being the attraction for Hingston. The remainder of the party made a short march and camped on the slopes of the Tang La, and as we progressed on our route we saw their camp being pitched in a fairly sheltered spot up a little valley.

Our route led us along the main route to Lhasa for some twenty miles or so, and Hingston and I amused ourselves by trying to round up some kiang,[1] and as a matter of fact we did get very close to them.

The road, although pleasant enough to ride, must be deadly boring for a pedestrian, notwithstanding the fact that the great North Ridge of Chomulhari, running for at least ten miles in a northerly direction, is really a most magnificent sight, and its terribly steep ice faces, almost terrifying in their steepness when regarded from a mountaineering point of view.

The main caravan had to take the ordinary Kampa Dzong route, which is necessary when much transport is employed, crossing the great ridges of the Donka La, and although starting in mild weather, were prepared for a severe time, and were not disappointed.

Even we encountered a very cold wind before reaching Tuna, as bleak and desolate a spot as one could wish to see.

The next morning I was down with a severe go of malaria, which obliged me to hand over the conduct of the Expedition to Norton.

In fact, even after I had begun to recover, Hingston was adamant. Hingston, although adamant, was interested, however, as my case showed the physiological effects on the human body produced by a sharp attack of malaria when it develops at an altitude of over 15,000 feet.

The fever, under his skilful treatment, yielded in four days, but I had to be carried out of Tibet completely incapacitated.

At any rate I did a bit of good to one member of the Expedition, for the exercise of carrying me for twenty miles back into Phari appears to have provided excellent training for my old henchman Llakpa, who afterwards so distinguished himself on the great mountain.

Naturally this *coup de jarnac* dealt me by the Fates was a terrible disappointment to me, but there are compensations for everything, and my compensation was Norton. Let me say at once that even if I had continued with the Expedition there was no step taken by Norton, no order issued by him, and no decision made by him of which I should not have been proud to have been the author. No doubt an extra hand who knew the ropes, at the Base Camp, would have been of advantage, but beyond that, in such a great matter as the continuity of the command, there is nothing to be said.

My own subsequent movements were simple enough, but one point

--------------------

1   Wild donkeys.

is certainly interesting, and that is the extraordinary rapidity with which strength was regained, even at such an altitude as Yatung, roughly 10,000 feet. So much so that after a few days' rest I was able to continue, riding and walking, my journey down to Gangtok, crossing the Natu Là in deep snow.

However, Hingston was just as adamantine when we reached Gangtok, and would not listen to what I was pleased to call reason.

He left me at the latter place – Gangtok – and travelled *via* Lachen direct to Kampa Dzong, writing to me on the way up, and giving descriptions of his enjoyment of the road through the forests, and that he had captured no less than 300 different kinds of bugs without even dismounting.

I must here thank Major and Mrs Bailey for the great care they took of me in Gangtok while I was convalescing.

From April 27 to August 8 there is a great gap: I waiting in comfort – that is physical comfort – while the rest were occupied with the great fight. A most humiliating and trying position.

I shall never forget receiving a most kind and sympathetic letter from Lord Lytton, the Governor of Bengal, enclosing the fateful telegram telling of our loss.

The whole history of that wonderful battle and the final sacrifice is told in the chapters which follow, and so I leave that to other pens.

––––––––

In a later chapter Colonel Norton fully discusses the problem of Everest, and especially that part which has not yet been entirely solved. But so many points in this year's attempt have been cleared up, and such great progress has been made, that we are in an infinitely better position to review and complete our task.

As will be seen, the Expedition in 1924 suffered from very unusual climatic conditions, and these not to do with the arrival of the monsoon, but due to depressions forming in the West, and travelling the whole length of Afghanistan, the Northern Panjab, and the Himalayas, causing until quite late into May rough and cold weather, and making a record low temperature for that month throughout the sub-montaine districts.

These disturbances brought to Everest hurricane after hurricane, and terrible cold at a time when clear, if not comparatively warm, weather is expected.

One of our great problems in the attack on Everest is to bring one's party burly and fit to the foot of the mountain, and to keep them so.

I am not exaggerating at all if I estimate that that great three weeks' struggle to establish the camp at the North Col reduced the efficiency of the party, whether European or Tibetan, by at least one-third. That is to say, that each member of the Expedition, with ordinary luck, would have been one-third a better man when engaged on the final assault.

To my mind the problem is solved, with the gods on our side, and given again a party of equal efficiency.

The minor matters that we have learnt, whether in organisation or deductions from physiological experience, count comparatively for little.

The greater problem is solved, whether oxygen is employed or not.

We have only got to get together a party to match that of 1924. To go there, and do it; utilising at the same time all the influence we have with the heavenly Authorities to supply us with propitious weather.

There is one subject, however, which I must not forget. We certainly, in 1924, did learn a great deal about the extent to which acclimatisation is progressive. It was also quite clearly established, I think, that those who had lived for considerable periods at a height of over 16,000 feet, even after the lapse of two years, got their acclimatisation more rapidly than beginners. Even in 1922 we noticed that Mallory was far fitter at high altitudes than anyone else at the start.

We put this down to innate capacity, very largely, but it was quite probably, in the light of our further experience, due to his training and experience of the previous year.

This is a fact worth remembering, and it might even be an assistance, if there is a long gap before the new Expedition takes place, for climbers to make a point of spending a considerable time on the way up to Tibet at the Gautsa rest-house, which is at about 12,000 feet, training themselves from there, and utilising the ample supplies obtainable in Chumbi, so as to get a great measure of acclimatisation before crossing the Tibetan plateau. I may say this is a favourite scheme of Colonel Norton's.

I seem to have dismissed the oxygen question with scant reference, but I think the conclusion is clear. Every effort should be made to attain a full acclimatisation, and that acclimatisation should be utilised, so to speak, to its utmost safe limit, and that oxygen should only be used to ensure success for the final dash.

I have every reason for thinking that it has been found possible to construct an adequate and infinitely lighter oxygen apparatus.

I will conclude my chapter by drawing attention to the psychological attitude which should be adopted.

The whole history of mountaineering bears out our experience. The steady progression of the most difficult climbs in Switzerland, from a reputation for 'impossibility' to 'an easy day for a lady,' exactly expresses the idea. The standard has been steadily rising, for but a few years ago a height of 23,000 feet to 24,000 feet was considered the limit of human capacity.

During our storming of Everest we always adopted the attitude, when thinking, considering, or talking of our great project, that it *began after 23,000 feet*, and that anyone should be expected to easily arrive at that point with or without a load on his back.

This, although probably an illogical conclusion, had the perfectly logical result that we had hoped for.

# 2 THE MARCH ACROSS TIBET

BY LIEUT. COLONEL E.F. NORTON, DSO

The first march from Phari is always something of an event. To begin with there is the great question whether sufficient transport animals will materialise to enable the expedition to start at all, and April 7, 1924, provided no exception to the rule, for the dilatory and obstructive methods of the Dzong Pen of Phari and his Gyembus (or head-men) were fully up to standard, and it took Geoffrey Bruce and Shebbeare six hours of arguing and driving before the last of our 300-odd transport animals were fairly on the road.

Then there is the joy of doing a whole march close under that most beautiful mountain Chomulhari, whose isolated position and perfect shape combine to produce a picture from which one can hardly take one's eyes. The peak is seen at its best from a mile or two south of Phari; this day's march takes one rather too close under it, and this detracts from its outline, but, on the other hand, one opens out a series of vistas of the spurs which form its western buttresses and which, viewed end on, are striking to a degree. As we neared camp we looked straight up a ridge which begins in a knife-edge of rock worthy of the Chamounix Aiguilles and is continued towards the mountain by what must be one of the steepest and narrowest ice arêtes in the world.

The route we were to follow for the next four days crosses the north-eastern spurs of a big snow mountain called Pau Hunri, and for some reason this area is the most inhospitable of any we meet on the Tibetan plateau. I have now crossed it four times, both in spring and summer, and never without encountering a blizzard or constant storms of snow and sleet. So we were not surprised to find it trying to snow as darkness came on; and for the first time we appreciated the joys of our new mess tent, which, specially designed as the result of our previous experience, proved of all this year's innovations the most complete and permanent success.

Our march on April 7 was a very short one, for we knew that transport difficulties would delay our start. On April 8 we lengthened our stride and covered twelve miles. The miles of the great Tibetan plains are long; sometimes they seem as long as Irish miles after a day's hunting. And towards the end of this day's march we began to marvel at our hardihood two years before, when we covered in one day the full twenty miles comprised in our first two marches this year, and that in a blizzard and for the most part on foot, only to go one better next day with a march of some twenty-five miles. And it must be remembered that we were now at an altitude somewhat greater than that of the top of Mont Blanc, and, unacclimatised as we were, this factor affected our going power more than a little.

Halfway through this second day's march we met a messenger from Hingston with a note to tell us that General Bruce was sick of a fever and lying up at Tuna – a piece of news that greatly disconcerted us.

On April 9, marching with the thermometer at 4° Fahrenheit and in a strong and bitterly cold wind, we crossed that series of three 18,000-foot passes which we know collectively as the Donka La, and got into camp at 5.30 p.m. The entry in my diary for the day finishes with: 'As often before I am lost in admiration of the servants, porters, etc., who walk eighteen miles in bitter weather, get into camp and work like beavers to get their sahibs (who have ridden much of the way) fed, clothed and housed.'

On the 10th we marched all day, only getting into camp at dusk. Our route lay over a vast gravelly plain, the very abomination of desolation; on the north the horizon was bounded by variegated limestone hills rising to 18,000 or 19,000 feet. To the south the plain rose gently to a skyline, perhaps ten miles away, over which appeared the great blunt snowcapped summits of Pau Hunri, Kinchenjhau and Chomiomo. At this season the plain appears utterly devoid of vegetation, yet herds of kyang and Tibetan gazelle surrounded us in every direction, all looking as sleek and round as if their chosen habitat were the finest pasture in Asia. To the best of my recollection we had not seen a human being for the last two days.

That evening certain anxieties we had already felt about the health of the party began to take a more definite form. Beetham was evidently suffering from a severe attack of dysentery, and Mallory had some very disquieting symptoms. Somervell suspected the possibility of appendicitis, and spent some hours into the night in making plans to deal with his case if the worst came to the worst.

Next morning we descended steeply on to Kampa Dzong. After the rough march from Phari, Kampa has each year been something of a haven of refuge, and this time it gave us a particularly warm welcome. Tucked away in a sheltered corner of the hills, this picturesque village is a veritable sun trap, and the descent from the great plateau we had crossed to a height of about 14,000 feet was itself a relief to our so far unacclimatised party. The scenery as you descend on the village is striking; the great flat plain of Kampa stretches ten miles to the west, and from this point of view has an iridescent quality which a closer acquaintance scarcely explains. The variegated foothills which border it look as if they were composed of knife-powder, rust and wood ashes, and the horizon is bounded on three sides by what appear at this season to be all snow mountains. On the south stretch the great peaks of the main range of the Himalayas, where Tibet borders on Sikkim and Nepal, and on the north is a range, snow-capped except for two summer months, which borders the valley of the Brahmaputra. Westward, the fine shapes of the Gyankar range merge into the giants of the Mount Everest system, though these, tinted golden by 100 miles of atmosphere, still seem to dominate the nearer range less than half as distant. This morning the familiar shapes of Everest and Makalu remained almost clear of cloud until the foothills shut them from our view, and only as we were losing them did they begin to fly the cloud banner which in this region always marks the master-peak.

Arrived at Kampa, we occupied the walled enclosure which has always been allotted to us by the courtesy of the local officials. There is an unchanging quality about Tibet which was brought home to me whenever we re-occupied one of our old camp sites; here at Kampa not a stone was changed: the same Tibetan hares hopped about, and the same snow cock cackled on the hill over our camp, and in the broken-down willow tree which our enclosure boasted lived the same magpie and the same little brown accentor.

At Kampa we were to change transport animals, and wherever this occurred the routine was much the same. The local Dzong Pen or Gyembu would meet us on our arrival, and having vaguely assured us that our requirements would be punctually fulfilled, would leave us to settle into camp after arranging for a meeting later in the day. In due course he would arrive, and Geoffrey Bruce and I would entertain him to tea in the mess tent. After preliminary courtesies and an interchange of gifts we would state our requirements and he the difficulties of meeting them; these we would counter by producing the passport provided by the Tibetan Government and carrying the Dalai Lama's seal, in which all officials of the specified districts were strictly enjoined to give us every assistance. The effect of this document would be varied: in some cases it would be treated with the greatest respect, in others it seemed to carry very little weight.

Prevarication and delay was generally our guest's strong suit – ours a polite firmness as to numbers and dates. Finally would come the battle royal as to the rate to be paid per animal – yak or donkey. The Dalai Lama's pass said that we were to receive transport at the 'current rate,' but the trouble was that this proved a *façon de parler*; there was no such thing as a current rate. Most fortunately the head Gyembu of Kampa Dzong – for the Dzong Pen was away – an ugly bucolic man, but straightforward and honest withal, proved singularly accommodating in this respect, and we founded our future ideas of a current rate largely on his modest demands, which were rather lower than the average prices paid in 1922. At some stages – notably Tinki Dzong – we had to arrange for a further interview, and then to take a very strong line before we could secure our transport at a reasonable rate. Our conversations, which were carried on through the medium of an interpreter, always finished on a friendly note, no matter how severe had been the tussle. Sometimes we were ourselves entertained in the Dzong, and if the negotiations were prolonged, we were apt to find the keen edge taken off our bargaining powers by a surfeit of macaroni and mutton, sweet-meats and Tibetan tea – that vile decoction flavoured with salt and butter – or chang (the local form of beer).

On this occasion our hopes of a speedy resumption of our journey were dashed, and we found that we must wait four days for our transport. But there were several reasons why this forced inaction was not unwelcome: it gave time for the invalids to recover, and, as we hoped, for the General, of whom we had no further news, to rejoin us; it enabled us to spread out kit, have a welcome bath, and generally ease off after our first taste of high-level marching. It gave us the chance also seriously to discuss our programme for climbing the mountain.

In this we had so far reached something of an impasse. As long ago as the previous Christmas in England I had circulated a paper containing my ideas on the subject, and with these Mallory had by correspondence disagreed in certain respects. At Darjeeling, and again at Phari, we had held lengthy discussions – Mallory, Somervell, Geoffrey Bruce, and myself – and, failing to agree altogether, had decided to continue our arguments across the endless plains of Tibet. At Kampa we hoped for a final decision and a cut-and-dried plan of which the details could be worked out on the fortnight's trek still ahead of us. Now was the chance, and each day we went at it, sometimes Mallory and I, sometimes he and I with the addition of Somervell and Bruce, and once in full committee of all the climbers.

But we were to leave Kampa with our plan still in the air; Mallory's and my points of disagreement were much narrowed down, but enough remained to preclude a final decision. I cannot now remember the exact points on which we split, but I do remember the very pleasant spirit in which we differed.

Mallory was, I think, impatient by nature; yet with me he showed throughout these discussions the most perfect patience and tact, and that despite the fact that, owing to his eleventh-hour decision to join this year's Expedition, I had been appointed leader of the climbing party, a role to which his previous record on the mountain might well have entitled him, and which he assumed as soon as I became leader of the Expedition.

On April 13 fell the blow that we had begun to fear. John Macdonald arrived alone with a couple of pack mules; the General, under Hingston's escort, had had to return to Phari on a stretcher and so by easy stages to Yatung and Darjeeling. A note from Hingston left little doubt as to the wisdom of this decision.

This was indeed a shot between wind and water, and we were a gloomy party in the mess tent that night. It is hard to explain to those who have not served under him what the loss of our leader meant to us. It was said of Wellington in the Peninsula that 'the sight of his old nose was worth 10,000 men' in a critical situation. General Bruce's nose may not be much like that of the Great Duke, but it might well have been worth the last 1,000 feet of the mountain to an Everest expedition. He had a peculiar genius for the leadership of such an expedition; his prestige among the Mongolian people of both Nepalese and Tibetan stock stood very high, for he understood these folk as few white men do, and his temperament was exactly suited to dealing with them; in the troublous times ahead of us his influence over the porters would have been invaluable, and he was both known and greatly trusted by the Tibetan officials with whom we were to deal. He had a happy knack of sweeping away difficulties in the most lighthearted and effective way, and, perhaps most important of all, he had the gift of uniting the British members of a party and of inspiring them with something of his own cheerful spirit. Looking back now I can see clearly that though we of the 1924 Expedition were perhaps as happy a family as ever faced together the trials inseparable from such enterprises, we lost from April 13th something of that lighthearted atmosphere which the General alone could maintain.

But if we were henceforth to be deprived of General Bruce's leadership, he left us as legacy a most efficient organisation; I doubt if so strong a party will ever again be got together to climb Mount Everest. Of the climbers Mallory, Somervell, Geoffrey Bruce and myself had all been high in 1922, while Mallory had carried out the climbing reconnaissance in 1921 as well. Odell, Beetham and Hazard were Alpine climbers of notable speed and endurance and of great experience. Young Irvine's record was somewhat different, for his mountaineering experience was limited (though sufficient to guarantee him a safe member of any climbing party); but he had rowed two years in the Oxford boat, and if further proof of the essential qualities of endurance and courage were necessary, he had given them amply while sledging in Spitzbergen with Odell the previous summer, and later ski-ing in Switzerland.

To anyone interested in 'make and shape' the party was an instructive study. By trial and error, so to speak, we have evolved a type to climb at extreme altitudes, and it is exactly the type which I have for many years believed to be the best all-round build for a man: five foot eleven inches in height and eleven stone seven pounds in clothes. Mallory, Somervell, Geoffrey Bruce and Hazard fulfilled these conditions so nearly that they might all have exchanged clothes very respectably, and in proof of the all-round usefulness of the type, I may add that Geoffrey Bruce is that rare combination – a horseman and an athlete of quite remarkable versatility. Hazard, perhaps the slimmest of the four, has been noted for feats of strength; Somervell has to his credit an astonishing record of consecutive performance on the first-class peaks of the Alps; while Mallory, the graceful and accomplished mountaineer *par excellence*, had also made his mark at football and rowing. Odell only deviated from type by an inch or two of extra height, and he also had a record second to none for toughness and endurance both in the Alps and in Spitzbergen.

Beetham and I were at opposite ends of the scale. Beetham, of stockier build than the rest, was active as a cat and – so Somervell declares – a perfectly heartbreaking man to live with in a long day in the Alps. Previous to this Expedition he had never been on a horse, but his force of character was more than equal to so mild a test as a twelve-hand Tibetan pony, and it was an inspiriting sight to see him scouring the plains of Tibet on 'Ginger,' whom he quite frequently persuaded to go in the direction he indicated. 'It was grand to see that mountain horseman ride.' As for me, I approximate to Euclid's definition of a straight line. Irvine, as befitted a rowing blue, was big and powerful – with fine shoulders and comparatively light legs; he was only twenty-two, while the remaining seven climbers were all between thirty-three and forty years of age.

Hingston being away, the only other members of the party at this time were Noel, Shebbeare, and John Macdonald. Noel accompanied us as cinema expert, and it was largely through him that the funds necessary to finance the Expedition had been provided. He ran a small organisation of his own and was self-supporting as regards equipment, transport and *personnel*. As he had been a member of the 1922 party and had been to the North Col that year, he knew the ropes and, placing the good of the Expedition always before his own interests, he was a most valuable member of the 1924 party.

Shebbeare shared with Bruce the duties of transport officer: an officer of the Indian Forest Department, he had made a speciality of elephants, tame and wild, but the wilder the better. Tibet, however, is curiously deficient in elephants, and he owed his place on the Expedition to his great knowledge of, and sympathy with, the Mongolian people of the foothills, and to a temperament which made him from the start as popular with the porters as he was with all of us. John Macdonald, the son of the British Trade Agent at Yatung, came with us to the Base Camp and thence returned to Phari, thus organising that most efficient service of mail runners which kept the outer world in touch with our doings. His intimate knowledge of the Tibetans and his cheerful willingness to help us out in all our negotiations with the local officials were a great asset to the Expedition.

Our seventy-odd porters, syces, cooks and domestic servants were all recruited in Darjeeling under General Bruce's auspices. For the moment I will only speak in general terms of this splendid body of men, on whose shoulders we literally climbed Mount Everest. All without exception were of Mongolian stock – Bhotias (or true Tibetans) and Sherpas (Tibetan by race, but hailing from the higher valleys of Nepal). Like the British members of the party these men were carefully picked, and picked to a definite type evolved by previous experience. Light and wiry must be your good high-altitude porter, for he cannot afford to carry, in addition to his pack, a load of brawn and muscle. More, he must be a good-class man of some intelligence: the bucolic bumpkin with coarse features and slow brain fails no less than the 'hefty' giant, under the stress of high-altitude conditions. To deal with individually and *en masse* these men are singularly like a childish edition of the British soldier, many of whose virtues they share. They have the same high spirit for a tough and dangerous job; the same ready response to quip and jest. As with the British soldier, the rough character, who is perpetually a nuisance when drink and the attractions of civilisation tempt him astray, often comes out strongest when 'up against it' in circumstances where the milder man fails.

A strong element in our organisation was a party of four Gurkha noncommissioned officers lent (for the second year in succession) by the kindness of the 2/6th Gurkha Rifles, the battalion which also lent the services of Geoffrey Bruce, and to which the Mount Everest Expedition owes a debt of gratitude.

In a later chapter their work will be described in greater detail, and all I shall say here is that in allotting tasks to the officers of the Expedition I always regarded these NCOs as so reliable that they could be employed in any position of trust – such as the care of our very considerable treasure chest – on an equal footing with officers. Perhaps the most salient characteristic which they all shared was a remarkable sense of duty. The subsequent loss of Lance-Naik Shamsherpun was a very sad blow to all of us and cut short what would undoubtedly have been a brilliant military career.

Such was the party that I was now to lead; and I must take this opportunity of acknowledging another debt of gratitude: for if we owed the excellence of the party to the organisation of General Bruce, I certainly owe the fact that we reached the mountain punctually, smoothly and without a hitch to the never-failing advice, guidance and organising power of his cousin, Geoffrey Bruce. In 1922 I had not dealt with many of the Tibetan officials, whereas Geoffrey had assisted at all the General's interviews, and so knew the ropes; but it was as much his character and general efficiency as his previous experience which made him my more than right-hand man in 1924.

If the *suaviter in modo* was my strong point, he supplied the *fortiter in re*, and I remember our very good friend the Dzong Pen of Shekar simulating a certain anxiety when he enquired if that very determined young soldier was to take part in our discussions. When we pulled his leg about this afterwards, he replied, 'Well, it's quite right that a soldier should be very firm.' Firm he could be, as some of the more obstinate and obstructive Gyembus and minor officials discovered, on those trying occasions when, by about midday, the last twenty loads were still lying on the ground and the empty plains of Tibet showed no signs of disgorging the last of the promised transport.

We left Kampa Dzong on April 15. Our route to Tinki lay due west across a wide plain relieved by one long hog-backed hill halfway through the first day's march. Crossing this, we regained the plain and camped that night at Linga, a pleasant camp surrounded by a swamp and a number of shallow ponds; here the ruddy sheldrake and bar-headed geese were already busy with domestic affairs and almost as tame as barndoor fowls. On April 16 our march skirted the swamp that leads to Tinki Lake. Shebbeare had preceded us by one day to Tinki to hasten the supply of transport, which we were to change at this stage, and which we had ordered some days previously from Kampa.

As we approached the village he, with the Dzong Pen and a party of retainers, rode out to meet us.

The Dzong Pen, a youth of twenty-one, held a temporary appointment, pending confirmation from Lhasa, to the post of his father, with whom we had dealt in 1922 and who had since died. The lad proved courteous and friendly, and though we had a good deal of trouble to fix a reasonable rate for our transport, we finally succeeded in doing so and arranged to continue our march after one day's halt.

On this day, in addition to a lot of useful work by all members of the party on stores and oxygen, we finally settled the outline of our plan of campaign. To Mallory goes all the credit of evolving, from the conflicting views held up to date by him and me, a plan which combined all the good points of both, and which was that evening unanimously approved by all the climbers in conclave. I will explain this plan later, for its details were worked out down to the last porter load and coil of rope before we reached the Base Camp. At the time we were all entirely satisfied with it, and though the Fates ruled that it should never be put into execution, I still think that, with the knowledge we then had of our resources and the task before us, we could not have bettered it.

It was at Tinki also that another load was lifted from my mind. Our invalids here showed clear signs of recovery. To be exact, Mallory's trouble had never become serious and had been mending from Kampa onwards, but it had been touch and go whether Beetham was not to leave us at that place and head for the Swedish Mission at Lachen in Sikkim, to rejoin us – possibly – on his recovery. In fact, I had advanced on his tent with an ultimatum to this effect, feeling like the executioner with the bowstring, and he must have recognised me as such, for never did victim put up a better fight for a few days' grace. I finally gave in, and sternly bade him recover by Tinki – or thence seek a lower altitude. That he did recover by Tinki was due, I believe, to sheer dogged determination, and it has always been a matter of keen regret to me that this obstinate quality, of which he has so large a share, was fated to be wasted in fighting up to Camp III, when it would have been so great an asset higher on the mountain. When I say that he recovered, I mean that he recovered from the acute stage, for you do not quickly recover from dysentery when you have been treating it for a fortnight in the Tibetan spring by marching fifteen miles a day at an average height of 15,000 feet.

So it was with light hearts that we marched from Tinki on April 18 and headed for the Bahman Dopté Pass and the Chiblung Chu route to the Phung Chu valley.

Our transport for the next six days consisted almost entirely of donkeys. These tiny creatures carry the same load as a yak – 160 pounds – at a distinctly faster pace and for any distance up to twenty-five miles a day over passes rising 3,000 feet above the plains. How their little legs – no thicker than walking-sticks – can do it, is a mystery.

By now we had got well into the swing of marching. The early mornings were usually still and gloriously sunny, and we breakfasted in the open about seven o'clock, by which time the big mess tent would be packed and away on a pair of fleet mules of our own which we had bought for this purpose in Kalimpong. By 7.30 or 8 the whole Expedition would be *en route*, strung out in little parties of donkeys, horsemen and pedestrians over a mile of country. We most of us rode and walked about half and half, for our experience of 1922 had taught us the necessity of saving the energies of the climbers for what was ahead. But there were some very determined pedestrians, notably Shebbeare, who seldom rode.

About 11.30 we would sit down by twos and threes, or collect into little parties in some sheltered spot – for by then the inevitable Tibetan wind would be going strong – and eat a light lunch of biscuit and cheese, chocolate and raisins. We usually got into our new camp about 2, though we were occasionally as late as 7 p.m. The mess tent would be pitched and waiting for us, and often its well-known outline would be a beacon to guide us the last mile or two. If all were well the position of camp would be further marked by a wisp of smoke from a yak-dung fire, indicating that the advanced cook had also arrived and had tea ready. In the grateful shelter of the tent we enjoyed a more substantial tiffin, and soon after our tents and belongings would begin to arrive. By 5 p.m. on most days the whole camp would be pitched and snug, and a visit to the porters' tents would disclose a circle of grinning faces sitting round a yak-dung fire right inside each tent, with a savoury brew sizzling in the pot and an atmosphere that no European could have stood for five minutes. Dinner would be about 7.30, and so to bed by 8.30. The minimum temperature at night during this stage averaged 10° Fahrenheit pretty consistently.

What a happy life it was! The more so for a feeling of optimism that began to be apparent about this time, due partly to confidence in our plan, the details of which were shaping under our constant discussions; partly to the increasing fitness and form of the party; partly also, I think, to the fact that we were beginning to know one another well – and with such a party mutual acquaintance could not but breed mutual respect and confidence.

I walked much with Mallory, and I remember how often we would wind up a long discussion on ways and means with the remark, 'If only a non-oxygen party can sleep at 27,000 feet and an oxygen party at 26,500 feet, the trick is done – both ways.' *Dis aliter visum.*

From Tinki we climbed to the Bahman Dopté Pass, at about 17,000 feet, and thence descended into the Chiblung Chu valley. This we followed for two days, and camped on the night of April 20 at its mouth, just above the quicksands and old lake-bed near Shiling. On the morning of April 21 we climbed a hill above camp and enjoyed, at about sixty miles' range, that most striking view of Mount Everest which the mountain presents to the east, for on this side it is a true snow-peak, its slopes running in clean straight lines from the summit 6,000 feet down to where its base is lost among the cluster of smaller peaks. A beautiful and a formidable mountain it seems from here.

On this day we entered the valley of the Phung Chu (or Arun, to give it its Nepalese name), whose left bank we followed for three days to Shekar Dzong. With the exception of our glimpse of Mount Everest from near Shiling we were now out of sight of the big snows, for the valley was shut in on both sides by unimpressive limestone hills rising 3,000 or 4,000 feet above the river. As we neared Shekar these grew always more completely barren and desolate, until one could picture oneself among the mountain scenery of the moon; utterly devoid of vegetation, they were of every shade of colour, from lemon-yellow to rust-red or purple.

On April 23 we reached Shekar Dzong, and the Dzong Pen, our friend of 1922, rode out to meet us, greeted us most courteously and promised every assistance in his power. It was a relief to hear that our fresh transport was to be ready for us in two days. All details were arranged at an interview in camp the same afternoon, and it was a real pleasure to deal with this straightforward and efficient gentleman – a man who was entirely master in his own house and who yet ran his subordinates so quietly. But quiet though he was, we did not fail to note that his Gyembus jumped to obey his orders.

I remember that through some slip or misunderstanding there was a small mistake made in the price fixed for our transport – a mistake in our favour – which, small though it was, was by no means negligible when multiplied by nearly 300. We at once offered to rectify this, but the Dzong Pen refused to go back on an undertaking he had once given.

April 24 was spent by all hands working in their various departments. It was here that Odell and Irvine, the oxygen experts, definitely ascertained that the apparatus supplied us had some very serious defects; a large proportion of its numerous valves were found to leak. Many of the cylinders were partially – some completely – empty, and various other defects came to light. The two experts, who had for days been working every afternoon, and often late into the night, put in a regular field-day, and finished by evolving a new and simplified arrangement of the apparatus, which was satisfactorily tested the same evening by Mallory and Somervell on the steep sides of the hill on which stand the fort and monastery. At my instance Odell wrote a comprehensive report on the faults of the apparatus, to be sent to the Mount Everest Committee.

I myself carried out a difficult duty here. This was to inform the various members of the climbing party in which attempt they were to take part. For some days, now that the plan of campaign had been decided in principle, I thought that I had detected a slight air of constraint and uneasiness in the party, and from my own feelings I judged that the sooner every one knew his place in the coming operations the better.

Our plan was briefly to attack the mountain at as early a date as possible by an attempt consisting of two parties of two climbers each, one pair equipped with oxygen, one without. The two parties after sleeping at 26,500 feet and 27,200 respectively (or as near these heights as the porters could put their camps) were to go for the top on the same day, independently, but ready mutually to support one another. Four more climbers would support this attempt or remain in reserve, and in the event of an initial failure, these four would repeat the attempt with any modifications dictated by the experience of the first attempt.

It was significant of our confidence at this stage that most of us felt the odds were against a second attempt being necessary, and it will be guessed how keen was the competition – unexpressed though it was – to take part in the earlier attempt. It was one of the penalties of leadership that I had to take on myself the entire responsibility of allotting climbers to one or other of the attempts: not that I kept the decision in my own hands; on the contrary, I had discussed it exhaustively with Mallory, Somervell and Bruce – the three veterans of 1922 – for some days.

As it turned out various considerations settled most of the places inevitably. A member of each party must know something either of Nepalese or Hindustani. The more experienced mountaineers must, as far as possible, be evenly distributed as well as those with previous knowledge of the mountain. Those who were fittest or promised to acclimatise early must take part in the first attempt, and each oxygen party must include one of the oxygen experts. My own position I left to Mallory and Somervell to decide.

The arrangement which resulted was as follows: first attempt, Mallory and Irvine with oxygen; Somervell and myself without. Second, Geoffrey Bruce and Odell with oxygen; Beetham and Hazard without. Of course this was to be subject to alterations dictated by the subsequent form of the members of the party. I explained this decision, with the reasons that led to it, at a conference of all the climbers the night before we left Shekar Dzong, and it was one of the first indications of the fine spirit which the 1924 party later showed so conspicuously that there was not a word of protest or dissatisfaction from any of the disappointed climbers.

We presented our friendly Dzong Pen with some of our most handsome and costly presents, but we subsequently heard that what his soul really yearned for was a cheap camp chair and a pair of the snow goggles with which our porters were equipped. The latter want was easily supplied, but we were short of chairs, and I could only promise to send him one from Darjeeling on our return – a promise I duly kept four months later.

On April 25 we started the last stage of our march, turning due south and heading directly for the mountain. The march from Shekar to Panglé is always a short and enjoyable one; our journey was nearing its end, and the knowledge that we had only four or five more of these pleasant marching days ahead of us made me, for one, enjoy each one more and more. We were a large enough party to assure constant change of companionship and the possibility of sharing diversity of interests with the others. In the absence of Hingston, our naturalist, Shebbeare, Beetham and I all did a bit in the bird line; Odell's geological knowledge was in great demand, and I spent many a pleasant hour watching Somervell sketching and feebly trying to emulate him.

These marches also afforded a good opportunity of getting to know the porters. Bruce, Shebbeare and I took every opportunity of watching their form on the march and of studying their characters. They were the most cheerful, friendly fellows imaginable, and responded instantly to a joke. One Mingma, a baby-faced lad whose character belied his innocent expression, had distinguished himself earlier in the march by biting off one of his friend's fingers – so he became Mingma Kukar (the dog), and we used to bark and growl at him when we passed him on the road. Shebbeare would yarn away with the porters by the hour, and Somervell, who hit it off with them famously, often threw additional light on their characters, as he took the daily sick parade, and had an equally unerring eye for a malingerer or for the stout heart that made light of a genuine ailment. Of serious sickness among them I cannot remember a single case from Phari to the Base Camp.

We camped the night of the 25th at Panglé and next morning, after a light sprinkling of snow in the night, we climbed the last high pass of our march. This pass, the Pang La, rises some 3,000 feet above our camp; it is distinguished from the many similar passes we had crossed by the fact that we reached it after just three weeks on the Tibetan plateau, and three weeks seems to be the period necessary to produce effective acclimatisation. So here we watched our own form and that of our companions with some curiosity, as probably affording for the first time some definite indication of how we were going to shape in the bigger trials ahead. I was elated to find, on reaching the pass, that I had beaten my 1922 time by a quarter of an hour – the more so as I had had some heart-searching over one or two of the earlier passes: on the Bahman Dopté, for instance, Mallory and Odell had quite run away from me.

From the Pang La a striking panorama of the main Himalayan range comes into view, with Mount Everest, its central point, some thirty-five miles away as the crow flies. Four of the highest mountains in the world are to be seen in one *coup d'œil*. Climb a small hill over the pass and you will add two more, one at each extreme flank. From right to left they run: Gosainthan, Cho Uyo, Gyachung Kang, Mount Everest, Makalu, and Kanchenjunga. And that nothing may be lacking from the grandeur of the view, each of the giants is so spaced from its neighbours that none is dwarfed, and each stands dominating the serried ranks of lesser peaks which stretch in a jagged wall from horizon to horizon. Above 20,000 feet or thereabouts all is snow and ice except where the cliffs are too sheer for snow to lie, with one exception. By some freak of the inclination of the rock to the impact of the perpetual north-west wind, the northern face of the whole topmost pyramid of Mount Everest – 6,000 feet of it – is at this season almost bare of snow.

The day was singularly windless, and the sun on the southern side of the pass hot enough to allow us to sit for perhaps an hour, and out came binoculars and telescope, maps, cameras and sketch-books. We took the climb to the north-east shoulder – over 27,000 feet – as done, and every eye was turned on the last 2,000 feet. When we had climbed Mount Everest by every conceivable route, we turned our attention to Makalu, and were promptly stumped. It is going to be quite a long time before Makalu reaches the last stage of the once-inaccessible Alpine peaks and becomes 'an easy day for a lady.'

This barren pass – for its character belies its name, which means the grassy pass – is for some reason a great place for early flowers, butterflies and lizards, and we all scattered after specimens on the way down, finding but little this year to reward us, though I saw a tern (apparently the common tern) flapping its way northward over the pass; truly spring migrants in Tibet must be inspired by the faith that moveth mountains.

That night we camped at Tashi Dzom, in the valley of the Dzakar Chu. We were now to follow it to its source, just above the Base Camp, where it emerges from the snout of the Rongbuk Glacier. Next day, April 27, we covered perhaps the dullest stage of all our journey, the fifteen miles to Chödzong, the last village we pass through before entering a land of utter desolation relieved only by the big monastery at Rongbuk.

The stage from Chödzong to Rongbuk bears to the wide plains behind and the big glaciers ahead somewhat the same relation as, in an approach march of the Great War, the ruined areas bore to the fertile fields of France behind and the stricken battlefield ahead. For it is a cheerless, desolate valley suggestive at every turn of the greater desolation to which it leads. The valley is narrow and the river absurdly small to represent the drainage of four great glaciers with some dozens of smaller tributaries. The hills on both sides are ugly brown humps of limestone devoid of any beauty of colour or form. For ten or fifteen miles on either bank of the river-bed stand the great moraines that once flanked the now shrunken glacier, for all the world like interminable railway embankments. Against the brown hillsides these moraines look almost white, for they are composed of crystalline rock which I, in my ignorance, should call granite (though Odell has another name for it). Every rock in them has fallen in some remote age from the cliffs of Mount Everest, Gyachung Kang, or their satellites. High above on the steep hillsides the snouts of glaciers begin to appear, almost hidden by their terminal moraines. The marked drop in temperature and the bite to the wind that blows straight off the big snow-fields above further serve to emphasise the fact that the land of ice and snow is getting very near.

Soon one gets a first glimpse of it, for the tributary valley of the Gyachung Chu opens up a peep of the great snowy amphitheatre of Gyachung Kang and its neighbours. Next a turn in the main valley shows a white shoulder which can only be the west peak of Everest. Soon comes another twist, and quite suddenly the familiar form of Everest itself and the Rongbuk monastery come almost simultaneously into sight.

We camped on the open stony shelf, itself the top of an old moraine, just in front of the monastery. It was a disappointment to hear that the head lama was sick and could not at present carry out the ceremony of blessing the whole expedition, on which, on behalf of our porters, we set considerable store. In addition to a selection of our best presents we sent him a yak-load of cement; this he had asked for in 1922, as he wanted it to carry out some repairs to the big 'chorten' which overlooks the monastery, and we had brought it all the way from Darjeeling. Hazard, our ex-sapper, volunteered to give some instruction in how to mix and use it and, on an opportunity occurring later, was able to do so.

On April 29 we covered the last stage of our journey to the site of our old Base Camp, four miles up the valley from the monastery. Before leaving Rongbuk we said good-bye to our good little ponies which had carried us so well for a large part of our 300-mile march from Darjeeling; the going above Rongbuk was too rough for them, and they turned back under the charge of our syces heading for a village in the valley below to enjoy a well-earned rest in its comparatively balmy climate and so-called pastures. I confess to having stifled a feeling of envy for them as we turned our faces in the opposite direction.

Picking our way through the tumbled heaps of old moraine, we found ourselves by 11.30 at the old camping-ground, which looked as if we had only left it yesterday. In another hour every yak had disappeared down the valley again, and the camp was as busy as an ants' nest.

That was a hard day; every one had his appointed task, and we now began to reap the fruits of all the work we had done with pencil and paper from Darjeeling onwards, for we were able to get to work with the minimum of delay and the maximum of organisation. The tents were soon up; nearly 300 yak-loads of provision boxes, rolls of bedding and stores of all sorts, dumped higgledy-piggledy off the yaks, began to sort themselves into orderly lines and piles; and a steadily increasing dump of boxes and bundles, all appropriately labelled, represented the loads to start no later than the very next day for Camp I on the shoulders of our local Tibetan porters who had been specially enlisted for the purpose from Shekar and the intervening villages by the good offices of the Shekar Dzong Pen.

And then down came the snow: whirling powdery stuff, blotting out the landscape and making us bitterly cold, but – and this is the saving grace of this country – so devoid of any wetting quality that you can be snowed on for hours without any need even to change your coat; a shake and a brush and it is all gone. My diary notes that this was one of the coldest days that I had ever known at the Base Camp, and we all worked muffled to the eyes in our full outfit of woollen and wind-proof clothes, ear-flapped caps and long mitts. But we kept at it without stopping until dusk, and by then were in a position to send off 150 porter-loads next day.

We had left Phari one day earlier than in 1922, and it had been my intention to make up one more day on the march so as to reach the Base Camp two days sooner than in that year, and in this we had succeeded. The reason for haste was this: we hoped if all went well to put in our first attempt on the mountain as early as May 17. If this failed, and even should the monsoon break, as in 1922 (an exceptionally early year), on June 1, we should still have ten days in which to make any necessary additions or modifications to the high camps before a second attempt; and this interval might serve to allow some climbers from the first attempt to recuperate sufficiently to take part in or to support the second attempt, or even perhaps to form a third.

But before the first attempt, the general organisation of which I have already described, could take place, there was much to be done. Camps I, II, and III had to be established and stocked; the route from Camp III to the North Col had to be reconnoitred by a party of climbers, for this route follows a steep glacier, and it was certain to have changed since 1922. Camp IV must then be established and stocked with stores and oxygen both for itself and the higher camps. Next Bruce and Odell were to escort a party of fifteen porters to a site for Camp V at about 25,500 feet, there to prepare the camp and dump tents and stores for it and for higher camps. Somervell and I were then to start from Camp IV, sleep one night at Camp V and another at Camp VII (at about 27,200) feet, and while we were climbing to the latter, Mallory and Irvine were to go from Camp IV to Camp VI at about 26,500 feet, there to sleep. With this programme to precede our combined attempt on the summit on May 17, it will be understood that time pressed.

Again it was considered important that the climbers should get above the Base Camp as soon as possible in order to continue the process of acclimatisation, or rather adaptation to altitude, for though we were by this time well acclimatised to marching and sleeping at an average height of, say, 14,000 feet, with occasional excursions over passes 3,000 feet higher, we were now confronted with another step in the ladder. The Base Camp is at about 16,800 feet and every step beyond it is a step higher. To me, though perhaps not to all, a marked change takes place at about 16,000 feet. Above this height the not very serious *malaise* that we experience on the outward march becomes something more definite and unpleasant. On first arrival at the Base Camp one is conscious of it all the time; the least exertion, such as getting into a sleeping-bag or putting on one's boots, is exhausting; lighting a pipe is quite a business, for one's breath gives out about the same moment as the match, and the pipe has gone out before it is recovered.

I confess that the first trip to Camp I is pain and grief to me. I remember that the first time I did it this year my right arm and shoulder became weary merely from the weight of my ice axe, and I thought I should have to find a lighter axe. Walking is a labour, and in the keenest air there is no exhilaration; rather is there an indefinable feeling of discomfort and distress.

After a trip or two to Camp I things improve, but the process is repeated with each new rung in the upward ladder until further acclimatisation is achieved, and though, on returning to the Base after a sojourn at Camp III or higher, one forgets much of this unpleasantness, I am convinced that life above 16,000 feet is never quite what it is below that level. There seems to be something lacking all the time, and indeed there *is* something lacking – and that something the very breath of life – oxygen.

So finished the first phase of the Expedition; we were up to time, and we had a surprisingly clean bill of health. So smoothly had the machine run so far that we may be pardoned if we were optimistic as to the future. If the party which met for dinner in the mess tent at 7 p.m. that night was not hilarious, all, I think, displayed the tempered cheerfulness of high altitudes; we little guessed what rude buffets the future had in store for us.

# 3 THE RONGBUK GLACIER

## BY CAPTAIN J.G. BRUCE, MC

As Colonel Norton has already described, the first attempt on the summit was fixed to take place on May 17, by which time it was calculated that the three glacier camps and the camp on the North Col would be established and stocked. There was, however, a great deal to be done in these few days. Not a moment could be wasted, and the great rapidity with which the first two camps were completed was due, firstly, to the very careful calculation and labelling of boxes and equipment done by Norton and Shebbeare before the Expedition left Darjeeling, and, secondly, to the tactful and skilful manner in which the Gurkha NCOs handled the local labour.

On arrival in the Base Camp, we had with us just over 150 local Tibetans, who had been recruited, with the permission of the Shekar Dzong Pen, from the area between Shekar and Rongbuk. Our arrangement with them was that they should be paid at the rate of four *tankas* a day (about a shilling), and given some rations. They were not to be employed on snow or ice, and were to be quickly released when the work was done as they had the sowing of their fields to attend to. They undertook to look after themselves as regards other amenities, which meant that they were quite satisfied to sleep in the open at 18,000 feet with no cover or blankets. Had they been of a less hardy race, their maintenance in such country would have been well-nigh impossible.

In order to save the climbers from any arduous work before it was absolutely necessary, I suggested to Norton that the Gurkha NCOs should be allowed to establish the first two camps, putting into Camp II all necessary stores and equipment for camps farther on. He agreed to this proposal, and on April 30 three of them set out from the Base Camp with a convoy of 150 Tibetans, men, women, and boys, carrying at least forty pounds each regardless of age or sex. I made considerable efforts before their departure to hand out the lightest loads to the women and boys, but it was no good, and I had to resort to the only plan that ensures swift allotment and complete satisfaction in Tibet. Tibetans all wear prettily woven garters of distinct colouring round the tops of their boots, and immediately recognise their own colours. The best method of distributing loads consists in collecting a garter from each person, shuffling them well, and throwing one on to each load. The owner of the garter then claims his or her load, and carries it all day without further complaint.

We were lucky in having a glorious day for this first move. From the Base Camp we could watch the coolies threading their way up the stony valley, singing and joking as they went, then taking to the higher route along the shelf, and finally disappearing from sight into the mouth of the East Rongbuk Glacier. This was a really good start, and we felt optimistic for the future. That evening in the Base Camp the dinner to celebrate our safe arrival was a large affair – five courses and champagne.

Two of the three NCOs conducting the convoy to Camp I had been with the previous Expedition of 1922, and could be relied on to reconnoitre the route from Camps I to II without assistance from us. Their orders were to send seventy-five coolies back to the Base Camp on arrival at Camp I, and to keep the other seventy-five with them for the first move to Camp II next day. Seventy-five came back all right from Camp I, but next morning we were greeted with the news that fifty-two had disappeared in the night. This was a very serious matter, for everything depended on these men, and a transport strike at this juncture would effectively cripple the whole pro-gramme. So Norton, Shebbeare and I went up to Camp I to see how the NCOs were faring. We were relieved to find no evidence of discontent, and that everything was running smoothly.

Just after we arrived the convoy of seventy-five Tibetans from Camp II came in. They were full of cheer. We told them that they were doing splendid work, and if they completed Camp II with all the necessary loads by the following evening we would give them extra wages and a good feed. They were delighted, and promised to see the matter through. Although we made full enquiries, no light could be thrown on the sudden departure of the fifty-two from the Base Camp.

The performances of the women are worthy of record. One carried her child of about two years on the top of her forty-pound load from 17,500 feet to 19,800 feet, deposited her load there and carried the child back again. She at once expressed her readiness to repeat the journey if necessary. Another woman of maturer age – she had grey hair – treated us to a little step dance before sitting down to her food. It was a great relief to find them like this, and we calculated that by using some of our own porters in place of the fifty-two deserters, the programme could yet be kept up to time. Moreover the NCOs told us that the route between Camp I and II had scarcely changed at all in the last two years, and had presented no difficulties.

Camp I was – for the Rongbuk Glacier – a snug retreat which managed to catch any sunshine going, while missing most of the wind. It was situated a few hundred yards from the junction of the main and East Rongbuk Glaciers. Away from it on both sides of the stream ran steep scree slopes culminating in vertical cliffs. Here and there one could see pillars of rock fashioned by the wind almost into the shape of men. The 'Sangars' built by the 1922 Expedition were still in good condition, and by stretching the flies of the Whymper tents over them, comfortable shelters for the NCOs had been made. Camp I was easily the best camp on the glacier, but unfortunately the one that could be least used by reason of its distance from the mountain.

After drinking a mug of hot tea with Tejbir, Hurke and Shamsher, we started for the Base Camp. On our way down we passed a party of Noel's photographic men, leading two of their mules laden with cinematograph outfit towards Camp I. They said that they had experienced little difficulty in getting mules along. They reached Camp I all right, and repeated the journey several times on subsequent days. But the inadequate supply of fodder for the mules, which had to be brought up from Chodzong to the Base Camp, a distance of about twenty-two miles, made the employment of coolies better worth the while in the end. For this reason I do not think animal transport on a large scale beyond the Base Camp is deserving of consideration.

In the meanwhile every one at the Base Camp had been busy perfecting the plans, and making ready for a move beyond Camp II as soon as news was received of its completion. On the evening of May 2 a note was brought into camp from Tejbir and Hurke, to the effect that all loads were safely deposited in Camp II, and that they were sending down the coolies to be paid off. This was indeed a great success, particularly as there had been a slight snowstorm during the day, and we had feared that it might interrupt the smooth working of the convoys. Towards evening the coolies arrived, and we gave them their promised feed and extra pay. It was delightful to see these simple folk enjoying a good feed and apparently satisfied with their lot. We were certainly satisfied with what they had done. Six of the best coolies among them were kept on for odd jobs about the camp, and the rest went happily back towards Rongbuk.

The next task before us was the transportation from Camp II of the necessary stores for Camp III and the higher camps. For this work our own porter corps was formed into two parties of twenty each, and a reserve of twelve. Briefly, these parties were to be utilised as follows:

No. 1 party was to go through with some of the climbers to Camp III, establish it, and remain based there for the purpose of getting the next camp on to the North Col. A day later No. 2 party was to move to Camp II, and work between II and III. The reserve party was to remain at the Base Camp ready to replace casualties among the first two parties, for in dealing with Everest, anywhere beyond the Base Camp may be considered as the 'danger zone,' and trouble may surely be expected in some form or another. To the Gurkha NCOs was given the responsible task of taking charge of a glacier camp each, which included seeing to the feeding and welfare of every one in it, and supervising the arrivals and departures of convoys.

As the success or failure of the attempt scheduled to take place on May 17 depended so greatly on the work of our porter corps during the next two weeks, a slight digression may here be permissible in order to give some idea of them and their limitations. Apart from cooks, syces, and bootmakers, we had enlisted seventy men as carriers in Darjeeling during March. News had preceded us that we should require men to accompany the Expedition, and volunteers were so plentiful that we found a small army of nearly 300 from which to pick. Among them were many who had taken part in the 1922 Expedition, and those who had done really well that year were at once re-engaged. The selection of the remainder with nothing but appearance to go by was a difficult matter, and bound to be in the nature of a gamble, since there were neither time nor means available to test them individually. The guiding principle was to take men of obviously good breeding who appeared lithe and active in preference to the thick-set and at first sight more impressive-looking giants. Among those finally chosen there were, nevertheless, several big men, but it is interesting to note that when the time came none of them were fit enough to take part in the really high climbs.

The journey from Darjeeling to the Base Camp afforded excellent opportunity for getting the porter corps into good physical condition for the hard work before them, and at the same time to study them closely with a view to ear-marking those likely to go high on the mountain. Throughout this period they always had the best of food, clothing, and tent accommodation, and were never burdened with heavy loads. This policy amply repaid us, for when we arrived at the Base Camp we had none of them on the sick-list. To keep them upon the straight and narrow path for several weeks had been no easy matter, for Sherpas and Bhotias are a light-hearted and inconsequent people with a thirst that has to be quenched.

As carriers they are unsurpassed, for they are brought up to it from their youth. When quite small children they learn to carry loads, fetching and carrying water and grain for the upkeep of their homes. Born and bred in the mountains they are sure-footed and self-reliant, and owing to the rigorous climate of their homes can withstand more than average exposure and fatigue. Some of our porters were inhabitants of Solah Khombu, a Sherpa settlement in Nepal, just to the south of the Nangba La. Solah Khombu lies on one of the main trade routes between Nepal and Tibet, and the two countries are separated by the high Nangba Pass, 19,000 feet above sea-level. That these people think little or nothing of traversing this high and wind-swept pass is clearly shown by the fact that there is continuous traffic across it for five months of the year, and that among the travellers are frequently to be seen women carrying their babies and small children on their backs.

The severe tests of this year showed us how extremely difficult it is to gauge the true form of the porter, and to estimate how much strength and determination he has left after a certain amount of hardship. One minute all goes well, the next he collapses both physically and mentally, having apparently reached a limit beyond which he cannot go. I do not say that this happened in every case. The 'Tigers,' for instance, whose exploits will be described later, never failed us, and very few ever gave in before they put their loads into camp.

May 3 was a cold, stormy day, with threatening clouds in the sky, when the first party of climbers and porters set out from the Base Camp. The climbers were Mallory and Irvine, whose intention it was to help with the establishment of Camp III, and then remain there for a few days to acclimatise and test their oxygen apparatus; and Odell and Hazard, who were to push on from Camp III and construct the route up the North Col. Noel, with a portion of his cinema outfit, accompanied them, and on the next day Havildar Umar and the second party of porters followed. The rest of us had another day or two to wait at the Base Camp in order to give the first lot time to accomplish their tasks.

The Base Camp daily presented scenes of considerable activity. Our chonzay[1] had his fuel (yak-dung) and meat supplies coming in regularly from below, and these had to be checked and paid for. One day a couple of enterprising Sherpas from Solah Khombu, remembering that the previous expedition had been glad to buy vegetables, came into camp with potatoes

---

1  A subordinate official of a Tibetan district.

to sell. We bought them all, and sent them back for more. Another day a suspicious-looking villain, leading two donkeys with equally suspicious-looking loads, was found to be a purveyor of Chinese spirit, and had to be removed outside the three-mile limit. On another occasion a messenger came in bearing a complaint from the Shikar of Tashi Dzom to the effect that we had 'beaten two of his subjects without reason at Rongbuk.' Untrue though the allegation was, we could not ignore it, for much of our supplies and the welfare of the ponies we had left with him depended upon this man's good-will. Accordingly Paul, the interpreter, was despatched to visit Tashi Dzom, and to do what he could to pacify the Shikar. This ambassadorial role exactly suited Paul's fancy, and as soon as he was able to procure a pony, he went off looking very important – a vain young man, but efficient. He carried out his mission most satisfactorily, and came back a week later with all kinds of friendly messages from the Shikar.

Before Norton left the Base Camp he gave the Gurkha surveyor, Hari Singh Thapa, who was attached to the Expedition from the Survey of India Department, full instructions about what he was to do during the next few weeks. The most important piece of country to be dealt with was the West Rongbuk Glacier, but it was thought unsafe to send the survey party without at least one expert climber to escort them. As there were no climbers available for the West Rongbuk Glacier, Hari Singh was told to do two important but easily accessible areas, one in and around Gyachung Kang Glacier, and the other to the east of the Rongbuk Monastery. He set off on May 5, with a small convoy of local coolies, on what subsequently proved to be a very successful survey expedition.

There was a further exodus on the 6th, when Norton, Somervell and Beetham moved out. Norton and Somervell were to go quietly through to Camp III, and gradually acclimatise themselves before their non-oxygen attempt on the 17th. Beetham was almost fit again. He had made a marvellous recovery, mainly by sheer determination not to give in and allow himself to be packed off to Darjeeling. As he could not yet be counted upon to take part in this first attempt, he volunteered to help generally all along the line, and particularly to assist Noel with his photographic work.

So far everything appeared to be running smoothly ahead. My turn to follow up the glacier came on May 7. Norton had asked me to follow up behind the rest of the party, make a thorough inspection of each camp *en route*, and ensure that the non-commissioned officers understood exactly what they had to do. I had to join Odell in Camp III by the 11th, ready to go

PLATE 1
A panorama of the central Himalaya showing the route from Darjeeling to Mount Everest. Drawn by Mr D. Macpherson for the Mount Everest Committee.

PLATE 2
View of Kanchenjunga from Darjeeling, painted by Norton before the start of the expedition in March 1924. *See page 8.*

Rongli Chu
29 3/24

PLATE 3
The Rongli-Chu at Rongli in Sikkim, painted by Norton. *See page 19.*

PLATE 4
Chomulhari on the Tibet/Bhutan border, photographed from near Phari with yak transport in the foreground. *See page 27.*

PLATE 5
Chomulhari from the west, painted by Somervell. *See page 170.*

PLATE 6
Kampa Dzong fortress. Unfinished watercolour by Somervell. *See page 28.*

PLATE 7
Kinchenjhau from Kampa Dzong, painted by Somervell. *See page 29.*

PLATE 8
From Linga looking west at evening during the monsoon. Watercolour by Somervell. *See page 34.*

PLATE 9
Gyachung Kang from Gyachung Chu. Watercolour by Somervell. *See page 41.*

PLATE 10

Looking north from Sichu camp, en route to the Rongshar Valley. Watercolour by Somervell. *See page 125.*

PLATE 11
Sunset on the snows of Cho Rapzang, painted by Somervell. *See page 127.*

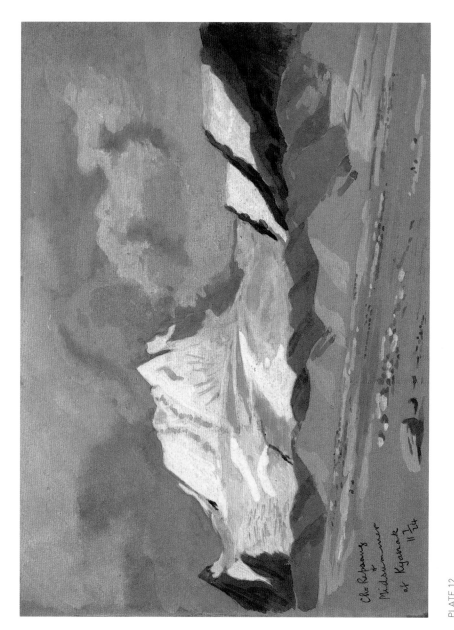

Within the image (artist's handwritten notes):

Cho Rapzang
+
Midsummer
at Kyetrak
11.7.24

PLATE 12
Cho Rapzang and midsummer at Kyetrak. Watercolour by Norton. *See page 126.*

In the image, handwritten: "First view of Gaurisanker from Tingsang 24 6/24"

PLATE 13
The first view of Gaurisankar from Tingsang, painted by Norton. *See page 134.*

Gaurisankar

26/4

PLATE 14
Gaurisankar rising above the clouds. Watercolour by Norton. *See page 134.*

PLATE 15

The Tingri plain from Sharto, painted by Norton. *See page 136.*

Tso. Mo-Tray Tang
$\frac{7}{14\,24}$.

PLATE 16
Tsomo-tre-tung lake, painted by Norton. *See page 141.*

on with him up the mountain and establish Camp V. I took with me the reserve party, among whom were some of the old hands of 1922. They had originally rather resented being relegated to this job, for they had all been told that the men to go highest would reap the greatest rewards, and they considered that they were not getting a fair start. I did my best to assure them that they were there for a good purpose, little thinking at the time how soon this would be proved.

We arrived at Camp II on May 8, and found the tents pitched in the same spot as they were two years ago, beside the frozen lake, with the high wall of glittering ice cliffs closing it in on the lower side. Instead of finding the camp empty except for a cook and an odd porter or two, we found it fully occupied. There had been a severe breakdown, which would undoubtedly have developed into a complete collapse of the porters had Norton not been present at the critical moment to keep them on their feet and restore their ebbing courage and spirits. He explained to me what had happened on the two previous days. He and Somervell reached Camp II on May 7 without incident, but on arrival discovered that No. 2 party based there had encountered such appalling weather that Mallory had decided to form a dump on the glacier, a mile short of camp, and send them back. That evening between four and six o'clock they observed some porters staggering wearily down the glacier from the direction of Camp III. These men belonged to the first party, and had made one journey to the camp with full loads two days before. They had since then been confined to their tents in Camp III, with only one blanket apiece, and a little uncooked barley to eat, and were now driven out unable to bear it longer, utterly exhausted. This meant that there was almost double the number of men in Camp II that it was calculated to accommodate, and all of them in need of nursing and comforting. Consequently all the stores and tents intended for the higher camp had at once to be broken open and distributed to meet this grave emergency. Mallory, Irvine, Hazard and Odell, with two or three men, were apparently still in Camp III, but no further news was forthcoming until Mallory himself came down to Camp II early next morning (a few hours before the reserve party and I arrived). His story amplified the information the porters had given. He said that a terrible wind with a temperature as low as -22° Fahrenheit had played havoc with the men, and had resulted in the failure of the second party to carry as far as Camp III. Consequently the party already in Camp III had been stranded with only the barest necessities of life for forty-eight hours. He had ordered them back himself, and, owing to their disheartened condition, only with the greatest difficulty induced them to leave their tents and move down. He also said that Odell, Hazard and Irvine were remaining in Camp III, and that the two former were to make an attempt that day to reconnoitre the North Col route.

This was the situation on May 8, and a very unenviable one, particularly for our leader, upon whose shoulders rested the responsibility of deciding what the next move was to be. Fortunately for us all, he was one of those really great leaders of men, who by their own resolution and courage inspire their comrades and followers with some measure of their own qualities. Norton is certainly one of these, though, characteristically, in his despatches he takes no credit for the resumed advance to himself. He wisely decided to rest the first party at Camp II, while Somervell, who was always a great favourite with the men, and who had a happy way of getting the best out of them, should take the second party up as far as the dump with loads, and get them to carry from there to Camp III sufficient stores and bedding to make the camp habitable. If the first party of porters could be pulled together again in twenty-four hours' time, they were then to be utilised to keep Camp III supplied from Camp II. The breaking up of stores and equipment intended for high camps, and the temporary dislocation of the programme, made it necessary to call up Shebbeare from the Base Camp to take charge of Camp II, where his knowledge of the men and their language would be of the utmost value. But he could not be removed from his important post at the Base Camp, leaving our money bags and the fuel and meat arrangements to look after themselves. So messages were despatched telling Hazard to relieve Shebbeare at the Base, and Shebbeare to come up to Camp II as soon as he had handed over the Base Camp to Hazard.

The rest of that day was spent in revising plans and cheering up the men for another effort. On the following morning Norton, Mallory and I, with twenty-six porters, started off for Camp III. The presence of the reserve party was a great asset, for being fresh they were able to do most of the heavy carrying, and their energy and keenness had a very favourable effect upon the others.

The route over the glacier was almost the same as in 1922, except that, instead of crossing the 'trough,' it followed up it until the general level of the glacier was almost reached. Even in this case blue pinnacles of ice surrounded us like a forest. Some of them were gigantic at the lower end of the 'trough,' getting smaller and fewer as we emerged to the glacier itself. The glacier surface consisted of absolutely smooth ice, varied by depressions and cracks full of powdery snow. Here, as well as in the 'trough,' crampons were of the utmost assistance, and the porters were quick in appreciating their value. Without them, this stage of the journey was always a very tiring and tedious one, and ordinary climbing nails were not sharp enough to grip the surface.

Snow began falling soon after we left Camp II, and continued to fall all day. About half-way Hazard met us, making his way down to the Base Camp to relieve Shebbeare. He told us that he and Odell had tried to reconnoitre the North Col the day before, but had been unable to get higher than some three-quarters of the way to Camp IV and to make a dump of some ropes and pegs at the foot of the ice slopes. We gathered from him that Camp III was an exceedingly unpleasant place. With the wind and snow increasing every moment it was obviously going to be even worse than he painted it, but it was little use trying to talk in half a gale, so we bade him farewell, and pushed on as rapidly as possible. From the dump we sent back to Camp II all except eight of the reserve party. By the time we reached Camp III (21,000 feet) the wind and snow had assumed proportions of a real blizzard, which was to last for forty-eight hours. Camp III was a picture of desolation. Though situated in the only possible place for a camp, it seemed to catch every icy blast that blew. No one moved about the camp; it seemed utterly lifeless. The porters there were wretched, and this terrible blizzard, coming immediately on top of their hardships of a few days ago, completely damped their spirits and energy. Many of them became so apathetic that they would not even attempt to cook for themselves, even when stoves and oil were pushed inside the tents for them. Our eight stalwarts of the reserve again proved their value in helping with the cooking and comfort of the others. But the fierceness of the wind made movement outside a tent almost impossible, so after a hasty meal we turned in, two to a tent, where the excellent sleeping-bags at any rate afforded warmth.

The blizzard continued with unabating violence, and snow drifted into our tents covering everything to a depth of an inch or two. The discomfort of that night was acute. At every slightest movement of the body a miniature avalanche of snow would drop inside one's sleeping-bag and melt there into a cold wet patch. It was a very severe test on the tents, and although the largest of them only weighed sixteen pounds not a single one gave way under the terrific strain. Morning came, and the snow stopped falling, but fallen snow was being driven along the surface of the glacier, producing the same effect as a blizzard. Up to ten o'clock it was useless to attempt to leave the shelter of a tent. It was then that Kami, our cook, produced for us a breakfast that none of us will ever forget. How he succeeded in cooking anything will remain a mystery. He announced that the meal was ready, and the five of us crowded into the tent nearest his to eat it, looking forward more than anything to a mug of hot tea. To our intense disappointment, however, tea was not yet ready. The first dish thrust into the tent contained what Kami was pleased to call 'monkri,' and which on closer investigation proved to be macaroni. Without wishing to appear ungrateful to Kami, I must say that it was a most unappetising dish. Unfortunately we could not have our tea until we had disposed of the 'monkri' and handed back the pot for the tea to be brewed in. After an hour's wait the tea came, and was most hot and comforting. We clamoured for more, although it had been brewed in the same greasy pot as the macaroni. At the time we were not particularly struck by the humorous side of this meal, but afterwards reference to 'monkri' and 'Kami cha'[2] never failed to produce a laugh.

After breakfast the situation was discussed, and it was decided that Mallory and Irvine should move down to Camp II that day, as both of them were showing signs of the strain that had been imposed upon them, and prepare for the possibility of evacuating altogether should this kind of weather continue. These two had been in the thick of it from the start, never sparing themselves for a moment. Irvine's capacity for work was immense. After the most gruelling day on the glacier, he would settle down with his tools inside a tent, improving the oxygen apparatus, or mending stoves, regardless of time or temperature, long after the rest of us were inside our sleeping-bags.

When Mallory and Irvine left us, the wind was still tearing across the glacier, snatching up the snow and hurling it through the camp. Later in the day Norton and Somervell did a fine piece of work in finding their way down to the dump with seventeen of the porters and bringing up nineteen loads, of which they carried one each. I was left in camp with Odell and a few men to make arrangements for a hot meal for every one, and to get the snow out of the tents. The porters who went to the dump with Norton and Somervell were just about played out when they returned. Struggling back against that piercing wind had taken all the strength out of them. They simply flopped into their tents and lay there. We forced them to eat and drink, took off their boots, and saw them safely tucked into their sleeping-sacks. I do not think I have ever seen men so tired, and it was not to be wondered at, for the majority of them had carried loads through wind and snow on five successive days.

........................
2   Kami's tea.

As evening came on, the wind blew still harder in tremendous gusts from every direction. All the tents were again filled with snow with all the consequent discomfort. The cold was intense, and the thermometer fell to thirty-nine degrees below freezing-point. Sleep was an impossibility with the noise of the wind and the wild flapping of the tents. Dawn came at last, but the wind still continued. It was now quite obvious that the North Col would be impracticable for several days even if the weather improved. So there was no other course open but retreat. As we were talking over plans at 9 a.m., the temperature was still below zero. The first step was to turn out the men and strike the tents, as it was not considered safe to leave them standing exposed to the elements during our absence. This was easier said than done, and it was some time before we were able to make the men move at all. They were huddled in their tents, not caring whether they lived or died, and even the idea of withdrawing to the Base Camp with its comforts, warmth and good food left them unmoved. Eventually, however, they were persuaded to face it, and while I struck the tents, Norton and Somervell made lists of what was left in the camp.

Then we took to what Norton has aptly described as the 'Via Dolorosa,' first down the wind-swept glacier to Camp II, then the rough miles of tumbled moraine, withdrawing every man to the Base Camp, with a melancholy procession of snow-blind, sick, and frost-bitten men, being shepherded down by their comrades.

Just outside Camp II we met Irvine. He told us that one of the porters – Tamding – had fallen with his load on the ice and broken his leg, and that Somervell's services were urgently required to set it. The man had been Somervell's servant on the journey across Tibet, and during that time Somervell had lost one or two articles of underwear, which had never been traced. Inspection of the fractured limb now revealed the fact that the missing garments had been 'borrowed' by Tamding. The condition of his leg was not very serious, though it gave him considerable pain, and arrangements had to be made to carry him down to the Base Camp.

By the evening (May 11) Mallory, Beetham, Irvine and Noel were at the Base Camp, Somervell and Odell with half the porters at Camp I, and Norton and I with the other half of the porters at Camp II.

Norton and I shared a tent there which had been put in order for us by Shebbeare, and turned in early to have a long sleep. When I woke up in the morning I remarked that I had enjoyed an extremely comfortable night's rest, and was surprised to find Norton not in the least enthusiastic about the manner in which he had passed the night. He appeared to be examining his bedding and comparing it with mine, and finally pointed out that while he had only one thickness of eiderdown between him and the East Rongbuk Glacier, I had been 'hogging it' on no less than two eiderdown quilts and two thick mattresses!

We started down from Camp II at 9.15 a.m., leaving tents and stores as they stood ready for reoccupation. Tamding had to be brought down in a carrier, and reached the Base Camp by evening. We found Somervell at Camp I with his hands full. Casualties were mounting up, and there were some very sick men. The worst case was Shamsher, one of the Gurkha NCOs, practically insensible, suffering from a clot of blood on the brain. Manbahadur, the cobbler, was in a fearful condition with both his feet frostbitten up to the ankles. Another man was down with severe pneumonia, while many had minor ailments. We managed to get them all away except Shamsher, who could not be moved, and a NCO and a couple of porters were left to look after him.

What a haven of rest the Base Camp seemed to be that night! Warm spacious tents, hot food in plenty, and luxurious camp beds. Best of all Hingston, whom we had already met near Camp I *en route* to visit Shamsher, was there to cheer us up and to administer comfort to the sick and needy. He had arrived on the 11th, just when he was most wanted, having conducted General Bruce safely to Gangtok and hastened across Tibet to rejoin us.

So ended the first attempt to reach the mountain.

This setback was a very great disappointment, but the Expedition, though much weakened as the result of it, was far from defeated. A few days' rest was the first consideration, during which time it was hoped that the weather would really clear up, and give us the chance we wanted. On the morning of May 13 Paul, the interpreter, was despatched to the Rongbuk Monastery to request the Holy Lama to bless all our men on the 15th. They were very anxious to obtain his blessing, and on our part we gave them every encouragement and assistance in arranging for it. A trip down to the monastery would do them a lot of good, while the influence of the Lama's blessing would be invaluable in helping to restore their *moral*. After only one night at the Base Camp they were beginning to look more like themselves again, but it was obvious that if we were to get the best out of them, some reorganisation would be necessary. After breakfast Norton and I talked it all over, and decided to make them up into three definite parties, each to be led by a selected porter, with the next best as his second-in-command to take charge if anything happened to the leader. These leaders and seconds-in-command would be given extra pay, and be generally treated as non-commissioned officers. The one advantage that accrued from the hardships of the past week was that we now had a really good idea of which were the outstanding men, and had little difficulty in selecting six as leaders. We then called them up, and explained what was expected of them. In arranging the parties we allowed them, as far as possible, to pick their own men. They seemed very pleased with the idea, and the scheme had the advantage of supplying a little healthy rivalry and *esprit de party* throughout the porter corps. Of the three originally selected as leaders, Narbu Yishé and Lobsang subsequently became famous, when with the strongest of their respective parties they carried loads to Camp VI at nearly 27,000 feet. In reorganising the porters, we were careful to have at least two men in each party detailed for training in the use of *meta* (solidified spirit) and the Primus stove.

Meanwhile Hingston was busy attending to the sick men in camp. Manbahadur, the cobbler, was still in a terrible state, and even if he had lived would undoubtedly have lost both feet as far as the ankle. All the rest were progressing well. Hingston and I with a stretcher party set out at about eleven o'clock for Camp I to see Shamsher, hoping that after a quiet night's rest he would be better, but Hurke met us as we came into camp, and said that he thought Shamsher was worse. This was indeed the case, and Hingston decided that the only hope of saving his life lay in moving him down to a lower altitude. He was placed on a stretcher, and although carried with the utmost care, was unable to last out the journey and died that evening half a mile from the Base Camp. By his death the expedition were the poorer of a gallant and loyal young man, who had worked with the most conspicuous and whole-hearted zeal throughout. Manbahadur died a few days later, and they were buried in a sheltered spot near the Base Camp.

The following day was a busy one, and though the camps as far as III were established and partially stocked, there was a great deal to do in correcting the lists and ensuring that nothing was left out. The porters' food and clothing also required much attention, and the men detailed as cooks had to be shown how to use the Primus stoves. The weather was still very unsettled, and that afternoon snow fell in the Base Camp, and the mountain looked impossible all day.

May 15 was the day fixed for the blessing. The whole expedition was to be blessed – climbers, Gurkhas and porters. Before we started each man was given two rupees with which to make an offering to the Lama, and then we all set out for the Rongbuk Monastery, four miles down the valley. On arrival the men were told to remain in the large outer court, while we were taken up a flight of narrow stairs to the Lama's antechamber, where a table was laid for a meal. The usual form of Tibetan dish, consisting of macaroni and spices, was handed round by some of the young Lamas of the monastery, and was quite appetising. We were then taken into the presence of the Holy Lama, who was seated at an altar on his roof-court, attended by a dozen lesser Lamas. We were given seats along the sides of the court opposite him, while our men filled up the space in the middle. In turn we walked up to his altar, and he touched each of us upon the head with his silver prayer wheel which he held in his left hand. The Gurkhas and porters followed us, and appeared to be deeply affected by the simple ceremony. The Lama then delivered a short but impressive address, encouraging the men to persevere, and assuring them that he would personally pray for them. Nothing could have been more satisfactory. The reverence with which the men entered and left the presence of the great Lama was eloquent proof of his influence over them. His prayers and blessing put fresh heart into them, and on the return journey to the Base Camp they were very nearly their cheery normal selves once more. That evening Paul came to the mess tent and announced that the porters were all very pleased and grateful 'to him and the Colonel Sahib' for having arranged for the ceremony.

The 16th was a brilliantly fine day, not a cloud in the sky, and the mountain clear and serene. It looked as if this weather had really come to stay, and so it was decided to make a fresh start next day. Since our return to the Base Camp on the 12th, Mallory had been busy making a new programme, showing the movements of each climber and each party of porters for the next ten days. The intention was to put the original scheme in motion again, with the date of the final attempt on the summit put back from May 17 to 29. As a preliminary move, the Gurkha NCOs and a small party of men left the camp on the evening of the 16th, and reoccupied Camp I, so that there should be no delay in making a real start on the morrow. Arrangements seemed as perfect as we could get them that night, and we were hopeful that great things might yet be accomplished. Next morning, however, trouble again appeared – Beetham was down with an acute attack of sciatica, and could scarcely move. It was hard luck that the Fates should have thus afflicted him just as he was recovering his true form and was so tremendously keen to take his place at the front.

By the evening of May 19 the Expedition was once more in full occupation of the glacier up to Camp III. Weather conditions appeared much more favourable, and the last day or two had been bright and sunny, though there was a certain amount of cloud about the mountain. The climbers were distributed as follows:

Norton, Somervell, Mallory, Odell at Camp III.

Irvine and Hazard at Camp II, *en route* for Camp III.

Shebbeare, in charge of the working of convoys up the glacier, at Camp II.

Noel and I at Camp I, *en route* for Camp III.

Hingston and Beetham at the Base Camp.

How the Expedition fared in this renewed advance will be described in the next chapter by Colonel Norton.

# 4 THE NORTH COL

BY LIEUT. COLONEL E.F. NORTON, DSO

This chapter deals with that phase of the campaign of 1924 in which we struggled to establish ourselves on the North Col. Looking back on it all now one realises that it was really the decisive one. In a sense we won, for we did succeed in establishing Camp IV on its selected position, yet the effort left the party so weakened that our ultimate failure became almost a foregone conclusion.

Throughout this phase it is important for the reader to remember that a vital consideration was our uncertainty as to the date of the arrival of the monsoon. In 1922 it had broken on June 1; the soft breath of the south-east wind had then its inevitable effect on the steep snow slopes below the North Col, and a party of climbers and porters was swept away in an avalanche which killed seven of the latter, the climbers and remaining porters only escaping by a miracle. Now we believed that the monsoon was a fortnight before its normal time that year, but we had no accurate data on this point, and in any case it was not safe to rely on its postponement to a later date. This year, when we were persistently assailed during the latter half of May by weather conditions which resembled the first stages of the monsoon, we were always obsessed by the fear that we were already too late and that its full force would be on us before we had even established ourselves on the North Col; for it must be remembered that its arrival does not always take an unmistakable form. It may do so, but it may also arrive in a half-hearted fashion, alternately advancing and clearing off again; and my diary at this time refers more than once to a 'preliminary monsoon current.' Hence the idea in our minds was that we must at all costs establish the North Col Camp; then a fine interval before the arrival of the monsoon proper might just give us the time to put in one serious attempt on the summit. This explains our exhausting attempts to compete with impossible weather – weather which, as we now know, had nothing to do with the monsoon, but was the outcome of conditions that from end to end of the Himalayas produced, in the latter half of May, low temperatures and a series of storms unprecedented in the memory of the oldest planter in Darjeeling.

Foreseeing this uncertainty we had, before leaving Darjeeling, made arrangements for telegrams to be sent us both from relations of Mallory's in Colombo and from the meteorological department at Simla, to keep us informed as to the progress of the monsoon, which generally takes at least three weeks to reach Northern India after it has broken in Ceylon and on the Malabar coast; these telegrams were duly sent, but, carried as they were by relays of mounted men or runners from Phari onwards, the first that gave us really useful information arrived just too late, for it met us on our final return to the Base Camp when all was over – a day or two before the monsoon broke in the Rongbuk Valley.

Camp III is pitched on the northern flank of the highest tributary glacier which flows down to join the East Rongbuk Glacier on its left or western side. This tributary glacier fills the great bay which lies between the north-eastern spur of Everest and the long parallel spur of the North Peak, and its source is actually the very top of the saddle connecting these spurs, which we call the Chang La or North Col, where, sheltered from the prevailing west wind, a great mass of snow accumulates immediately under and up to the crest, and thence pours down the steep slopes below in the form of a hanging glacier to join the more placid surface of the sea of ice which fills the bay I have already-described. It follows that the route up this steep glacier must vary in detail from year to year. In 1924, in one place, a great line of ice cliffs represented the upper lip of what in 1922 had been a narrow crevasse a few feet across, and which then ran transversely across the top of the steep traverse just below Camp IV; for the lower lip had fallen away some hundreds of feet in the intervening two years, as the mass of ice poured down the slopes below.

The last chapter describes how the first party, which started on May 8 to work out a route to the North Col, had to turn back somewhat short of the position of Camp IV, owing to insufficient acclimatisation and bad snow conditions. Time now pressed, and as this next step in our ladder was one of vital importance it was decided that in the renewed attempt Odell should be accompanied by Mallory and Somervell, a pair who not only knew the old route better than any of the rest but who, working together, could be relied on to succeed if success were humanly possible. As, however, I judged that neither Mallory, who was suffering from the prevalent 'high-altitude' throat, nor Somervell, who had a touch of the sun, might prove fit to go, I also decided to accompany the party, at least as far as the foot of the steep slopes below the Col, in case either of the others dropped out. Lhakpa Tsering, a wiry and active porter, was to come and carry a load of Alpine rope and pickets with which to affix it in the more difficult places. I asked him if he thought he was up to the climb, and he replied with a fine scorn:

'Why, didn't I go twice to 25,000 two years ago?'

Our route from Camp III followed the left lateral moraine of the glacier for perhaps three-quarters of a mile, and up this we trudged on the morning of May 20. It is an Alpine tradition to start at a very steady pace in the early morning; but at 21,000 feet and over it is not only tradition which enforces what might more truthfully be called a crawl: it is the lowered vitality of the early hours – or so I have always imagined; for upward-bound parties leaving Camp III always made a very poor showing and often returned many hours later looking brisker than when they started.

This morning was no exception, and it soon became evident that one of the party – Somervell – had more the matter with him than the early morning lassitude; he was in fact suffering rather severely from the sunstroke he had contracted in the windless glare of the 'trough' the day before. I believe he had had a high temperature all night, and as, leaving the moraine, we crossed the smooth and glassy bosom of the glacier and approached the foot of the steep slopes, it became evident that he was in no condition to go on. Obvious though this was, it needed a concerted attack by both Mallory and myself to convince him, and it was with the greatest reluctance that he at last conceded the logic of our arguments and, turning on us a back view eloquent of protest, headed down the glacier again.

A very short examination of the slopes above now decided our plan – for Mallory and I in the little sixteen-pound tent we shared had discussed and agreed on the principle that dictated it. The obvious and easy route of 1922 – the scoop in which the fatal avalanche took place – must be avoided; but this year a large crescent-shaped crevasse, some quarter of a mile long, crossed the whole face of the steep slopes on its right in such a fashion that its left or southern end just reached the top of the scoop; a series of slightly convex snow slopes, mostly at a comparatively gentle angle, gave access to the right or northern end of the crevasse, and as these slopes ran right down to the level surface of the glacier with no serious *bergschrund* or ice cliffs at their base, we argued that they offered a fairly safe approach to the crevasse, by following the lower lip of which we could safeguard this portion of our route from the danger of avalanches and so regain the top of the scoop in safety. From this point to the shelf on which it was hoped to pitch Camp IV it appeared unlikely that we could under any circumstances select a route that would be safe under dangerous snow conditions, but this mattered less as an upward-bound party would have had ample warning of danger and could turn back before reaching that point – as was, in fact, done by Bruce and Odell three days later.

In their previous attempt Odell and Hazard had followed the 1922 route, and they had made a *cache* of rope and pickets at the bottom of the slopes; so it was now decided that, while Mallory and I headed half right to the proposed new route, there to get on with any step-cutting that we found necessary, Odell and Lhakpa Tsering should collect the dumped stores and, cutting across the foot of the slopes, join us higher up.

Of our ascent to the crevasse there is little to tell; we led in turns, sharing the laborious work of cutting or stamping steps. Mallory and I always climbed well together at these altitudes, for though on his day he was often too fast for me lower down, up here we always went very comfortably in double – or perhaps I should say tandem – harness. We met two minor crevasses and crossed them without difficulty. The last pitch up to the big crevasse, taken straight up the slope, was as steep as was pleasant, but we were satisfied that we could make this bit good with a fixed rope from above. Arrived at the crevasse, certain suspicions we had felt below were confirmed: the lower lip on which we now stood was broken about half-way across, and in order to regain it beyond the break it became necessary to descend into the bottom of the crevasse and climb out again by what looked a nearly vertical wall of broken ice leading up to a narrow crack or chimney; this seemed to lead once more to the lower lip beyond the break and an easy route to the far end of the crevasse. The handle of the sickle, so to speak, took us to the break; to reach the curved blade, of which we proposed to follow the inner, or cutting, edge, we must climb the wall and chimney.

All impatience to know if our labours so far were to prove vain, we pushed quickly on after a few words with Odell and Lhakpa, who were plugging along in our footsteps below, within easy shouting distance.

Confronted with a formidable climbing obstacle Mallory's behaviour was always characteristic: you could positively see his nerves tighten up like fiddle strings. Metaphorically he girt up his loins, and his first instinct was to jump into the lead. Up the wall and chimney he led here, climbing carefully, neatly, and in that beautiful style that was all his own. I backed him up close below, able now and then to afford him a foothold with haft or head of my axe. The wall, like most walls, was not as steep as it looked and needed only careful step-cutting; but the chimney, on this our first experience of it, was the deuce, for it was very narrow (it widened later under the influence of a hot sun), its sides were smooth blue ice and it was floored – if the term 'floor' can be applied to a surface that mounts almost vertically – with soft snow which seemed merely to conceal a bottomless crack and offered little or no foothold. The climb was something of a gymnastic exercise, and one is little fitted for gymnastics above 22,000 feet. I suppose the whole 200-foot climb to a most welcome little platform at the top took us an hour of exertion as severe as anything I have experienced. From the platform we looked down on the very top of Odell's and Lhakpa's heads and, with a shouted word or two, pushed on to make good the remaining half of the crevasse. Odell was carrying a light load of pickets – wonderfully constructed hollow wooden pegs, some eighteen inches long and only weighing a few ounces, which we used for attaching fixed ropes. Partly owing to this load and partly to the fact that he was one of those who acclimatised slowly and did not at this time show his subsequent wonderful form, he was feeling the effects of altitude pretty badly. However, by the time Mallory and I, after an abortive attempt, discovered the right way on, Odell and Lhakpa were close behind us.

Our route from the platform ran steeply upwards along a narrow ridge of ice with the crevasse on our right and airy space on our left. Here we cut good steps and soon reached more level going on a narrow knife-edge of snow, the lower lip of the crevasse, which soon brought us to its far end. Beyond this we were on steep snow slopes and shortly had to traverse the concave scoop, which represented the upper part of the alternative route followed in 1922. All this part was subsequently made as good as ingenuity and an elaborate system of fixed ropes attached to the pickets already described could make it, and I remember one very comforting rope which was tied right round a great 'serac' or ice pillar. Just beyond this serac we were confronted by the steepest bit of the whole climb – some 200 feet of snow slope at the extreme angle on which snow would lie, falling away at the bottom in a great ice cliff; and this slope we had to traverse diagonally before arriving on the shelf just above it and the old site of Camp IV. We both had unpleasant recollections of this traverse, which had changed little since we last crossed it on our descent in deep fresh snow two years before, when at every step it looked as if the whole surface of snow was bound to peel and carry us with it into the abyss below; and for Mallory it recalled an even more sinister incident, for in 1921, when he first discovered this route to the North Col, the whole surface *did* peel off between his party crossing it in the ascent and their descent an hour later.

Mallory's nerves responded as usual to the call on them, and he again insisted on taking the lead. We agreed that the safest way to negotiate the place was to climb nearly vertically up the steepest pitch and only traverse to the left at its top where the slope began to ease off towards the edge of the shelf above. Odell, who was going better and better as the day wore on, was now with us, and he and I prepared to hold Mallory from below from a safe corner by the big serac if the treacherous surface should slip and carry him past us. But all went well, and perhaps half an hour later we each followed in turn up the steep ladder of steps which he had cut with such labour in the half-ice, half-snow surface.

It was a good moment when we arrived about 2.30 p.m. on the shelf, still bathed in sunlight and pleasantly sheltered from the west by a wall of ice above. Our first thought was to look for signs of our old camp left all standing in 1922, but of course there was no trace of it, for the whole jumble of snow hummocks and ice cliffs was, as I have explained, part of a true glacier and so all on the move. The shelf was narrower than in 1922, and now formed a hog-backed ridge of untrodden, glistening snow barely affording level space for our proposed row of little six-foot square tents.

We were well pleased at our success in establishing once more the most difficult portion of the whole route up the mountain. I would say we were elated, but that I think one is never elated at 23,000 feet; at these heights one's emotions are all in half tones, and we were not a little weary, for we had not been content merely to climb: every footstep of the way had been kicked or cut with the axe to leave a clear and safe track for the laden porters to follow next day. Stretched on the snow in the sun we ate a hasty snack and feasted our eyes on the wonderful view over the Lhakpa La and Khartaphu to the maze of peaks which encircle Everest to the east, away sixty miles to the Gyankar Range and beyond where the eye of faith might pick out distant Kanchenjunga; yet fine though it was we knew it to be tame compared to the view in the opposite direction, now hidden by the ice cliff at our backs – a view whose savage grandeur is unequalled by anything I have seen.

Nothing now would please the indomitable Mallory but that the route onwards from our shelf to the actual Col must be reconnoitred, and Odell at once volunteered to lead the way. For myself I discovered an urgent need to drive some pickets for a fixed rope which should hang down the steepest part of our ladder of steps below – a ten-minute job.

The task of the other two proved the affair of a long hour, and Mallory, who had borne the heaviest brunt of the previous work, looked nearly at the end of his tether by the time they rejoined me, for the site of Camp IV is separated from the Col by a maze of snow ridges and partially concealed crevasses – cruel hard work for a tired man. In 1922 all access by this most direct route was denied by an impassable crevasse, and a devious way surmounting the ice cliff over the camp had to be worked out. Here it was that Mallory, Somervell, Morshead and I, returning from our highest climb that year, spent the hours between 7 and 11 p.m. groping our way over some 300 yards by the light of a candle lantern. This year Odell happily succeeded in finding a bridge across the most serious crevasse and established a feasible route to the Col which served us throughout the campaign; this put the finishing touch to a good day's work.

We started down at 3.45, and the less said about the descent the better. We took the 1922 route and, going very fast, had a series of slips and tumbles into crevasses, for which there could be no explanation but sheer carelessness. I must exempt Odell from this stricture, but even he pleaded guilty to allowing Lhakpa Tsering to tie himself on to the rope with a reef knot, with the result that when once he slipped the rope came undone, and he was only saved from fatal consequences by a lucky patch of soft snow. It was indeed an instructive sight to see this superior young gentleman, who had climbed all day in excellent style and rather scoffed at our solicitude for his inexperience on snow and ice, suddenly converted into the veriest worm, clinging like a wet towel to steep ice slopes where safety is only found in an upright position.

Herein lies a moral for those of us (and I was among them) who have advocated adding a good Sherpa porter to a party of two climbers for the 'last lap' on Mount Everest. These men are not really all-round mountaineers; they have little knowledge of snow and ice, and are as subject as other inexperienced amateurs to sudden loss of nerve if something goes wrong.

We were back in Camp III by 6.30 p.m. – a weary party; and our satisfaction at a good day's work was tempered by a very persistent doubt as to how it would be possible, even with the aid of fixed ropes, to get loaded porters up the ice chimney. My diary for this day finishes with the following remarks: 'Indifferent night – head too full of the very apparent difficulties and dangers of the whole business; overcast and warm, light snow in early a.m. Don't like the look of weather much. Pray Heaven it's not the beginning of monsoon, as no power on earth can make parts of North Col route safe under monsoon conditions.'

In describing the work which was now carried out by other members of the party I am handicapped by having only my own brief diary and imperfect memory to remind me of their fine performances, and I hope I shall not be accused of egotism if I appear to pass lightly over some of these, while I describe in more detail events in which I myself took an active part. It was a busy and a strenuous time, and as each tired party returned to

Camp III, one listened almost perfunctorily to its story, satisfied that the work was going on, and then immediately turned one's attention to the next step; and later, when it was all over, these doings were overshadowed by more dramatic events, so that much of the story remained untold.

During all this phase Camp III was a truly horrid spot. The stones of the moraine on which it was pitched, stones which in 1922 radiated pleasantly the heat of the sun, were always covered with fresh snow; the little trickle of running water which their warmth should have produced was frozen stiff, and every drop of drinking or cooking water (I omit the usual reference to washing!) had to be melted over a Primus stove. Never a meal was eaten in the open, and I remember particularly the hatefulness of the evening meal, with the camp in cold shadow and one's feet like stones. We made rather a point of collecting in a spare tent pitched for the purpose to eat our meals – a last flicker of the social amenities. We had a real live cook at Camp III this year. Three of our total staff of four cooks took it turn and turn about at each of Camps I, II and III; and if I shudder now at the recollection of some of those hateful meals, I am fain to admit that seldom has food been cooked under more difficult conditions. Tea made with water which boils at a temperature in which you can bear the hand isn't very palatable even if it does not contain an admixture of paraffin oil and last night's 'mutton and veg.' Kami, Tsering and Kancha – we owe those cooks a debt of gratitude: alas, poor Kancha died of ptomaine poisoning in his own home a few days after our return to Darjeeling. Before turning in, feet had to be warmed up somehow, and as the moraine was too rough and the glacier too glassy to admit of a tramp, we used to carry out that military manoeuvre known as 'double mark time' on a flat stone, sometimes for ten minutes, and even then, perhaps, without much effect; but then it was a poor imitation of a 'double.' We mostly slept two in a tent; Mallory and I shared a tent, with Somervell and Odell next door. 'How's Sandringham?' we would ask, the right answer being, 'All snug, how's Balmoral?'

On May 21 Somervell, who now professed himself recovered, Irvine and Hazard got off about 8.30 with a convoy of twelve porters laden with tents, stores and provisions to establish Camp IV; the morning was unduly warm with a lot of light cloud about. Light, dry snow kept falling at intervals, but, the sun coming through now and again, we anticipated no trouble. The plan was that Somervell and Irvine were to accompany the party as far as Camp IV to help the loaded porters up the chimney and fix ropes in various places noted by our party the day before. They were then to return, leaving Hazard for one night alone at Camp IV with the twelve men. The following day Odell and Bruce were to join him, and after sleeping the night at Camp IV, go on with the twelve porters to 25,500 feet and establish Camp V.

To quote again from my diary: 'Up to 1 p.m. North Col slopes remained clear, but no sign of party along big crevasse; soon after it began to snow in earnest and nothing more could be seen. As I write at 6.20 p.m. Somervell and Irvine have not returned, and it is still snowing – very soft, wet snow. I am anxious. G. Bruce with nineteen porters arrived from II about 2 p.m., having cleared II and practically all dumps (of stores). I spent the whole day on loads, stores and "bundobust," and am now so sick of it that I can hardly bear to think any more about it.

'6.35 p.m. Somervell and Irvine just in – Hazard and party reached Camp IV – so all is more or less well.'

This is a very bald outline of a gruelling day's work. To begin with, fresh fallen snow had practically – and later entirely – obliterated the tracks Mallory, Odell and I had been at such pains to make. The snow soon became deep enough to make the going exceedingly laborious, if not dangerous. The climbers drove a quantity of pickets and attached all the necessary fixed ropes before the porters followed them.

Then came the chimney; they decided that it would be best to haul all loads by hand up a vertical ice cliff in one pull from the bottom of the wall clear up to the little platform at the top, and then to let the porters climb the wall and chimney unladen. Somervell and Irvine took their stand on the platform, Hazard directing operations from the bottom, and the two former hauled the twelve 20- to 30-pound loads clean up the cliff, experiencing great difficulty with an obtrusive bulge half-way up. They afterwards described it as heart-breaking work, and I can well imagine it; the wonder is that they escaped frost-bitten hands. Young Irvine was a perfect tower of strength, and his splendid physique never stood him in better stead. Somervell, yesterday an invalid with a temperature, did his full share of what must have been – I speak from memory – a two or three hours' job. Having seen Hazard and his none-too-merry men on to the shelf where they were to pitch the camp, with snow falling heavily, Somervell and Irvine returned, as already described, to Camp III.

Next morning, May 22, found it snowing hard; in fact, snow had been falling all night, and it continued without stopping until 3 p.m., so that there was never any question of Bruce and Odell starting for the Col. Our preparations in camp being finished, we all spent the day in our sleeping-bags with feet like stones, reading our home mail and papers which had arrived from Camp II with Bruce's party the day before. It was a miserable day, for we were haunted by the idea that this might be a first taste of the monsoon, and it was followed by an even more miserable night. The thermometer fell to -24° Fahrenheit – the coldest ever recorded in these parts, and I would emphasise the fact – for the benefit of those who are accustomed to figures like sixty 'below' in Canada or Arctic regions – that, with an insufficient supply of oxygen and the lowered vitality of these heights, -24° Fahrenheit is a more serious matter than the bare figures indicate. Many of the party got little or no sleep.

May 23 broke cloudless, windless and brilliantly fine, though the air was keen as a knife. After such a cold night we concluded that the fresh fallen snow on the slopes below the Col should be safe, and as every day was now precious, it was decided that Bruce and Odell should carry on with their programme. Bruce was very much 'all there,' in spite of the trying experience of the last twenty-four hours, and got the party of seventeen porters off in fairly good heart at 9.30.

About 1 p.m. it once more began to snow steadily, shutting out all view of what was going on above, but not before we had seen considerable movement on the traverse just below Camp IV – rows of little black dots slowly moving downwards and to the right like flies on a whitewashed wall. We concluded that Hazard had decided to evacuate Camp IV and return with his party; this was a relief, as if this were really the monsoon, the sooner they were back at Camp III the better. About 3 p.m. Bruce, Odell and their porters were sighted coming down the moraine: they had reached a point just short of the big crevasse, where they decided that the snow was in a dangerous condition and that it would be unsafe to go on. Their decision to turn back was confirmed by seeing Hazard's party descending the chimney above them, but though they spent some time trying to communicate by shouting, they could not make themselves heard.

Looking back now I am puzzled at our constant failure to make ourselves heard on the mountain. I can think of three occasions when our voices failed to carry distances of 200 yards or under, and that in a land of absolute silence, in shelter from the wind. Our voices were often feeble, of course, but I am not satisfied that this was enough to account for it.

We spent an anxious two hours waiting for the arrival of Hazard's party; some instinct must have warned us that all was not well. At 5 p.m. he arrived, accompanied by only eight of his twelve men. It appeared that he had gone first across the traverse to test the condition of the fresh surface snow, which rendered it a very dangerous passage; eight men had followed him, one crossing at a time, but the last four had turned back, either because they were sick – the remaining porters said that two of them were suffering from frostbite – or, more probably, because one of them had started a patch of the surface snow slipping and they had been afraid to come on. Certain marks on the steepest part of the traverse next day gave colour to this explanation.

The situation had suddenly taken a very serious turn. The snow was falling persistently and – an ominous sign – had begun to take the form of soft feathery flakes, such as we had been accustomed to associate with nothing but monsoon conditions. The four men were alone at Camp IV, a prey to the superstitious terrors to which those of their race are always prone on the big snow mountains. Two of them were reported frostbitten, and we now learnt for the first time that, during their ascent two days before, a load of assorted food had been lost over an ice cliff. They were thus restricted to a diet of barley-meal, unless they had the initiative (and the tin-opener) to use the small amount of sahib's food already in the camp. It was quite evident that they must be rescued, and that no later than next day; for the frostbite question alone made it imperative to avoid even one more day's delay.

It was equally obvious that it was at present out of the question to continue our attempts on the mountain; the whole party at Camp III was already in a bad way. Mallory and Somervell were both suffering from very bad high-altitude throats. Odell had had hardly any sleep for several nights; Irvine had diarrhoea, and Hazard had just had a very trying three days. The porters were for the most part quite unfit, morally and physically, for further efforts at present.

Both above and below the North Col there was sufficient fresh snow to put any attempt to climb the mountain out of the question for the present, while we were all more or less convinced that this was really the beginning of the monsoon.

Sitting huddled in our dining-tent by the light of a candle lantern, we made our plans for next day. Mallory and I had had a longer period of rest at Camp III than any of the others, and as a party of at least three was required to bring down the four men, it was decided that Somervell should accompany us; we three had climbed together in 1922, and we knew we could go well as a party. Bruce, with Hazard and Irvine, was to evacuate Camp III, leaving only Odell and Noel (the latter having arrived from Camp II) with half a dozen porters to wait for our return in case there should be casualties to carry down the glacier.

It was a gloomy little conference; we could not but recognise that to turn our backs once more on the mountain at this date might well mean the abandonment of all hope of success for the year. We were about to send three of the four climbers detailed for the first attempt on what must be a severe test of endurance, and this would still further diminish our chances of success if a change in the weather permitted a resumption of the attack. But at the time these seemed but minor considerations; the only thing that mattered was to get the men down alive. Personally my one fixed determination had all along been that we must on no account have any casualties among our porters this year, and here we were, faced with the very real possibility of losing four men; for it must be admitted that our chances of rescuing the marooned porters did not appear rosy at this time. We were all distinctly the worse for wear; both Mallory and Somervell had very bad coughs and sore throats, which hampered them badly in climbing; the condition of the North Col slopes must make climbing exceedingly slow and laborious, and there was the danger of avalanche. As we lay in our tent that night and listened to the soft pattering of the snow on its walls, I now know that neither Mallory nor I would have taken a bet of two to one against a successful issue to our undertaking next day, though at the time we kept such pessimistic views to ourselves. About midnight the snow stopped falling and the moon came out.

By 7.30 next morning we were off. Though the sun had been up two hours, the temperature was still only -2° Fahrenheit.

Of the climb which followed I remember only certain phases distinctly; the rest was just treadmill – with the snow anything from a foot to waist deep. As usual we were at our worst when we first started, and we looked so like a party of hospital convalescents that my hopes sank to zero. Mallory, who on these occasions lived on his nervous energy, kept urging us on: I remember his chiding us sharply for some momentary delay and later apologising for his impatience. I wore crampons, and owing to the constriction of their straps I suffered all day from cold feet.[1] At the foot of the chimney I had to take off my boots while Somervell rubbed my feet, but I never properly restored the circulation that day.

The three of us did the wall and chimney in fifty minutes. Arrived at the top we could see one of the marooned porters, one Phu, standing on the edge of the shelf, and I repeatedly hailed him to find out what was the condition of the four. I had the greatest difficulty in getting an answer out

---

1   A contrivance of eight sharp spikes fitted to the boot after the fashion of skates.

of him, and it was only when we arrived at the foot of the final traverse that the following conversation took place: 'Hi, Phu! Are you all fit to walk?' This had to be repeated several times. At last came the answering query, 'Up or down?' (so little apparently did he realise the seriousness of their situation). 'Down, you fool.' Whereupon he disappeared, and almost at once reappeared with the remaining three. They said that one, Namgya, had all the fingers of both hands badly frostbitten, and that another, Uchung, had some toes slightly affected, but that all were fit to come down. This was a relief, for though I had brought one of our 'one-man carrier' frames to be prepared for the worst, I very much doubt if we could have got a man down on it – certainly we could not have done so before dark.

Up to the final traverse the condition of the surface snow had proved less dangerous than we had anticipated, but it was obvious that the traverse was to be the crux of the climb. Here Somervell insisted on going across, while Mallory and I prepared to belay the 200 feet of rope that we had brought with us, driving both our ice axes into the snow up to their heads as a hold-fast, round which we passed the rope, paying it out yard by yard as Somervell slowly and laboriously made his way diagonally upwards and across; he punched big safe steps and continually stopped to cough and choke in the most painful manner. After one or two of these fits of coughing he leant his head on his forearm in an attitude of exhaustion, and so steep was the slope that the mental picture I have of him as he did this shows him standing almost upright in his steps with his elbow resting on the snow level with his shoulder.

Some five or ten yards short of where the crest of the slope formed the edge of the shelf on which the four men were waiting, Somervell reached the end of the rope; the full 200 feet were out, and by eye we judged it a near thing whether, in the event of his slipping, the length of the rope was not too great to stop him before he disappeared over the lip of the ice cliffs below. It was now 4 p.m. Time was all too short if we were to get down in daylight, and a brief shouted consultation decided us that the men must chance the unbridged ten yards and join Somervell unroped as best they could. Each man as he reached Somervell was to be passed across the taut rope in turn to where Mallory and I, securely anchored by my old friend the big serac, represented safety.

The first two reached him safely. One of them was across with us and the second just starting when, with my heart in my mouth, I saw the remaining two, who had stupidly started from the edge of the shelf together, suddenly flying down the slope. A big patch of the fresh snow surface had given way and the men were going down on their backs, feet first, in an almost upright position. For one paralysing second I foresaw the apparently inevitable tragedy, with the two figures shooting into space over the edge of the blue ice cliff, 200 feet below; the next they pulled up after not more than ten yards, and we breathed again. The accumulated snow under their feet had been bound, by the cold of the early morning and the hot sun which followed, to a holding consistency. Somervell, as cool as a cucumber, shouted to me, 'Tell them to sit still,' and still as mice they sat, shivering at the horrid prospect immediately beneath their eyes, while quite calmly Somervell passed the second man across to us, chaffing the wretched pair the while – so that one of them actually gave an involuntary bark of laughter.

Somervell then untied the rope from his waist, drove his ice axe in up to its head in the soft snow, passed the rope round it and strained it so as to make every foot he could, while Mallory and I held our end at extreme arm's length. Holding his own end in the same way he then let himself down to the extreme length of the rope and of his own arm, while with the other hand he grasped, one after the other, the two porters by the scruff of the neck and pulled them back to the anchor of his axe. Somehow they got across to us, for their nerve had gone and they slid and slipped, ruining the steps all the way across, and only saved themselves from repeating their previous performance by the rope handrail. Finally Somervell followed, after again tying the rope round his waist; and it was a fine object lesson in mountain craft to see him, balanced and erect, crossing the ruined track without a slip or mistake.

At 4.30 we started down; the slopes were already in chill shadow and it was evident that we were in for a race with darkness. Mallory led with one porter on a rope, then followed Somervell shepherding two; and I brought up the rear with Namgya and his frostbitten hands. Many times during the descent, but particularly in the chimney, I blessed my crampons, for Namgya's hands were useless and more than once I had to hold his full weight; but he put up a gallant showing until, at dusk, we reached the glacier and safety, when he rather broke down. Poor lad! He must have suffered a lot in those two and a half hours.

About 7.30 p.m., as we were leaving the glacier for the moraine three-quarters of a mile from home, some figures loomed up out of the darkness ahead, and we found Noel and Odell waiting for us with hot soup in a liquid-air flask – almost as memorable a drink as the never-to-be-forgotten coffee and brandy which greeted us in nearly the same place after another trying descent two years before. I think a laconic entry in my diary is the most sincere tribute I can pay to Noel and Odell, for it was written at the time: 'Both awfully good to us here and, later, in camp.' Noel had a peculiar genius for coming out strong on times like this, and I look back with gratitude to more than one occasion on which the shelter of his specially designed tent or some of his own private delicacies comforted me marvellously after a hard day.

Mallory's cough and the condition of my feet (which never really warmed up till next morning) precluded our enjoying, that night, the sleep we had earned, and we lay awake exchanging a murmured word from time to time. But our feelings were somewhat different from what they were when we had lain in the same tent the night before listening to the rustle of the falling snow and counting our chances for the morrow. Next morning we thankfully turned our backs on Camp III and, escorting a miserable little convoy of the halt, the lame and the blind, reached Camp II in due course in the teeth of a north-east wind and with snow falling again. The following day, May 26, Somervell and I reached Camp I.

The party was now disposed as follows: Odell, Noel and Shebbeare remained at Camp II with some twenty porters; Mallory, Somervell, Bruce, Irvine and I with another twenty porters were at Camp I. Hazard had gone right through to the Base, where he had joined Hingston and Beetham. About a dozen of the least useful porters were by now permanently kept at the Base and used only for the daily fuel and ration fatigues as far as Camps I or II.

The idea in thus stringing out the party in echelon was to enable us to resume operations with the minimum of delay should the weather let us. Those intended for the next trip to the North Col were to be at Camp II so that when once the word was given Camp IV could be reoccupied with only one day's delay. On May 15 Beetham had retired to the Base suffering from a very severe attack of sciatica; it was a cruel blow, no less to him than to the rest of the party, that just as he was really recovering from the weakening effects of his previous illness he should be thus smitten down again. If ever man conquered a physical disability by sheer will power Beetham had done so once, and though this same will power of his was going to have another very determined and obstinate try for it, for the moment Hingston had him in his clutches and safely tucked into bed at the Base.

On this same afternoon we held a council of war at Camp I. Several facts made it obvious that if the Fates were to give us one more chance, we must be prepared to put into operation some simplified plan. Firstly, Shebbeare and Bruce were agreed that not more than fifteen – at first Shebbeare, by no means a pessimist, said twelve – out of our original fifty-five porters could now be counted on to reach Camp IV, though it was rightly estimated that those who could do this might well go much higher. I was horrified at this idea, and went through the list of porters on paper very carefully, only to arrive independently at exactly the same result. The number physically disabled was very small; but a high proportion had shown by now that the unusual and unexpected conditions of the year had taken all heart out of them and they would not come up to the scratch again. This was cutting down our transport with a vengeance, for so far we had barely established Camp IV with four tents and sleeping-bags for twelve porters and one climber; all the food and fuel had still to be carried up, as well as every oxygen apparatus and cylinder required on the mountain, and the whole of the tents and stores for the higher camps; and it may be remembered that after Camp IV had been fully stocked the next step in our original plan was to send a party of fifteen porters, escorted by two climbers, to establish and stock Camp V.

Then there was the vital question of time. For the moment things looked a little better, and we again began to doubt if the weather we had experienced was really anything to do with the monsoon. At this time I developed a parrot cry which used to lead to concerted 'booing' whenever I started the well-known formula: 'I have a theory ... ' My theory, which I certainly only half believed myself, was to the effect that for the monsoon to gather sufficient impetus to carry right up to and over the main Himalayan range, the great oven represented by that part of Northern India adjoining the range must be stoked up by a fortnight's really hot weather; and that, therefore, we could still count on a sufficient spell of climbing weather before the true monsoon. Bruce's rival theory that, whatever happened below, it was always brilliantly fine over 27,000 feet, was obviously only a childish attempt to produce some alternative optimistic theory. But theories fade away in the hard light of facts: here we were within six days of the date on which the monsoon broke in 1922; we must have two or three days' rest, and we must waste one more day reaching Camp III. Our plan must obviously be such as would enable us to stage a serious attempt on the summit with the least possible delay when we again advanced to the assault.

There were a number of minor considerations, with which I will not weary the reader, except to mention our uncomfortable doubt as to whether those who had already tried it had derived any real benefit from the oxygen apparatus.

The council of war was long and undecisive, and I summoned another for next day, sending messengers to Camp II and the Base to invite Odell,

Shebbeare and Hazard to join in these important deliberations. They were resumed next day with the addition of Odell and Shebbeare, and the whole matter was most carefully thrashed out, every possible combination of our seven available climbers being tried. In the end the simplest possible plan carried the day and was adopted *nem. con.*, after I had made a careful analysis of the transport it entailed, as compared with that required by any other form of attempt. We decided to scrap oxygen altogether and to assault the mountain in a series of attempts, each of two climbers: the parties to leave Camp IV on consecutive fine days and to sleep twice above that point, once at Camp V, at about 25,500 feet, and once at Camp VI, at about 27,200 feet, or as near to those heights as we could induce porters to carry for us. I insisted on a supporting party of two climbers to be at Camp IV always, and this seemed to indicate that not more than two attempts could be made, for we could hardly believe that, after what we had already undergone, anyone would be found to do more than one really high climb. But here we judged by the standard of 1922, and Mallory and Odell were yet to show us what was to be the standard of 1924.

In allocating the climbers to these various roles I stipulated that Mallory had the right to join the first party if he wished. His throat was markedly better, and though he had so far borne the brunt of the hardest work, yet the energy and fire of the man were reflected in his every gesture, and none doubted his fitness to go as high as any. Of the remainder Bruce was now palpably the strongest; he had been strong all along, always showing a flat back and a free easy carriage, when some of us had been fain to bend and crawl, and chance had arranged it that he had so far done less above Camp III than the rest. So Mallory and Bruce were to make the first pair – and I must say they looked a pair to inspire confidence in success if, at this stage, success were humanly possible. Somervell's throat was benefiting a little by the warmth of Camp I, but was still far from right; but Somervell's prestige since 1922 was enormous, and his last performance with the marooned porters had enhanced it. Anyhow, Mallory and I had little doubt that he must be one member of the next attempt. For choice of the second member, as I was in the running, I again stood down and asked Somervell and Mallory to choose between Odell, Irvine, Hazard and myself. They chose me, and in this connection it must not be forgotten that physical fitness and technical proficiency were not the only considerations: there was the vitally important question of providing each party with a climber who could talk sufficient Nepalese to carry the porters with them when their resolution began to flag, as we expected it to do at Camp V. Odell and Irvine were to play the all-important role of supporters at Camp IV, Hazard to remain in reserve at Camp III.

May 28 (as had been the 27th) was cloudlessly fine and hot, and the firebrands – Somervell and Noel – wanted to be up and away; but much as I hated losing another day, I was so impressed with the improvement in the general health of the party after two days' rest that I decided to postpone our departure for one more. The day was not wasted; the picked fifteen porters on whom now all our hopes centred, and whom we nicknamed the 'Tigers,' were collected at Camp II; Irvine joined Odell there, and the famous 'old firm' produced perhaps their most useful mechanical contrivance in the shape of a magnificent rope ladder of Alpine rope and tent pegs destined to enable loaded porters to climb the steep ice wall below the 'chimney.'

The rest of us finished a communiqué to *The Times*, wrote home letters, continued the endless jigsaw puzzle of allotting porters' loads for the work ahead, and generally basked and revelled in a sun which was at times almost too hot.

Camp I has always been a good place; never has its sunny welcome proved more beneficial than during this brief three days of recuperation.

The climbing parties reached Camp III on the 30th, accompanied by Noel and cinema outfit. Hazard, destined to support from Camp III, arrived a day later. And with the climbing parties were assembled that picked gang of fifteen porters, the 'Tigers,' who were considered still reliable for going high.

The weather continued perfect, and on June 1 Mallory and Bruce, accompanied by nine of the 'Tigers,' camped at the North Col, establishing *en route* a rope ladder. Odell and Irvine were to remain in support at Camp IV.

On June 2, still apparently under perfect weather conditions, the two climbers and eight porters started up the great North Ridge to establish Camp V. But the weather on Everest is not always what it seems. Once past the jumble of crevasses and seracs separating Camp IV from the true col, a bitter north-west wind, one of the most formidable foes we have to face on Everest, smote the little party on the flank. This wind must be felt to be appreciated. Every member of the party was equipped with every device of windproof clothing which experience could invent. Yet such was the keenness of the wind that it appeared to have the double quality of penetrating through their clothes and yet nearly blowing the laden porters out of their steps.

Progress up the North Ridge of Everest does not lend itself to description. It is a fight against the wind and altitude, generally on rock, sometimes on snow, at an average angle of forty-five degrees. It will appeal to those who have ever tried mountain climbing over 23,000 feet. Camp V was to be situated on the east or sheltered side of the ridge at about 25,300 feet. At about 25,000 feet the endurance of the porters began to flag, and of eight only four made Camp V under their own steam. The remainder deposited their loads, unable to go on. While Mallory set to work to organise the camp, Bruce and one Lobsang, meriting the distinction of being one of the leaders of the 'Tigers,' made two trips back from the level of the camp and brought up the missing loads on their own backs. But white men cannot carry loads at these altitudes with impunity, and it is scarcely to be wondered at that Bruce's heart was strained, happily only temporarily, in this fine performance.

Camp V was now established – two fragile ten-pound tents perched on an almost precipitous slope. The tents occupied by the non-oxygen party in 1922, collapsed and held in position by big stones, were clearly seen 200 feet below. According to plan, five porters now returned to Camp IV, three picked men being retained to stay the night and carry a still tinier camp some 2,000 feet higher on the morrow. Obviously everything depended upon the physical condition and *moral* of these three men. But the most persuasive powers of Bruce could elicit from them little enthusiasm for their next day's task. Apparently the wind had taken the heart out of them. And after the truly miserable but inevitable routine in high altitudes of cooking the dinner the party went to bed with the sun still gilding the tops of the surrounding mountains, but with no rosy anticipations for the morrow.

It was intended to make an early start next morning. This had been done before, therefore it was not impossible, but where Sherpa porters are concerned it certainly approaches the limit of the possible. Making a long story short, a series of visits to the men's tents while the climbers' breakfasts were being prepared produced nothing but the unwelcome information that only one was fit to proceed. The other two professed to be sick and totally unable to carry a load. Bruce talks their language fluently and has great influence over them, and if anyone could have stimulated them to go it was he. But it was fairly evident that the three porters had shot their bolt and that nothing more was to be got out of them. So after a brief consultation it was decided to return to Camp IV.

Mallory and Bruce, on arrival at the North Col, were met by Odell and Irvine, who were fulfilling, for the first time in the history of Everest climbing, the official role of supporters. Since 1922 we had recognised the necessity of this role, picturing the comfort to a returning party of weary climbers such support might afford. The most optimistic imagination fell short of the reality as produced by that 'well-known firm,' Odell and Irvine. For over a week those two lived on the North Col (23,000 feet), and cooked every meal – and only those who have done it can appreciate the recurring hatefulness of this operation. They went out day and night to escort and succour returning parties and climbers over the intricate approaches to the camp, carrying lamps and drinks, and even oxygen to restore the exhausted. They ran the camp and tended the sick, and Odell for one went down to Camp III and returned to Camp IV, escorting parties or fetching provisions on three consecutive days. No members of the climbing party pulled more weight in the team than these two by their unostentatious, unselfish gruelling work.

# 5  NORTON AND SOMERVELL'S ATTEMPT

## BY LIEUT. COLONEL E.F. NORTON, DSO

Somervell and I started off from Camp III on June 1 to follow in Mallory and Bruce's steps. But before starting it became my sad duty to return Beetham to the Base. The reader will wonder how he came to be at Camp III, for I last mentioned him as safely tucked into bed at the Base suffering from sciatica, under Hingston's charge. I regret to say it was simply a case of mutiny: Hingston was told that he could go to the devil, and that he, Beetham, was not going to miss all share in the great doings that were projected; if he could do nothing else he could cook or carry a small load – anything to pull some weight in the team. So, limping and hobbling and taking wonderful photographs, he had reached Camp III on May 30. But he was too obviously a cripple to permit of any thought of using him on the mountain, and as we might now be very glad of our doctor in a day or two, when parties of porters and climbers who had been high came filtering back to Camp III, Beetham must return to take his place in charge of the Base Camp. It was never possible to leave the Base entirely without an Englishman, for we had a considerable sum of money in notes and copper coins in the treasure-chest, and it was always possible that some important communication might arrive from the outside world.

So for the second time I risked making Beetham my enemy for life – and I really thought I had done it this time – as I sent him, volubly protesting and limping like a cripple, down the glacier. He has, I believe, long since forgiven me. And in justification of my own brutal conduct I may add that Hingston's medical skill was very badly required almost as soon as he arrived at Camp III.

Throughout the operations which followed, Shebbeare remained at Camp II, with periodic visits to Camp III. He was in charge of what might be described as the reserve porters' rest-camp, and was responsible for the whole of the Lines of Communication from the Base to Camp III. Enjoying as he did the complete confidence of the porters, he was an ideal transport officer, for the men were perfectly happy under his charge, and he knew more about stores than anyone in the Expedition. We at Camp III never had to give a moment's thought behind us, but were free to concentrate our attention on the mountain, knowing that our supplies would arrive punctually as required, and that when porters were sent up to us they would arrive well fed and in good heart.

The porters told off to accompany Somervell and me, and to establish our camp at 25,500 feet, were six in number, and of these three were to come on to 27,000 feet. Bruce and I had tossed for first pick, and then chosen alternately from among the 'Tigers,' so that each party should be equally strong. My first three picks were Narbu Yishé, Llakpa Chédé and Semchumbi. Narbu Yishé was a plausible rogue, a Mongolian replica of a well-known type in the British Army – the old soldier: his nickname the 'Purana Miles' will convey as much to those whose scholarship is both classical and oriental. Here was a man who, whatever his failings below, was, I knew, capable of great things high up.

Llakpa Chédé will be familiar in person to all who have seen the 'Epic of Everest' film at the Scala Theatre – probably giving the impression of a very small, shy and frightened-looking man. In his own milieu nothing could have been more different – quiet still, but with the quietness of complete self-confidence; independent, sturdy, of irreproachable character, and a brilliant man on the mountain. As to Semchumbi, Geoffrey Bruce will tell you that he was a loafer, a cadger round the officers' mess kitchen, and a ne'er-do-weel. My view of him is different, as will appear.

At 3 p.m. on June 1, Somervell and I with our six porters reached Camp IV, where Odell and Irvine took charge of us, allotted us tents and cooked and served us our meals, for they were now installed in their new role as 'supporters.' And a thankless job this was, for almost the whole day was taken up with performing alternately the menial duties of cook, waiter, or scullion; going out to escort returning parties of porters or climbers across the crevasses and seracs leading to the North Col, or, not infrequently, descending to Camp III for more stores, while more fortunate climbers passed through and disappeared in succession up the mountain. Yet, thankless though the task may have been, Odell and Irvine gave such an exhibition of how it should be done that those of us who once passed through their hands are now spoilt for life: never again shall we enjoy such support as we were given by the 'old firm.' In a year when, to a conspicuous degree, all played for the side, none did so more conscientiously or with less thought of self than these two.

The morning of June 2 broke fine, and by 6.30 Somervell and I were off with our little party of six porters. The reader will understand that Mallory and Bruce were to have established Camp V overnight; this morning they should have been heading up the North Ridge for Camp VI, carrying with them the tent and sleeping-bags in which they had slept the night before.

Our loads, therefore, must comprise one 10-pound tent, two sleeping-bags, food and 'meta' (solid spirit) for ourselves for a possible three nights and for the porters for one; above the North Col porters' loads were always cut down to a maximum of twenty pounds a man, preferably a little under that weight. I cannot remember the exact details of the loads our men carried, but I know they were laden so near the limit that Somervell and I had to carry (as we had done the day before) a light rucksack apiece, with compass, electric torch, a few spare woollen garments, a change of socks, etc., for our own personal use.

Our route crossed the actual Col just below the western lip and, as we emerged from the snow hummocks to traverse it, we suddenly found ourselves in shadow and exposed to the full force of the west wind – from which we were completely sheltered both at Camp IV and in the intervening section; that was a bad moment, its memory is still fresh. The wind, even at this early hour, took our breath away like a plunge into the icy waters of a mountain lake, and in a minute or two our well-protected hands lost all sensation as they grasped the frozen rocks to steady us.

Some little way above the Col we emerged into sunlight again, and though we got the full benefit of the wind all the way up the ridge we never again experienced anything quite so blighting as those few minutes in the shady funnel of the Col. Nevertheless the wind was all day a serious matter. Though it seemed to cut clean through our windproof clothes, it yet had so solid a push to it that the laden porters often staggered in their steps.

I should here explain that our kit was specially designed to exclude the wind. Personally I wore thick woollen vest and drawers, a thick flannel shirt and two sweaters under a lightish knickerbocker suit of windproof gaberdine the knickers of which were lined with light flannel, a pair of soft elastic Kashmir putties and a pair of boots of felt bound and soled with leather and lightly nailed with the usual Alpine nails. Over all I wore a very light pyjama suit of Messrs Burberry's 'Shackleton' windproof gaberdine. On my hands I wore a pair of long fingerless woollen mitts inside a similar pair made of gaberdine; though when step-cutting necessitated a sensitive hold on the axe-haft, I sometimes substituted a pair of silk mitts for the inner woollen pair. On my head I wore a fur-lined leather motor-cycling helmet, and my eyes and nose were protected by a pair of goggles of Crookes's glass, which were sewn into a leather mask that came well over the nose and covered any part of my face which was not naturally protected by my beard. A huge woollen muffler completed my costume. Somervell was dressed in much the same style, and the porters were equally well equipped – each in a light green canvas windproof suit over a variety of woollen and leather garments. We got used to one another's appearance in time, but every now and then I was struck afresh with the absurdly 'gollywog' appearance of the party.

We followed our old route of 1922 – the blunt ridge known as the North Arête. For the first 1,500 feet or more the edge of a big snow-bed forms the crest of the ridge, representing the very top of that great mass of hanging ice which clothes the whole of the eastern slopes and cliffs of the North Col. Ascending, we stuck to the rocks just clear of this snow-bed; descending, it is possible to glissade the whole length of it down to the Col. The rocks are quite easy, but steep enough to be very hard work at those heights. About half-way up this day's climb was the spot where two years before I had, while taking a short rest, placed between my feet my rucksack, containing a few woollen comforts for the night, and something starting it off, it slipped from my grasp and in a second was leaping and bounding like a great football with the evident intention of stopping nowhere short of the main Rongbuk Glacier below. This gives a fair picture of the general angle of the climb.

Somewhere about this same spot we heard something above and, looking up, were not a little disconcerted to see one Dorjay Pasang, descending to meet us. He was Mallory's and Bruce's leading porter, their first pick and one of the men on whom our highest hopes centred. We had hardly heard his tale of woe and read a note he brought from Mallory when we saw above Mallory, Bruce, and three more porters descending in his tracks.

The wind was too cold for a long conversation, and their story was distressingly simple. On the preceding day they had met a very bitter wind all the way up the arête on which we now stood – so bitter that it had quite taken the heart out of their porters. They had pitched two tents at Camp V at a little over 25,000 feet and spent the night, but next morning nothing – not even Bruce's command of the language and well-known influence over these men – would induce any of the porters to go higher, and the end of it was that they had to return. Incidentally, Bruce had had to help the last two or three porters into camp the night before, carrying their loads for them for a short distance, and it was quite evident to us that these excessive exertions had affected him in some way – a surmise which was later confirmed by the discovery that he had strained his heart. So he himself was in no fit state to go on, though none who know him will doubt that he would have done so could the porters have been induced to accompany him. Now there is a moral attached to this story. My diary (written at Camp IV) for the day when this fatal wind was encountered mentions the fact that the weather was 'quite perfect'; the porters who failed were the pick of the 'Tigers,' presumably among the best men we had. Yet these picked men, under the one Sahib of all our party who knew best how to lead the Sherpa porter and on a day which at Camp IV appeared 'quite perfect,' were clean knocked out by wind and couldn't be induced to advance beyond 25,200 feet. How evident it becomes that it will never be possible to ensure success on any given day at these extreme altitudes!

As Camp V had been left all standing with tents and bedding destined to go higher that morning, Somervell and I were able to detach two of the porters who had accompanied us so far, to return with the descending party, and we now continued with four men, the three whose names I have already given and one Lobsang Tashi, a simple, good-natured giant from the eastern borders of Tibet. We reached Camp V without incident about 1 p.m. We had no difficulty in finding the camp from Mallory's description and from certain strips of coloured cloth which each party carried to serve as sign-posts and which had been put up at the point where we were to leave the ridge. The two tents were pitched one above the other on crumbling platforms built on the steep slope just over the edge, and on the east or sheltered side of the North Arête.

The afternoon was spent as every afternoon must always be spent under these conditions. On arrival one crawls into the tent, so completely exhausted that for perhaps three-quarters of an hour one just lies in a sleeping-bag and rests. Then duty begins to call, one member of the party with groans and pantings and frequent rests crawls out of his bag, out of the tent and a few yards to a neighbouring patch of snow, where he fills two big aluminium pots with snow, what time his companion with more panting and groans sits up in bed, lights the meta burner and opens some tins and bags of food – say a stick of pemmican, some tea, sugar and condensed milk, a tin of sardines or bully beef and a box of biscuits.

Presently both are again ensconced in their sleeping-bags side by side, with the meta cooker doing its indifferent best to produce half a pot of warm water from each piled pot of powdery snow. It doesn't sound a very formidable proceeding, and it might appear that I have rather overdrawn the panting and groans; but I have carried out this routine on three or four occasions, and I can honestly say that I know nothing – not even the exertion of steep climbing at these heights – which is so utterly exhausting or which calls for more determination than this hateful duty of high-altitude cooking. The process has to be repeated two or three times as, in addition to the preparation of the evening meal, a thermos flask or two must be filled with water for to-morrow's breakfast and the cooking pots must be washed up. Perhaps the most hateful part of the process is that some of the resultant mess must be eaten, and this itself is only achieved by will power: there is but little desire to eat – sometimes indeed a sense of nausea at the bare idea – though of drink one cannot have enough.

When we had done our duty, I visited the tent where the four porters were packed like sardines, to persuade them to do theirs. For some time I could elicit nothing but grunts, but I succeeded at last in infusing some life into the comatose, unwilling figures, and it then appeared that some stones had fallen from our tent platform and, landing on the porters' tent, had cut Lobsang Tashi's head – a slight affair despite a good showing of blood – and Semchumbi's knee. The latter was a much more serious matter – a nasty gash right across the knee-cap.

With one last look at the panorama of glacier and mountain spread out below – a world composed of three elements only, rock, snow and ice, the mountain-tops now gilded by the declining sun and Camp III just discernible in the cold shadow of the North Peak under our feet – we turned in for the night, with gloomy forebodings for the morrow; for there was nothing whatever in the attitude of our porters to-night to encourage us to hope that we should next day succeed any better than Mallory and Bruce.

My diary records that we spent a 'fair night'; only some 200 feet below we had seen the collapsed forms of two tents in which two years before Mallory, Somervell, Morshead and I had spent a truly miserable night, scarcely any of us getting any sleep. The difference was largely accounted for by improvements in our equipment and in the organisation of our camp, and it is by this progressive raising of the standard of comfort high on the mountain that we shall some day reach the top.

On the morning of June 3 we were up at 5 a.m., and while Somervell busied himself with preparations for breakfast I climbed down to the porters' tent with some misgivings as to what their condition would prove to be. My fears were justified, and for some time groans were the only answer to my questions. But having at last, as I thought, inspired the men sufficiently to induce them to cook and eat a meal, I returned and had breakfast. I then again tackled them, for they seemed incapable of making any sort of a move without much stimulating, and it was at once evident that Lobsang Tashi was finished and useless for any higher climbing. His head wound was nothing, but he complained of sickness, and it was evident that his heart was not in the task of going any higher. Semchumbi was genuinely lame, his knee was much swollen, and he looked an unlikely starter, despite the fact that he showed a good deal more spirit than the other wounded man.

Llakpa Chédé I judged fit and willing to go higher provided that any of the others would, and so I concentrated most of my persuasive powers on Narbu Yishé. I talked for a long time to these men, pointing out the honour and glory that they would achieve if they would but carry their loads another 2,000 feet – thus passing by 1,500 feet the highest point to which loads had ever been carried.

I remember saying, 'If you put us up a camp at 27,000 feet and we reach the top, your names shall appear in letters of gold in the book that will be written to describe the achievement.' To make a very long story short I succeeded in inducing the three – Narbu Yishé, Llakpa Chédé and Semchumbi – lame as he was – to come on, and we actually started from camp at 9 a.m. – four hours after we had got up. Truly it is not easy to make an early start on Mount Everest! Lobsang Tashi was sent down alone to Camp IV; as soon as his face was turned in the right direction he showed considerable alacrity, and we had the satisfaction of seeing him reach that camp in safety an hour or two later.

Of our ascent of the ridge there is little to tell; it was a repetition of the climb of the day before and was over ground familiar to Somervell and myself, as we had traversed exactly the same route when making for our highest point two years before. Narbu Yishé and Llakpa Chédé went splendidly when once they were started. Somervell was feeling his throat very badly and had constantly to stop and cough, so he took on himself the task of shepherding Semchumbi, who, to do him justice, performed a very fine feat indeed in climbing for four and a half hours with a twenty-pound load, and, though inevitably slow and a drag on the whole party, he remained cheerful and willing and did his very best. The weather continued fine and the wind was markedly less severe than on the day before.

Some time after midday we recognised and passed the highest point that Mallory, Somervell and I had reached in 1922. As I have said before, one's sensations are dulled at these altitudes, but I remember a momentary uplift at the thought that we were actually going to camp higher than the highest point ever reached without oxygen. With a clear day ahead of us, and given favourable conditions, what might we not achieve!

About 1.30 it became evident that it would be impossible to urge the gallant Semchumbi much farther, so I selected a site for our tent, a narrow cleft in the rocks facing north and affording the suggestion – it was little more –

of some shelter from the north-west wind. Here I set the two leading porters to scrape and pile the loose stones forming the floor of the cleft into the usual platform for a tent. I can safely say that in two excursions up and down the whole length of the North Arête of Mount Everest I have never seen a single spot affording the six-foot square level area on which a tent could be pitched without having to build a platform. As Somervell helped and encouraged Semchumbi up the last steep pitch, I went off for three-quarters of an hour to reconnoitre the beginning of next day's climb.

About 2.30 we sent the three porters down. They had nearly 4,000 feet to descend, for we have since estimated the height of Camp VI at about 26,800 feet, and one of them was lame: so there was not too much time for them to reach Camp IV by daylight. I gave the men a note to be shown to the Sahib in charge of each camp to say that they had done splendidly, and were to be fed on the fat of the land and passed comfortably to the Base Camp and a well-earned rest.

We afterwards learnt that on this day, Odell and Hazard, the latter of whom had reached Camp IV the day before, climbed to Camp V, returning to Camp IV the same night. Odell was after fossils, and actually found the first ever collected on Mount Everest, and Hazard accompanied him for air and exercise. This little stroll is a curious commentary on the fact that two years before the scientists were debating whether human beings could exist without oxygen at 25,000 feet.

Somervell and I spent the afternoon as on the day before, with the exception that we had now no porters to stimulate, and this was fortunate, for as you near 27,000 feet you have no great surplus of determination. My diary for the day finishes with the surprising entry: 'Spent the best night since I left Camp I,' yet it was true in my case, and Somervell was at least fairly comfortable if he didn't sleep quite so well as I did. As one of our doubts had always been whether it would be possible to sleep, or even rest well, at 27,000 feet, this is an interesting point. Besides my boots I took to bed with me in my eiderdown sleeping-bag two thermos flasks filled with warm tea; towards morning I found that one of these had got rid of its cork, and its contents – no longer warm – had emptied into my bed.

Once more our hopes of an early start were shattered; snow had to be fetched and melted to provide the essential drink for breakfast. If – as I have before described – vitality is low in the early hours at Camp III at 21,000 feet, it can be guessed how near the limit 6 a.m. found us at 27,000. Yet somehow the job was done and we were off at 6.40.

Perhaps an hour beyond camp we encountered the bottom edge of the great 1,000-foot-deep band of yellow sandstone that crosses the whole north face of Everest from shoulder to shoulder, and is so conspicuous a feature of the mountain as seen from the north. This afforded easy going as we traversed it diagonally, for it was made up of a series of broad ledges running parallel to its general direction and sufficiently broken up to afford easy access, one to the next.

The day was fine and nearly windless – a perfect day for our task – yet it was bitterly cold, and I remember shivering so violently as I sat in the sun during one of our numerous halts, dressed in all the clothes I have described, that I suspected the approach of malaria and took my pulse. I was surprised to find it only about sixty-four, which is some twenty above my normally very slow pulse. I was not wearing snow goggles except when actually on snow – a very small proportion of the day's climb – as I had found that the rims of my goggles somewhat interfered with a clear view of my steps. At a height of about 27,500 feet I began to experience some trouble with my eyes; I was seeing double, and in a difficult step was sometimes in doubt where to put my feet. I thought that this might be a premonitory symptom of snow-blindness, but Somervell assured me that this could not be the case, and he was undoubtedly right, for I have since been told that it was a symptom of lack of control and due to the insufficiency of oxygen in the air I was breathing.

Our pace was wretched. My ambition was to do twenty consecutive paces uphill without a pause to rest and pant, elbow on bent knee; yet I never remember achieving it – thirteen was nearer the mark. The process of breathing in the intensely cold dry air, which caught the back of the larynx, had a disastrous effect on poor Somervell's already very bad sore throat and he had constantly to stop and cough. Every five or ten minutes we had to sit down for a minute or two, and we must have looked a sorry couple.

The view from this great height was disappointing. From 25,000 feet the wild tangle of snowy peaks and winding glaciers, each with its parallel lines of moraine-like cart tracks on a snowy road, was imposing to a degree. But we were now high above the highest summit in sight, and everything below us was so flattened out that much of the beauty of outline was lost. To the north, over the great plateau of Tibet, the eye travelled over range upon range of minor hills until all sense of distance was lost, only to be sharply regained on picking up a row of snow-peaks just appearing over the horizon like tiny teeth. The day was a remarkably clear one in a country of the clearest atmosphere in the world, and the imagination was fired by the sight of these infinitely distant peaks tucked away over the curve of the horizon.

Towards noon we found ourselves just below the top edge of the band of sandstone and nearing the big couloir or gully which runs vertically down the mountain and cuts off the base of the final pyramid from the great northern shoulder. The line we had followed was one roughly parallel to and perhaps 500 to 600 feet below the crest of the North-east Arête; this was the line Somervell and I had always favoured in preference to the actual crest, which Mallory advocated.

At midday Somervell succumbed to his throat trouble. He declared that he was only delaying me, and urged me to go on alone and reach the top. I left him sitting under a rock just below the topmost edge of the sandstone band and went on. I followed the actual top edge of the band, which led at a very slightly uphill angle into and across the big couloir; but to reach the latter I had to turn the ends of two pronounced buttresses which ran down the face of the mountain, one of which was a prolongation of a feature on the skyline ridge which we called the second step, and which looked so formidable an obstacle where it crossed the ridge that we had chosen the lower route rather than try and surmount it at its highest point. From about the place where I met with these buttresses the going became a great deal worse; the slope was very steep below me, the foothold ledges narrowed to a few inches in width, and as I approached the shelter of the big couloir there was a lot of powdery snow which concealed the precarious footholds. The whole face of the mountain was composed of slabs like the tiles on a roof, and all sloped at much the same angle as tiles. I had twice to retrace my steps and follow a different band of strata; the couloir itself was filled with powdery snow into which I sank to the knee or even to the waist, and which was yet not of a consistency to support me in the event of a slip. Beyond the couloir the going got steadily worse; I found myself stepping from tile to tile, as it were, each tile sloping smoothly and steeply downwards; I began to feel that I was too much dependent on the mere friction of a boot nail on the slabs. It was not exactly difficult going, but it was a dangerous place for a single unroped climber, as one slip would have sent me in all probability to the bottom of the mountain. The strain of climbing so carefully was beginning to tell and I was getting exhausted. In addition my eye trouble was getting worse and was by now a severe handicap.

I had perhaps 200 feet more of this nasty going to surmount before I emerged on to the north face of the final pyramid and, I believe, safety and an easy route to the summit. It was now 1 p.m., and a brief calculation showed that I had no chance of climbing the remaining 800 or 900 feet if I was to return in safety.

At a point subsequently fixed by theodolite as 28,126 feet I turned back and retraced my steps to rejoin Somervell. In an hour I had gained but little – probably under 100 feet in height, and in distance perhaps 300 yards – on the position where we had separated. Surveying is an exact science, and I must not quarrel with Hazard for fixing our highest point twenty-four feet below the height of Kanchenjunga, the third highest mountain in the world.

I feel that I ought to record the bitter feeling of disappointment which I should have experienced on having to acknowledge defeat with the summit so close; yet I cannot conscientiously say that I felt it much at the time. Twice now I have had thus to turn back on a favourable day when success had appeared possible, yet on neither occasion did I feel the sensations appropriate to the moment. This I think is a psychological effect of great altitudes; the better qualities of ambition and will to conquer seem dulled to nothing, and one turns downhill with but little feelings other than relief that the strain and effort of climbing are finished.

I was near the end of my powers, and had for some time been going too slowly to hope to reach the summit. Whether the height I had reached was nearing the limit of human endurance without the artificial aid of oxygen, or whether my earlier exertions and hardships in the month of May accounted for my exhaustion, I cannot, of course, say, but I incline to the latter opinion; and I still believe that there is nothing in the atmospheric conditions even between 28,000 and 29,000 feet to prevent a fresh and fit party from reaching the top of Mount Everest without oxygen.

One small incident will serve to show that I must have been very much below my proper form at this time, and that my nerve had been shaken by the last two hours of climbing alone on steep and slippery going. As I approached Somervell I had to cross a patch of snow lying thinly over some sloping rocks. It was neither steep nor difficult, and not to be compared to the ground I had just left, yet suddenly I felt that I could not face it without help, and I shouted to Somervell to come and throw me the end of the rope. Here again I remember the difficulty I had in making my voice carry perhaps 100 yards. Somervell gave me the required aid, and I could see the surprise he felt at my needing it in such a place.

Then came the descent. Soon after we started down, at about 2 p.m., Somervell's axe slipped from his numb fingers and went cart-wheeling down the slopes below. This must have been somewhere about the point where an hour or two before he had taken his highest photograph; and it is a proof of the deceptive picture of the true angle of the mountain conveyed by these photographs that it does not give the impression that a dropped axe would go any distance without coming to rest, yet his never looked like stopping, and disappeared from our view still going strong.

We retraced our steps of the morning; we made very poor going, descending at a very much slower pace than we had made two years before when we turned back from our highest point some 1,000 feet lower.

We looked in at our tent at Camp VI, finding it without difficulty, collected one or two of our belongings and a section of tent pole as a substitute for Somervell's axe, collapsed and weighted the tent with stones, and started down the interminable North Arête. Sunset found us level with Camp V, which we left below us on the right without departing from the blunt crest of the Arête. We were unroped, for here the going was both safe and easy. Arrived on the big snow-bed I glissaded for some little distance before I realised that Somervell had stopped behind, and I had to wait quite half an hour for him to catch up. I concluded that he had stopped to sketch or photograph the effect of the sunset glow on the great panorama of peaks surrounding us – a proof that I had by no means realised his condition. Actually he had been stopped by a more than usually severe fit of coughing which had ended by very nearly choking him, and he was probably only saved by coughing up the obstructing matter along with a lot of blood. When he rejoined me, coming very slowly down the rocks, as he could not trust himself to glissade on the snow, it was already dark and I lit up my electric torch.

As we neared the Col I began to shout to Camp IV, for it was one of our rules that any party of porters or climbers descending from the mountain must be met at the Col and escorted and roped over the intricate route into camp by one or more of the supporters, who knew the way by heart. At last I made myself heard, and an answering shout informed us that our escort was coming and was bringing an oxygen apparatus and cylinder. But there was something we wanted far more than oxygen, for we were parched and famished with thirst. I remember shouting again and again, 'We don't want the d—d oxygen; we want drink.' My own throat and voice were in none too good a case, and my feeble wail seemed to be swallowed up in the dim white expanse below glimmering in the starlight.

A hundred feet or more above the Col, Mallory and Odell met us, and told us that Irvine was in camp hard at work preparing our dinner. Somervell had a go at the oxygen, but seemed to get little benefit from it, and I tried it with the same result. But we were perfectly fit to get along without it, and perhaps another three-quarters of an hour saw us arrive in camp. Mallory and Odell were kindness itself, and they kept congratulating us on having reached what we estimated as a height of 28,000 feet, though we ourselves felt nothing but disappointment at our failure. We reached Camp IV at 9.30 p.m., and what a different welcome it gave us to that we had received at the same place two years before on our arrival at eleven at night in an empty and deserted camp! Young Irvine had both tea and soup ready for us, and we had something to eat; but our appetites were meagre, and herein lies one of the difficulties of high climbing: one eats from a sense of duty, and it is impossible to force oneself to take enough food even to begin to make good the day's wastage of tissue.

As Mallory and I lay in our tent, he explained that he had decided that if we two failed to reach the summit, he was determined to make one more attempt, this time with oxygen, and how he had been down to Camp III with Bruce and collected sufficient porters to enable the attempt to be staged.[1]

I entirely agreed with his decision, and was full of admiration for the indomitable spirit of the man, determined, in spite of his already excessive exertions, not to admit defeat while any chance remained, and I must admit that – such was his will power and nervous energy – he still seemed entirely adequate to the task. I differed with him in his decision to take Irvine as his companion – for two reasons: firstly, that Irvine was now suffering from the prevalent throat trouble, though certainly not as badly as Somervell had been before the start of our climb; secondly, that he was not the experienced climber that Odell was, while Odell was obviously fit and strong, and, acclimatising very slowly as he had done, was now beginning to show unmistakably that we had in him a climber of unequalled endurance and toughness. Mallory's reasons for his choice were that though Odell and Irvine were both thoroughly *au fait* with every detail of the oxygen apparatus, yet the latter had a peculiar genius for mechanical expedients, and had taken the lead in devising means to obviate its numerous shortcomings; and he insisted that those who were to use the apparatus must have faith in its efficacy. Odell, having used it with Bruce on the day of their abortive attempt to reach Camp IV without apparently benefiting from it, certainly had not this confidence.

---

1   It may be asked how it came that sufficient porters were now available for an attempt with oxygen, seeing that we had decided against an oxygen attempt at Camp I on the grounds of inadequate transport.
      Mallory and Irvine decided to use practically no oxygen up to Camp VI; two or three porters, who had returned from Camp V after the abortive attempt, were employed again; the continued fine weather had so heartened the porters that two extra volunteers over and above the fifteen 'tigers' were found; and, lastly, Camp VI having been established with tents and bedding by Somervell and me, nearly every available porter could now be used for carrying oxygen cylinders.
      It was to Bruce's energy (despite his strained heart) that the successful organisation of the transport for this attempt must be credited.

But it was obviously no time for me to interfere with the composition of the party, and when I found that Mallory had completed his plans I made no attempt to do so.

Some time after eleven o'clock that night, as I was dozing off to sleep, I was suddenly wakened by sharp pain in my eyes, and found that I had been smitten with a severe attack of snow blindness. In the morning I found myself completely blind, and I remained in this condition for the next sixty hours, suffering a good deal of pain.

June 5 was spent in the usual preparations for Mallory and Irvine's climb, on which they were to start next day. I was only able to help by periodically coming to the door of my tent and talking to the porters, for, poor though was my knowledge of Nepalese, there was no one else at Camp IV who could do so even as effectively as I; Mallory had learnt a sufficient smattering of Hindustani to communicate with these men to a certain extent, but it was evident that his party might have considerable trouble in getting their porters on from Camp V to Camp VI (though we hoped that their reluctance would be reduced to some extent by the fact that the carry had now been once successfully accomplished), and I had to do my best to stimulate the porters in advance for this crucial moment. That afternoon Somervell descended to Camp III and thence next day went on down to the Base Camp, and Hazard arrived from Camp III to take Irvine's place, with Odell as supporter at Camp IV.

On June 6 at 7.30 a.m. we said good-bye to Mallory and Irvine, little guessing that we should see them no more. My last impression of my friends was a handshake and a word of blessing, for it was only in my imagination that I could see the little party winding its way amid the snow humps and ice crevasses leading to the Col – the two climbers, never to return, accompanied by four or five porters.

About 10.30 a.m. Hingston arrived from Camp III with two porters, to see what could be done for my eyes, of which Somervell had told him. Hingston is nothing if not efficient; he had already proved himself a remarkable goer on the glacier as far as Camp III, and we were scarcely surprised when he arrived in Camp IV with the matter-of-fact ease of an experienced mountaineer. Yet with a view to what followed it is worthy of note that he had never previously climbed a mountain in the Alpine sense.

An examination of my eyes showed that nothing could be done to restore my sight at the moment, though there was little question that they would recover in a day or two; but I was anxious not to remain a useless encumbrance on the supporters at Camp IV and, Hingston volunteering to escort me with his two porters, I decided to go down, blind as I was, to Camp III.

Hazard offered to accompany us as far as the top of the ice chimney to rope me from above down this steepest portion of the route, including the chimney itself and the wall below it. Accordingly, about 11 a.m. we started the descent. The two porters, Nima Tundrup and Chutin, were both strong and steady climbers, and between them and Hingston – the last doing all the really responsible work – my every footstep was guided and my feet placed for me the whole way down, while Hazard held me with a rope down each steep section in succession. It was indeed a remarkable performance on the part of Hingston: he gave me the impression of having the steadiness and confidence of an Alpine guide. I was shod with crampons, and thanks to them and to the help of my companions I never had an anxious moment, though it was necessarily a most laborious and tedious process. To make a long story short we reached the glacier without incident and hence sent one porter on to fetch six men, with the one-man carrier, from Camp III to meet me where our route took to the moraine; for on its rough boulders I could never have made any progress at all.

These six men took it in turns to carry me, and did so over the most appalling going – boulders, ice, and frozen scree – without a single false step until, about 5 p.m., we reached Camp III; there I was welcomed by Bruce and Noel with that extraordinary solicitude and kindness which I have come to recognise as the one great reward that awaits the unsuccessful Everest climber.

Next morning I was beginning to see a little, and in two more days was completely recovered. Bruce, Noel, Hingston and I decided to remain at Camp III until the fate of Mallory and Irvine's attempt was decided. During the next four days we were to pass through every successive stage of suspense and anxiety from high hope to hopelessness, and the memory of them is such that Camp III must remain to all of us the most hateful place in the world.

# 6 MALLORY AND IRVINE'S ATTEMPT

BY N.E. ODELL

Of all our long line of camps from the Base Camp to Camp VI, No. IV on the North Col was perhaps the most remarkable and the most distinctive in character. It was the only one in which we had perforce to forsake the warmth and dryness of a rock foundation and take to the dubious alternative of snow. The experience of at least two of us in the Arctic had taught us that, unless altogether impossible, it was worth while going to infinite trouble to pitch on rock. Snow may be delightful for a temporary siesta, if Nature has provided one with a good hide and a low coefficient of thermal conductivity, but it is remarkable how soon it congeals to the consistency of the hardest rock, and how difficult it is to smooth out the relief of one's anatomy first impressed upon it! But there have been many worse camps on snow than that on the North Col at 23,000 feet; indeed, in my experience it was one of the best. Perched on an ice-ledge in about the same position as the camp of 1922, it had four tents: two for sahibs and two for porters. The ledge was a shelf of *névé* with a greatest breadth of about thirty feet, and a high wall of ice which rose above it on the western side gave comforting protection from the chilly winds that constantly blew from that direction. Indeed, had it not been for this natural screen the camp could never have been occupied for such long periods as it eventually was. To the east one looked out over the upper *névé* basin of the East Rongbuk Glacier, and beyond its high border and the Hlakpa La, to the distant rugged range of Gyankar outlying the wide depression of the Arun River: a commanding view which, when in addition the effulgence of sunrise touched and tinted the nearer rock spires of Chomo Lönzo, formed a picture that made it worth while leaving the warmth of one's sleeping-bag at 4 a.m. to gaze upon in an ecstasy of adoration. During my eleven days' residence here I experienced all kinds of weather conditions, not the least remarkable being two days when the sun temperature at midday was 105° Fahrenheit, while the air temperature at the same time was only 29°. It is a question if the air temperature up here ever exceeds that of the freezing-point, and it is probable that the fallen snow wastes away entirely by direct evaporation. The snow was consequently very dry and unconsolidated, and in the complete absence of any running water supply, snow melting and water boiling was a rather protracted occupation of mine as camp cook. The ledge was fortunately extensive enough to allow of an ample area of clean snow being reserved for water supply, and the preservation of this and all the other little duties attendant on camp life fell to my lot while in charge. One is so often asked what it feels like living up at these altitudes, and the only reply that can be given is that after some degree of acclimatisation one's sensations are really quite normal, and it is only when great exertion is necessary that one feels 'like nothing on earth'! And certainly the adverse effect of high altitude on one's mentality has been exaggerated: the speed of one's mental processes may perhaps be slowed down, but their capacity is but little impaired. And this is not self-delusion, as some physiologists would wish to make out, from evidence derived from unacclimatised subjects!

To reach the actual saddle of the North Col, which lay nearer the foot of the North Ridge of Everest than the ledge on which the camp was situated, it had been necessary in 1922 owing to the presence of difficult 'schrunds to make a way up towards the North Peak and then back again along the crest of the Col. An annoying and time-wasting necessity this had proved to be, especially when tired climbers were returning from the mountain at dusk, and we were anxious at the outset to try and cut it out. And this we succeeded in doing, as on the occasion of our first reaching the site of Camp IV, on May 20, Mallory and I found it was just possible to force a somewhat complicated route from the southern end of the camp ledge direct up to the Col. This route, though a little treacherous from two doubtful snow-bridges, proved to be negotiable until the end.

On June 1 I had gone down to Camp III, and on getting back to IV next day with a fresh supply of stores, I had been surprised to see Mallory and Geoff Bruce returning from V, their attempt to get higher having been rendered abortive by the refusal of the porters to go on. Mallory was not a little disap-pointed and upset about this, and he took the view, possibly on account of the strained condition of Bruce's heart, that a further attempt should not be made except with the use of oxygen. He went down with Bruce and Irvine that same day to Camp III, intent on investigating afresh with Bruce's aid the question of available porterage. It was found just possible to collect to-gether sufficient men, who were not indisposed, to carry up oxygen supplies for such an attempt. Irvine occupied himself meanwhile in putting the final touches to the recreated oxygen-breathing sets. I was still in charge of IV, and in the meanwhile with Hazard had been up to V in support of Norton and Somervell's wonderful attempt on the summit without oxygen, and to conduct their porters back to the North Col.

On the evening of June 4 Mallory and Irvine with a few coolies came up from III, the two former using oxygen. They were able to cover the distance in the fast time of two and a half hours, and seemed well pleased with a performance which had no doubt been prompted by the wish to demonstrate the real efficacy of oxygen. But in my opinion the demonstration was hardly justified, and Irvine's throat at any rate, that had already given him considerable discomfort from the cold dry air, that at these altitudes can reduce this delicate passage to the consistency of cardboard, was palpably aggravated by the effect of the oxygen. Mallory's throat was less affected, though it was undoubtedly causing him some little irritation; and, besides, his usual equanimity was perhaps a little disturbed by the feeling of responsibility consequent upon this being probably the turning-point in the success or failure of the campaign. Who with the fighting spirit of Mallory, or with the long-tried obsession of attainment of the greatest goal of his ideals, could be otherwise than impatient to be off on the culminating challenge of a lifetime, nay even of a whole generation of active mountaineers! And Irvine, though through youth without the same intensity of mountain spell that was upon Mallory, yet was every bit, if not more, obsessed to go 'all out' on what was certainly to him the greatest course for 'pairs' he would be ever destined to 'row'! I had frequently shared a tent with Sandy Irvine in one or other of our glacier camps, but it was the previous year on our sledging journey across Spitzbergen that I had first got to know him intimately. The effects of high altitude somewhat enhanced his natural reserve, but he told me on more than one occasion how much he hoped he would have a real chance of 'a shot at the summit.' And careful and devoted though his work was on making the oxygen apparatus efficient for use, he did not hesitate to tell me that he would rather reach the foot of the final pyramid without the use of oxygen than the summit by means of its aid! He thought that if it were worth while doing at all, it was worth while doing without artificial means. Nevertheless when the call came from Mallory for this one last effort with every means at our disposal, he saw the necessity of foregoing any personal preference in the matter, and welcomed almost with boyish enthusiasm a chance that he had little thought would come his way.

It was late the same evening of Mallory and Irvine's arrival at Camp IV that the former and myself went up to meet Norton and Somervell returning from their record climb, the events of which have already been described. June 5 was spent quietly at the North Col, one and all of us feeling a sense of impotence at our inability to diminish the suffering that poor Norton was undergoing from his painful attack of snow-blindness, and Somervell on account of his severely relaxed throat. The latter, however, with his customary fortitude and resolution, announced that he was fit enough to go down to Camp III, and down to Camp III in the evening, of course, he went. Hazard was signalled for from Camp III by means of our usual code of blankets placed against the snow, and Irvine and I busied ourselves with re-testing and putting further final touches to the oxygen apparatus. It was a brilliant day with a maximum midday sun temperature of 105°, though the air temperature never rose above freezing. We had to darken the tent where Norton was lying by an outside covering of sleeping-bags. I took the precaution of wearing a sun helmet up here on the North Col, and at times on the glacier below, though I could never get an authoritative opinion from either of our medical experts as to the necessity of such a procedure, so detached, or arbitrary, in their counsel can the advanced thinkers in that dignified profession become! But though blessed with a fairly thick skull, I was taking no risks, and while in respect of the sun considerations of latitude rather than altitude were perhaps uppermost in one's thoughts, yet the altitude and prevailing air temperature never allowed to go far out of mind the possibility of one's shaded side freezing!

I think most of the party, with perhaps the exception of the unfortunate Norton, slept well that night, though Irvine admitted his sorely sun-scorched face had caused him distinct discomfort at times. Hazard and I were up early the morning of the 6th, and soon had frizzling and crackling over the Primus stove a choice fry of sardines, to be served up in Mallory and Irvine's tent with biscuits and ample hot tea, or chocolate. On the announcement of this breakfast they seemed pleased enough, but I must admit that either owing to excitement or restlessness to be off they hardly did justice to the repast, or flattered the cooks! At 8.40 they were ready to start, and I hurriedly 'snapped' them as they were loading up with the oxygen apparatus. Their personal loads consisted of the modified apparatus with two cylinders only and a few other small items such as wraps and a food ration for the day, amounting to not more than perhaps twenty-five pounds. This may sound to many a very heavy load to carry at such altitudes, and in actual fact it is, but it is an easy load compared with the total of forty pounds or more that the original breathing apparatus as well as the items of extra clothing, etc., that must be carried, amounted to. The eight porters, who accompanied them from Camp IV, carried provisions, bedding, and additional oxygen cylinders, but of course no breathing apparatus for their own use. It always amazed us how little on the whole our Sherpas were affected by moderate loads, though as a matter of fact at these altitudes we contrived to give them no more than twenty to twenty-five pounds to carry. The party moved off in silence as we bid them adieu, and they were soon lost to view amidst the broken ice-masses that concealed from view the actual saddle of the North Col and the lower part of the North Ridge of the mountain.

Though a brilliant morning, my diary records it as very cloudy in the afternoon and even snowing a little in the evening. It was at 9.45 that morning that Hingston arrived and conducted Norton in his sightless condition down to Camp III, Hazard going down as far as the rope ladder and then returning to me on the North Col. I occupied myself meanwhile with various camp duties and observations. That evening, soon after five o'clock, four of Mallory's porters returned from Camp V, where his party was spending the night, and brought me a note saying, 'There is no wind here, and things look hopeful.'

On the 7th Mallory's party was to go on up to Camp VI, and I that same day with Nema, who was the only porter of the two available at the North Col, followed up in support to Camp V. This method of support, a stage as it were behind, was rendered necessary by the limited accommodation at these two high camps, consequent upon the inadequate number of porters available to carry up sufficient tentage, etc. I had expected on my way up to Camp V to find a spare oxygen-breathing set that had been left there earlier, but discovered that Irvine the previous day had taken the mouthpiece from it for a spare, and so rendered it useless to me. However, I carried it on up to Camp V in case another mouthpiece were available there; but this was not so, though it did not bother me, since I found I was able to get along as well without its aid, and better without the bulky inconvenience of the whole apparatus. Not long after my arrival Mallory and Irvine's four remaining porters returned from Camp VI, their advent having been heralded by stones falling unpleasantly near the tent that had been unwittingly displaced by them during their descent of the steep slopes above. The exposure of Camp V in this respect had been borne in on me during my first visit with Hazard, when Norton and Somervell's returning porters had likewise unknowingly bombarded our frail tents with stones and struck a porter of ours, though fortunately with no severe results. Mallory's porters brought me the following message:

Dear Odell, –

We're awfully sorry to have left things in such a mess – our Unna Cooker rolled down the slope at the last moment. Be sure of getting back to IV to-morrow in time to evacuate before dark, as I hope to. In the tent I must have left a compass – for the Lord's sake rescue it: we are without. To here on ninety atmospheres[1] for the two days – so we'll probably go on two cylinders – but it's a ——load for climbing. Perfect weather for the job!

Yours ever,

G. Mallory.

Nema, my porter, was obviously much affected by mountain sickness, which made it very unlikely that he would be able to go higher next day, and consequently I decided to send him down that evening with the other four returning men. It is wonderful how soon that strange malady, so often described as 'mountain sickness,' seems to disappear not only with the descent, but when the decision to descend has been made: at any rate I have noticed it time and again with these native porters, if not with other climbers! When no further effort is to be called for, the psychological effect is such that a fresh stimulus to normality is given, and sickness and other effects disappear. And as the little party started down Nema seemed as active and fit as the rest of them. However, I was not loath to let him go, as I knew by so doing I should be freer on the morrow to wander about over the North Face and make a more thorough geological examination of it on my way up to Camp VI. After a short search within the tent I duly found Mallory's missing prismatic compass. That evening as I looked out from the little rock ledge on which my tent was situated, the weather seemed most promising, and I knew with what hopeful feelings and exultant cheer Mallory and Irvine would take their last look around before closing themselves in their tiny tent at VI that night. My outlook, situated though I was 2,000 feet lower down the mountainside than they, was nevertheless commanding and impressive in the extreme, and the fact that I was quite alone certainly enhanced the impressiveness of the scene. To the westward was a savagely wild jumble of peaks towering above the upper Rongbuk Glacier and its many affluents, culminating in the mighty Cho-uyo (26,750 feet) and Gyachung Kang (25,910 feet), bathed in pinks and yellows of the most exquisite tints. Right opposite were

1  This refers to the pressure, and consequent amount, of oxygen they had been using. For full supply, the pressure stood at 120 atmospheres.

the gaunt cliffs of Everest's North Peak, their banded structure pregnant with the more special and esoteric interest of their past primeval history, and in this respect not detracting by its impression from the vision of such as can behold with more than single eye. This massive pyramid of rock, the one near thing on God's earth, seemed only to lend greater distance to the wide horizon which it intercepted, and its dark bulk the more exaggerate the brilliant opalescence of the far northern horizon of Central Tibet, above which the sharp-cut crests of distant peaks thrust their purple fangs, one in particular rising supreme among them. To the eastward, floating in thin air, 100 miles away, the snowy top of Kanchenjunga appeared, and nearer, the beautifully varied outline of the Gyankar Range, that guards the tortuous passages of the Arun in its headlong plunge towards the lowlands of Nepal. It has been my good fortune to climb many peaks alone and witness sunset from not a few, but this was the crowning experience of them all, an ineffable transcendent experience that can never fade from memory.

A meal of 'Force' and a little jam varied with macaroni and tomatoes completed my supper, and then by dint of two sleeping-bags and the adoption of a position to avoid the larger stones of the floor I stretched myself diagonally across the tiny tent in an endeavour to obtain what sleep I might pending a visit from the notorious Sukpas, or even the watchdogs of Chomolungma! For all I know none put in an appearance, and even the wind did not attain its usual boisterous degree, or threaten to start the somewhat precarious built-up platform on which the tent was perched from a glissade down the mountain-side. I kept reasonably warm and consequently had a fair amount of sleep. I was up at 6, but the great efforts necessitated and energy absorbed at these altitudes, by the various little obligations of breakfast and putting on one's boots, etc., prevented my starting off before eight o'clock. Carrying a rucksack with provisions in case of shortage at Camp VI, I made my solitary way up the steep slope of snow and rock behind Camp V and so reached the crest of the main North Ridge. The earlier morning had been clear and not unduly cold, but now rolling banks of mist commenced to form and sweep from the westward across the great face of the mountain. But it was fortunate that the wind did not increase. There were indications though that this mist might be chiefly confined to the lower half of the mountain, as on looking up one could see a certain luminosity that might mean comparatively clear conditions about its upper half. This appearance so impressed me that I had no qualms for Mallory and Irvine's progress upward from Camp VI, and I hoped by this time that they would be well on their way up the final pyramid of the summit. The wind being light, they should have made good progress and unhampered by their intended route along the crest of the north-east shoulder.

My plan was to make a rather circuitous route outwards over the northern face in order to examine the geological structure of the mountain. The lower part of it is formed of a variety of gneisses, and on these rest a mass of rocks, mainly highly altered limestones, which compose the greater part of its upper half, and here and there are to be seen in small amount light granitoid rocks which break across, or are interbedded with, all the other series. But for a fuller description I would direct the reader's attention to Part 3, the above being sufficient to indicate roughly the general character of the rock met with. The whole series dips outwards from the mountain at about thirty degrees, and since the general slope of this face, above 25,000 feet, is about forty to forty-five degrees, the effect is to make a series of overlapping slabs nearly parallel with the slope, and presenting a number of little faces often up to fifty feet in height, which can be climbed, usually by an easy though sometimes steepish route, while most can be entirely circumvented. The rocks are not on the whole rotten in texture since they have been considerably hardened by the igneous intrusions of granitoid rocks. But the slabs are often sprinkled to a varying degree with debris from above, and when to this is added freshly fallen snow, the labour and toil of climbing at these altitudes may perhaps be imagined. It is not so much the technical difficulty as the awkwardness of a slope of uncertain footing not quite steep enough for the use of one's hands.

At about 26,000 feet I climbed a little crag which could possibly have been circumvented, but which I decided to tackle direct, more perhaps as a test of my condition than for any other reason. There was scarcely 100 feet of it, and as I reached the top there was a sudden clearing of the atmosphere above me and I saw the whole summit ridge and final peak of Everest unveiled. I noticed far away on a snow slope leading up to what seemed to me to be the last step but one from the base of the final pyramid, a tiny object moving and approaching the rock step. A second object followed, and then the first climbed to the top of the step. As I stood intently watching this dramatic appearance, the scene became enveloped in cloud once more, and I could not actually be certain that I saw the second figure join the first. It was of course none other than Mallory and Irvine, and I was surprised above all to see them so late as this, namely 12.50, at a point which, if the 'second rock step,' they should have reached according to Mallory's sche-dule by 8 a.m. at latest, and if the 'first rock step' proportionately earlier.

The 'second rock step' is seen prominently in photographs of the North Face from the Base Camp, where it appears a short distance from the base of the final pyramid down the snowy first part of the crest of the North-east Arête. The lower 'first rock step' is about an equivalent distance again to the left.[2] Owing to the small portion of the summit ridge uncovered I could not be precisely certain at which of these two 'steps' they were, as in profile and from below they are very similar, but at the time I took it for the upper 'second step.' However, I am a little doubtful now whether the latter would not be hidden by the projecting nearer ground from my position below on the face. I could see that they were moving expeditiously as if endeavouring to make up for lost time. True, they were moving one at a time over what was apparently but moderately difficult ground, but one cannot definitely conclude from this that they were roped together – a not unimportant consideration in any estimate of what may have eventually befallen them. I had seen that there was a considerable quantity of new snow covering some of the upper rocks near the summit ridge, and this may well have caused delay in the ascent. Burdened as they undoubtedly would be with the oxygen apparatus, these snow-covered debris-sprinkled slabs may have given much trouble. The oxygen apparatus itself may have needed repair or readjustment either before or after they left Camp VI, and so have delayed them. Though rather unlikely, it is just conceivable that the zone of mist and clouds I had experienced below may have extended up to their level and so have somewhat impeded their progress. Any or all of these factors may have hindered them and prevented their getting higher in the time.

I continued my way up to Camp VI, and on arrival there about two o'clock snow commenced to fall and the wind increased. I placed my load of fresh provisions, etc., inside the tiny tent and decided to take shelter for a while. Within were a rather mixed assortment of spare clothes, scraps of food, their two sleeping-bags, oxygen cylinders, and parts of apparatus; outside were more parts of the latter and of the duralumin carriers. It might be supposed that these were undoubted signs of reconstructional work and probable difficulties with the oxygen outfit. But, knowing Irvine's propensities, I had at the time not the slightest qualms on that score. Nothing would have amused him more – as it ever had, though with such good results – than to have spent the previous evening on a job of work of some kind or other in connection with the oxygen apparatus, or to have invented some problem

---

2   *Vide* diagram in *Geograph. Journal*, Vol. LXIV, No. 6, p. 457.

to be solved even if it never really had turned up! He loved to dwell amongst, nay, revelled in, pieces of apparatus and a litter of tools, and was never happier than when up against some mechanical difficulty! And here to 27,000 feet he had been faithful to himself and carried his usual traits, though his workshop for the purpose would be decidedly limited, and could not have run to much more than a spanner and possibly a pair of pliers! But it was wonderful what he could do with these. I found they had left no note, which left me ignorant as to the time they had actually started out, or what might have intervened to cause delay. The snow continued, and after a while I began to wonder whether the weather and conditions higher up would have necessitated the party commencing their return. Camp VI was in rather a concealed position on a ledge and backed by a small crag, and in the prevailing conditions it seemed likely they would experience considerable difficulty in finding it. So I went out along the mountain-side in the direction of the summit and having scrambled up about 200 feet, whistled and jodelled in case they should happen to be within hearing. I then took shelter for a while behind a rock from the driving sleet. One could not see more than a few yards ahead, so thick was the atmosphere, and in an endeavour to forget the cold I examined the rocks around me in case some new point of geological significance could be found. But in the flurry of snow and the biting wind even my accustomed ardour for this pursuit began to wane, and within an hour I decided to turn back, realising that even if Mallory and Irvine were returning they could hardly yet be within call, and less so under the existing conditions. As I reached Camp VI the squall, which had lasted not more than two hours, blew over, and before long the whole north face became bathed in sunshine, and the freshly fallen snow speedily evaporated, there being no intermediate melting phase as takes place at lower altitudes. The upper crags became visible, but I could see no signs of the party. I waited for a time, and then I remembered that Mallory had particularly requested me in his last note to return to the North Col as he specially wished to reach there, and presumably if possible evacuate it and reach Camp III that same night, in case the monsoon should suddenly break. But besides this the single small tent at Camp VI was only just large enough for two, and if I remained and they returned, one of us would have had to sleep outside in the open – a hazardous expedient in such an exposed position. I placed Mallory's retrieved compass that I had brought up from Camp V in a conspicuous place in the corner of the tent by the door, and after partaking of a little food and leaving ample provisions against their return, I closed up the tent.

Leaving Camp VI therefore about 4.30, I made my way down by the extreme crest of the North Ridge, halting now and again to glance up and scan the upper rocks for some signs of the party, who should by now, it seemed to me, be well on their downward tracks. But I looked in vain: I could, at that great distance and against such a broken background, little hope to pick them out, except by some good chance they should be crossing one of the infrequent patches of snow, as had happened that morning, or be silhouetted on the crest of the North-east Arête, if they should be making their way back by that of their ascent, as seemed most likely. I was abreast of Camp V at 6.15, but there being no reason to turn aside to visit it, situated as it was a hundred yards or so off the main ridge east-ward along the face, I hurried downwards. It was interesting to find, as I had earlier, that descending at high altitudes is little more fatiguing than at any other moderate altitudes, and of course in complete contrast to the extraordinarily exhausting reverse of it, and it seemed that a party that has not completely shot its bolt and run itself to a standstill, so to speak, on the ascent, and in any attempt on the summit, should find itself unexpectedly able to make fast time downward and escape being benighted. And as I shall mention later, the unnecessity of oxygen for the properly acclimatised climber seems never more evident than in this capability of quick descent. I was able to speed up my headlong descent upon the North Col by taking to the crest of the snow cornice to the leeward of the North Ridge, and finding the snow between 24,800 and 23,500 feet hard and conveniently steep, it was possible to indulge in a fast standing glissade that brought me to Camp IV by 6.45 p.m. It was rather surprising and withal useful to know that this distance between Camps IV and V, which upwards necessitated at any time three to four hours of arduous toil, could be covered in barely thirty-five minutes descending by means of a glissade; but it was a glissade that involved care and judgment to avoid the Scylla of the rocks on the one hand, and the Charybdis of the cornice edge on the other![3]

Hazard welcomed me at Camp IV, and right glad was I of his wonderful brew of hot soup made from a mixture of at least six varieties of Maggi. Fortunately I am not habitually cursed with thirst on a mountain, but I was rather surprised to find how little Everest with its excessive dryness affected me in that way. However, whatever necessary moisture had been evaporated from my constitution during the last two days was now speedily replaced

---

3  The place is well seen, though foreshortened, in the background of the frontispiece of the *Assault on Mount Everest*, 1922.

from the amazing quantities of soup and tea put in front of me by Hazard. And what a two days had it been – days replete with a gamut of impressions that neither the effects of high altitude, whatever this might be, nor the grim events of the two days that were to follow could efface from one's memory! A period of intensive experiences, alike romantic, aesthetic, and scientific in interest, these each in their various appeals enabling one to forget even the extremity of upward toil inherently involved, and ever at intervals carrying one's thoughts with expectancy to that resolute pair who might at any instant appear returning with news of final conquest. They would be late, for were they not behind their scheduled time when last seen! And hence they would succeed in reaching Camp VI only, or Camp V possibly, before darkness. The evening was a clear one, and we watched till late that night for some signs of Mallory and Irvine's return, or even an indication by flare of distress. The feeble glow that after sunset pervaded the great dark mountain face above us was later lost in filtered moonlight reflected from high summits of the West Rongbuk. We hoped that this would aid them if perchance some incident had precluded their return as yet to Camp V or VI.

Next morning we scrutinised through field-glasses the tiny tents of those camps far up above us, thinking they must be at one or other, and would not as yet have started down. But no movement at all could be seen, and at noon I decided to go up in search. Before leaving, Hazard and I drew up a code of signals so that we could communicate to some extent in case of necessity: this was by a fixed arrangement of sleeping-bags placed against the snow for day signals, and as far as I was concerned Hazard was to look out for them at stated times at either of the upper camps. Answering signals from him were also arranged. For use after dark we arranged a code of simple flash signals, which included, of course, in case of need, the International Alpine Distress Signal. We had by this time three porters at the North Col Camp, and two of these I managed after some difficulty to persuade to come with me. We started off at 12.15, and on our way up the North Ridge we encountered that bitter cross-wind from the west that almost always prevails, and which had really been the means of rendering abortive Mallory and Bruce's earlier attempt. I found my two Sherpas repeatedly faltering, and it was with difficulty that one in particular could be persuaded to proceed. We reached Camp V, however, where the night was to be spent, in the fairly good time of three and a quarter hours. I hardly expected, I must admit, to find that Mallory and Irvine had returned here, for if they had, some movement must have been seen from below. And now one's sole hopes rested on Camp VI, though in the absence of any signal from here earlier in the day, the prospects could not but be black. And time would not allow, even if I could have induced my men to continue in the conditions, of our proceeding on to Camp VI that evening. We made ourselves as comfortable at V as the boisterous wind would permit, but gusts sweeping over the North Ridge would now and again threaten to uproot our small tents bodily from the slender security of the ledges on which they rested, and carry them and us down the mountain-side. Fleeting glimpses of stormy sunset could at intervals be seen through the flying scud, and as the night closed in on us the wind and the cold increased. The porters in their tent below mine were disinclined for much food, and were soon curled up in their sleeping-bags, and I went down and added a stone or two to the guys for the security of their tent. I did likewise to mine and then repaired inside, and fitted up for use next day the oxygen apparatus that had lain idle here since I brought it from the ridge two days previously: having with me another mouthpiece, it was now ready for use. I managed to cook a little macaroni and tomatoes on the Meta stove, and that with tea and 'Force' comprised my meal. The cold was intense that night and aggravated by the high wind, and one remained chilled and unable to sleep – even inside two sleeping-bags and with all one's clothes on.

By morning the wind was as strong and bitter as ever, and on looking in at the porters' tent I found them both heavy and disinclined to stir. I tried to rouse them, but both seemed to be suffering from extreme lassitude or nausea. After partaking of a little food myself I indicated that we must make a start, but they only made signs of being sick and wishing to descend. The cold and stormy night and lack of sleep had hardly been conducive to their well-being, and to proceed under these conditions was more than they could face. I told them, therefore, to return without delay to Camp IV, and seeing them well on their way downwards I then set off for Camp VI. This time with an artificial oxygen supply available I hoped to make good time on my upward climb. But the boisterous and bitter wind, blowing as ever from the west athwart the ridge, was trying in the extreme, and I could only make slow progress. Now and then I had to take shelter behind rocks, or crouch low in some recess to restore warmth. Within an hour or so of Camp VI, I came to the conclusion that I was deriving but little benefit from the oxygen, which I had been taking only in moderate quantities from the single cylinder that I carried. I gave myself larger quantities and longer inspirations of it, but the effect seemed almost negligible: perhaps it just allayed a trifle the tire in one's legs. I wondered at the claims of others regarding its advantages, and could only conclude that I was fortunate in having acclimatised myself more thoroughly to the air of these altitudes and to its small percentage of available oxygen. I switched the oxygen off and experienced none of those feelings of collapse and panting that one had been led to believe ought to result. I decided to proceed with the apparatus on my back, but without the objectionable rubber mouthpiece between my lips, and depend on direct breathing from the atmosphere. I seemed to get on quite as well, though I must admit the hard breathing at these altitudes would surprise even a long-distance runner.

On reaching the tent at Camp VI, I found everything as I had left it: the tent had obviously not been touched since I was there two days previously: one pole had, however, given way in the wind, though the anchorages had prevented a complete collapse. I dumped the oxygen apparatus and immediately went off along the probable route Mallory and Irvine had taken, to make what search I could in the limited time available. This upper part of Everest must be indeed the remotest and least hospitable spot on earth, but at no time more emphatically and impressively so than when a darkened atmosphere hides its features and a gale races over its cruel face. And how and when more cruel could it ever seem than when balking one's every step to find one's friends? After struggling on for nearly a couple of hours looking in vain for some indication or clue, I realised that the chances of finding the missing ones were indeed small on such a vast expanse of crags and broken slabs, and that for any more expensive search towards the final pyramid a further party would have to be organised. At the same time I considered, and still do consider, that wherever misfortune befell them some traces of them would be discovered on or near the ridge of the North-east Arête: I saw them on that ridge on the morning of their ascent, and presumably they would descend by it. But in the time available under the prevailing conditions, I found it impossible to extend my search. Only too reluctantly I made my way back to Camp VI, and took shelter for a while from the wind, which showed signs of relenting its force. Seizing the opportunity of this lull, with a great effort I dragged the two sleeping-bags from the tent and up the precipitous rocks behind to a steep snow-patch plastered on a bluff of rocks above. It was the only one in the vicinity to utilise for the purpose of signalling down to Hazard at the North Col Camp the results of my search. It needed all my efforts to cut steps out over the steep snow slope and then fix the sleeping-bags in position, so boisterous was the wind. Placed in the form of a T, my signal with the sleeping-bags conveyed the news that no trace of the missing party could be found. Fortunately the signal was seen 4,000 feet below at the North Col, though Hazard's answering signal, owing to the bad light, I could not make out. I returned to the tent, and took from within Mallory's compass that I had brought up at his request two days previously. That and the oxygen set of Irvine's design alone seemed worth while to retrieve. Then, closing up the tent and leaving its other contents as my friends had left them, I glanced up at the mighty summit above me, which ever and anon deigned to reveal its cloud-wreathed features. It seemed to look down with cold indifference on me, mere puny man, and howl derision in wind-gusts at my petition to yield up its secret – this mystery of my friends. What right had we to venture thus far into the holy presence of the Supreme Goddess, or, much more, sling at her our blasphemous challenges to 'sting her very nose-tip'? If it were indeed the sacred ground of Chomolungma – Goddess Mother of the Mountain Snows, had we violated it – was I now violating it? Had we approached her with due reverence and singleness of heart and purpose? And yet as I gazed again another mood appeared to creep over her haunting features. There seemed to be something alluring in that towering presence. I was almost fascinated. I realised that no mere mountaineer alone could but be fascinated, that he who approaches close must ever be led on, and oblivious of all obstacles seek to reach that most sacred and highest place of all. It seemed that my friends must have been thus enchanted also: for why else should they tarry? In an effort to suppress my feelings, I turned my gaze downwards to the North Col far below, and I remembered that other of my companions would be anxiously awaiting my return, eager to hear what tidings I carried. How then could I justify my wish, in face of such anxiety, to remain here the night, and prolong my search next day? And what hope, if I did, of finding them yet alive?

Alone and in meditation I slowly commenced my long descent. But it was no place for silent contemplation, for buffeted by storm-blasts that seemed to pierce one through, it needed all one's attention and calculation to negotiate safely the exposed slabs of the ridge and prevent a slip on their debris-sprinkled surfaces. Hampered as I was with the unwieldy oxygen outfit, which I had no need to use but wished to recover, these slabs were in places, under these conditions, decidedly awkward. I quickened my pace on the easier ground farther down, but at times found it necessary to seek protection from the biting gale in the lee of rocks and reassure myself that no symptoms of frostbite were imminent. Hazard had seen me coming, and sent his one remaining Sherpa to welcome me at the foot of the ridge. Arrived at the

North Col Camp I was pleased to find a note from Norton and to discover that I had anticipated his wishes that I should return and not prolong my search on the mountain, seeing that the monsoon seemed likely to break at any moment. Next day Hazard, the porter and myself, leaving the tents standing and loading ourselves up with all we could save, evacuated the North Col Camp, and went down in good weather, and in quick time, by the 'avalanche route' to Camp III, where we found the rest of the party gone, save Hingston and Shebbeare who were about to evacuate it. After a rest and good meal here, we proceeded on down the changed and wasted glacier to Camp II, where we spent the night, and the following day rejoined the main party at the Base Camp, to revel in the joys of opening spring, so long withheld and now let loose on us in all their glory of flower and insect life, as we plunged forth from our erstwhile Arctic environment.

I have already mentioned the possible reasons why Mallory and Irvine were so late in reaching the point at which they were last seen, which if the 'second rock step,' as referred to earlier, would be an altitude of about 28,230 feet, as determined by theodolite from the Base Camp by Hazard; if the 'first rock step,' then not more than 28,000 feet. And in the latter event we must assuredly and deservedly attribute the *known* altitude record, the greatest mountain height definitely attained by man, to Norton, who reached not less than 28,100 feet. I propose, therefore, very briefly just to speculate on the probable causes of their failure to return. From the 'second step' they had about 800 feet of altitude to surmount, and say 1,600 feet of ground to cover, to reach the top, and if no particularly difficult obstacle presented itself on the final pyramid they should have got to the top at about 3 to 3.30. Before, however, he left Camp VI Mallory had sent a note to Noel at Camp III saying he hoped to reach the foot of the final pyramid (about 28,300 feet odd) by 8 a.m. So on this schedule they would be perhaps five or six hours late in reaching the top, and hence they would find it almost impossible to get down to Camp VI before nightfall, allowing five or six hours for the return. But at the same time it must be remembered there was a moon, though it rose rather late, and that evening it was fine and the mountain clear of mist as far as could be seen. In spite of this they may have missed their way and failed to find Camp VI, and in their overwrought condition sought shelter till daylight – a danger that Mallory, experienced mountaineer that he was, would be only too well aware of, but find himself powerless to resist. Sleep at that altitude and in that degree of cold would almost certainly prove fatal. Norton, I know, finds it difficult to reconcile this explanation with the fact that no light was seen on the mountain after dark, and I am well aware it is a potent argument against it. But to me it is by no means conclusive since anything might have happened, in the way of damage or loss of their lantern or flash-light, to have prevented their showing a light. And the same applies to the magnesium flares which we supposed that they carried. In the tent at Camp VI I found one or two of the latter, which indicates the possibility of their having forgotten them the morning of their departure.

The other likely possibility, that many will not unnaturally subscribe to, is that they met their death by falling. This implies that they were roped together, a suggestion that I have mentioned earlier need not necessarily be inferred from their observed movements when last seen. It is at the same time just possible that though unroped they may have been climbing, on the ascent or descent, on some steepish pitch in close order, and the one above fallen on the lower and knocked him off. But, it is difficult for any who knew the skill and experience of George Mallory on all kinds and conditions of mountain ground to believe that he fell, and where the difficulties to him would be so insignificant. Of Sandy Irvine it can be said that although less experienced than Mallory, he had shown himself to be a natural adept and able to move safely and easily on rock and ice. He could follow, if not lead, anywhere. Such had been my experience of him in Spitzbergen, Norway, and on our own home mountains. They were, of course, hampered by the oxygen apparatus – a very severe load for climbing with, as Mallory had mentioned in his last note to me. But could such a pair fall, and where technically the climbing appeared so easy? Experts nevertheless have done so, under stress of circumstances or exhaustion. Following what we called the 'ridge route,' i.e. by the crest of the North-east Arête, there seemed to be only two places which might in any way cause them trouble. The first was the 'second step,' already referred to more than once. This seemed steep, though negotiable at any rate on its north side. And if it were this step, as I thought at the time it was, that I saw the first figure (presumably Mallory) actually surmount within the five minutes of my last glimpse of them, then we had been deceived as to its difficulties, as at the distance we might well be. The only other part of the ascent that might have presented any difficulty, and probably not more than awkwardness, is the very foot of the final pyramid, where the slabs steepen before the relatively easy-looking ridge to the final summit can be attained. Norton at his highest point was close below this section, and he has expressed the opinion that these slabs, sprinkled with snow, might constitute a considerable source of danger in the case of a slip. But with all due deference to Norton's actual view of this place, from what can be seen of the local detail both in Somervell's photograph taken at 28,000 feet and in Noel's wonderful telephotograph of the final pyramid taken from above Camp III, the difficulties here look decidedly as if they could be circumvented by a nearly horizontal traverse to the right to the actual foot of the ridge of the final pyramid. In any case, to a leader of Mallory's experience and skill such moderate difficulties as these would present cannot long have detained him, much less defeated him, and during the descent such places as the above, and the probable consequences of a slip thereon, would be so impressed upon him, as well of course as on Irvine, that the greatest care and attention would be exercised.

Again, it has been suggested that the oxygen apparatus may have failed and thereby rendered them powerless to return. I cannot accept the validity of this argument, for from my own personal experience, to be deprived of oxygen – at any rate when one has not been using it freely – does not prevent one from continuing and least of all getting down from the mountain. On my second journey up to Camp VI, as related earlier, when I was using oxygen, I switched it off at about 26,000 feet and continued on, and returned, without it. Mallory in his last note to me said they were using little oxygen, and that they hoped to take only two cylinders each, instead of the full load of three each, from Camp VI. But even if later they were using much oxygen, they had both during the previous weeks spent adequate time at extreme altitudes, namely 21,000 feet and over, to become sufficiently acclimatised and not liable to collapse in the event of the oxygen failing. The importance of this factor of acclimatisation is discussed elsewhere.

Hence I incline to the view first expressed that they met their death by being benighted. I know that Mallory had stated he would take no risks in any attempt on the final peak; but in action the desire to overcome, the craving for the victory that had become for him, as Norton has put it, an obsession, may have been too strong for him. The knowledge of his own proved powers of endurance, and those of his companion, may have urged him to make a bold bid for the summit. Irvine I know was willing, nay, determined, to expend his last ounce of energy, to 'go all out,' as he put it, in an utmost effort to reach the top: for had not his whole training in another hardy pursuit been to inculcate the faculty of supreme final effort? And who of us that has wrestled with some Alpine giant in the teeth of a gale, or in a race with the darkness, could hold back when such a victory, such a triumph of human endeavour, was within our grasp?

The question remains, 'Has Mount Everest been climbed?' It must be left unanswered, for there is no direct evidence. But bearing in mind all the circumstances that I have set out above, and considering their position when last seen, I think myself there is a strong probability that Mallory and Irvine succeeded.

# 7 THE RETURN TO BASE CAMP

## BY LIEUT. COLONEL E.F. NORTON, DSO

June 12 saw all the surviving members of the Expedition collected at the Base Camp, with the exception of Shebbeare. He, with all the porters, was occupied in clearing all camps from III downwards of those stores which we considered worth transporting back to Darjeeling; and so efficient was his organisation that he arrived at the Base on the 13th with his task completed. There was no question of any further resumption of hostilities on the mountain; at my request Hingston examined the whole party and reported that, without exception, all those who had been above Camp IV had their hearts dilated to a greater or lesser extent, and, though there was no reason to anticipate lasting ill effects to anybody, he warned us that further exertions at high altitudes would be liable to cause serious permanent disability.

One of those who had apparently suffered least was Odell; this was indeed a testimonial to his remarkable physique and an indication that the man who acclimatises slowly to altitude may well prove in the long run the most enduring; for Odell's performances have no equal in our short record of high climbing. In addition to three previous attempts to reach the North Col, one successful and two abortive, he, between May 31 and June 11, went three times up and down from Camp III (21,000 feet) to Camp IV (23,000 feet), once from Camp IV to Camp V (25,200 feet), and twice from Camp IV to Camp VI (26,800 feet), these last two ascents occupying four consecutive days; during these twelve days he slept every night, with one exception, at 23,000 feet or higher.

We were a sad little party; from the first we accepted the loss of our comrades in that rational spirit which all of our generation had learnt in the Great War, and there was never any tendency to a morbid harping on the irrevocable. But the tragedy was very near; our friends' vacant tents and vacant places at table were a constant reminder to us of what the atmosphere of the camp would have been had things gone differently. To several of us, particularly to those who, on previous expeditions to Mount Everest or Spitzbergen, had been close friends with the missing climbers, the sense of loss was acute and personal, and until the day of our departure a cloud hung over the Base Camp. As so constantly in the war, so here in our mimic campaign Death had taken his toll from the best, for they were indeed a splendid couple.

PLATE 17

Everest from the north-east, showing the east face of the mountain. Painted by Norton from near Jikkyop, about sixty miles away. *See page 37.*

Mt Everest
from Pang La
26/4/24

PLATE 18
The north face of Everest from Pang La, about thirty-five miles away. Watercolour by Norton. *See page 40.*

PLATE 19

Everest from Chogorong, high above the Rongbuk valley *(see page 125)*. Norton believed that this view gave a much better impression of the upper parts of the north face of Everest than the more familiar views from the Rongbuk monastery or Base Camp *(see plate 20)*. The latter were taken from viewpoints both much lower than Chogorong and much closer to Everest, and therefore show the upper parts of the mountain considerably foreshortened, as does the diagram showing the heights reached by the various summit parties in 1922 and 1924 *(see plate 43)*.

PLATE 20

The north face of Everest from Base Camp, painted by Somervell in 1922. Comparison with plate 19 shows that the upper parts of the mountain were comparatively free of snow in 1924.

PLATE 21

Members of the 1924 expedition, photographed at Base Camp shortly before they left Everest. Norton is wearing soft shoes because of frostbite sustained during his summit attempt with Somervell. Mallory and Irvine are conspicuous by their absence. From left to right, back row: Hazard, Hingston, Somervell, Beetham, Shebbeare; front row: Geoff Bruce, Norton, Noel, Odell.

PLATE 23
Two portrait heads of Geoff Bruce (wearing hat with hatband), and one of Odell, sketched by Norton, probably at Everest.

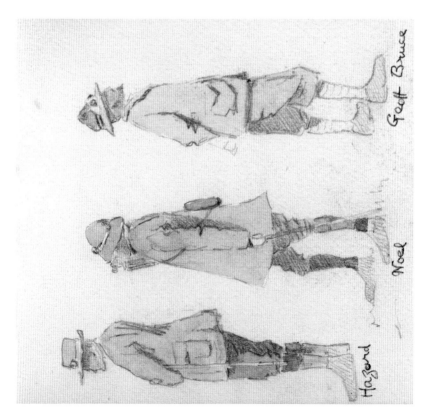

PLATE 22
Hazard, Noel and Geoff Bruce, sketched by Norton probably early in the expedition.

PLATE 24
Porters at Base Camp loaded with supplies for the higher camps.

PLATE 25
Camp II on the East Rongbuk Glacier. *See pages 47 and 51.*

Camp IV
(On this ledge)

PLATE 26
The head of the East Rongbuk Glacier and the North Col, showing the site of Camp IV. *See pages 61–62.*

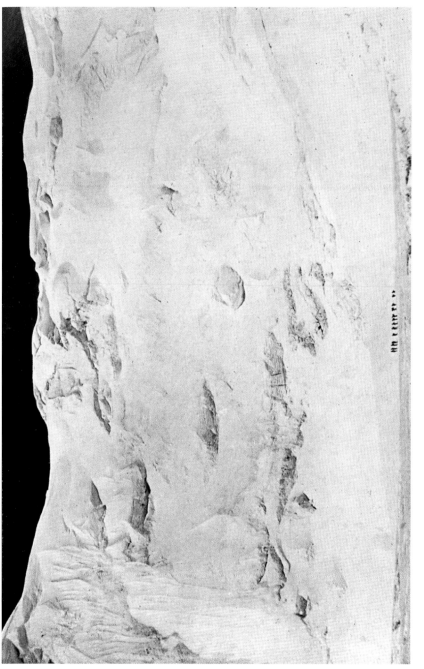

PLATE 27
The ice wall beneath the North Col, with a climbing party at its base. *See page 62.*

Camp IV

PLATE 28
The route up the Chimney to Camp IV at the North Col. *See page 63.*

PLATE 29
Pencil sketches by Norton of a climber, probably Geoff Bruce.

PLATE 30
Climbing the Chimney en route for the North Col, using the rope ladder constructed by Irvine. This had been fixed in position on 31 May *(see page 77)*. The photograph was probably taken by Somervell the next day as he and Norton climbed to the North Col with six porters prior to launching their summit attempt. *See page 81.*

PLATE 31
Somervell's evocative photograph of Norton climbing solo above 28,000 feet on 4 June en route to a world altitude record without oxygen of 28,126 feet, with the summit of Everest in the background. It was published at the time as 'the highest point in the world at which photographs have been taken.' *See page 89*.

more or less windless but so cold that one shivered continually despite layers of windproof clothing, & when in sun

Near big couloir at about noon T.H.S had to give it best ... I went on alone but almost at once encountered v. bad going. No footholds on sloping slabs & much snow lying soft & powdery on these slabs. Crossed big couloir but only made perhaps 500* & 100 feet on T.H.S & at 1pm turned back, — (28,128 ft) Joined him by 2 pm when we turned home. He lost his ice axe.

After some scrambling, made VI picked up sacks & so down ridge — horrid sliding scree. T.H.S going v slow sick man. Got to ft level with V at sunset & onto snow at dusk — Here I glissaded but T.H.S dropped ½ hour behind & I had to sit & wait. Eventually hailed IV. Gave T.H.S my axe & took his tent pole.

Mallory, Odell & Irvine with oxygen met us 200 ft above Col & escorted us back to IV (9.30) fed & looked after us royally

At 10 pm I developed real bad go of snow blindness v painful, stone blind.

---

PLATE 33
Portrait of Somervell, taken probably after the summit attempt.

PLATE 34
Studio portrait of Norton.

Mallory's was no common personality. Physically he always seemed to me the beau ideal of the mountaineer; he was very good looking, and I have always thought that his boyish face – for he looked absurdly young for his thirty-seven years – was the outward and visible sign of a wonderful constitution. His graceful figure was the last word in wiry activity and he walked with a tireless swing which made him a man with whom few could live uphill; he was almost better downhill, for his years of mountain training had added balance and studied poise to his natural turn of speed.

But it was the spirit of the man that made him the great mountaineer he was: a fire burnt in him and caused his willing spirit to rise superior to the weakness of the flesh; he lived on his nerves, and throughout two campaigns on Mount Everest (I never climbed with him elsewhere) it was almost impossible to make out whether he was a tired man or not, for he responded instantly to every call that was made on him, and while the call lasted his would remain the dominant spirit in any enterprise. The conquest of the mountain became an obsession with him, and for weeks and months he devoted his whole time and energy to it, incessantly working at plans and details of organisation; and when it came to business he expended on it every ounce of his unrivalled physical energy.

Such was Mallory the mountaineer; but there was another and quite different Mallory, whom we knew in the mess tent and at times when there was no call for action. This aspect of him was curiously at variance with the other; it showed us a nature aesthetic and gentle combined with a keen and cultured intelligence; though here too a flash of the same impatience with which he urged on our flagging footsteps on the mountain would sometimes break out in our arguments and discussions; for his views were always clear-cut and decided and his nature masterful. We used to dub him a 'high brow' and in fancy I can hear Longstaff chaffing him in 1922: 'Mallory, you know the one good thing the Bolsheviks have done in Russia? They've obliterated the Intelligensia.'

His death robs us of a right loyal friend, a knight 'sans peur et sans reproche' amongst mountaineers and the greatest antagonist that Everest has had – or is like to have.

Young Irvine was almost a boy in years – he was twenty-two; but mentally and physically he was a man full grown and able to hold his own with all modesty on terms at least of equality with the other members of our party, who averaged twelve years older than he. Physically indeed he was not only a man full grown, he was a splendid specimen, as befitted an

Oxford rowing blue, with the powerful shoulders and comparatively slim legs characteristic of the best oars.

His experience as a mountaineer was limited to the rocks of the British Isles and a climb in which he distinguished himself in Spitzbergen; but the previous summer he had been a member of the Oxford Expedition to those islands, and it was largely the outstanding reputation he had there gained for endurance, initiative, and all those moral qualities which go to make the right man for such an enterprise that had led to his being selected for the Mount Everest party. He had further added to his reputation by the extraordinary aptitude he had shown for ski-ing as a novice in Switzerland the preceding winter. One more invaluable characteristic was his turn for things mechanical, for in this respect he was nothing short of a genius, and he became our stand-by in dealing with the troubles and difficulties we encountered over this year's oxygen apparatus, and, for the matter of that, in every department – from a lampshade to a rope ladder.

He shares with Odell the credit of having shown us all how to 'play for the side,' stifling all selfish considerations, for nothing in the record of 1924 was finer than the work these two put in as 'supporters' at Camp IV.

Sandy Irvine's cheerful camaraderie, his unselfishness and high courage made him loved, not only by all of us, but also by the porters, not a word of whose language could he speak. After the tragedy I remember discussing his character with Geoffrey Bruce with a view to writing some appreciation of it to *The Times*; at the end Bruce said: 'It was worth dying on the mountain to leave a reputation like that.' Men have had worse epitaphs.

Work is the best specific against depression, and fortunately we had work to do in plenty, for the transport animals to take us away were ordered for the 15th, and we had more than enough to keep us all busy for the next three days. But before we tackled our various tasks I assembled a conference to discuss the disaster. With one dissentient, Odell, we were agreed that it was in all probability due to a simple mountaineering accident – a slip and sudden death. Odell inclined to the belief that the missing climbers had delayed their return too late and, after very probably reaching the top, had found themselves exhausted and benighted, and, unable to find Camp VI, had wandered about in the darkness looking for it until they finally succumbed to exhaustion and exposure. The truth must always remain a matter of pure speculation, but it may be of interest to put down here the reasons which led to these diverse views: Odell argued that two climbers of Mallory's and Irvine's skill could scarcely have fallen on what, at least at lower altitudes, would be considered an easy rock peak; that both were men of indomitable spirit, and to such the lure of the summit, so close, with the last serious obstacle surmounted by one o'clock, might have proved irresistible, while a brief calculation makes it evident that to have reached the summit from the place where they were last seen just before 1 p.m. might well have delayed their return to a dangerously late hour.

Against this view I argued that a slip is always possible in the case of the most experienced mountaineers; and from my own observation of the rock in the neighbourhood of the point where they were last seen a serious slip for one of a roped party of two might well spell destruction for both. More particularly would this be so when – as on the day in question – these sloping slabs are covered with a thick powdering of fresh snow. I knew Mallory's innermost thoughts and intentions, for I had discussed our prospective climbs with him a score of times, and on one point he had most definitely made up his mind – that as leader of a party the responsibility lay heavy on him to turn back, however near the summit, in good time to ensure a return to safety. I cannot agree with Odell that Camp VI was pitched in a place that would be difficult to find, even after dark, for it was on the very backbone of the North Arête, just below the point where the steepest part of the upper Arête alters its character and becomes a gently rounded hump. Finally, and most conclusive, if the pair were benighted on the mountain, why was their torch (it is inconceivable that Mallory, after his experience in 1922, could have started unprovided in this respect) not visible to the eyes of those of us who watched for them so anxiously from Camps IV and III? For a watch was kept on the mountain until long after dark from both camps; the night was clear, and from both probably, certainly from Camp IV, a light moving on the mountain must have been detected after dark. We had even arranged a signal – the letters S.O.S. in Morse code – which was to be sent repeatedly to Camp IV by any climbers benighted high on the mountain and unable to reach Camp VI. Briefly these were the arguments on both sides.

The much-debated point as to whether, in either case, they reached the top before the disaster occurred can never be settled until, perhaps, some day a successful party discovers there some sign – such as an oxygen cylinder – to prove that success was theirs too. They were last seen at 12.50 roughly 800 feet from the top, which they might conceivably have reached by 3 or 3.30 p.m., and so have had four hours of daylight in which to descend to Camp VI; such a programme would not have been incompatible with what I knew of Mallory's intentions, for he and I were both agreed that a party might be justified in leaving the top as late as 4 p.m., returning to Camp VI for the night. It remains a case of 'not proven,' and that is all that can be said about it.

Another matter remained to be settled: one of the subsidiary tasks allotted to the 1924 Expedition was to survey certain areas, the map of which the 1921 Expedition had not been able to complete; the most important of these was the area about the head of the West Rongbuk Glacier. The Survey of India had lent us the services of a Gurkha surveyor, and throughout the time that we had been occupied on the mountain he, with a small party, had been diligently employed on a plain table survey of the required areas. He had by now mapped all of these with the exception of the most important – the head of the West Rongbuk Glacier. It was thought that this was too serious an undertaking until the party could be led by an expert mountaineer.

Hazard, despite the hard time he had had, at once expressed himself willing to undertake this duty, and Beetham, who was now beginning – just too late – to recover from his attack of sciatica, volunteered to accompany him. After some discussion it was decided that Hazard only should go, for we needed Beetham's skill as a photographer to record the fine views we hoped to obtain on a short expedition to the Rongshar Valley – one of the great gorges running down into Nepal to the west of Mount Everest. The party was now bound there for a brief period of recuperation at lower altitudes before beginning the homeward march.

Hazard appeared thoroughly to enjoy the prospect of a return to snow and ice and all the discomforts of a tiny tent, under glacier conditions, and set to work to organise the transport and supply of his party with enthusiasm, and this despite the fact that every indication pointed to the immediate break of the monsoon. It did, in fact, break the day after he started; but, though the resultant cloud and snowstorms limited the possibilities of his task, he successfully achieved the main object of his expedition and brought back a valuable survey of the doubtful area.

The rest of us now got to work on the tasks that remained to be done before we left the Base Camp. To Somervell and Beetham was allotted the building of a monument to commemorate the names of the twelve men, British and Himalayan, who in three years have lost their lives in the attempt to climb Mount Everest. A committee, consisting of Hingston, Noel and Hazard, redistributed the stores for our next move, for, besides the main body bound for the Rongshar Valley and Hazard's party, another under Noel was to start at once for Shekar Dzong and the Chumbi Valley. Bruce and

Shebbeare, in addition to their routine work as transport officers, redistributed our porters into three parties: one to accompany Hazard, one to accompany the main body, and one, the largest, to return with Noel to the Chumbi Valley and so on to Darjeeling, where arrangements were made to pay them off on their arrival. In addition they made a selection of stores, the value of which would not pay for hire of transport back to Darjeeling, and which were either left with the lamas of the Rongbuk Monastery or destroyed. The sad task of disposing of the belongings of Mallory and Irvine was undertaken by Odell; and I was fully occupied in writing reports, Press communiqués and letters.

The construction of the monument for which Somervell and Beetham were responsible was a big undertaking. Beetham with a gang of assistants cut a simple inscription on certain large flat slabs of blue slaty rock which left a white surface when chipped. Somervell, with the aid of all the porters who could be spared from other duties, built a solid square plinth of big rocks, three feet high and some fifteen feet square, on the most prominent of the rounded moraine heaps overlooking the Base Camp. On this plinth he raised a cone of glacier-worn rocks, and the inscribed slabs were let into that side of it which overlooked the Base Camp; the height of the whole structure was perhaps ten feet. The inscription read: 'In memory of three Everest Expeditions.' Then followed, '1921, Kellas,' '1922' – with the names of the seven porters killed in the avalanche; '1924, Mallory, Irvine, Shamsher, Manbahadur.'

The few days we spent at the Base Camp before leaving represented the height of summer in the Rongbuk Valley. The monsoon actually broke on the mountain the day after we left and, judging from the experiences of 1921 and 1922, this meant a return to bleaker conditions with constant snowstorms; so the week which precedes the monsoon is presumably the nearest approach to summer that this region knows. After our experiences higher up we found it very pleasant; the sun was often almost too hot, and though the inevitable wind down the valley always got up about nine or ten o'clock and blew till sundown, it seldom cut with the keenness of six weeks earlier.

At a casual glance the valley was bleak and bare as ever, and no hint of green relieved the grey and yellow hillsides; but look more closely and you would find that the last month had worked a miracle. The tiny creeping or low-growing plants that sparsely dotted the moraine heaps were all doing their best to flower; as far up the moraine as just below Camp I a little pink primula and the charming *amœna* gentian – a white bell with emerald markings inside and a chocolate streak outside each petal – coyly revealed themselves here and there to the seeing eye; the prickly brown grass that surrounded the spring at the Base Camp was quite unmistakably trying to look green, and amongst and around it the little clumps that looked like pincushions or half-buried stones had burst into thick clusters of tiny white flowers with pink or yellow centres – almost indistinguishable at a little distance from the whitish granite stones.

Butterflies were common and of strangely familiar types; swallow-tails, tortoise-shells, Apollos, and a kind of clouded yellow predominated. The birds walked about all round our feet, the hill rock-dove, the alpine chough, the little brown accentor – true friend of man like all his species – Adam's snowfinch and Brandt's ground-linnet, most of them actually nesting in the vicinity. And one day a herd of 'barhel' – one of the shy and wary wild sheep of the Himalayas – grazed within twenty-five yards of our tents, all fear of man banished by the fact that the solitary lama inhabiting the hermit's cell just above the camp made a practice of feeding them. Fully to appreciate these things you must have spent six weeks up the East Rongbuk Glacier in the land of rock and ice where life is not.

From motives of economy we had arranged – as already described – to send the bulk of our porters straight back to Darjeeling with Noel, there to be paid off. The privileged dozen or fifteen who were to accompany us to the Rongshar Valley and on the homeward march were selected from among those who had gone highest and done best on the mountain; these men were mostly required to perform the duties of our personal servants, and to Odell was allotted the ruffianly but stout-hearted Narbu Yishé, who had accompanied Somervell and me to nearly 27,000 feet, and of whom I have already spoken more than once.

Now if you know no Oriental language and have to talk to a man who has no English, there is more than one way of doing it. Beetham adopted the ordinary methods of John Bull on the Continent: he talked good simple English rather loudly and slowly and produced surprisingly successful results. Odell adopted a more sonorous style, and addressed the Sherpa porter in rolling periods worthy of Doctor Johnson. I was much intrigued one day at overhearing a conversation between Odell and his new valet in the tent next to mine. The latter, to my surprise, did know one word of English, which was 'yes,' but I'm not sure that this really helped matters. It went something like this:

*Odell.* 'Ah, good morning, Narbu Yishé. I understand you are undertaking the duties of my personal servant.'

*N.Y.* 'Yes, Sahib.'

*Odell.* 'Well, I have been excellently served in the past by Pu and Namgya and I am very sorry to part with them, but I am convinced that if you display the same spirit that they have done we shall get on together to our mutual satisfaction.'

*N.Y.* 'Yes, Sahib.'

*Odell.* 'Let us examine my luggage and I will show you how my various belongings are disposed.'

*N.Y.* 'Yes, Sahib.'

After this auspicious beginning there must have been a hitch in the proceedings, and in a few minutes Narbu Yishé appeared at my tent with his best military salute. 'Please ask the Sahib,' said he, 'to give me his keys and leave the rest to me; I quite understand the duties of a bearer, and he will find that his kit will be looked after and all his work perfectly done.' But I am sorry to say that Narbu Yishé proved himself a good deal more addicted to the flowing bowl than to pitching his sahib's tent and looking after his belongings, and we finally parted from him with mutual esteem but with little regret soon after we started our homeward march. He decided to return to his home in the Solah Khombu district of Nepal, where, I believe, he now wears with all honour a bronze medal presented by the Committee of the 8th Olympiad. For the qualities which take a porter with twenty pounds on his back up to 27,000 feet are not necessarily those of Jeames de la Pluche.

By midday on June 15 the last yak had left the Base Camp and headed down the valley, winding in and out among the hummocks of old moraine, and the last members of the party, following in its track, could turn back and look on what had for six weeks been so busy a scene, now once more reverted to solitude: that grim, forbidding little basin which could yet seem a very haven of refuge to the weary traveller from the bleaker land above. But now there is a new feature in the landscape; the cairn built by Somervell and Beetham stands conspicuous on the highest stony hillock over the camp, outlined against the great mountain which lured to their death those whose names it commemorates.

Who can tell what white men will next turn that corner and see – for nothing ever changes in Tibet – the cairn, 'In memory of three Everest Expeditions'?

# 8 THE RETURN JOURNEY

BY BENTLEY BEETHAM

June 15 saw the evacuation of the Base Camp and the beginning of the journey to the Rongshar Valley.

Our last view of the Base – a place of many different memories – is likely to remain with us to the end. Geoffrey, Somervell and I, the last to leave, stopped to look back. In the foreground was the now empty camping site; away in the background towered Everest, aloof and expressionless as ever, and now partially veiled by drifting cloud and mist, while between stood out with startling boldness the dark moraine and its memorial cairn. It was a silent, impressive picture. Slowly we turned away from it, thinking much but saying nothing.

It was the end of the third round. We had taken punishment; we were retiring to a corner to recuperate. There was to be another round, or rounds, of course. The mountain could and would be climbed – when depended more upon the Fates, the vagaries of weather, than upon the plans of men. Such, I think, was the burden of our thought. There was no repining. The deepest wish of every member was that he might take a part in the next attempt. That stillborn question, 'Is it worth while?' is surely a product of town life: it could never arise like a canker to infect our thoughts out there on the plateau, in front of the great mountain.

What a different Rongbuk Valley, what a different atmosphere, mental as well as meteorological, was this on the downward journey in June from that of the upward march in April. Then all was speculation, every one was tense and striving; now it was over, and we knew; we were relaxed and going easy – we were on holiday. On the way up everything had been sterile, inhospitable and dreary, but now as we sauntered down we soon began to meet familiar little alpine blossoms peeping out from overhanging rocks or pushing up between the stones. As the supply of nectar increased, winged insect life became more and more plentiful and Hingston got busy with his net. Geoffrey, whose sporting nature was aroused by the quest of anything, also got busy, but in his own particular way. It was scarcely pure science with him – if you like, it was a blending of the interests of polo and entomology. As he rode he carried a male bamboo and with it took his insects on the wing. The amazing thing about it was not so much the number of insects he brought down as the slight damage many of them suffered. Fancy striking an Apollo in full flight with a heavy cane and picking it up almost undamaged! How many 'biggest bees in Asia' he winged and bottled in this way only Hingston will know, for Hingston was the recipient of all our catches.

It is surprising that this Rongbuk Valley, the main artery leading from the greatest mountain in the world, is so featureless, so unimposing; it is just one vast wilderness of stones. There are no fine precipices, no shapely aiguilles, no noble glaciers abutting on its flanks to break its grey monotony. Yet, as we passed down even this dead valley, all about Za Rongbuk seemed to be trying to put on a vernal smile; true, it was a very wan, thin smile, but one just perceptible in the warm June sun.

Opposite the old monastery we camped, arriving early and thoroughly enjoying the holiday spirit now pervading the whole party. Norton and Bruce, ever critical of horses, had their ponies' manes close-cropped – Shebbeare, Somervell and I performed a like office on each other's hair. We had not seen our ponies since they were sent down to recuperate at Tashi Dzom, nearly two months before. It was now all too evident that they had been neglected, ill-fed, and villainously shod. Hazard's mare was in a sorry plight and was not ridden again.

During the evening two of us crept into the great hall of the monastery where a service was in progress. Hitherto we had felt nothing but repulsion for the lamas, their mode of life and everything that pertained to them. We were therefore hardly in a mood to be prepossessed. Yet it must be admitted that that was the most impressive, the most moving service I, for one, have ever attended. Perhaps it was the unexpectedness of the whole thing, and especially of the worshippers' profound devotion. In any case it must have been only an appeal to eye and ear, and not to the conscious mind, for we could not understand one word of what was said. It was an instinctive acquiescence in their earnest consecration. The building was in such darkness that at first we could see nothing, but as the eyes grew accustomed to the gloom, row upon row of lamas were revealed seated motionless as images upon the floor. Only the unimpassioned faces of the lamas chanting the deep guttural prayers appeared, their crouching bodies, swathed in dark togas, remained unseen. Such light as entered illumined the faces of the idol-buddhas and filtered down between a maze of old silken banners reaching from the roof nearly to the worshippers. The music was supplied by a large number of deep drums, cymbals and some reed instruments, and as it rose and fell the air vibrated as with an organ. At intervals the worship ceased, and tea – the ultra-Tibetan type – was brought round by little boys; then the service was resumed.

Looking back we lose much of the glamour, but one thing remains which makes this and other Eastern services so impressive. It is the obvious fervour of the people. They may be misguided, but with them there is no pretence. It is merely the crowd spirit, if you like, but it is just this that makes the difference. We see a trace of it in our revival meetings. These Tibetans may be wrong, they may be deceived, but they are obviously in earnest: an English congregation may not be deceived, but are they in earnest?

The next day Noel, with his own bandobast and part of the Expedition's native *personnel* and stores, left us in order to rejoin his wife as quickly as possible. She, with Helps the artist, was awaiting him at Chumbi. We were all very sorry to lose him.

Hazard had already gone with Hari Singh and the surveyors to the West Rongbuk Glacier, so the main party, that heading for the Rongshar, was now reduced to seven – Norton, Bruce, Somervell, Hingston, Odell, Shebbeare, and myself.

A little below the monastery the Dzakar Chu, which has so far run in an open dreary course, now cuts through a spur of rock. The precipitous gorge so formed is short, but is spanned by a frail plank bridge. Some of the ponies shied and refused. Somervell had much trouble with his, and just as he had got it across it suddenly backed and almost sent him headlong over the edge into the cauldron beneath – but the rider was Somervell, so of course it didn't quite.

We continued down the left side of the valley, gradually bearing away to the west, and crossed a torrent, the result of the melting snows on Gyachung Kang. Here we had lunch and lazed, and though still at over 15,000 feet the stones were almost too hot to sit on. Myriads of large black bugs (Rynchota) like small cockroaches were swarming over the rocks just above the water-line. What *they* found to eat on this glacial stream even Hingston could not suggest, but we watched some choughs up-stream who were busily feeding on *them* and gobbling them up at a great rate.

That night we camped in a grassy basin high up among the hills. Below was a delightful alpine pasture spangled with dwarf primulas of a rich carmine. Already everyone was feeling and looking better. The air was getting softer – moister. Somervell's throat and breathing were the most obvious legacies of the Everest blizzards. We were ostensibly going to the Rongshar to recuperate, but it must not be imagined that we were a very decrepit party: far from it! From the experience gained in 1922 we had absolutely escaped frostbitten face or fingers; we were unmaimed. But, for all that, though our bodies did not need what might be termed structural repair, they sorely needed refitting, refurnishing. The last reserves had been used up long ago, and our limbs would have moved a cannibal chief to tears, but we were in excellent health and spirits.

From a hill some 18,000 feet high just behind the camp there was a wonderful view of Everest and the great valley leading down from it which we had just left. The view-point was far enough away to allow the foreground, the foothills, to take their true perspective, yet close enough to enable us to see every detail.

That night as I lay in my sleeping-bag looking out through the doorway of the tent, I could see the whole of the historic ground, the scene of the protracted adventure, spread out like a map and bathed in soft, full moon-light. And what a strange impelling light it is! Poets and lovers have always extolled it, but even to the most unromantic there is something in it pecu-liarly moving, especially when it is experienced in solitude and in the desolate spaces of the earth. Never is its spell more potent than in the presence of great mountains. By day we see things and facts in their normal guise, as we are wont to think of them; by moonlight we review them afresh, and they then appear perhaps more nearly as they really are, shorn of all convention and preconceived ideas.

Without labouring the point too far – by daylight we view matters in an eminently earthly, worldly aspect; moonlight seems to bring us face to face with greater and more lasting ideas: it lends a touch of the supernatural to our vision. That night and with that scene in front of one, it was quite easy to realise that the price of life is death, and that, so long as the payment be made promptly, it matters little to the individual when the payment is made. Somewhere, up there, in that vast wilderness of ice and rock, were two still forms. Yesterday, with all the vigour and will of perfect manhood, they were playing a great game – their life's desire. To-day, it was over, and they had gone, without their ever knowing the beginnings of decay. Could any man desire a better end? It seemed not.

Next morning we trekked on up and over the gentle Lamna La (17,400 feet), and down the other side – pleasant going all the way. Then across huge mile-wide stone fans which bygone glacial torrents had deposited in the plain and through which now gushed numerous streams, the dwindling descendants of the parent flood. The camping site at Sichu was provided with a splendid spring of water issuing below a *chorten* bedecked with a thousand votive prayer-canes. Paul (our interpreter) said that here the offering was for the purpose of seeking a blessing on the spring from the gods and not, as was more usual, to drive away the devils. However, in Tibet the procedure in each case appears to be identical, so I suppose the gods and evil spirits are left to settle the point of ownership between themselves.

On June 18 we came into full view of Cho Rapzang at the head of the Kyetrak Valley, while over on our right lay a beautiful mass of unnamed and wholly unknown mountains, whose slender, shapely summits rose to over 23,000 feet. Many of us planned future climbing holidays here – and elsewhere!

The lateral moraines in the lower valleys hereabouts were the largest any of us had ever seen. They were estimated to be at least a thousand feet high and extended for miles, like great snakes writhing across the land. When moraines, especially terminal ones, become grass-grown they often form a pleasant feature in the landscape, as in so many of our English Lakeland dales, but in their original nakedness they are perhaps the ugliest thing in nature. Surrounded as it is by these great featureless heaps of whitish-grey stones, the village of Kyetrak, built of the same material, is the most dreary and forlorn of human habitations. The hovels are of the most primitive and insanitary description. Nevertheless Kyetrak is in its way an important place. Its *raison d'être* is its position on an old trade route between Tibet and Solah Khombu in Nepal. The pass is still freely used and so this desolate village acts as a market for the exchange of goods passing either way – wool, salt and cloth from Tibet; rice, sugar, grain and sheet copper from Nepal. Hardy traders these, to take their merchandise over an icy pass 19,000 feet high. Some of our porters had their homes in the Khombu Valley and their comely sisters, with fine sisterly spirit, but without invitation, came over the pass to accompany their brothers and help them bear their loads, somewhat to the embarrassment of the rest of the Expedition.

At Kyetrak we were able to buy our first sheep – about four shillings and sixpence apiece. True, they were not fat, but their wool hid some of their angularity, and their owners handled their limbs with pride, and called the sahibs' attention to parts where flesh might be distinctly felt. Fortunately their interiors were better furnished, and their livers quite out of proportion to the rest of the carcase.

With us on the northern side of the main watershed the weather was still gloriously fine, the tumult of monsoon cloud boiling up from Nepal along the southern edge of the Himalayas only serving to improve the view and emphasise our good fortune.

Our way was now over the Pusi La to Tazam on the southern side. As usual we could get no definite information as to the extent of the journey. Estimates varied from two days to four hours – the latter by a party who said they had just crossed. In point of fact we left at 8 a.m. and reached the camping site soon after 5 p.m. Either they or the four hours must have had winged heels, or we must have been still more exhausted than we thought.

The pass itself, though something over 17,000 feet, is at an easy gradient in its upper parts, though some of its lower earthy slopes are very steep. On the way up we turned aside, and by climbing the old lateral moraine got a magnificent panoramic view with Cho Rapzang, smothered in tumbled glaciers from head to foot, right in front of us and Cho Uyo and Gyachung Kang away to the left – the east. It is between the first two that the route to Solah Khombu lies.

Immediately over the pass we could see the beginning of the stream which forms part of the head waters of the Rongshar Chu, the river we were about to follow to Nepal. The glacial runners soon carved out a valley which quickly deepened and became more contracted, the mountains seeming to advance upon it till nought was left but a narrow rocky gorge without a scrap of alluvial bottom, the torrent usually occupying the whole bed. As we descended, the lichens, starveling grasses and dwarf alpines rapidly succeeded each other and in turn gave place to larger growths – azaleas and heath-like plants, and then to low-spreading junipers and cypresses, not growing upright but closely following the contours of the rocks they clothed almost, as it were, a giant woody moss. Following them came other conifers, small birches, mountain ash, and here, just on the tree-line, we made our camp, revelling in a crackling fire of fir branches – the first we had seen for several months.

The scenery was majestic and impressive, but always extraordinarily curtailed. The rocky mountain walls on either hand went up and up till lost in the pall of monsoon clouds overhead, which latter ceaselessly drifted up the valley from the south. Nowhere had the gorge a straight course, so that all one saw was a length of V-shaped tunnel leading ever downward. When a black thundercloud closed in the roof the whole effect was most weird: it might well have been the realisation of Jules Verne's road to the centre of the earth.

All next day we continued down the gorge, following a crazy path on the right side. The temperature was steadily rising as we descended, though rain and mist had now taken the place of sunshine. By the end of another march we had reached a zone warm enough to allow one to indulge in utter idleness: we had reached our goal – a place for rest and recuperation. But so narrow was the defile and so steep were its sides that the difficulty was now to find a site on which to place the camp. At last in a small branch glen a suitable place was found, and here our Rongshar Base was made. It was an altogether delightful place. Set in a steeply terraced jungle of flowering shrubs and trees its most beautiful feature was the profusion of pale blue irises of exquisite form that grew on every open patch of ground. It seemed sheer vandalism to pitch one's tent on top of them: instead, we gathered them. We knew that the great mountain Gaurisankar lay directly opposite to our camp, but even in the early mornings the clouds never lifted far enough to reveal more than a peep of the lower ends of the glaciers and of shapely ridges in between.

On June 24 Bruce, Hingston, Shebbeare, Odell and I set off with a mini-mum bandobast to penetrate as far down into Nepal as we could. To our surprise, instead of the gorge opening out, as it had shown some signs of doing, its sides became even higher and more steep. Often great walls of rock rose straight up from the water for a thousand feet or more without a break, then a few shattered ledges or a terrace, then up again till lost in the clouds. Some of these huge slabs of rock had their faces slightly cavernous, the upper parts overhanging menacingly. Such walls were of course utterly impassable, and had two occurred opposite each other the valley would have been permanently sealed, but as they did not, by crossing and re-crossing the river we could continue the descent. We had now reached a zone of sub-tropical forest where magnificent timber grew. The branches of the trees were festooned with hanging lichen and crowded with creepers and epiphytes – ferns and others. Often the host was itself dead, but was greener and more leafy than it had ever been in life. Very little animal life of any kind revealed itself, though occasionally high up about the tree-tops we saw, as it were, flocks of gorgeous butterflies, no doubt drawn together by some nectared tree blossoms.

Earlier in the day we had already passed the Tibet-Nepal frontier and, greatly to our surprise, found it was marked by a boundary stone. True, de-limitation of territory may well have prompted some of man's earliest erections, yet in its trim formality this boundary stone looked strangely out of place in this remote and inaccessible gorge. One wonders if there are like stones in each of the other valleys leading down into Nepal from the Himalayas.

A very creditable erection it was too. It looked rather like a shrine. There was a stepped plinth, surmounted by a large well-dressed slab of gothic tombstone shape. On this was cut an inscription in two languages, Nepalese and Chinese. One of our cooks, Tenchutta, who claimed to be able to read both languages, told me that the notice was to the effect that Tibetans were forbidden from descending the valley beyond that point, while the Nepalese were prohibited from ascending past it. He seemed rather perturbed about the notice; but fortunately, as we were neither Nepalese nor Chinese, we felt free to do both! This same Tenchutta had one strong point in his favour as an Expedition cook – he was a really excellent forager. He could conjure up chickens or eggs where no fowl appeared to be. In holy valleys, too, when no life was allowed to be taken and when I had to arrange for a murrain (a form of cervical hæmorrhage) to fall upon the birds during the night, he would solemnly report their death to me in the morning. Moreover, he was always on the look-out for any gifts Nature might have to offer in the way of wild fruits, herbs, etc. One of his quite most successful efforts was *bamboo au gratin*. This dish was composed of the thick, soft young shoots of the plant, peeled and stewed with cheese and covered with white sauce. It really was most delicious. But the shoots *must* be young and tender. Sometimes his zeal to produce the dish overcame his discretion in selection, and – well, every one knows what bamboo is like! Another discovery of which he was inordinately proud was a kind of fungus. It grew as a jelly-like slime on rotten wood and decaying trees, whence he diligently scraped it with his finger-nails – certainly admirable implements for the purpose. The stuff itself was nearly translucent, but with it came chips of rotten wood and bits of lichen, and when the collection had been duly transferred to his cap for transit, it really did look a horrid mess. At first I felt a certain responsibility in allowing it to be served, but the anxiety was allayed by watching his preparation of it, which showed that the venture was no new one to him and that he was quite familiar with the process. Arrived at camp he immersed the mass in water, and by working it about he brought to the surface all the chips of wood and bits of lichen, and the stuff was cleaned. When cooked it had little flavour and was certainly not worth the trouble it involved. Later, we got some fine 'horse' mushrooms at about 15,000 feet, which we greatly enjoyed.

The gorge was still getting more and more precipitous and the route more and more crazy. Really some bits of the way tracked out across the face of a slab might have given Mr Heath Robinson an inspiration. The faith the engineers had in a few wisps of bamboo fibre as lashing was hardly reassuring to the European mind. The ladder portions of the way were all fastened with this material, but as if to give the thing an air of stability, though probably to prevent its being blown bodily away, large slabs of stone were inserted at intervals between the treads. These hardly facilitated one's passage and looked heavy enough in themselves to bring the whole thing down. Airy horizontal traverses were thus often almost paved with stones, but if one was indiscreet enough to pry over the edge and examine the substructure one found that the stones were laid on brushwood, which was in turn supported by the flimsiest and most sketchy framework of branches, attached to the cliff apparently by faith alone: then only did one appreciate even the bamboo lashing!

Considering our position on the south side of the Himalayas and the time of year, the weather was kind to us, for although a great deal of rain fell it was mostly precipitated in the evenings and during the night: the early mornings and sometimes a large part of the day were fine; but the clouds always closed our valley in, as by a lid, and hid the tops of the rocky walls.

We knew that we were trespassing on a grand scale, and wondered more and more that no one had turned up to bar the way. The next day, June 25, provided what was probably the explanation of our freedom. We had not been descending long that morning before the cliff on our side of the gorge became utterly impassable, even as an acrobatic feat of rock-climbing, and it was therefore obvious that a bridge had existed hereabouts to lead to the other side. Unfortunately it was equally apparent that no bridge remained: it had been swept away, only a few tattered fastenings showing where its near end had once been anchored. The spot was most impressive. If I have used the word impressive rather frequently I must be forgiven, for I can think of no other that suits the lower Rongshar quite so well. The scenery is simply overwhelming: one is almost appalled by the display of terrestrial force – potential in the overhanging rocks, kinetic in the water.

The river, which throughout its course is one mad cataract, here takes a sudden plunge of 200 or 300 feet. On the very edge of the abyss there stands up out of the racing water two jagged points of rock, and it was by these that in three lengthy spans a way across had once existed. From the middle span the view must have been marvellous.

The failure of the bridge had brought about an interesting situation, and incidentally no doubt accounted for our unopposed descent. The first Nepalese village of any account lay still farther down the valley, and none could now ascend from it beyond the broken bridge, so that the upper part of the gorge (cut off, as it were, in the rear, by the Himalayan Chain) was isolated from the rest of the world almost as effectively as if it had been an oceanic island. One wondered who in this wild place would take the initiative, and have the means to reconstruct the bridge, and when. Would it be months, or years, before the people, caught as in a trap in the depths of this stupendous gorge, again have access to their neighbours other than by the lofty mountain passes? If the initiative had to come from the Tibetan side, one felt one knew the answer!

Shebbeare, a forest officer, looked longingly at the job, but after he had reluctantly satisfied himself of the impossibility of our making a temporary way across, there was nothing for it but to retreat to a good camping site we had passed a little higher up-stream. Here on a gravel spit we pitched the tents just as the rain began in earnest. Opposite the camp on the other shore was a dark overhanging cliff. Presently someone noticed suspended from the roof of this overhang nine large combs of honey and four lesser ones. Through glasses we could see that they were covered black with crawling bees: in fact no comb was visible, and they looked exactly like gigantic swarms. Heavy rain and leeches made exploration of the jungle round about less inviting than it at first appeared, and before long every one found occupation in his tent.

Under some rotting balks of timber Hingston and I turned out some great furry spiders. They were such ugly-looking customers that one felt inclined to shoot them first and pick them up afterwards! But they were soon pushed unceremoniously into the cyanide bottle.

Next morning agitation among the coolies awoke me soon after 5 a.m. It was the bees! The smoke from the newly kindled mess fires had been wafted up the opposite cliff to where the combs were hanging, and the bees had come down to see about it. From then onwards until the sun became obscured about 8.30 things grew increasingly lively. They were huge bees – the largest of the three forest species – and were nearly black. They came straight at us and stung as they alighted. They were so big that we could watch them in flight for quite a long distance and clearly follow their tactics. They came swooping down the drift of smoke and then began systematically to quarter the ground, looking for the enemy and keeping about fifteen inches above the surface. So long as you remained quite still they usually passed by, but move a leg and you were at once their quarry. Instantly they came straight for you, but when within a few inches of your puttee, instead of alighting there they suddenly shot upwards and pitched unerringly on the top of your head. This was our salvation, as nine times out of ten they stung the hat. Occasionally on the upward swoop they spotted a patch of fur and dived for it, and we had hastily to knock them out of our beards before they reached the skin. Tippoo, one of our cooks, was simply splendid.

He was wearing a woolly helmet, and each time he passed from the cook-house to the mess-tent he was bespattered with bees, and you could hear an angry buzz as he approached. I shall never forget his cheery face, framed in bees, appearing in the doorway. We had to make him thin them out a little before we allowed him inside, lest, while handing round the welcome break-fast, he should also distribute with it a liberal sprinkling of the angry bees. What a jolly meal that was! Every one got his share of stings, and so provided mirth for others. I can see old Tippoo now standing in the doorway and plucking the bees off his hat and beard with his fingers. If he didn't nip them hard enough as he threw them from him – and one doesn't linger in the handling of a live bee – they flew straight back again as if attached to his head by an elastic string. Fortunately the poison inserted by their sting was as mild as the bees were large and vicious, and seemed to cause less swelling than that of an English bee. The coolies were half afraid and half amused – they loved to see each other, or a sahib, stung, but they ran madly about when their turn came. Shebbeare said their fear was not unfounded, as he had known of several cases where attack by these forest bees had ended fatally to men and horses. In such cases, however, it is not the attentions of a few skirmishers, but the descent of the whole colony which is the danger.

From this camp we got our only glimpse of what we imagined to be Gauri-sankar, or rather a part of it, for I do not think that what we saw can have been the actual summit. It looked fine, but not as grand as we had anticipated. Perhaps, if indeed it was Gaurisankar, the stupendous nature and verticality of the foreground killed it, as well it might.

On June 26 the return march to Tazam was begun. On the way we re-passed the only little stretch in the river's course that was not a wild descent, elsewhere it is almost one continuous cataract throughout. Here a landslide on a grand scale had dammed the valley, momentarily holding up the waters before they took a plunge more profound than usual. There was shingle in this pent-up reach and on it as we passed down we had seen birds I took to be ibisbills. They were not in evidence when Hingston passed, and he was very much disappointed to have missed them. Now on the ascent the same thing happened. As we went by they were there, evidently nesting, and as noisy as oystercatchers, but an hour later when he was at the place there was no sign of them. As soon as he came into camp and learned that they had again been seen at the same place, with his usual enthusiasm he set off back immediately without waiting for a meal. He was well rewarded, for not only did the old birds show up, but he saw their chicks, nearly as large as themselves, running about and being fed on a gravel islet in mid-stream. The young of this species he believed to be unknown to ornithologists, and he was very anxious to examine it. There was the priceless chick running about in full view of him, but between them was half the Rongshar torrent. Much though Hingston coveted it, he would not allow Geoffrey or me to try to swim across to get it. We had no cord to act as a life-line, and if the swimmer failed to make the island – well, the first stop would have been Nepal. Tell it not in South Kensington, but I really felt rather glad that the chick escaped. It looked so forlorn on its scrap of shingle, with its parents calling mournfully around, while half an expedition sat on the bank and plotted for its capture.

Near this spot we found in the forest a little encampment – a family in three generations – of primitive paper-makers. I got quite friendly with these simple, jolly people, and was able to follow the whole of their ancient and interesting process from start to finish – from the growing plant to the folded paper. Small trees, rather like our elder, were cut down and stripped of their 'bark' to the cambium layer. The naked branches were left lying on the ground, not being needed for fuel, of which there was an abundance everywhere, but the 'bark' was carried home through the forest in baskets. There women laboriously tore and cut the tough white bast fibres from its inner side, using fingers, knife, and teeth. The outer corky part was waste and was used only as fuel, but the bast was macerated and later boiled in large copper cauldrons over slow wood fires, until it went down into a jelly-like pulp of a light reddish-brown colour. Then shallow wooden frames like window-sashes, but glazed with fabrics, were got ready and immersed in clean cold water. The pulp was ladled into them, there to be deftly worked and spread under water until it formed a thin even layer upon the fabric. Then the frames were gently raised above the surface and allowed to drain, first in a horizontal position and then vertically, propped up in a circle round a great wood fire. When thus hardened off the paper was stripped easily from the canvas backing and was ready for use. The people told me that they had come from Lhasa to make the paper, that they and their ancestors had always made it in this valley, and that it was required in Lhasa for official purposes. Fancy an entire family making a yearly journey from Lhasa to the Rongshar in order to make a few sheets of paper!

When we got back to the Rongshar Base, Norton and Somervell, who had remained there, were bubbling over with enthusiasm about a view they had had – or purported to have had – of Gaurisankar. In fact they were so effervescent about it that we began to doubt the seriousness of the vision. Certainly their sketches of it tallied, as did their stories; but had they not had ample time in which to prepare both, and did we not often in these leisured days extend each other's hind limbs? Moreover there was a suspicious absence of photographic evidence. Gradually, however, we realised that it had all happened – that they had seen a mountain-peak which eclipsed all others, and we were filled with a desire to see it ourselves. Their view-point had been an alpine meadow some 1,500 feet above the camp. Here was a small Tibetan village and the remains of a much larger one, evidently of great antiquity. The mani-walls (prayer-stones) had once been of an unusually imposing nature, but were now so weather-worn that only the faintest trace was left of the inscription they once bore. Bruce, Odell and I took tents and sleeping-bags up to this meadow next day, and, as if to show *bona fides*, Somervell accompanied us. All that day the clouds looked like dispersing, but they never did so. Late in the evening we got some delightful views looking down the gorge towards Nepal between piled-up masses of coppery cumulus clouds, but of Gaurisankar we saw not a trace. I looked several times during the night and just at dawn, but a steady rain was falling. In the morning Bruce and Somervell went down to the Base. After breakfast Odell and I mounted higher in an endeavour to get above the clouds, but the rain got steadily worse, so he too gave it up. In the hope of getting photographic records I stayed another night – our last before the homeward trek – but with no better fortune. Never a glimpse of the great mountain appeared, although the clouds that hid it were in ceaseless motion – forming, rising, dispersing, and reforming. By eight o'clock on June 30 my coolies had come up for the things, as the camp below was being struck, so the last hope of getting pictures of Gaurisankar vanished.

On July 3 we re-crossed the Pusi La, now much more snowy than on the outward journey.

Norton and I had a very pleasant morning. Many new flowers had appeared since we passed; some of them, he thought, were new and unrecorded species, as they had not been noted on the 1922 Expedition. One pleased us particularly. It was of a rich azure blue and had blossoms not dissimilar to those of *Ranunculus glacialis* only rather smaller, the flowers being so closely set as to form a cushion. Snow-cock were disporting themselves on every side (how wonderfully invisible they are among the stones!), while a pair of lammergeiers behaved as if their eyrie were somewhere close at hand. In point of fact we saw no nest of any species of vulture in Tibet, and we wondered where these birds, which play such an important role in the disposal of the dead, could have their nurseries.

Having descended from the Pusi La we found that the numerous streams furrowing the great stone waste below the snout of the Kyetrak Glacier were in full spate, and we just managed to get across without our horses being swept away. These Tibetan ponies are willing, plucky little fellows; they faced the icy water time after time till every one was safely over.

It was now full summer, but Kyetrak had not smiled to greet it. How could it? Whitish-grey stones look much the same in July as in December. It is altogether a most unlovely place.

We were now leaving the Himalayas behind and passing out into the open spaces of Tibet. Wide brown plains were everywhere bounded by bare barren hills, the whole rimmed round by distant blue-grey mountains and white glaciers. Here and there on the vast horizon dark thunder-clouds were gathered and from their under-surfaces we could see drifting curtains of descending rain. Behind these isolated little storms and to the right and left of them the country was bathed in sunlight, which made them look strangely artificial, theatrical, one might almost say. The major span of the horizon was in places some 200 miles across, and the area of country seen was so great that though these storms were always on the move it was some days before one actually crossed our path.

We had not been down on the plain long before we saw and were seen by a herd of kiang. They watched us interestedly for a time and then retreated towards a small nullah. We held on our course until the last one had disappeared over the ridge, then pulling our ponies round we galloped hard for a point some way higher up the nullah where we judged they might now be. It was our first kiang hunt and one of our most successful. As we topped the ridge and looked over it there, right below us, were thirteen of the beautiful animals trotting leisurely in single file up the middle of the valley. Instantly on seeing us they were off with a shaking of necks and a kicking of heels, and without the slightest prompting on our part our ponies were off after them in a mad gallop down the nullah side, heedless of rocks and pika burrows. Shebbeare and I, who were rather farther up than Geoffrey, tried to head them off while he rode straight at the last one. In the first dash the ponies seemed almost as fast as the kiang and he got to within some fifteen yards of them, but as soon as they settled down to an easy swinging gallop they proved too swift, and quickly drew away from us. Still, it was all great sport.

A couple of miles away we could see Norton trying, single-handed, to manoeuvre a herd of about twenty towards us. Kiang are certainly inquisitive beasts, but withal somewhat stupid. Several times they broke past him on the flank and then stopped and turned round to stare at him, so each time he regained his position and began to drive them in our direction, till finally they took alarm and galloped past him like a flash and were quickly out of sight. The Tibetans told us that they were very good to eat, and I can well believe it, though we never had an opportunity of tasting their flesh. To shoot these in the nullah would have been an easy matter, but it may well be otherwise sometimes. Later, we saw a herd that would not allow an approach within half a mile.

We camped that night at Sharto. The country was beginning to get fertile; there were little enclosures of barley coming up strongly, notwithstanding that the altitude was close upon 15,000 feet, and there was quite a profusion of plant life. Terrific rain fell that evening, and the cookhouse had an impromptu river running through it – a golden opportunity for washing grimy utensils which was taken full advantage of. In the morning the village brought out its halt and sick. The Tibetans imagined that all the bugs and beetles, lizards and grass-hoppers that Hingston caught and bottled were for medicinal purposes, and the fame of him soon spread abroad. We did not correct this opinion as it allowed him to collect these lowly things in holy places, where otherwise such action would probably have given offence. Unfortunately on this occasion the medical equipment had gone on before this impromptu sick parade began. But Hinky was never at a loss. Most of us would have bungled – have said that the medicine-chest had already been despatched and that we were sorry we could do nothing. Not so he. Having examined the patients with professional mien – pustular skin diseases, withered limbs, acute conjunctivitis – he handed round bull's-eyes and acid-drops; the former to be taken in hot water on retiring, the latter, twice a day in milk. It was rather pitiful to see them borne away rejoicing, but faith might do something for them, and a refusal to tend them certainly could not do anything and would almost surely be misunderstood. Moreover, as all his colleagues were careful to assure him, all his medicines were equally good! Lest this action of spontaneous tact be misunderstood, let it be stated that Hingston, and Somervell too, were able to relieve much suffering on our way across Tibet. At this very village of Sharto the previous night, I believe, he had opened out a dangerous abscess and probably saved a life.

Tingri was reached on July 5, and turned out to be a much more important place than at first sight it appeared to be. It has a considerable trade, possesses much arable land, and is a garrison town. Not that this last qualification signifies much, as I think the only trace of soldiery which we saw was a little group cleaning Martini rifles, and I remember we thought that the men so employed might with great advantage have turned their attention upon themselves – or is it that these Tibetan outposts are advanced students of the art of camouflage. The top of the hill above the village is crowned by a commanding-looking Dzong. From a distance its battlemented walls look sound, but in reality the whole place is dreadfully dilapidated and entirely unoccupied. The roofs are now gone, floors and ceilings are tumbling in and the walls everywhere are crumbling down. Some hazardous 'first ascents' were achieved as we explored the place, one member disappearing through a floor, as if it had been through a hole in ice, but judging by the volume of sound that issued from the under chamber his lungs at least were quite uninjured. Had we been able to read Tibetan and Chinese we might have found much of real interest here. Some of the rooms had evidently formed a sort of muniment store, and on stone shelves amid the collapsing walls were bales of folded manuscript. Large sheets, of the same type as those we had seen made in the Rongshar, were folded and packed away as it were in quires. These writings no doubt dealt with matters pertaining to the fort and might have revealed much information on past days, knowledge which is so lacking in Tibet. The libraries of the monasteries with their great wooden-backed tomes, each in its stone pigeon-hole, are said to contain nought but Buddhist, or rather Lamaic, theology.

The people of Tingri were noticeably less shy and more interestedly inquisitive than those met with elsewhere. They had heard of the wonders of my 'picture box' as our coolies called my reflex camera. They knew that if you looked into it you could see a picture in all its colours and motion, so they followed me about in droves. Unfortunately their knowledge of the instrument was imperfect, and they persisted in trying to peer in through the lens. The result of this was that as I looked in at the hood, in the orthodox method to photograph anything, all I could see was a sea of Tibetan faces – mostly out of focus, instead of the picture I sought. Gradually I got them to understand that it was necessary to have an open space in front of me in order to take a photograph, and therefore I found myself at the apex of a V-shaped lane of craning necks. In their desire to look in at the lens they continually encroached upon this open space, and I had to keep them back by playfully throwing stones at the intruders, for which purpose I kept my pockets filled with missiles. These Tibetans are by nature an easily amused and cheery people, and provided one does such actions as this in the right spirit, they will take anything in good part. This widening of the 'V' they regarded as a sort of game, and every time anyone was hit, the others roared with laughter. In fact they made so much noise that soon half the village was attracted, and the only way I could manage the crowd was to sit down and point the camera in the wrong direction and let them form up in a hopelessly encroaching V, then turn round quickly and take the picture before the crowd had time to reform on the new front. Their appreciation of tactics was bad for a garrison town, for during the whole morning they never spotted the meaning of this simple manoeuvre. Now and then I allowed a few of them to look through the camera at the moving picture of their fellows reflected on the ground glass. It simply delighted them and they were never tired of watching it. It made me wince to see them press their filthy, greasy heads into the hood. Many of them had skin eruptions with open sores, but I only had to hope that such were not contagious.

Every member of the Expedition was now in splendid form and health, and we began to seek outlets for our spare energy. From the bottom of a kitbag I unearthed a rope quoit we had used for training on the *California*, and with it we improvised 'Tibetan tennis.' The court we marked by scratching the surface of the plain; ice axes and a bandage made the net. It was astonishing how soon one got out of breath. We were, so we thought, perfectly acclimatised. We went about our ordinary daily routine as easily as if it had been at sea-level instead of over 14,000 feet above, but immediately we did anything in the least violent, or impeded the breathing in any way, as by stooping, then altitude began to assert itself again in no uncertain manner. By nothing was this more emphasised than by this tennis. There were only three of us who played: Bruce, Somervell and I – Norton, who would have made a fourth at any sport, was lame through foot trouble during most of the homeward march – so we had to play singles. We started feeling fit enough for a wrestling bout or a cross-country run, but if the game was in the least fast in ten minutes we were completely done. At Yatung, some three weeks later and 4,000 feet lower, there was a marked improvement in our form; our state there was perhaps what at home would be described as one of 'rank bad training.' Now it is noteworthy that at 14,000 to 15,000 feet the Tibetans can run up steep hillsides chasing and shouting at their yaks, and return unwinded. How long, I wonder, would it take a European to acclimatise himself thus far – is it a matter of months or years, or is it one of generations of heredity?

This matter of acclimatisation is a fascinating subject. It is so very real, such a vital factor to success, and yet it is so indefinite, so immeasurable. That is it – we want somebody to devise a simple meter. It is no measure of acclimatisation that one man takes a pass gaily and as if he likes it, while another plods heavily along and seems to labour. The real difference in the two may be masked entirely by opposite temperaments, by spirit and the exercise of will power. The one may be exhausting his reserve of strength, while the other who envies his companion his seeming fitness may unconsciously be husbanding his own resources. One of those who made the 'heaviest going' over the passes on the outward journey was Odell, yet it was he who later gained by far the greatest victory over altitude that has ever been achieved by man. Of course the estimation of the number of red corpuscles in a given quantity of blood provides a direct indication of the response the blood system has made to the change in altitude, but, altogether apart from the trouble of making this test in the field, it may be questioned whether it gives the measure of acclimatisation of the man as a whole.

Perhaps it might be well if, on a future Expedition, a longer time was spent between leaving Calcutta and reaching the Base Camp. After the voyage and the heat of the plains of India there is useful acclimatisation to be done in the neighbourhood of Darjeeling, and again, later, in that of Yatung, before finally going up on to the plateau. Three days, and one day respectively, at these places, as in 1922, is perhaps hardly enough.

It is so difficult not to confuse ordinary bodily training, i.e. condition of the muscles, with acclimatisation, i.e. adjustment of every organ concerned with a reduction in atmospheric pressure. Anything in the nature of long or exhausting marches on the outward journey may well be a mistake – acclimatisation does not lie that way. Presumably the men chosen for the expedition will be muscularly fit and will not require much hardening off in that direction – and in any case they will have had it by the time they reach Base Camp – all this is required to get their whole bodies in tune with their new surroundings. The evidence all seems to point to the advisability of going easy until the great final effort; but there is something harder than to put the brake upon oneself when feeling fit in any form of sport nor would it be a much easier task for the leader to curb his team; but it may be worth the doing.

From Tingri we marched by Memo, and arrived at Shekar on the evening of July 7. Here we were able to replenish our stores from a dump left with the Dzong Pen on the outward route. Some cases of sugar were particularly welcome. We made him a handsome present of surplus stores, and received a sheep and some eggs – assorted ages – in exchange. There was every reason to be grateful to this headman: he had had more to do for us than any other Dzong Pen and he had carried out his contracts well. Here Geoffrey had a kit inspection for the men, a necessary proceeding every now and then. Otherwise there is no limit to what the coolies would carry back – the carriage at our expense. In this case he cut the transport down by several mule-loads. The marches to Shekar were very pleasant ones: we dawdled through the country, birds'-nesting as we went along. Now it was a sand-lark that started up from her eggs at our ponies' feet and ran fitfully about amongst the desert scrub, her deep cup-shaped nest sunk to the rim in sand and usually beside a tuft of vegetation, but whether this was for concealment or protection against the wind was a matter of dispute. Now it was a pair of showy hoopoes that held the attention, flying in and out of their nesting site in the crumbling earthen walls of some old building; or it might be nobler species. Here a white-tailed eagle was seated on a rocky ridge performing its toilet and quite disinclined to move; then, a lordly lammergeier, beating the mountain-side, was sweeping by in majestic flight, the tip of its great primaries straining and bent upwards with the rush of air. Yonder, on a steep crag overlooking the plain, an upland buzzard had its nest and young. Lizards – no two seeming quite alike – scuttled across the sand; frogs we found in water up to 15,000 feet, and grasshoppers everywhere were indiscreet enough to hop and so disclose their presence to Hingston, who had a perfect mania for bottling them. There was always something to interest or amuse.

On the route between Shekar and Tinki it was very noticeable that now in midsummer the distant landscape looked more wintry than it had done in April. Hills that were then quite bare and brown were now white nearly down to the plain. Of course the mean temperature would be far lower in April than in July, but at the former time precipitation was nil, while now it was abundant and fell as snow. I remember that on the way up from India we had noticed a similar phenomenon. Looking back, southwards and downwards towards Sikkim, the country seemed snowbound and Arctic, while looking northwards and upwards to higher elevations, the land was snow-free. No doubt this effect was accentuated by the greater melting power of the sun's rays on the southern slopes (which alone you see when looking north) than on the northern faces, but it was chiefly due to a difference in precipitation.

The streams were now at their maximum and often afforded excitement in crossing them. Soon after leaving our camp near Jikkyop on the 12th we had to negotiate the Puchung Chu, a river coming down from the Brahmaputra watershed. It was considered doubtful whether we should be able to get across. It appears that in such a difficulty the Tibetan method is to drive a herd of cattle over in order to consolidate the bottom and so prevent the single-hoofed ponies and donkeys from sinking in too far. After less than the usual delay the herd was forthcoming and was with much forcible persuasion driven over and back again. The route was now declared open. Our transport at this time consisted of small donkeys, some of which were now pushed in. But though the cloven-hoofed cattle had managed it, the donkeys couldn't. Their small hoofs and heavy loads made them sink too deeply, and they were soon swept off their feet and carried down-stream. Three were all but drowned – one had to have artificial respiration (not provided for in the Royal Life Saving Society's handbook). After this it was evident that there was nothing for it but to unstrap the loads and to man-handle everything across: three hours' hard work for 200 yards! Most of our coolies and all the Tibetans from whom we had hired the transport entered the water willingly enough, carrying the loads on their backs. The bottom was none too good, yet they worked so steadily that not a single case was dropped. One old Tibetan excelled all others by bearing four cases at a time – a fine feat of skilful balance as well as strength.

So we jogged on, past Chiblung and Khenga and over the Bahman Dopté, the 'steepest pass.' Here Norton, Bruce, Somervell and I branched off to visit the Tsomo-tre-tung Lake, an arm of which one could see from the top of the pass, peeping round invitingly from behind some intervening hills. Even now, after many disillusionments, we were again hopelessly deceived in the matter of distance. It seems impossible to read into the Tibetan landscape the mileage that is really there. The marvellous clearness of the atmosphere simply does not allow vision to take heed of distance. Another factor in deception is the flatness of the plains that lie between the hills. Standing on the level the horizon is, I suppose, about three miles away, and since the effects of space have been optically cancelled the nearest hills seem to be about that distance away. Mount an eminence and the horizon of course recedes, taking with it, so to speak, the hills. This will continue until the horizon passes beyond the actual base of the hills, after which they recede no farther. But whatever the explanation, the lake was at least twice as far away as we expected it to be, and the last descent to it from a little col not less than three times the distance we estimated. When at last we reached it, we found it was alive with duck. They were resting on the shore, but put out at once on our approach. They were not at all tame, and even had we been allowed to shoot it is doubtful if we should have got many, though a punt-gunner might have had his wildest dream fulfilled. The lake showed evident signs of the rapid desiccation which the district generally appears to be undergoing. That part of the Tibetan Plateau through which we travelled now supports only a fraction of the population that formerly existed there. Whole districts, sections of valley systems, are now uninhabited, dotted over with ruins which speak of considerable former population. Three recent successive conquests of this land,[1] the first at least of a very bloody nature, must have thinned out the inhabitants, but increasing desiccation may well have been a potent factor in depopulation. Unfortunately of this latter cause we have no dates or data, though evidences of its effect are plentiful enough.

The homing instinct was now beginning to draw us back. Unconsciously we experienced an unwillingness to tarry: only one night was spent at each of Tinki, Kampa, and Phari. Not that there was much inducement to linger at the Donka La, for the weather was bitterly cold and wet. The cooks had rather a rough time of it hereabouts through absence of a cookhouse, but they were always cheerful, and never sulked. As typical of the good spirit of our men, I remember that here, after they had had a particularly miserable time struggling with a refractory stove in driving sleet, they came joyfully to tell me that there were fish to be caught in the stream near by. I think that most people would have sat tight about those fish at the end of a long day's march and under those conditions, especially as the only method of catching them was by thrusting our arms into the icy water, but not so they. In half an hour we had got enough for a fry, but they were not the bright 'snow trout' we had caught before. They were a species of loach, slimy and muddy, and that evening I came to the conclusion that Jan Ridd's taste in fish-flesh was not the same as mine.

At Kampa, Odell went off to 'solve some more problems' of a geological nature in a valley to the south. Shebbeare went with him to look after the transport, so our party was still further reduced. We did not see them again until they arrived in Darjeeling the day after we got there.

The ride into Phari was a cold and soaking one, and our ponies were dull and listless. They were feeling the wet far more than they had done the zero temperatures in the dry cold. Even a promising 'pie-dog' well out in the

---

1  First the Gurkhas came up over the Himalayas from Nepal and pillaged the country to such an extent that the Tibetans, unable to cope with them, sought and received the help of China. By what must have been a wonderful military expedition the Chinese crossed Tibet and drove out the Nepalese, but themselves occupied the land. There they remained until quite recently, when the Tibetans were at last strong enough in turn to drive them out.

open failed to rouse their spirits, much to the chagrin of Norton and Geoffrey – joint masters of the Everest pack. The whole party was just attuned thoroughly to appreciate the comfort the Phari bungalow offered. Chairs and a fire, china cups and plates, a tub and a house – how little one felt to have missed them, but what real pleasure they afforded at their reappearance!

John Macdonald had come up from Chumbi to meet us, and had thoughtfully sent on in advance fresh garden produce: lettuces and peas, turnips and potatoes. How delicious everything tasted!

Accommodation in the Phari bungalow was limited, so the specimens, Hinky and I, shared a room and tried to dry off a little before a roaring fire. Mould was attacking the botanical collection, and we had to spread all the sheets out in turn to try to arrest its ravages. It was not until you began thus to handle the collection that you fully realised Hingston's zeal and untiring patience. Besides the collection of plants I believe the Expedition brought back nearly 10,000 zoological specimens, mostly beetles, bugs, and other invertebrates. This was 10,000 dead, official specimens – there were many others which travelled with us unofficially as stowaways.

Leaving Phari and the plateau on July 21, the descent through the upper Chumbi Valley was nothing but a sheer joy: no quantity of rain could hide or mar the wonderful flora of this gorge. Up to this point I admit that I had been rather disappointed with the Himalayan flowers. Individually they are unsurpassable – the magnolias and rhododendrons; *Primula Sikkimensis* and all its kind; the yellow meconopsis sending up great pyramidal spikes like a giant Canterbury-bell; the dwarf blue things of the higher terrain, and the perfectly delightful iris of the Rongshar, are each as fine as, or finer than, anything I had seen before – yet nowhere had we met that almost wanton profusion, alike of variety as well as mass, that is seen on Alpine slopes and meadows. But here at the head of the gorge such floral wealth was spread with lavish hand. One could have stayed here for days merely to enjoy, not necessarily to collect, the flowers. Perhaps most of them were of familiar form, but of new variety – old friends in a new guise. Many, however, were utterly strange to us who had only an acquaintance with European blossoms. Some of these exotics were of striking grace and beauty, and would be an asset anywhere. One longed to be able to show them to flower-lovers one knew at home, but it is almost impossible to transport roots from such a place, and seeds were not yet ripe.

The next day we reached Yatung, and were at once entertained to lunch by the Macdonald family. The hospitality we were shown by them and by

Captain and Mrs Noel was beyond all thanks: they simply could not show us kindness enough. I think their best reward must have been our whole-hearted appreciation of it! For there is nothing so satisfactory as to see that which one has prepared be unreservedly enjoyed – in this, I suppose, lies much of the pleasure which children afford their elders.

We had already given away to various Dzong Pens as much of our spare stores as we could without risk of spoiling the pitch for a subsequent Expedition, and now finding that the rates for transport to Darjeeling were exorbitantly high we decided to hold an autumn clearance sale of tents, stores, and general equipment. It was an event of no small importance in the valley. It was, in fact, a unique sale – it contained bargains. We had no front-page advertisements in the Press, but we had a goodly company of prospective purchasers. It was in every way a sale befitting the dignity of the Expedition, though perhaps the salesman's style was a little cramped by the use of an interpreter, and by the necessity for little explanations of the different shades of use of such similar looking articles as dubbin and golden syrup. The sale was voted a great success all round, and certainly every purchaser got very good value for his money. It was interesting to notice how well to the fore was the feminine element in the advent of a sale even in Tibet; and incidentally, it may be added, it was only one of the fair sex that changed her mind and brought her purchase back! For what it is worth, let me suggest to sociologists that this sale mania, which is so noticeable a feature of the modern woman, is nothing more than a new expression of the deep-seated collecting, husbanding propensity typical of the female sex in its widest biological sense.

A small native garrison, an outpost of the empire, is stationed at Yatung, and the men were very anxious to play the Expedition at football. Geoffrey with great good-nature arranged the match, but omitted to turn out himself. Naturally it was an event of first importance in the village, but the monsoon, now at its height, did its best to wash the fixture out. Though failing in this, it was more successful with the field: that it quite obliterated, substituting for much of it a rippling sheet of water. All the preceding night and that morning the rain roared down unceasingly, yet about the appointed hour the spectators began to turn up smilingly. Something had to be done. Apart from that wretch Geoff, who was not to be found, there were only three of us fit enough to play – Hingston, Somervell and myself – so filling up gaps in a somewhat sketchy side with likely looking coolies, and borrowing two men (our best) from the garrison reserve, we took to the water.

It must have been one of the strangest games of football ever played. We won the toss, and elected to play down-stream, hoping thereby that we might get a goal washed through. Nailed climbing boots made large enough for three pairs of woollen socks do not tend to make one nimble, especially when they are filled with water; nor was the going what would be described as fast, but perhaps this was just as well, for we were soon very short of breath. We found this sort of football, played at 10,000 feet, an exhausting game, and it says much for our acclimatisation that we were able to stick it out. The spectators revelled in the game. Yatung was beating an 'English' team! There was no doubt about the beating: they were far too good for us; the only doubt was in their designation of our side. They played most sportingly and took everything in good part. When anyone was sent sprawling in the water the people roared with delight, just as heartily if it was one of their men as when it was one of ours. Nothing really exciting happened, no one actually got out of his depth, but when the whistle went for full time with the score 5-1 for them, they were wild with delight. It seemed a pity to stop their fun, every one looked expectant, so we gave them ten minutes more each way. They put on two more goals, and were enjoying it so much that we gave them a last ten minutes, but, thanks to the current, they failed to score again. It is up to the next expedition to avenge our defeat; but Yatung will always prove a difficult side to beat on its home ground!

Before we left the Chumbi Valley we invited the Macdonalds and the Noels to a little lunch à la Base Camp, served, with true local colour, in the mess-tent. Perhaps it was not a strict copy of the meal as usually served in that well-known restaurant, but at least every course was founded on fact, that is to say it had been evolved and more or less approved of at some period of the Expedition. The only real innovation was the lettuce.

Every one entered thoroughly into the spirit of the thing and was very jolly, and if some of the courses did get a little mixed and somebody was offered, and in all innocence accepted, brandy sauce while still busy with chicken pie, it only helped to enliven the proceedings. The menu, as it appeared, was as follows:

Kalimpong Beer.                    God bless Kalimpong.

Lunch à la Base Camp.
———————

Sardines, hard-boiled eggs, potato cream and Chumbi herbs.
Quails in pâté de foie gras and lettuce.
———————

Pea soup, Erbowurot; fried bread and grated cheese.
———————

Mutton cutlets, sauce Kyetrak; green peas.
Chicken-and-ham pie à la Teuchutta; new potatoes.
———————

Plum pudding; sauce, trois étoiles cognac.
Baked custard, French plums, très ordinaires.
———————

Cheese omelette à la Rongbuk.
———————

Tea, mixed biscuits, crystallised ginger.
———————

Grace – anglaise.

July 24, 1924.

July 25 saw the beginning of the last stage in our journey, and I think every one felt sorry that it was coming to a close. We took a different route from that followed on the outward march and camped a few miles short of the Natu La, at the beautifully situated Champetang bungalow. In one village we passed through we saw hanging suggestively outside the Depen's house the various implements of punishment for evildoers: whips, thorny sticks, nailed batons and chains for beating, small flat-faced bats for smacking the cheek and sole of the feet, and the usual large square wooden Chinese collars of detention – altogether a most chastening sight.

The Natu La is on the boundary between Sikkim and Tibet. It was very noticeable that the moment we crossed it and entered British territory the forest track became an efficient road, in parts built up and engineered like a railway embankment. All day we passed through what must be most magnificent country, but the monsoon was busy and we could only see, as it were, a horizontal slice of it: the tops of the gorges were lost in cloud, the bottoms were filled with swirling mist. That night at Karponang the ponies had a dreadful time with leeches. The place was swarming with them. From the damp woodwork of the bungalow alone we collected more than Hinky needed. While he was busy bottling them we noticed dangling from behind his ear, like an onyx pendant, a fine well-fed specimen: so that too went in with the others. It is strange how often you may be unaware of a leech's presence even when it is drawing your blood. Quite a large one may have been hanging on the back of your neck for a long time before you are vaguely conscious of something being there and put up your hand and find it. Often when the boots were taken off at night they were found to be a bloody mess inside – the unfelt work of small leeches that had wormed their way through eyelet-holes and stockings. They are strange creatures – blind, deaf, and without apparent senses, there they sit in the streaming forests poised on a leaf waving their 'tails' about in the hope of touching some passer-by. It sounds to be a precarious mode of existence, but is evidently one by which the species is able to thrive exceedingly. What their sense organs are, how they scent their prey, we hadn't time to investigate, but it was obvious that they could detect your presence. Those on the woodwork of the bungalow became agitated and waved their tails about every time we passed them closely.

Soon we were down into the hot steaming forest where the cicadas, sitting on the bark, deafened one with their strident notes – surely, all things considered, one of Nature's strangest noises. This zone, about the rice line, is one of great luxuriance alike in fauna and in flora. Gorgeous butterflies were flitting by on every side, but Hingston was superior to their gaudy charms; they were already well-known and catalogued and therefore ceased to interest him. Whereas the wonderful variety of bugs and hemiptera in quaintest forms might well reveal new species, and of these he welcomed as many as we could bring him. But though Hinky ignored the painted scraps of life, they had a quixotic effect on Geoff. He rode the forest paths doing battle all the way: once nearly going over the khud in a magnificent encounter with a fine Apollo.

At night in the forest bungalows the moths were attracted by the lights and flickered across the whitened ceilings. This was the signal for post-prandial exercise. Mounted pick-a-back upon each other's shoulders, the top man armed with cyanide bottle, we chased the moths around. Sometimes, in order to reach the apex of the roof, we had to build a three-man pyramid, which often collapsed just as the moth was about to be secured. How we laughed and panted! What honest fun it was: we were back at school again, and revelled in the free good-fellowship!

Now we were getting back to the modern world, and as we approached the Tea, the planters showed us every kindness in their delightful homes, and the days sped all too fast. On August 1, when only a few miles out from Darjeeling, we were met by General Bruce and a fleet of cars to take us in. How glad we were to see him looking as fit and being as cheery as ever, and what a hearty, boisterous welcome he gave us all! His joviality infected every one as usual, and even supported us during the baneful attentions of the inevitable Press photographer. Very tactfully the sahibs were taken back severally from here to our head-quarters at the Mount Everest Hotel, while a processional entry into Darjeeling was arranged for the native *personnel* of the Expedition. It was exactly what would most appeal to them. The procession was really an imposing affair, headed by the Police Band. All the town was on holiday, and every one was in the market-place to welcome them. We lent our servants our ponies; some of the coolies borrowed others, the remainder walked. The 'make up' of the whole thing we left entirely in the hands of the men, and as the procession passed us we noticed that some of the best fellows, the men who had gone really high, were walking almost shyly in the rear, while some of the less worthy rode almost ostentatiously in front – all the world, all alike.

Everywhere there was great excitement and enthusiasm. Her Excellency Lady Lytton made a little speech of welcome, General Bruce replied, and the procession started off again; in fact the men liked 'processing' so much that it seemed doubtful if they would ever stop. Every one was very indulgent; and I feel that anything that can be done to show these Sherpa porters that we appreciate them is not too much. They are splendid fellows, and it must always be remembered that success in reaching the summit depends almost as much on them as on the actual climbing party. Some of these men have sprung from families living at 12,000-14,000 feet, and have habitually crossed passes over 16,000 feet, and so it comes about that when the Expedition has reached 20,000 feet, these fellows are only some 6,000 feet above their normal habitat, while the European members are feeling the effect of a change in altitude of the full 20,000 feet. Thus it is that it is possible for them to carry a light load where a sahib can only manage to stumble along un-encumbered. It has been said that these men could easily reach the top if they themselves really wished to do so. I do not believe it for one moment. I think we are no less necessary to them than they are to us – they have the acclimatised bodies, but lack the right mentality; we have the will power, the necessary spirit, but are woefully deficient in acclimatisation. It is just one example of the splendid team work that is so noticeable a feature of these Everest Expeditions: we are mutually dependent, and one day we shall help each other to the top. I believe that some of the local Tibetans have an even better natural equipment than our Sherpa men, and it might well be worth making a strenuous effort to get a few of them to go high. I believe they did not go above the Base Camp in 1922; last year they went to Camp II, but would not go beyond it, because that involved crossing the open glacier with its crevasses, in each of which an evil spirit was supposed to lurk. Nothing we could do or offer would induce them to go on, though physically they were magnificently fit. But surely some way can be devised by the next expedition of laying the evil spirits for them. Great lamas can give charms potent against any ill – they gave the Tibetan soldiers charms infallible against the English bullets during the 1903 campaign, and when the men complained that their comrades were shot down without regard to talisman, the lamas decided that the artful English must have changed the nature of the bullets for which the charms were valid, and it was therefore necessary for them to prescribe new ones. Such was the faith of these simple people that this explanation did duty again and again, and so the sad game went on. Now great lamas are not wholly without regard to mundane things, and might be willing to help a future expedition, and it seems to me that a similar charm, with equal faith, might work much better against the glacier devils than did the others against the rifle bullets. If these genii of the ice were once laid, the only difficulty of this kind remaining would be to appease the anger of the goddess on the mountain top. She unfortunately resents all intrusion upon her snowy sanctuary. It will be remembered how the four porters marooned on top of the North Col lay listening to the bark, bark, barking of the watchdogs which guard her throne. When we visited the Rongbuk Monastery on the way up to the Base Camp we saw a new mural painting that had been executed since the 1922 Expedition. It was, in a way, commemorative of that event: it was designed to record the defeat of the party in their endeavour to reach the summit, and in particular to call attention to the tragic accident when seven coolies were swept to their death by an avalanche. In the painting, there was the party being pitchforked down the mountain-side by hoofed devils and sent spinning into the colder hell. I like this idea of a twofold nether region. They have the ordinary variety, the place of heat and flames, almost identical with ours; but since the idea of fire is suggestive of comfort, almost of bliss to the Tibetan mind, the lamas have conjured up a second Gehenna, a place where nought but ice and snow and perishing winds prevail. The latter was destined for us.

But to return to Darjeeling before the Expedition finally breaks up. However unlooked-for it may be, some word of appreciation, of honest thanks, must be offered to the residents of this hill station for the wonderful kindness and hospitality they showed to us. For about a fortnight we were engaged in settling up accounts and in bringing the Expedition to an orderly conclusion, and throughout that time we enjoyed a constant round of entertainment. To particularise in such a matter may seem invidious, but certain memories of that time stand out so prominently as to compel some mention of them. First and foremost was the hospitality in its widest sense, so freely offered by Her Excellency Lady Lytton and by all at Government House. Nothing could have been kinder, more in sympathy with our needs – formality at a minimum; welcome at the maximum. Then there was the never-to-be-forgotten 'Planters' Dinner' on August 9 and 10! The dignity of the first part, followed without break or discord by the athletics of the second, could only co-exist with perfect fellowship. It reminded me of an adult – very adult – edition of the juvenile 'tea and games.' Yet it is said – and truly – that we take our pleasures sadly – yes, but not always! Then, too, we had the great privilege of being Honorary Members of the Planters' and Gymkhana Clubs. There were delightful, strenuous hours in the Canadian Tennis Courts, and other memorable ones, not less strenuous, when some of us, under protest, made our first essay on roller skates. There was a pleasant afternoon with Mr English at the Museum, when *Hirudo glacialis* (and other strange new beasts of very recent evolution) were first revealed to the world of science! Finally, there was the generosity of Mr Stephen, who not only housed the Expedition in his two splendid hotels in Calcutta and Darjeeling for as long as its members chose to stay, but who also invited us all to a unique luncheon-party at his country residence. Little wonder that we were loath to disband. But, as ever, the best of friends must part, and so the different members slipped away down the little mountain railway from Darjeeling to the plains, and then, by various routes, to home. The Mount Everest Expedition of 1924 was ended: ended, that is, in an active state; as a cherished memory it will remain an undying possession for each of us to the last.

# 9 FUTURE POSSIBILITIES

## BY LIEUT. COLONEL E.F. NORTON, DSO

(Reprinted from *The Alpine Journal*, May, 1925. By permission.)

Turning to the future, the difficulties which will confront another expedition may be summarised as:

(i) The Weather.

(ii) Physical Mountaineering Difficulties.

(iii) Porter Organisation.

(iv) The Physiological Problem and the Use of Oxygen.

*(i) The Weather.* – As regards the weather. I hope it may be assumed that the weather met with in May of last year was exceptional; the Darjeeling tea-planters said that for at least twenty years no such weather had been known at this season.

On the other hand, Odell has an interesting paper by a man in Calcutta who has compiled very convincing statistics to show that the weather in India runs in cycles of sixteen years, and that we are now at the bottom of a wave corresponding to a series of wet years; he claims that he foresaw that last year's Expedition was foredoomed to failure, and he says that no new expedition should be undertaken until 1929.

But it must not be forgotten that the year 1924 would have been sufficiently favourable if we could have foreseen what was coming; Camp III could have been established and stocked, but not used for sleeping, and an advance to Camp IV and onwards only undertaken with the beginning of the spell of three weeks' fine weather which begun on May 26. This would have sufficed, though it would be preferable to have more margin; the point is, can we – or can we not – reckon on three clear weeks of fine warm weather before the monsoon? I believe that normally we can.

There is one more point about the weather: it must be recognised that during any spell of fine weather it is impossible to guarantee that within three days there may not be a snowstorm or a particularly severe wind on the mountain – in this respect the Himalayas do not differ from other mountains – and so a party starting from the North Col gambles on three suitable days running. If it encounters bad weather it runs the risk, not only of temporary failure, but also that its members may have shot their bolt for the year; we are not all Odells to go repeatedly to 25,000 and 27,000 feet.

*(ii) Physical Difficulties.* – In all probability these exist only in two places – the slopes leading to the North Col and the approach to the final pyramid a little above 28,000 feet; with these two exceptions the route is all easy and safe, except perhaps after new snow.

The approach to the North Col is simply a steep glacier, and the route evidently varies from year to year; unexpected difficulties may always confront a future expedition here.

The obvious route, the zigzag trough used throughout the 1922 attempts, was avoided last year on account of the dangers of avalanche, for it was here that the whole party was swept away during the last attempt of that year, and seven porters were killed.

The alternative route adopted in 1924 avoided the dangers of the trough, but entailed some very laborious climbing and carrying.

The final steep traverse before arriving on the shelf, where Camp IV has been pitched for two years, is unavoidable, and will always be a source of possible danger.

The approach to the final pyramid appears to be the only other place entailing any danger, except perhaps when new snow is lying. Here there are two possible routes; the first, which Mallory always favoured, and which he followed in his last climb, is by the crest of the North-east Arête.

There was always the doubt that a feature in this route, which we called the second step, might cause considerable difficulty; it presents a vertical face to the south and east, but seemed surmountable, though evidently steep, to the north. Mallory and Irvine were last seen on the top of the step, and so must have climbed it; but this is not quite sufficient to guarantee this route, as they may well have fallen from it on the descent.

From the point where they were last seen to a point some 300 feet below the summit it is all steep, but almost certainly easier than the place they had just surmounted; the last 300 feet is obviously easy.

The alternative route which I favoured, and which Somervell and I followed, is roughly parallel to the crest, but 500 to 1,000 feet below it on the north face. This route becomes steep and rather dangerous, though nowhere difficult – if I may so differentiate – in, and just west of, the big couloir, which cuts off the final pyramid from the great north-east shoulder of the mountain. For a short distance, perhaps 200 feet, the going is very steep, and composed of overlying slabs approximating to the general slope of the mountain; there is always apt to be a sprinkling of snow here, which conceals the foot-holds and constitutes the principal danger of a slip, for, sheltered as it is from wind and sun, the snow is powdery (of the consistency of coarse salt) and nowhere supports the foot.

About 200 feet above the point I reached, all of which is of the steep slabby rock I have described, you emerge on to the face of the final pyramid, and, as far as we could judge from the Base Camp, there should be no further difficulty up to the summit.

Thus by either route there is some steep climbing at about 28,200 feet, steeper than anything on rock below; this factor must not be forgotten in estimating times both in ascending and descending, for over portions of it it may be necessary to move one at a time on a belayed rope.

*(iii) Porter Organisation.* – Our principle was that, in the early stages, parties of porters must always be escorted by climbers on the glacier between Camps II and III, and between Camps III and IV. When the route and the generally negligible crevasses between Camps II and III became well marked, and when the elaborate system of fixed ropes which we used below Camp IV was established, such escort could be dispensed with if necessary. On the North Arête of the mountain, between Camps IV and VI, it has always been considered justifiable to send down returning porters without escort.

Above the North Col the whole difficulty – a very real and vital one – will always be the lowered vitality at high altitudes and its effects on the *moral* of the porters; it becomes necessary to stimulate their will-power to carry out what their physical powers are certainly capable of.

*(iv) The Physiological Problem and the Use of Oxygen.* – Is it possible to climb the last 1,000 feet without oxygen?

After our experience at 27,000 feet in 1922, we were somewhat disappointed at the bad progress we made last year near 28,000 feet. It was merely a ques-tion of pace: our going-power seemed steadily to diminish, there were no other symptoms; one could sit down and smoke a pipe in comfort, and my pulse after sitting for some minutes was only some twenty above normal. The trouble was that one went so miserably slowly uphill; downhill, on easy going, one could always go all right.

As regards pace at this height, we have no satisfactory figures to guide us, for though it is true that I only mounted something under 100 feet and progressed horizontally about 200 yards in my last hour, this hour included the only comparatively difficult going we met.

I was precluded from mounting by a series of buttresses, which forced me to traverse until I reached the big couloir: I had twice to retrace my steps and select a new route, and I was bothered by the powdery snow, and some trouble with my eyesight (the beginnings of snow-blindness, which attacked me the same evening).

I was alone, unroped, and had to be exceedingly careful. Finally, I was not in a fit condition to provide a test case, as I had lost too much condition throughout the month of May, and the same applied in a greater degree to Somervell – owing to his throat trouble.

I myself believe that an average rate of 200 to 500 feet an hour could be maintained for the last 1,000 feet of Mount Everest by a fit party without oxygen.[1]

Is the oxygen apparatus, in its present form – viz. compressed gas in steel cylinders entailing a weight of twenty to thirty pounds on the climber's back – sufficiently beneficial to outweigh the time, labour, and organisation it involves? It is very hard to say; in its favour are:

(a) The experience of Finch and G. Bruce two years ago.

(b) A somewhat vague statement by porters that Mallory and Irvine were going well up to 27,000 feet (though Mallory wrote to Odell that they had used very little oxygen up to this point).

(c) A record I have discovered in the Camp diaries of a quick climb from Camp III to IV by Mallory and Irvine in which they are stated to have used oxygen.

(d) The very optimistic note from Mallory, written from Camp VI, telling Noel to be on the look-out for them with his cinema at the foot of

--------

1  The following times are the quickest recorded for a party of two or more. Some exceptionally quick times by a single climber are omitted. With one exception all are without oxygen.

| | | | UP | | DOWN | |
|---|---|---|---|---|---|---|
| | Stage | Difference in Height | Hours | Feet per Hour | Hours | Feet per Hour |
| III<br>to<br>IV | 21,200<br><br>22,700 | 1,500 feet | 3<br>with O$_2$<br>2 ⅔ | 500<br>564 | 1 ½ | 1,000 |
| IV<br>to<br>V | 22,700<br><br>25,300 | 2,600 feet | 6 | 433 | 1 ¼ | 2,000<br>(glissading) |
| V<br>to<br>VI | 25,300<br><br>26,800 | 1,500 feet | 4 ½ | 333 | 1 ¾ | 857 |
| VI<br>to | 26,800<br>28,100 | 1,300 feet | 6 ½ | 205 | about 2 ½ | about 520 |

the final pyramid at 8 a.m. This surely must indicate that they had reason to anticipate great things from the oxygen next day.

Against it are:

(a) The experience of G. Bruce and Odell, who both obtained very little – if any – benefit from it up to 23,000 feet.

(b) The subsequent experience of Odell, who used it up to 27,000 feet with similar results. He admits that he used it very economically, but states that when he turned on the full two litres it did him no more good.

(c) Mallory's and Irvine's actual appearance, at 12.50 p.m., at a point still below the foot of the final pyramid, indicating a rate of progress but little better than Somervell's and mine without oxygen.

Personally, I think that this unaccountable delay was, at least partly, due to some mechanical defect in the apparatus, which postponed their start while Irvine was putting it right, but I do not propose to touch on the mechanical question here: this must be the subject for discussion by experts.

There you have the data about the oxygen: it remains the unknown quantity – the $x$ of Mount Everest.

Other physiological problems are those of food and acclimatisation.

There is no doubt that it is exceedingly difficult to hit on the right form of food for high altitudes. It should be palatable, for men will not eat enough of anything which is not; it should be so easily digestible as not to handicap the climbers' going-power for the next three hours, during the process of digestion; yet it must be sufficiently sustaining to prevent a hollow feeling soon after it is eaten, to support life for several days of severe exertion, and to offer resistance against cold.

Of acclimatisation we have learnt a good deal this year, though we have, no doubt, much still to learn.

There appears to be a certain permanent acclimatisation which lasts over a period of at least two years, for there is small doubt that those of the party who had been there before adapted more readily than the new-comers.

The undoubted superiority of Mallory in pace and general going-power over all of us, in both 1922 and 1924, may have been partly due to his having a year's start over the rest.

I believe that everybody has a certain limit up to which he improves under favourable conditions, and that this limit varies from, say, 19,000 to 23,000 feet.

There is also no doubt that some men adapt faster than others, and that some of those who adapt slowly prove the strongest in the long run: Somervell in 1922 and Odell in 1924 are good examples of this.

For some, three weeks' acclimatisation at each advance in altitude would be desirable – were it possible.

On the other hand, during five days at Camp III, in the third week in May this year, when the weather conditions were very bad, the whole party deteriorated so rapidly that it became imperative to retreat; the general ill-effects of hardship, cold, and lack of sleep far outweighed the question of acclimatisation.

The difficulty will always be to strike a balance between these conflicting considerations.

*Solution.*

I will now give you, as briefly as I can, my own suggestions as to how the difficulties I have described may be dealt with.

*(i) The Weather.* – The Meteorological Department at Simla should be approached for any data as to:

(a) The probability of a cycle of unfavourable years in the near future; for the reasons I have already given I do not consider this so important as:

(b) Whether a spell of fine hot weather immediately preceding the monsoon is normally to be expected.

If the answer to this latter question were in the affirmative, it would be a great help to the leader of a future expedition in making up his mind when to 'drop the flag.'

With the same object in view, another possibility is the provision of a wireless receiving set to accompany the expedition, who would thus be enabled to receive messages as to the progress of the monsoon. Last year we made arrangements for such telegrams to be sent us both from Simla and Colombo, but they inevitably arrived too late: the first useful message we received met us at the Base Camp just as we had finished for the year.

Armed with this knowledge, the leader of a future expedition should be able to avoid the exhausting process of unnecessarily fighting severe weather conditions.

*(ii) Physical Difficulties.* – I would not advocate any attempt to find an alternative route to the North Col. The approach from the west via the main Rongbuk Glacier may well be as liable to avalanche as the present route; it is more exposed to the danger of falling stones, it entails a climb of nearly 1,000 feet more, and both it and the camps below would be exposed to the full force of the west wind.

Our experience of two years tends to show that the 1922 route, what I have called the trough, may probably be used with safety until the advent of the true monsoon and the soft south-east wind, for even after a new fall of snow the hot sun and cold nights, which are characteristic of the pre-monsoon north-westerly weather, soon render it safe. An alternative route on the same side, like the one used last year, should, if possible, be worked out to provide a bolt-hole if necessary.

The final traverse should never be tackled from below immediately after a fresh fall of snow; if it becomes necessary to descend by it, a judicious use of ropes, fixed and otherwise, one man only moving at a time, should make it reasonably safe.

As regards the route to be followed for the last 1,000 feet, I think that the experienced climbers who will lead future attempts must form their own conclusions from their reconnaissance of the ground and the data of last year's experiences.

For myself I still incline to the lower route.

*(iii) Porter Organisation.* – There is only one way of overcoming the difficulty I have mentioned – that of inducing porters to go to somewhere near their physical limit on their highest day – and this is for a large proportion of the climbers to acquire such influence over the porters that the latter will follow them.

To do this the first essential is that they must learn at least something of their language. I have learnt something of four Oriental languages, and I speak from experience when I say that, given the necessary determination and goodwill, much can be done between leaving England and arriving at Rongbuk; but I would go farther, and insist that, with the aid of the London School of Oriental Languages, of retired officers of Gurkha regiments, or some such means, members of a future expedition should, before sailing from England, acquire a foundation on which to build rapidly when once they get among the hill folk.

In addition, every climber should know every porter by name – here again I speak with certainty when I say that it is perfectly easy to know fifty or sixty men by name in a week or two; and more, not only must he know the men, the men must know and trust him.

Without these fundamentals the small amount of leadership required is impossible; surely I do not ask too much when the success or failure of the whole expedition may – nay, must – depend on this one link in the chain.

*(iv) The Physiological Problem and Oxygen.* – As regards the use of oxygen, the balance of probability is now that men can reach the top without; but it is by no means certain. I do not think it would be justifiable to send an expedition unequipped in this respect.

It must be for the experts – using Odell's invaluable experience – to rectify as far as possible the faults of last year's apparatus. I believe there is little – if any – hope of materially lightening it.

I would suggest that a future expedition would do well to confine themselves to using it only above 27,000 feet, for the acclimatisation acquired in climbing to that height without oxygen is the surest safeguard against serious effects of a breakdown of the apparatus high up.

I would deprecate any attempt to influence beforehand the decision of the leader of an expedition as to the extent to which oxygen is to be used; supply the best apparatus that can be made, and leave the party a free hand whether – or when – it is to be used.

Without oxygen the surmounting of the last 900 feet resolves itself into a question of 'time and space.'

With or without, I now consider it essential to sleep two nights – and only two – above 23,000 feet; to sleep three nights above this height would entail impossibly big intermediate camps.

I am quite satisfied that Camps V and VI can be pitched 250 and 500 feet higher, respectively; we have always aimed at putting Camp VI just under the north-east shoulder, at about 27,200 feet, but if a suitable site can be found nearer the summit at this level it would be much better.

This would leave 1,800 feet for the last day against, say, 1,300 covered by the non-oxygen party this year. This party started at 6.40 a.m., having been delayed an hour by an accident to a thermos flask. They turned back at 1 p.m. and reached Camp IV at 9.30 p.m.

I should say here that an early start in the Alpine sense seems impossible on Mount Everest; I can only suppose that this is due to the lowered vitality of the early hours. But assume a start at 5.30 a.m. and a return to Camp V only; we save at least three hours in which to cover the remaining 500 feet – up and down. This runs it very fine indeed, but I am taking the rate of progress of this year's party, and I think the pace ascending – but particularly descending – should be considerably faster with a fitter party.

The position of Camp VI will be the deciding factor. The nearer it is to the summit the greater the chance of success – obviously – but also the greater the risk that a party, with the tempting goal so close, will postpone their return until too late to reach safety. Leaders of future climbing parties should keep a clear sense of their responsibility in this respect.

As regards the food question, I can only suggest that some keen biologist might be asked to tackle the matter scientifically – it is worth all possible investigation – but I am not hopeful of improving very much on what we had last year.

Finally, as regards acclimatisation and the conservation of energy, I would take a leaf from Longstaff's book and say, *if conditions are bad*: 'Go as often as possible to 20,000 feet – even to 23,000 feet – but do not stay there.'

Sleep no higher than you can sleep well, than the highest point where you can to some extent enjoy your food, but spend as long as possible at this height.

In any case, I would not advocate going higher than 23,000 feet, until it is necessary, for above that point most people lose more in general condition than they gain in red corpuscles.

It must be the aim of a future expedition to make Camp III almost as comfortable as the Base Camp was this year; it is an impossible ideal, but we can get very much nearer it than we ever have before.

I have alluded to what Longstaff said about acclimatisation; I should like to pay a tribute to his remarkable insight into the whole problem under discussion. In many other respects his prognostications, made years before the 1921 Expedition first reconnoitred the mountain, have been proved accurate: the height of the snow-line on the northern side of the range, the height of the Base Camp, the organisation and positions of intermediate camps, the composition of the climbing party and the best type of porter, the minimum rate of progress necessary to ensure success – in all these matters he has been a true prophet, and I hope that a future expedition will not fail to benefit by the advice and help which he is always willing to give.

# PART 2
# MALLORY'S LETTERS

NOTE: THESE LETTER DIARIES WERE WRITTEN TO
MRS MALLORY DURING THE PROGRESS OF THE EXPEDITION
AND HAVE KINDLY BEEN PLACED BY HER AT THE DISPOSAL
OF THE MOUNT EVEREST COMMITTEE.

# LETTERS TO HIS WIFE

## BY GEORGE LEIGH MALLORY

1

HOTEL MOUNT EVEREST. DARJEELING.
MARCH 25. 1924.

These have been full days since we came up here on Friday, and to-morrow, Wednesday, early we start for Kalimpong – so that our stay has been short enough, and much taken up with packing and arrangements of one sort and another. Norton has got the whole organisation under his hand, and we shall economise much time and money by dumping some of our boxes *en route*; all the stores for the high camps have practically been settled already. The party looks very fit altogether. We had a very hot journey through India. The hot weather apparently came with a rush this year just before we landed, and the temperature must have been up to 100° a good part of the time we were in the train, as it was reported to be 99° in Calcutta; it's a grimy dusty business, and I was glad to get to the end of our train journeying. I was feeling a bit short of sleep, otherwise very fit. The only doubts I have are whether the old ankle one way or another will cause me trouble. Four of us walked up to Seneschal Hill yesterday afternoon to see the magnolias – I was trying my new boots from Dewberry; they are going to be good, but my right ankle didn't feel too happy.

The magnolias were magnificent – a better show than last year – four different sorts, white and deep cerise pink and two lighter pinks between – they do look startlingly bright on a dark hillside. The country here is very dry at present and a haze of dust blown up from the plains hangs about. We haven't seen the mountains until this morning when Kanchen [Kanchenjunga] has very dimly made an appearance. Somervell and Odell, besides the General, Geoffrey Bruce, and Norton, etc., were here before us; it was very nice to see Somervell again, and Odell is one of the best. Really, it is an amazingly nice party altogether; one of the best is Hingston, our MO, an Irishman, a quiet little man and a very keen naturalist. The only one I don't yet know is Shebbeare, who belongs to the Forestry Department and is said to be a particularly nice man; he knows all about trees and shrubs, which is a very good thing, but nothing about flowers – so that we shall once more be without a real botanist.

To-morrow we go to Kalimpong all together, as before, and then separate in two parties; I shall be with the second, with Norton, Hingston, Irvine and Shebbeare, I believe. Noel's movements are independent.

The English mail should have come in yesterday, but the ship was twelve hours late and we shan't get it until to-day and consequently will have precious little time for answering.

2
RONGLI CHU.
MARCH 29, 1924.

This is the great day of valley-ease and warmth and languor and the delights of the lotus-eater, and I must write to you here with my feet in the splashing stream and heaven all about me as I look up. We started from Pedong this morning – sloped easily down the 2,000 feet to the stream where I bathed last time while Noel immortalised the event; there Irvine, Odell and I bathed, properly this time, even finding a pool to dive into, and at length. Thence on ponies up to Rheenok – you should be able to follow all this on one of my old maps of Sikkim – where I made some attempts at photographing the remarkable houses, and thence, not up over the pass by Ari to get here by the shortest way, but contouring the hill until we could drop into this valley six miles below the bungalow. It is a very lovely valley, quite one of the best parts of Sikkim, and we had a good walk up, quite energetically carrying heavyish rucksacks. I was wearing my new boots for the first time for a whole march and found them pretty comfortable, my ankle and hip and all going quite well too, so that I quite expect by the time we reach Phari I shall have ceased to think about them. The weather is perfectly fine, but very hazy, owing to the great number of fires in the valleys. It is the custom of the country to burn a good deal of undergrowth and dead leaves in the forests in order to get better new grass in the spring – but I can't remember anything like so much haze as this last year. Consequently we have had nothing at all of a view all the way from Darjeeling, and the country is looking more dry and dead than last year; it has, in fact, been very dry. I hear there has been exceptionally little snow in Tibet and that the plains are already beginning to look green – but this is hardly credible. Incidentally, there are signs of a change of weather this afternoon – but then we had a thunderstorm in Kalimpong which made absolutely no difference!

It has, apart from views, been a pleasant journey so far. We started in motors for six miles from Darjeeling, and half-way down the hill Norton, Hingston, Somervell and self had breakfast with a tea-planter called Lister – it is a famous tea-garden, I believe, and he certainly gave us to drink Orange Pekoe of the most delicious flavour (a series of violent splashes at this point). After that pleasant interval we took all the short cuts, hurrying down to Tista Bridge, where we arrived dripping and found our ponies; my pony which is to carry me to Phari is quite a good beast – the best I have had at this stage, and my saddle is comfortable, and I feel very well off altogether; we went straight up the hill on our ponies and were in Kalimpong at 1.30 for tiffin.

At Kalimpong next day last time's performances were repeated – a 'tamasha' for boy scouts and girl guides and a wonderful little ceremony in the big schoolroom with all of us on the platform singing the metrical version of Psalm CXXI to the tune of the Old Hundredth, and prayers and speechmaking divinely mixed. Old Dr Graham is really a wonder, and if one were going to be a missionary one couldn't do better. He has between 600 and 700 children under his charge, and does them well all round. When the old Scot is short of money he goes down to Calcutta and collects a few lakhs of rupees from the big business-men, who all know and believe in him, and so his institutions flourish.

I think I told you the name of the second party, but omitted Odell. Shebbeare the forest officer is an excellent fellow. We went a little walk into the forest above Pedong last evening and we saw quite close a very fine jungle cat, about as high as Raven, but with the proportions of Agapanthus, or rather perhaps of the other Westbrook cat, which it also resembled in colour. Shebbeare didn't get a very good view of it and couldn't tell me what it was; but it is extraordinary how it makes the whole forest seem alive to see a beast like that. We couldn't be a nicer party – at least I hope the others would say the same; we go along our untroubled way in the happiest fashion.

Since I began writing the air has become unbearably stuffy and a thunderstorm is brewing. The one crab about this place is that there is no water supply which is at all likely to be unpolluted – and so one drinks tea, but our tiffin-tea has left me very thirsty and I long for a long lemon squash or whisky-and-soda. You see how completely a physical animal one has become.

I'm spending a certain amount of time and effort as we come along learning Hindustani; it is very unsatisfactory because the coolies themselves are so bad at it, but I do find already that I get on with them more easily. We shall be very short of men who can speak to porters higher up.

I'm really enjoying myself now with a good holiday feeling. To-morrow's march is all up hill to Sedongchen, and the next, still up to Gnatong (12,500), is the great rhododendron march, but only the very lowest will be in flower. I have in mind another little detour, by way of variety, from Kapup, diverging to the Natu La instead of by the Jelap La as before.


3
YATUNG.
APRIL 2, 1924.

It seems I ought to get off a letter to you to-morrow morning in order to be certain of catching the mail. I don't know that I have a very great deal to tell you.

All goes well with me. The march from Sedongchen to Gnatong was glorious, Kanchenjunga and his neighbours appearing magnificently; I haven't seen any distant mountain view before from this part and we counted ourselves very lucky. Gnatong (12,500 feet) was not so cold this time, though the verandah was bunged up with snow, and from there we made two easy stages here, stopping the night in a little rest-house an hour down this side of the Jelap La. Norton and I walked up to the pass (14,500 feet) together and were pleased to think that we felt fitter than last year. I certainly am feeling very fit now. I sleep long and well and can walk as fast as anyone. We have had a few good signs of spring – on the Sikkim side a most lovely little primula flourishing from 9,000 to 11,000 feet, with the habit of our English primrose, only somewhat smaller and neater, and of a delicious crimson colour; and *Rhododendron falconeri*, the big bright red fellow, was flowering freely a bit lower. On this side we have another primula, *denticulata*, paler in colour and of the polyanthus type, very freely scattered over the meadows; and we have our old friend Daphne, I know not what species. The conifers too in this valley are all showing green.

It has been a wonderfully pleasant journey so far, with bright sun and pleasant conditions altogether. And it has been a very jolly company. We found the first contingent here no less happy than ourselves. The General has not been quite well and has stayed here to-day while Norton takes on the first party. The slack day has been very pleasant. I have had a long ramble with Irvine.

4

ONE MARCH FROM PHARI.
APRIL 7. 1924.

I stupidly didn't write from Phari – not realising that I should probably have no chance of sending a letter back on the way to Kampa. But it happens there may be a chance to-morrow, so I will write a few lines in bed to-night. It isn't easy to write because the site of my tent dips slightly towards the head of my bed and no amount of propping seems quite to overcome the difficulty. If I had my bed the other way round my head would be at the mouth of the tent and this would create a difficulty about light; besides, it is snowing slightly and may snow more, and though I don't mind having my feet snowed upon for the sake of fresh air, I am unwilling to have my head snowed upon during the night. As it is my tent is a wonderfully comfortable spot. The little table made for me by our friend in Maid's Causeway is at my bedside and on it my reading-lamp: I expect I shan't always be able to have oil for this, but so long as I can I shall burn it. Did I tell you about the Whymper tents? We each have one to himself: they have two poles at each end, a much more convenient plan than the other with single poles. A ground-sheet is sewn into the sides so that draught and dust are practically excluded if one pitches in the right direction; and, a great blessing, the tent has plenty of pockets. Moreover, it is by no means small – seven feet square or very near it. The mess-tent also is a great improvement on last year's: there is ample head room, and the mess-servants can pass round without hitting one on the head with the dishes; the tables are wooden (three-ply wood varnished), and it is supposed that messes will be wiped off without difficulty; and they fit conveniently round the poles. The lamps, which burn paraffin vapour (assisted by some clockwork arrangement inside), are also good and an enormous improvement on the dim hurricane lamps used last time. In short, a certain amount of care and forethought has made us much more comfortable without spending a great deal of money.

I must tell you how wonderfully fit I have been these last days, much better at this stage I'm sure than either in '21 or '22. I feel full of energy and strength and walk up hill here already almost as in the Alps; I sleep long and well; my digestion is good, and in short I haven't a trouble physically, unless one may count my ankle, of which I'm often conscious, but the leg seems perfectly strong and I'm sure it won't let me down.

The General is not coming with us to Kampa Dzong (last year's route), but in six days instead of four, by another way which will allow him to camp lower. It is difficult to know how much to make of his trouble; I think it is ten to one he will be all right.

I can't write much more in this position and my arms are getting cold. I was going to tell you something about our plans, but I will leave that until next letter. Tibet is much warmer this year, though this afternoon was pretty cold.

5

KAMPA DZONG,

APRIL 12, 1924.

As I sit in my tent writing I have at my side a pot of grease into which I occasionally dip my finger and then rub a little on to the sorer parts of my face. The wind and sun between them have fairly caught us all these last three days. Norton says that he was accused by his people after the last Expedition of having acquired a permanent dint in his nose, and he is determined to prevent the same thing happening again – but how to do it? Personally I limit my desire in that direction to keeping my nose the same size as usual; I don't like to feel it swollen with sunburn. Somervell, who started with a complexion tanned by Indian suns, is now exactly the colour of a chestnut, and, as he greases freely, no less shiny. Beetham so far has the best beard, but then he had a start as he didn't shave after Kalimpong, and I'm inclined to back Geoffrey Bruce against him in the long run, as his will be blacker. The face with greatest number of flaky excrescences and crevasses is undoubtedly that of Hazard, and the underlying colour in his case is vermilion.

In my last letter I told you how well I was. But I have not been altogether well since then – something wrong with my tummy – a slight colitis or something of the kind. Consequently I have felt very feeble, and as I am strictly dieted have little to sustain me beyond biscuits and jam. We shall have two clear days here and I shall have time to get better, and in fact I am already much better and haven't the least doubt I shall be perfectly strong again when we are on the move once more.

Though we have almost exactly followed our tracks of 1922 from Phari to Kampa, it has been a very different journey – not only different companions and incidents, but a rather different Tibet. The second march from Phari landed us half a mile beyond the 'Blizzard Camp' of '22; we had no blizzard this time, but neither had we the bright high lights of Tibet. Chomulhari, a mountain which impresses one more each time one sees it, was veiled at first in thin grey mist, and then apparently caught it properly from the north; we were continually threatened at the other side of the great Tuna Plain and had a nasty wind in our faces, but escaped worse. I can't tell you how much I am interested by the weather – it's so difficult to make out what causes it, or what the signs may mean, or how it is to be compared with what we experienced in '21 and '22. This day I'm talking of was more like a day during the monsoon; in the evening smoky grey clouds were clinging to the hill-sides as though the air were laden with moisture; and yet all the weather reports from India have shown a deficiency of moisture in Bengal. One of the novelties this year is our mess-tent, Norton's special child. It goes on in advance on a mule so as to be ready for us when we arrive – at least that is the idea; on the night I'm speaking of some of us were the first to arrive in camp and set to work pitching our ample green marquee. The first procedure is to lay down a string in the chosen spot marking the perimeter of the pegs; a place is marked on this string against which each peg has to be driven in – driving pegs into stony ground at these altitudes makes one puff; the floor, a large sheet of green canvas, is placed in the correct position with the line of pegs and upon this the tent is hoisted. I must say it is a great success. It has perpendicular sides about four feet high below the slant of the roof and consequently there is ample headroom. The floor dimensions I should guess at eighteen feet by nine feet. The mess waiters have plenty of room to pass behind us. The tables, which are none of your gim-crack canvas-topped X pattern or other, but pukka wooden tables with three-ply wooden tops and screw-in legs, are two feet six inches square, made to fold into half that size, and are arranged in series down the middle of the tent – and then, cunningest device of all, there is a piece to go round the pole in the centre and fitting on to two half-tables, so that no gap is left. We have no tablecloths, as it was thought that our tables duly wiped would prove a cleaner way.

On the night of the second march from Phari (i.e. April 8), having pitched our tent, we lay about in it waiting the arrival of (1) the cooks, (2) the yaks. The former, whose business it is to go on ahead and have a meal ready if possible, or as soon as may be, had lost themselves on this occasion. The yaks are in very poor condition and go even slower than I remember; the men with them (about 300 beasts) were too few, so that loading up was very slow (two to three hours) in the morning, and one could hardly expect the bulk of the animals at the end of a long march before nightfall. So there we sat, or rather lay, out of the wind in our green tent, chatting

– chaffing, until gradually one by one nearly every one had a snooze; and as they lay there snoozing with faces rendered ghastly by the green light they looked like a collection of corpses.

The night of the 8th was decidedly chilly – the wind got up from an unexpected quarter and blew violently into our tents; the minimum temperature was 4°. I should have told you, however, that before we turned in we were cheered by a clear view of Chomulhari. The point of Chomulhari is the way it dominates the plain. The view of it from Do-chen reproduced in *The Reconnaissance* gives you some idea of what I mean; but coming across this way to Kampa Dzong we don't go so far north, and the farther you go from the mountain the more its great wall of rock presents itself as the barrier of the world in which you are. Good-bye to Chomulhari – I should like to have a whack at him one of these days.

The march of the 9th corresponded with that of 1922, except that we stopped about four miles short of our last time's camp, but it was a bitter journey; the wind blew in our faces all day, often very strongly and terribly cold, and the sky was white or overcast and the sun had no warmth. And I had a bad tummy; I walked almost the whole way to keep warm, and it was very tiring work under those conditions. We camped in a good spot looking up nullah to Pau Hunri. The wind died down in the evening; the stars were bright, and the temperature fell to two degrees below zero. Beetham was up fifteen times in the night.

The 10th was supposed to be a short march and a comparatively short day. The yakmen had had enough of it on the previous day, and consequently we made a very late start, 10.45 I think. It was supposed that if we didn't stop in last time's camp, four to five miles farther on, we should be able to stop three miles farther on again. However, no water was met with for another ten miles. We went on and on over the wide plain sloping upwards; in the distance at last we saw a little cloud of smoke and a little later some flash of bright green near it – the smoke was from our cook's fire and the green spot was our mess-tent, which we reached towards sundown; and then turning to look back towards the east I saw the black battalions of yaks still a long way off, and beyond them in the distance once more across the plain, nearly forty miles away, the great wall of Chomulhari, appearing as though the spurs of Pau Hunri, which we had crossed with so much labour, had no existence. A beautiful camp this one with a velvet-sided hill to the south of us, and to the north a long line of hills near at hand, while the snowy side of Chomiomo appeared through a gap; and a good night, not so cold.

On the 11th to Kampa; a pleasant and easy march with much looking at snow-mountains, Chomiomo and Kanchenjunga principally. Everest was not clear as we came down to Kampa, though we could make out where it was.

*April 14.* Yesterday we had the news that the General is not coming on. The possibility had been in the back of our minds since Yatung. We are all very sorry for him. We've lost a force, and we shall miss him in the mess.

Meanwhile Norton takes command. He has appointed me second-in-command in his place and also leader of the climbers altogether. I'm bound to say I feel some little satisfaction in the latter position.

I've been very busy the last two days formulating a plan of attack to be discussed as a commentary on Norton's plan, and we have just been having a general powwow about the two schemes. I don't know whether I told you anything about this before. Roughly Norton proposes (a) two without oxygen establish Camp V at 26,500 and sleep there. Next day they go on and get as near as possible to the summit, partly by way of reconnaissance, partly by way of taking the chance if it exists of getting to the top.

(b) The day they go on a party of three with oxygen come up to V and are there to receive the first two, and themselves go on next day.

The valuable points in this scheme are: (1) that the oxygen party should not this way be let down by their load failing to arrive at V; (2) that one attempt supports the other. The weakness, I think fatal weakness, is that you spend two men making an attempt without the best chances of success, the best chance gasless being with two camps above Chang La; from the point of view of making the best possible gasless attempt supposing the first gas attempt fails two men have been wasted.

We had a very useful and amicable discussion of various points arising from these two plans and hope to get something settled by Tinki.

We are on the eve of resuming our march. The worst news is about Beetham, who has not yet properly recovered from dysentery and is a very weak man. It is not yet decided whether we shall send him down to Lachen to-morrow. If he comes on and gets bad and Somervell (in the absence of Hingston with Bruce) has to take him back we shall have lost two of the best and be left without a medical officer, a very serious position. Beetham is just on the turn; but even if he is going to get better up here it might pay better to send him down at once with a fair prospect of his rejoining us at the Base Camp about May 8 to 10.

This letter is full of news and very impersonal. Now about myself. I was able to feel definitely this morning that my trouble has passed. The tenderness in my gut is no longer sensitive, like an old bruise rather, and I feel strong and full of energy and myself, and I haven't the least doubt I shall remain fit: I shall take every care to do so. The warm pleasant days here have done us all good.

I'm happy and find myself harbouring thoughts of love and sympathy for my companions. With Norton, of course, I shall work in complete harmony; he is really one of the best. I read little what with Hindustani words and Sherpa names to learn, but I have occasional hours with Keats' letters or the *Spirit of Man*, which give perhaps more pleasure here than at home. I have had no mail since I last wrote. If the English mail had been sent off as soon as it reached Phari we should have received it by now; but the arrangement is for the runner to come through and return so as to fit the out mail to England (a very bad arrangement on the surface) and consequently we shan't get our letters before we get to Tinki. I've written to no one but you this time. Please do what you can – at all events write to my people.

6

TINKI DZONG.

APRIL 17. 1924.

This is only a hurried line at the end of a full day – to tell you:

(1) that my tummy is in perfect order again, and I feel as fit as possible. It was a funny go altogether and quite inexplicable. Naturally there was a small appendicitis scare as the tenderness was on the right side, but Somervell was practically sure from the start that I was free from that.

(2) Beetham came on with us. It was Somervell's decision on the very morning of leaving Kampa Dzong – that is to say Somervell had to decide that Beetham would get better; and no doubt he is right. But it is one thing to have no more dysentery and another to get really fit again after all that when living at this altitude. At present Beetham looks years older, in much the same way as Raeburn did in '21, only at a younger stage and has quite lost all kick, and there was no one more energetic earlier.

(3) I've had a brain-wave – no other word will describe the process by which I arrived at another plan for climbing the mountain:

(a) A and B with fifteen porters (about), starting from IV (North Col), establish V, building emplacements for four tents at about 25,500, and descend.

(b) C and D, gasless party, go to V with another fifteen porters, of whom seven carry loads, and descend, the other eight go up without loads, practically speaking, and sleep.

(c) C and D proceed to establish a Camp VII at 27,300 (about) with these eight porters carrying up six loads.

(d) E and F, gas party, on the same day as (c) start with ten porters (about) from IV, go without loads to V and from that point E and F, using oxygen, they take on the stores and gas previously dumped at V about 1,000 feet higher to VI at 26,500.

(e) Then the two parties start next morning and presumably meet on the summit.

You will readily perceive the chief merits of this plan; the mutual support which the two parties can give each other; the establishment of camps without waste of reserve climbers (A and B will not have done so much that they can't recover); the much better chance this way of establishing VI without collapse of porters. And then if this go fails we shall be in the best possible position to decide how the next attempt should be made; four climbers we hope will be available and the camps either way will be all ready.

This plan has such great advantages over all others that Norton has taken it up at once and this evening we had another powwow and every one has cordially approved. I'm much pleased about this, as you may imagine – if only for this it seems worth while to have come. It is impossible yet to say who the parties will be. Norton and I have talked about it; he thinks Somervell and I should lead each one of these two parties; he puts himself in my hands as to whether he should be one of them – isn't that generous? We shall have to judge as best we can of people's fitness when we reach the Base Camp. Either Odell or Irvine must be of the gas party.

We have stayed one day here for transport, as against three last year when Longstaff was ill; and we hope only to stay one day at Shekar, and so we should be two or three days up at the Base Camp.

No mail yet – one should have arrived to-day. I didn't tell you that I bought a pony at Kampa Dzong, a very good animal, though too thin.

7
CHIBLUNG.
APRIL 19, 1924.

I don't know whether you will easily find this place on the map. We have come north from Tinki, avoiding unpleasant customers at Chushar and Gyanka Nampa, and this valley is divided from that in which Rong Kong lies by a low range of hills. We are encamped just at the corner of the Chiblung Chu; Sanghar Ri and the ridge where Somervell and I climbed in 1922 is our view to the west.

To-day, at last, an English mail has reached us.

Karma Paul, who brought our mail, also brought news of the General, whom he left in Phari; he must be pretty ill still as he was unable to walk and was to be carried down to Chumbi; Hingston will accompany him to Gang-tok and should rejoin us at the Base Camp about the middle of May. Meanwhile Beetham gets on slowly and can't be said to have got rid of dys-entery yet, let alone picking up after it – however, I think he's on the mend.

I heard from Mary to-day with news of the weather in Colombo, and it looks as if the earliest breath of the monsoon is a fortnight early! But that doesn't necessarily mean much. The bad sign is the weather here, which is distinctly more unsettled than in '22, and the last two nights have been unhealthily warm. To-day we have been in a regular storm area, though no rain or snow has actually fallen here.

*April 24, at Shekar Dzong.*

I've left it rather late to go on with this letter. That is partly because one way or another I have been spending a good many spare moments on the elaboration of our plans. The difficult work of allotting tasks to men has now been done – Norton and I consulted and he made a general announcement after dinner two days ago. The question as to which of the first two parties should be led by Somervell and which by me was decided on two grounds: (1) On the assumption that the oxygen party would be less exhausted and be in the position of helping the other, it seemed best that I should use oxygen and be responsible for the descent. (2) It seemed more likely on his last year's performance that Somervell would recover after a gasless attempt to be useful again later. It was obvious that either Irvine or Odell should come with me in the first gas party. Odell is in charge of the gas, but Irvine has done the principal engineering work on the apparatus – what was provided was full of leaks and faults and he has practically invented a new instrument, using up only a few of the old parts and cutting out much that was use-less and likely to cause trouble; so Irvine will come with me. He will be an extraordinarily stout companion, very capable with the gas and with cooking apparatus.

Norton, if he is fit enough, will go with Somervell, or, if he seems clearly a better goer at the moment, Hazard. Beetham is counted out for the moment, though he's getting fitter. Odell and Geoffrey Bruce will have the important task of fixing Camp V at 25,500.

The whole difficulty of fitting people in so that they take a part in the assault according to their desire or ambition is so great that I can't feel dis-tressed about the part that falls to me. The gasless party has the better adven-ture, and as it has always been my pet plan to climb the mountain gasless with two camps above the Chang La it is naturally a bit disappointing that I shall be with the other party. Still, the conquest of the mountain is the great thing, and the whole plan is mine and my part will be a sufficiently interesting one and will give me, perhaps, the best chance of all of getting to the top. It is almost unthinkable with this plan that *I* shan't get to the top; I can't see myself coming down defeated. And I have very good hopes that the gasless party will get up; I want all four of us to get there, and I believe it can be done. We shall be starting by moonlight if the morning is calm and should have the mountain climbed if we're lucky before the wind is dangerous.

This evening four of us have been testing the oxygen apparatus, and com-paring the new arrangements with the old. Irvine has managed to save weight, four or five pounds, besides making a much more certain as well as more convenient instrument. I was glad to find I could easily carry it up the hill even without using the gas, and better, of course, with it. On steep ground where one has to climb more or less the load is a great handicap, and at this elevation a man is better without it. The weight is about thirty pounds, or rather less. There is nothing in front of one's body to hinder climbing, and the general impression I have is that it is a perfectly manageable load. My plan will be to carry as little as possible, go fast and rush the summit. Finch and Bruce tried carrying too many cylinders.

I'm still very fit and happy. Tibet is giving us many beautiful moments. With these abnormal weather conditions it is much warmer than in 1922 and the whole journey is more comfortable. It is nice having one's own pony – mine is a nice beast to ride, but he's not in good condition, and to-day has had a nasty attack of colic; however, he'll have a long holiday to come soon and I hope he'll fatten up and arrive fit and well in Darjeeling, where I shall sell him.

Only four marches, starting to-morrow morning, to the Rongbuk Monastery! We're getting very near now. On May 3 four of us will leave the Base Camp and begin the upward trek, and on May 17, or thereabouts, we should reach the summit. I'm eager for the great events to begin.

Now I must say good night to you and turn in to my cosy sleeping-bag, where I shall have a clean nose sheet to-night, one of the two you made to fix with patent fasteners. Considering how much grease my face requires and gets, that device has been very useful.

The telegram announcing our success, if we succeed, will precede this letter, I suppose: but it will mention no names. How you will hope that I was one of the conquerors! And I don't think you will be disappointed.

8

RONGBUK BASE CAMP.

APRIL 30. 1924.

We've had unexpected notice of a home-bound mail to-morrow and I've no letter ready. We arrived here only yesterday, and I have been very busy ever since, the reason for this is in part that we have arranged for our army of Tibetan coolies to carry our loads up the glacier to No. II Camp; 150 have actually gone up to-day; consequently we have had a great rush getting our loads ready to go up. My special concern has been with the high-climbing stores and provisions for high camps. Yesterday morning as the animals arrived here I got hold of the boxes I wanted – most of which I knew by sight – from among the feet of the donkeys and yaks and had them carried to a place apart. So I was able to get ready thirty loads, apart from food stores, yesterday afternoon. Later Norton and I had a long powwow about the whole of our plan as affects the porters. It is a very complicated business to arrange the carrying to the high camps while considering what the porters have been doing and where, during the previous ten days, so as to have sufficient regard to their acclimatisation and fitness. Further, one has to consider the fitting up of Camp III, which will still be going on after we have begun the carrying to IV; the accommodation at the various camps; and, finally, the escorting of porters from III upwards. However, I have made a plan for the porters which fits in with that previously made for climbers, and though a plan of this kind must necessarily be complicated it allows for a certain margin, and even a bad day or two won't upset our apple-cart.

Irvine and I with Beetham and Hazard start from here on May 3, and after resting a day at Camp III the last two will establish Camp IV while Irvine and I have a canter up to about 23,000, up the east ridge of Changtse, partly to get a better look at camping-sites on the mountain and partly to have a trial run and give me some idea of what to expect from Irvine. Beetham and Hazard, two days later, will escort the first lot of loads to IV; Odell and Geoffrey Bruce the second, establishing Camp V on the following day; Norton and Somervell, and lastly Irvine and self follow; Irvine and I will get two or three days down at Camp I meanwhile.

The Rongbuk Valley greeted us with most unpleasant weather. The day before yesterday and the following night, when we were encamped outside the Rongbuk Monastery, a bitterly cold wind blew, the sky was cloudy, and finally we woke to find a snowstorm going on. Yesterday was worse, with light snow falling most of the day. However, to-day has been sunny after a windy night and the conditions on Everest have gradually improved until we were saying to-night that it would have been a pleasant evening for the mountain. It is curious that though quite a considerable amount of snow has fallen during these last few days and the lower slopes are well covered, the upper parts of Everest appear scarcely affected – that is a phenomenon we observed often enough in 1922, and notably on the day when we made the first attempt.

I shall be busy with details of personal equipment amongst other things these next two days. But I also hope there'll be a mail from you and time to send letters and think of you at home, and perhaps write you another letter, though the Lord knows when the next mail will go away from here.

We continue to be a very pleasant party – Beetham has had a truly marvellous recovery, but I can't quite believe in his being really strong yet, though he makes a parade of energy and cheerfulness, and I'm a little doubtful about his being one of the first starters.

Sorry to write so poor and hurried a letter. I'm very fit – perhaps not just so absolutely a strong goer as in '21, but good enough, I believe – and anyway I can think of no one in this crowd stronger, and we're a much more even crowd than in '22, a really strong lot, Norton and I are agreed. It would be difficult to say of any one of the eight that he is likely to go farther or less far than the rest. I'm glad the first blow lies with me. We're not going to be easily stopped with an organisation behind us this time.

9

MAY 11, 1924.

Now I must give you a brief record of the days that have passed since leaving the Base Camp. It has been a very trying time, with everything against us. The porters have seemed from the first short of acclimatisation and up against it.

*May 3.* Irvine, Odell, Hazard and self to Camp I. Half the porters lagged badly. Having added a good deal of stuff on their own account to what we had given them to carry they had big loads.

*May 4.* I decided to leave five loads not urgently required at Camp I and have five men to carry all the porters' blankets, etc. The result was good and the men must have gone well. Irvine and I had gone ahead and reached Camp II at about 12.30; we had hardly finished a leisurely tiffin when the first porters arrived. Camp II looked extraordinarily uninviting, although already inhabited by an NCO and two others in charge of the stores (150 loads or so) which had already been carried up by Tibetans. A low irregular wall surrounded a rough compound, which I was informed was the place for the Sahibs' tents, and another already covered by the fly of a Whymper tent was the home of an NCO. The Sahibs' compound was soon put sufficiently in order; two Whymper tents were pitched there for the four of us, while a wonderful brown tent of Noel's was pitched for him. No tents were provided here for porters: the intention was to build comfortable huts or 'sangars,' as we call them, using the Whymper flys for roofs, but no sangars had yet been built, and accommodation for twenty-three men is not so easily provided in this way. However, I soon saw that the ground would allow us to economise walls, and Irvine and I with three or four men began building an oblong sangar, the breadth only about seven feet; other men joined in after resting. It is an extraordinary thing to watch the conversion of men from listlessness to some spirit of enterprise; a very little thing will turn the scale: on this occasion the moving of a huge stone to form one corner started the men's interest, and later we sang! And so these rather tired children were persuaded to do something for their comfort; without persuasion they would have done nothing to make life tolerable. Towards 3 p.m. Odell and I (Irvine seemed tired after prodigious building efforts) went to reconnoitre next day's march over the glacier. We began by going along the stones of the true left bank, the way of 1922, but the going was very bad, much more broken than before. To our left on the glacier we could see the stones of a

PLATES 35 (↖) AND 36 (↗)
Mallory (left) and Irvine, sketched by Norton, probably early in the expedition.

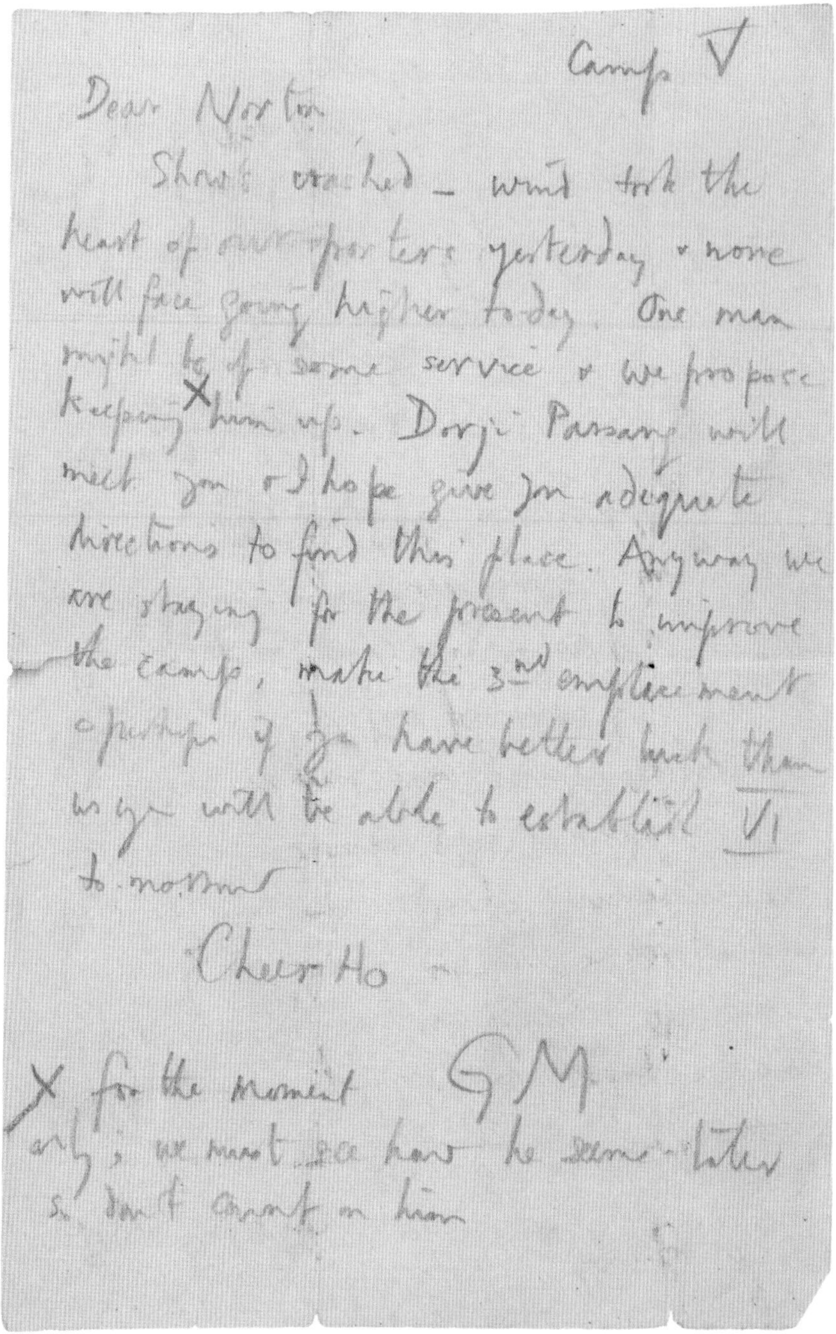
Camp V

Dear Norton

Show's cracked – wind took the heart of our porters yesterday & none will face going higher to-day. One man might be of some service & we propose keeping X him up. Dorji Passang will meet you & I hope give you adequate directions to find this place. Anyway we are staying for the present to improve the camp, make the 3rd emplacement & perhaps if you have better luck than us you will be able to establish VI tomorrow

Cheer Ho

GM

X for the moment only; we must see how he seems later so don't count on him

PLATE 37
Mallory's last note to Norton, sent down from Camp V on the morning of 2 June 1924, announcing the abandonment of his first summit attempt with Geoff Bruce. *See page 83.*

PLATE 38
The famous last photograph of Mallory and Irvine, taken by Odell as they were about to leave Camp IV on the morning of 6 June 1924 for their summit attempt. In one of the tents in the background Norton was lying incapacitated with snow-blindness. *See page 98.*

to IV

No sign of others — nor any signal from IV with
whom we had arranged signal to indicate success or
failure of climbers

9⁶/₂₄ No III

Rough cold day — very stormy high wind on mounts
mostly from N. but conflicting with other currents from E.
Spent whole day in camp with people watching
into No IV + V Camps &c all day.
Anxiety momentarily increased.
By 11.0 decided disaster probable — sent letter of
instructions to Odell + Hazard
(i) Reconnoitre to VI if could do it within 24 hours
+ if they considered it possible climbers could be there unseen
(ii) Clear Camp IV by 4 pm Tomorrow or earlier if dangerous
snow begins
(iii) Principle to risk no more lives in trying to retrieve
the inevitable
(iv) Within these limits act on discretion

PLATES 39–40
'Of all the truly miserable days I have spent at [Camp] III this [is] by far the worst.'
Norton recorded in his diary the anxious wait for news of Mallory and Irvine on 9 June 1924,
and the decisions he took when it seemed inevitable that disaster had overtaken them. *See page 110.*

Soon after this letter left saw what we took to be Odell + 2 porters leave it, apparently for V tho' could not spot them arriving there.

Shebbeare + some 30 porters arrived from III at 11 am to evacuate Camp, but could do little under existing circs so sent them back with 4 or 5 loads at 2.30 pm to return on 11th.

Of all the truly miserable days I have spent at III this by far the worst — By now it appears almost inevitable that disaster has overtaken poor gallant Mallory + Irvine — 10 to 1 they have 'fallen off' high up.

6 pm my messengers to IV returned

Hazard has "sent Odell" (God knows why he didn't go himself) to V — one porter to go on to VI if possible tonight — Odell not to go beyond VI

Mallory + Irvine were last seen by Odell from VI (12.50 pm on 8th) 'going strong' about the final step before the pyramid — This appears to confirm my fears as above

# MT. EVEREST TRAGEDY.

## TWO CLIMBERS KILLED.

## FATE OF MR. MALLORY AND MR. IRVINE.

**(" The Times " World Copyright.)**

The Mount Everest Committee have received with profound regret the following telegram from Lieut.-Colonel E. F. Norton, the leader of the expedition, dispatched from Phari Dzong on June 19, at 4.50 p.m. :—

"Mallory and Irvine killed on last attempt. Rest of party arrived at base camp all well."

The Committee have telegraphed to Colonel Norton expressing their deep sympathy with the expedition in the loss of their two gallant comrades, which must have been due to the most unfavourable conditions of weather and snow which have from the first arrival at the scene of operations impeded the climbing this year. The last message from Colonel Norton, dated May 26, told how the party had been driven out of their high camp for the second time by heavy snow. It seems probable that they had been able to return to the assault early in this month, and that the lamentable accident which has cost the lives of two of the best climbers occurred about June 6.

The tragic death of these two men—George Leigh Mallory, who alone of all those engaged in the present attempt had also taken part in the two previous ex-

## MALLORY'S LAST CLIMB.

This ends Dr. Somervell's story. Colonel Norton, resuming his narrative, says :—

"The two attempts without oxygen failed to reach the summit. I hope to discuss later in your columns the vexed question whether success on these lines was possible or not. In any case, I was delighted to find on my arrival at Camp Four on the night of June 4 that Mallory had rightly determined in my absence that there must be one more attempt, and that immediately and, if possible, with oxygen. Bruce, the condition of whose heart definitely prevented him from taking part in another attempt, had already gone down to Camp Three to see if it were possible to supply sufficient porters to put on oxygen so as to make the attempt with an absolutely minimum load. The men were forthcoming. Mallory had already decided that the climbers to make this final assault should be himself and Irvine. Unremitting and indefatigable work which had been put in by the latter on the most defective of the oxygen apparatus fully justified his inclusion in the party. On the morning of June 6 these two, with eight porters, started for Camp Five, intending to sleep the following night at Camp Six and to make the assault on the summit to-day.

Their movements are shrouded in a mist of mystery, but one brief note reached us yesterday from their perch near the top of the North Ridge by the hand of a returning porter. It is to the effect that Noel, with the cinema, should be on the look-out for them about the base of the final pyramid that starts 650ft. from the top at 8 o'clock this morning. The returning porters report that this pair were going exceedingly strongly with oxygen yesterday ; from every point of view the situation is dramatic. One more small incident is worth noting.

During the night of June 4-5 on the North Col I was smitten with acute snow-blindness, and for 60 hours was completely and absolutely blind. At 10 a.m. on June 6 Hingston and two porters arrived from Camp Three to relieve and, if possible, escort me down. I was anxious to descend, as my presence at Camp Four could only be an embarrassment to Odell and Hazard, who had now taken the place of Irvine in the *rôle* of supporters. Hingston, being unable to perform the miracle of restoring my sight at the moment, performed, with the help of Hazard and the two porters, another miracle.

The route to North Col is admittedly an Alpine climb. They shepherded me down some 1,500ft. of sheer ice and snow, placing my every footstep, leading me by the hand, and supporting me with ropes, fixed and unfixed, with complete security. Hazard turned back after roping me from the top of the chimney to the bottom, and Hingston saw me the rest of the way into Camp Three.

Hingston is a famous goer on a hill-side and has a limited experience of snow and ice conditions in the Pamirs, but he has never done any Alpine climbing, so I think it must be admitted that his performance was remarkable, and it was certainly one that I shall not forget in a hurry.

## MALLORY AND IRVINE'S FATE.

BASE CAMP, June 11.

With the deepest regret I add these few lines continuing the above dispatch. Mallory and Irvine perished on the mountain beyond all doubt. They were last seen by Odell from Camp Six going strong for the top. I have not yet seen Odell, but estimate that this was about 11 in the morning of the 8th, and that the point reached at that time by the climbers was about 28,000ft. Nothing has been seen or heard of them since. Odell returned to Camp Four that night, and until about noon on the 9th the absence of news occasioned only anxiety, as the climbers might well have passed the night in Camps Five and Six.

At noon on the 9th Odell and two porters started from Camp Four and spent the night at Camp Five. About 1 p.m. on the 10th Odell reached Camp Six, whence he signalled that there was no sign of the missing men. Camps Five and Six were under continuous observation by Hazard from Camp Four throughout. These were provided with magnesium flares for distress signals, and there is no doubt that the climbers did not return to them. This puts any possibility of their survival out of the question, for no one could spend two nights on the mountain under existing conditions except in one or other of the two high camps and live.

The only likely explanation of the tragedy is that there was a mountaineering accident, unconnected with question of weather or the use of oxygen. This is borne out by my own observations four days previously of the nature of the ground they were crossing when last seen. I remained at Camp Three, directing operations by messenger, watching for a signal through the telescope, until 5.30 in the afternoon of the 10th, by which time I saw Odell reach Camp Four safely. My condition and that of Captain Bruce, the only climbers with me, precluded our reaching Camp Four in time to be of any help, and, beyond a letter of instruction to give the supporting party in Camp Four a free hand. They appear to have done all that was humanly possible.

I should add that I myself forbade any reconnaissance beyond Camp Six, as the weather was extremely threatening and conditions on the mountain appeared to be as bad as they could be, and I had to consider the lives of the two British and three Himalayan members of the Expedition who were still at or above Camp Four. I shall, of course, give you all details in my next dispatch.

---

PLATE 41

*(Left)* News of Mallory and Irvine's death was announced to the world in a brief telegram from Everest. Carried across Tibet by special runner, it was cabled from Phari and published in London by *The Times* on 21 June.
*(Centre and right)* On 26 June *The Times* published a communiqué from Norton. Begun at Camp III on 8 June, the day of Mallory and Irvine's summit attempt, it included a postscript dated 11 June in which Norton gave the first account of their deaths.

# THE LAST CLIMB.

## MR. ODELL'S STORY.

Mr. Odell's story of the final attempt on Everest—and victory?—is as follows:—

"Colonel Norton has requested me to relate the events connected with the last great climb of Mallory and Irvine, a climb a good many aspects of which I had the advantage of witnessing during a protracted period of 11 days, while acting in support at the North Col (23,000ft.). The duty of being in support, from meaning readiness to support at need any exhausted member of the party on the mountain, largely transformed itself into cooking and preparing meals for whatever climbers made the North Col Camp a place of call. This function kept us fully occupied, particularly as all the water had to be obtained by melting snow, snow that at this altitude was of an exceedingly dry and powdered variety.

"On June 6, following an early breakfast of fried sardines, joyfully acclaimed and moderately partaken of, Mallory and Irvine left the North Col Camp for Camp V. (25,000ft.), accompanied by five porters, with provisions and reserve oxygen cylinders. Using oxygen, they had already ascended from Camp III.; 2,000ft. below, in 2½ hours. They were highly pleased with their performance, which seemed to augur well for the final attempt on the mountain. The next day they ascended to Camp VI. (27,000ft.), which had been established by Norton and Somervell in a 'record' climb three days previously. The same day I ascended to the supporting Camp No. V. Hazard at this time arrived at the North Col to replace me. Porters returning from Mallory that night were the bearers of a hopeful message in a note which said that they had only used the minimum oxygen up to 27,000ft., and that the weather was perfect for the job. The latter I could well appreciate, for, looking out that evening from the little rock ledge on which the tent was pitched at Camp V., I saw that the weather indeed seemed most promising for the morrow.

"The situation of the camp was unique and the outlook a commanding one. Westward there was a savage, wild jumble of peaks, culminating in Cho Uyo (26,750ft.), bathed in pinks and yellows of most exquisite tints. Right opposite were the gaunt cliffs of Everest, the north peak, intercepting a portion of the wide northern horizon, of a brilliant opalescence which threw into prominence the outline of a mighty peak far away in Central Tibet : was it General Pereira's supposed rival to Everest ? Eastward, floating in the thin air, the snowy top of Kangchenjunga appeared, and at last the beautifully varied outlying Gyangkar range. Sunset and after at that altitude were a transcendent experience never to be forgotten.

"At early morning of June 8 it was clear and not unduly cold at such an altitude. The two porters I had brought with me to Camp V. complained of sickness and headache, and altogether I was not unthankful for an excuse to send them down to Camp IV. at the North Col, for I especially wished to be free during an ascent I was to make for as wide a geological survey of the mountain face between Camps V. and VI. as possible. Soon after I had started on my task banks of cloud began to form, which periodically immersed one in gloom, but the wind remained quite light for such an exposed ridge. Now and then there would be an accompaniment of sleet and light snow. I could see above me frequently during these squalls that there was a glow of light, indicating clearness at a higher altitude, and hoped that Mallory and Irvine were above the mist.

"At 12.50, just after I had emerged in a state of jubilation at finding the first definite fossils on Everest, there was a sudden clearing of the atmosphere, and the entire summit, ridge, and final peak of Everest were unveiled. My eyes became fixed on one tiny black spot silhouetted on a small snowcrest beneath a rock-step in the ridge, and the black spot moved. Another black spot became apparent and moved up the snow to join the other on the crest. The first then approached the great rock-step and shortly emerged at the top ; the second did likewise. Then the whole fascinating vision vanished, enveloped in cloud once more.

"There was but one explanation. It was Mallory and his companion moving, as I could see even at that great distance, with considerable alacrity, realizing doubtless that they had none too many hours of daylight to reach the summit from their present position and return to Camp VI. at nightfall. The place on the ridge mentioned is a prominent rock-step at a very short distance from the base of the final pyramid, and it was remarkable that they were so late in reaching this place. According to Mallory's schedule, they should have reached it several hours earlier if they had started from the high camp as anticipated. That they had encountered bad conditions and snow-covered rocks and other obstacles was likely. However, in my opinion, from the position in which they were last seen, they should have reached the summit at 4 p.m. at latest, unless some unforeseen and particularly difficult obstacle presented itself on the final pyramid. This seemed to be very unlikely, for we had scrutinized the last slopes with telescopes and binoculars and had seen that technically the climbing was easy. Perhaps the two most likely explanations of their failure to return were a fall or inability to reach camp before darkness set in. I rather incline to the latter view, and consider it very probable that they sheltered in some rock recess and fell asleep, and a painless death followed, due to the excessive cold at those altitudes.

## THE SEARCH.

"After the brief glimpse of the party above described I continued up to Camp VI., which was reached just as a rather severe blizzard started. The camp consisted of one small mountain tent perched on a ledge, backed by a step of rocks by no means conspicuous or easy to find. I brought up with me provisions for the camp, and, after placing them in the tent and sheltering for a while, I decided to go out in the direction of the peak along the mountainside, in case bad weather should compel the party to turn back. I whistled and yodelled through the driving sleet to give the returning party the right direction, but soon realized that in point of time it was a worthless task, for they would still be beyond hearing even if they were returning. Perhaps they were right above the blizzard in sunshine. Within two hours the storm had blown over and the whole north face was bathed in sunshine. I searched the upper crag for another glimpse of the party, but nothing could be seen.

"In accordance with earlier arrangements suggested by Mallory himself, I returned to the North Col, and with Hazard kept watch till late for signs of the returning party. As they had not returned on the morrow it was assumed that perhaps they were still sleeping at Camp VI., having reached it at a late hour the night before, but we were unable with field-glasses to detect any movement around the distant tent. At noon I decided to ascend to Camp V., stay the night, and proceed to Camp VI. the next day to ascertain if they had returned and whether help was needed in consequence of some mishap. I arranged a code of signals with Hazard, by means of sleeping bags placed conspicuously on the snow in case assistance, medical or otherwise, should be required. Two porters again came with me to Camp V., but again they had to return to Camp IV. because of indisposition.

"After a very cold night I pushed on to Camp VI., this time carrying with me an oxygen apparatus, and also provisions for the missing party. I reached the tent of Camp VI. in the afternoon, only to find everything as I had left it two days previously, as Mallory and Irvine had left it on the morning of their climb. Leaving the tent, I climbed some distance, and worked out along the face in the direction of their route, searching for some clue. But what hope was there on such a vast mountain-face ? Weeks of diligent search by a party fully equipped for such difficult and particularly trying work at that altitude might not produce any result or unravel the mystery.

"At length, as the day was drawing to a close, I reluctantly gave up the search and signalled down to Hazard at the North Col, over 2,000ft. below, that no trace could be found. Closing up the tent, and leaving it with the last relics of our lost companions, I made my way down the north ridge, having now and then to take shelter behind rocks from the violent and bitterly cold west wind and to restore warmth and prevent frostbite, and at dusk reached the North Col Camp, with its profound comforts and hot soup. The next day we evacuated the camp and the others in succession down to the East Rongbuk Glacier.

"Has Everest been climbed ? Colonel Norton has referred to this question. It will ever be a mystery. Considering all the circumstances and the position they had reached on the mountain, I personally am of opinion that Mallory and Irvine must have reached the summit. At least they have established a mountain altitude 'record.'"

PLATE 42
Norton's communiqué of 14 June, published by *The Times* on 5 July, included Odell's account of his final sighting of Mallory and Irvine on 8 June and his fruitless search for them on the following days. *See page 119.*

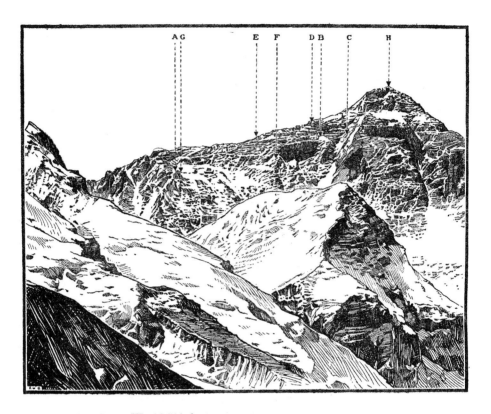

A.  Camp VI, 26,700 feet.
B.  The point reached by Somervell in 1924.
C.  The point reached by Norton in 1924.
D.  "The Second Step," where Mallory and Irvine were last seen.
E.  "The First Step."
F.  The point reached by Finch and Geoffrey Bruce in 1922.
G.  The point reached by Mallory, Norton, and Somervell in 1922.
H.  The summit, 29,002 feet.

PLATE 43
Diagram of the positions reached by the various summit parties in 1922 and 1924.
*See also caption to plate 19.*

PLATE 44

The porters who went highest. *From left to right:* 'Bom, Narbu Yishé, Semchumbi, Lobsang, Llakpa Chedi, Angtenjin. Narbu Yishé, Semchumbi and Llakpa Chedi carried loads to about 26,800 feet with Norton and Somervell to establish Camp VI on 3 June 1924. The others carried oxygen cylinders and equipment for Mallory and Irvine a few days later, and were the last people to speak to them before they disappeared. *See pages 57, 81, 85–87 and 98–99.*

PLATE 45
The memorial cairn erected to commemorate the twelve men, climbers and porters, who lost their lives on the Everest expeditions in 1921, 1922 and 1924. *See page 119.*

PLATE 46
The last to leave. A final view from Base Camp, with the memorial cairn silhouetted against the snows of Everest. *See page 121.*

TELEPHONES: REGENT 1710, 1711

TRAVELLERS' CLUB,
PALL MALL,
S.W.1.

June 25. 24.

My dear Norton,

The news of poor Mallory & Irvine's death was a frightful blow. It came like a great thud, and, as usual with these mechanical contrivances of the day, it came without warning. I heard it casually on the telephone from an odd newspaper man. But I want

immediately to say this that we all have the greatest confidence in your leadership. The full account of what happened is not in yet and we have only the bare details that they were killed. But I feel sure that it was through no want of foresight or arrangement on

PLATES 47–48
Letter from Sir Francis Younghusband to Norton dated 25 June 1924. It was written shortly after the telegram announcing the deaths of Mallory and Irvine had been published *(see plate 41)*, but before any details of their disappearance had reached London.

your part. and I have it in
Wallace's own hand writing that he
had the greatest confidence in you
as leader and not only confidence
but admiration.

The King has sent a very
kind and feeling message of
condolence to the relatives and
they also telephoned to me from
Buckingham Palace asking whether
you would appreciate a telegram
and of course I said you would

I hope the telegram will be reaching
you in a few days and that
it will help to cheer you all up
and make you feel that people
here are intensely admiring
your great struggle and are
highly appreciative of what you
have done.

Please remember me to all
the party.

Yours very sincerely
Francis Younghusband

Westbrook,
July 2                Godalming

Dear Teddie Norton

This letter must get to you before you come home. I have been and am so dreadfully sorry for you. One of my greatest comforts is to know that George was with Mr Somervell & you. So that he had people to be really happy with.

I must also say how filled I am with admira- at the great courage you all showed.

I am glad you let no one try to go higher searching. It would have done no good & might so easily have ended in more disaster

I dont think that passing from this life to the next matters at all for George. Its not difficult to believe he was ready. Of course I know he didn't want to & didn't mean

PLATES 49–50
Letter from Mallory's widow, Ruth, to Norton dated 2 July. It was written after the publication of Norton's communiqué recounting the deaths of Mallory and Irvine on 26 June *(see plate 41)*, but before Odell's account was published on 5 July *(see plate 42)*. At this point Ruth Mallory had almost certainly not yet received Norton's personal letter of condolence written at Base Camp on 14 June. Her letter reached him in Sikkim shortly before the end of the expedition.

to.

Please give Mr Somervell my love. I'll write to him sometime. Letters are so difficult to write I can't now. Perhaps he will write to me then I can answer it.

George lived as much in his life as most people in the whole of a long one & I think had quite his share of joy.

I shall see you when you come back I know and it will be a great pleasure. I don't know if Mr Somervell will come to England but he will let me know if ~~you~~ he does I am sure.

I am at Westbrook Godalming for some time now I could not stay in Cambridge. So would you address everything here.

Yours very sincerely<br>
Ruth Leigh-Mallory

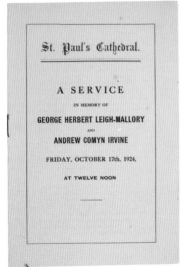

PLATE 51 (↖)
A studio portrait of Mallory.

PLATE 52 (↗)
Irvine photographed by G. Binney during the 1923 expedition to Spitsbergen.

PLATE 53 (↙)
Front cover of the order of service for the memorial service for Mallory and Irvine held at St Paul's Cathedral on 17 October 1924.

PLATE 54 (↘)
The final pyramid of Everest, photographed by Noel with a telephoto lens from above Camp III.
*See page 112.*

moraine appearing among the great ice pinnacles. We gained this by some amusing climbing, retraced our steps a little way along it towards Camp II, and then on the far side reached a hump from which the whole glacier could be seen rising to the south; from a point quite near us it was obvious there could be no serious obstacle, and that point we saw could be gained in a simple way; it only remained therefore to make a good connection with Camp II. We followed easily down the moraine, which is a stony trough between high fantastic ice pillars and a beautiful place, and just as we were nearing camp found a simple way through the pinnacles, so in an hour and a half the first most difficult part of the way from II to III had been established.

*May 4 to 5.* An appalling night, very cold, considerable snowfall and a violent wind.

*May 5.* Result: signs of life in camp very late. The first audible one in camps up to and including II is the blowing of yak-dung fire with Tibetan bellows.

The men were an extraordinarily long time getting their food this morning. The NCO seemed unable to get a move on, and generally speaking an Oriental inertia was in the air. It was with difficulty in fact that the men could be got out of their tents, and then we had further difficulty about loads; one man, a regular old soldier, having possessed himself of a conveniently light load, refused to take a heavier one I wanted taken instead. I had to make a great show of threatening him with my fist in his face before he would comply, and so with much difficulty about it and about what should be left behind in the way of coolie rations and blankets and cooking-pots, and the degree of illness of those reported sick, we didn't get fairly away until 11 a.m.

Now, making a new track is always a long affair compared to following an old one, and on this occasion snow had fallen in the night. The glacier which had looked innocent enough the evening before was far from innocent now. The wind had blown the higher surfaces clear. The days, I suppose, had been too clear for melting and these surfaces were hard, smooth, rounded ice, almost as hard as glass and with never a trace of roughness, and between the projecting lumps lay the new powdery snow. The result of the conditions was much expenditure of labour either in making steps in the snow or cutting them in ice, and we reached a place known as 'The Trough,' a broken trough in the ice, fifty feet deep and about one-third of the way up, knowing we should have all that we could do to reach Camp III. We followed along in the trough some way, a lovely warm place, and then came out of it into the open glacier where the wind was blowing up the snow maliciously. The wind luckily was at our backs until we rounded the corner of the North Peak, and then we caught it blowing straight at us from the North Col. As the porters were now nearly exhausted and feeling the altitude badly our progress was a bitter experience. I was acting as lone horse, finding the best way, and consequently arrived first in camp. It was a queer sensation, reviving memories of that scene with the dud oxygen cylinders piled against the cairn which was built to commemorate the seven porters killed two years ago. The whole place had changed less than I could have believed possible, seeing that the glacier is everywhere beneath the stones. My boots were frozen hard on my feet, and I knew we could do nothing now to make a comfortable camp. I showed the porters where to pitch their tents at 6.30 p.m., got hold of a rucksack containing four Unna cookers, dished out three and Meta for their cooking to the porters and one to our own cook; then we pitched our own two Meade tents with doors facing about a yard apart for sociability.

The porters seemed to me very much done up, and considering how cold it was even at 6 p.m. I was a good deal depressed by the situation. Personally I got warm easily enough. Our wonderful Kami produced some sort of a hot meal, and I lay comfortably in my sleeping-bag. The one thing I could think of for the porters was the high-altitude sleeping-sacks (intended for Camp IV and upwards), now at Camp II, which I had not ordered to come on next day with the second party of porters (two parties A and B each of twenty had been formed for these purposes, and B were a day behind us). The only plan was to make an early start next morning and get to Camp II in time to forestall the departure of B party. I remember making this resolve in the middle of the night and getting up to pull my boots inside the tent from under the door. I put them inside the outer covering of my flea-bag and near the middle of my body – but of course they remained frozen hard and I had a tussle to get them on in the morning. Luckily the sun strikes our tents early – 6.30 a.m. or a little later at Camp III, and I was able to get off about 7. I left directions that half the men, or as many less as possible, should come one-quarter of the way down and meet the men coming up so as to get the most important load to Camp III.

I guessed that B party, after a cold night, would not start before 9 a.m., and as I was anxious if possible to find a better way over the glacier I wasted some time in investigations and made an unsatisfactory new route, so that it was after 8.30 when I emerged from the trough, and a little farther on I saw B party coming up. It was too late to turn them back. I found some of them had resolved they would not be able to get to Camp III and go back to Camp II the same day and consequently increased their loads with blankets, etc., determining to sleep at Camp III. This was the last thing I wanted. My chief idea at the moment was to get useful work out of B party without risking their *moral* or condition as I saw we were risking that of A. So after dispatching a note to Noel at II I conducted B party slowly up the glacier. After making a convenient dump and sending down B party I got back to Camp III early in the afternoon, somewhat done and going very slowly from want of food at the last. In camp nothing doing. All porters said to be sick and none fit to carry a load. Irvine and Odell volunteered to go down to the dump and get one or two things specially wanted, e.g. Primus stoves, which was done. The sun had left the camp some time before they returned. A very little wall-building was done this day, notably round the NCO's tent, otherwise nothing to improve matters. The temperature at 5 p.m. (we hadn't thermometers the previous night) was observed to be 2° Fahrenheit, i.e. 30° of frost an hour before sunset; under these conditions it is only during the sunny, windless hours that anything to speak of can be done; this day there were such hours, but I gather that sahibs as well as porters were suffering from altitude lassitude.

*May 7.* The night had been very cold: -21½°, i.e. 53° of frost. Personally I slept beautifully warmly and yet was not well in the morning. Odell and Irvine also seemed distinctly unfit. I decided to send Hazard down with some of A party to meet at the dump and bring up some of B party (it had been arranged that some of this party should come up again). Investigation again showed that no porters were fit to carry loads; several were too unwell to be kept up at III. They had to be more or less pulled from their tents. An hour and a half must have been taken in getting their meal of tsampa, which they must clearly have before going down; and much time too in digging out the sicker men who tried to hide away in their tents – one of them, who was absolutely without a spark of life to help himself, had swollen feet and we had to pull on his boots without his socks; he was almost incapable of walking; I supported him with my arm for some distance and then told off a porter to do that; eventually roped in three parties in charge of the NCO I sent them off by themselves from the dump, where shortly afterwards I met Hazard. Four men of B had gone on to Camp III, but not to sleep. Three others whom we now proceeded to rope up and help with their loads alone consented to stay there. A second day therefore passed with only seven more loads got to Camp III, and nothing done to establish the camp in a more comfortable manner, unless it counted that this third night each of the six men would have a high-altitude sleeping-sack; and meanwhile the *moral* of A party had gone to blazes. It was clear to me that the *moral* of porters must be established if possible at once by bringing B party up and giving them a day's rest to make camp.

*May 8.* I made another early start and reached Camp II at 9 a.m., and here met Norton and Somervell. By some mental aberration I had thought they would only reach Camp II on this day – they had proceeded according to programme and come to Camp II on the 7th. We discussed plans largely while I ate breakfast, in the mild, sheltered, sunny alfresco of Camp II (by comparison). Norton agreed with my ideas and dispatched all remaining B party to Camp III with Somervell, to pick up their loads at the dump and carry them on. A had been filled up the previous night with hot food and were now lying in the sun looking more like men; the only question was whether in future to establish the correct standard and make them carry all the way to Camp III and back as was always done in 1922. I was strongly opposed to this idea; the best way of re-establishing their *moral*, I thought, would be to give them a job well within their powers and, if they improved as I hoped, they might well carry loads the three-quarter journey to the dump on three successive days – while B could ferry the last quarter once or twice on the two of the days when they would not be engaged in making camp. This was agreed to more particularly by Geoffrey Bruce, who really runs the porters altogether and who had now come up from Camp I.

A day of great relief this with the responsibility shared or handed over; and much lying in the sun and untroubled sleep at Camp II.

*May 9.* I intended going ahead of the party to see how things were moving at Camp III, for this day the camp was to be made wonderful. Seven men with special loads, fresh heroes from the Base, were to go through to Camp III; the A men to return from the dump to Camp II. As it turned out I escorted the first batch who were going through to Camp III. The conditions when we emerged from the trough were anything but pleasant; under a grey sky a violent wind was blowing up the snow; at moments the black dots below me on the glacier, all except the nearest, were completely lost to view. The men were much inclined to put down their loads before reaching the dump and a good deal of driving had to be done. Eventually after waiting some time at the dump I joined Norton and Geoff and we escorted the last three loads for Camp III the last bit of the way. On such a day I did not expect Camp III to be more congenial than it had been. However, it was something to be greeted by the cheery noise of the Roarer Cooker: the RC is one of the great inventions of the Expedition;

we have two in point of fact, one with a vertical, and one with a horizontal flame – a sort of super-Primus stove. Irvine and Odell had evidently been doing some useful work. It had been a triumph getting the RC to Camp III – it is an extravagant load weighing over forty pounds and it now proved to be even more extravagant of fuel than had been anticipated; moreover, its burning was somewhat intermittent, and as the cook, even after instruction, was still both frightened and incompetent when this formidable stove was not functioning quite sweetly and well, a sahib had often to be called in to help. Nevertheless the RC succeeded in cooking food for the troops, and however costly in paraffin oil that meal may have been it made the one great difference between Camp III as A party experienced it and Camp III now. Otherwise on this day, set apart for the edification and beatification of this camp, the single thing that had been done was the erection of one Meade tent to accommodate two more sahibs (only two more because Hazard came down this day). And no blame to anyone; B party was much as A party had been – in a state of Oriental inertia; it is unfair, perhaps, to our porters to class them with Orientals in general, but they have this Oriental quality that after a certain stage of physical discomfort or mental depression has been reached they simply curl up. Our porters were just curled up inside their tents. And it must be admitted that the sahibs were most of the time in their tents – no other place being tolerable. Personally I felt that the task of going round tents and seeing how the men were getting on and giving orders about the arrangements of the camp now naturally fell to Geoffrey Bruce, whose 'pigeon' it is to deal with the porters. And so presently in my old place, with Somervell now as a companion instead of Hazard, I made myself comfortable, i.e. I took off my boots and knickers, put on my footless stockings, knitted for me by my wife for the last Expedition and covering the whole of my legs, a pair of grey flannel bags and two pairs of warm socks, besides my cloth-sided shoes, and certain garments too for warming the upper parts, a comparatively simple matter. The final resort in these conditions of course is to put one's legs into a sleeping-sack. Howard and I lay warmly enough, and presently I proposed a game of picquette and we played cards for some time until Norton and Geoff came to pay us a visit and discuss the situation. Someone a little later tied back the flaps of the two tents facing each other so that after Norton and Geoff had retired to their tent the other four of us were inhabiting, as it were, one room, and hopefully talked of the genius of Kami and the Roarer Cooker and supposed that a hot evening meal might sometime come our way. Meanwhile I produced

*The Spirit of Man* and began reading one thing and another. Howard reminded me that I was reproducing on the same spot a scene which had occurred two years ago when he and I lay in a tent together. We all agreed that Kubla Khan was a good sort of poem. Irvine was rather poetry shy, but seemed to be favourably impressed by the Epitaph to Gray's Elegy. Odell was much inclined to be interested and liked the last lines of Prometheus Unbound. Somervell, who knows quite a lot of English literature, had never read a poem of Emily Brontë's, and was happily introduced. And suddenly hot soup arrived.

The following night was one of the most disagreeable I remember. The wind came in tremendous gusts and, in spite of precautions to keep it out, the fresh snow drifted in; if one's head were not under the bedclothes one's face was cooled by the fine cold powder, and in the morning I found two inches of snow all along my side of the tent. It was impossible to guess how much snow had fallen during the night when one first looked out. The only certain thing was the vile appearance of things at present. In a calm interval one could take stock of a camp now covered in snow – and then would come the violent wind and all would be covered in the spindrift. Presently Norton and Geoff came into our tent for a powwow. Geoff, speaking from the porters' point of view, was in favour of beating a retreat. We were all agreed that we must not risk destroying the *moral* of the porters, and also that for two or three days no progress could be made towards the North Col. But it seemed to me that, in the normal course of events, the weather should now re-establish itself and might even be sufficiently calm to get something done that afternoon, and that for the porters the best thing of all would be to weather the storm up at Camp III. In any case it would be early enough to decide for a retreat next day. These arguments commended themselves to Norton and so it was agreed. Meanwhile one of the most serious features of the situation was the consumption of fuel. A box of meta, and none could say how much paraffin (not much, however), had been burnt at Camp II; here at Camp III no water had yet appeared, and snow must be melted for every one at every meal – a box of meta had to be consumed here too, and Primus stoves had been used before the Roarer made its appearance yesterday. Goodness knows how much oil it has used. It was clear that the first economy must be in the number of sahibs (6) at Camp III. We planned that Somervell, Norton and Odell should have the first whack at the North Col, and Irvine and I finish the good work next day – Irvine and I therefore must go down first. On the way down Irvine suffered very much and I somewhat from the complaint known as glacier lassitude – a mysterious complaint, but I am pretty certain in his case that the sun and the dazzling light reflected from the new snow had something to do with the trouble.

A peaceful time at Camp II with Beetham and Noel.

*May 11.* The weather hazy and unsettled looking. I dispatched fifteen loads up to the dump and arranged for the evacuation of two sick men, of whom one had badly frostbitten feet, apparently a Lepcha, unfit for this game, and the other was Sanglu, Kellas's old servant, who had been attached to Noel this Expedition and last, a most valuable man, who seemed exceedingly ill with bronchitis. The parties had been gone half an hour before we were aroused by a shout and learned that a porter had broken his leg on the glacier. We quickly gathered ourselves into a competent help party, and had barely started out when a man turned up with a note from Norton to tell me, as I half expected, that he had decided to evacuate Camp III for the present and retire all ranks to the Base Camp. The wounded man turned out to be nearer at hand than, and not so badly wounded (a bone broken in the region of the knee) as I feared.

This same evening Beetham, Noel, Irvine and I were back at the Base Camp, the rest coming in next day.

Well, that is the bare story of the reverse so far as it goes. I'm convinced that Norton has been perfectly right. We pushed things far enough. Everything depends on the porters and we must contrive to bring them to the starting point, i.e. Camp III, at the top of their form. I expect we were working all the time in '22 with a smaller margin than we knew – it certainly amazed me that the whole bandobast, so far as porters were concerned, worked so smoothly. Anyway this time the conditions at Camp III were much more severe, and not only were temperatures lower but the wind was more continuous and more violent. I expect that these porters will do as well in the end as last time's. Personally I felt that I was going through a real hard time in a way I never did in '22. Meanwhile our retreat has meant a big waste of time. We have waited down here for the weather – at last it looks more settled and we are on the point of starting up again. But the day for the summit is put off from the 17th to the 28th, and the great question is, Will the monsoon give time?

10

MAY 27, 1924.

It has been a bad time altogether. I look back on tremendous effort and exhaustion and dismal looking out of a tent door into a world of snow and vanishing hopes – and yet, and yet, and yet there have been a good many things to set on the other side. The party has played up wonderfully. The first visit to the North Col was a triumph for the old gang. Norton and I did the job, and the cutting of course was all my part – so far as one can enjoy climbing above Camp III I enjoyed the conquest of the ice wall and crack, the crux of the route, and the making steps too in the steep final 200 feet. Odell did very useful work leading the way on from the camp to the Col; I was practically bust to the world and couldn't have led that half-hour though I still had enough mind to direct him. We made a very bad business of the descent. It suddenly occurred to me that we ought to see what the old way down was like. Norton and I were ahead unroped and Odell behind in charge of a porter who had carried up a light load. We got only ground where a practised man can just get along without crampon (which we hadn't with us), chipping occasional steps in very hard snow or ice. I was all right ahead, but Norton had a nasty slip and then the porter, whose knot didn't hold, so that he went down some way and was badly shaken. Meanwhile I, below, finding the best way down, had walked into an obvious crevasse; by some miscalculation I had thought I had prodded the snow with which it was choked and where I hoped we could walk instead of cutting steps at the side of it – all the result of mere exhaustion, no doubt. But the snow gave way and in I went with the snow tumbling all round me, down, luckily, only about ten feet before I fetched up half blind and breathless to find myself most precariously supported only by my ice axe somehow caught across the crevasse and still held in my right hand – and below was a very unpleasant black hole. I had some nasty moments before I got comfortably wedged and began to yell for help up through the round hole I had come through where the blue sky showed – this because I was afraid my operations to extricate myself would bring down a lot more snow and perhaps precipitate me into the bargain. However, I soon grew tired of shouting – they hadn't seen me from above – and bringing the snow down a little at a time I made a hole out towards the side (the crevasse ran down a slope) after some climbing, and extricated myself – but was then on the wrong side of the crevasse, so that eventually I had to cut across a nasty slope of very hard ice and farther down some mixed unpleasant snow before I was out of the wood.

The others were down by a better line ten minutes before me. That cutting against time at the end after such a day just about brought me to my limit.

So much for that day.

My one personal trouble has been a cough. It started a day or two before leaving the Base Camp but I thought nothing of it. In the high camp it has been the devil. Even after the day's exercise I have described I couldn't sleep, but was distressed with bursts of coughing fit to tear one's guts – and a headache and misery altogether; besides which of course it has a very bad effect on one's going on the mountain. Somervell also has a cough, which started a little later than mine, and he has not been at his physical best.

The following day when the first loads were got up to Camp IV in a snow-storm Somervell and Irvine must have made a very fine effort hauling loads up the chimney. [Unfortunately on the next day four porters were left on the North Col.]

Poor old Norton was very hard hit altogether, hating the thought of such a bad muddle and himself not really fit to start out next day – nor were any of us for that matter, and it looked ten to one against our getting up with all that snow about, let alone getting a party down. I led from the camp to a point some little distance above the flat glacier – the snow wasn't so very bad as there had been no time for it to get sticky, still that part with some small delays took us three hours; then Somervell took us up to where Geoff and Odell had dumped their loads the day before and shortly afterwards Norton took the lead; luckily we found the snow better as we proceeded. Norton alone had crampons, and was able to take us up to the big crevasse without step-cutting. Here we had half an hour's halt, and about 1.30 I went on again for the steep 200 feet and so to the point where the big crevasse joins the corridor. From here there were two doubtful stretches. Norton led up the first, while the two of us made good at the corner of the crevasse – he found the snow quite good. And Somervell led across the final slope (following Hazard's just discernible tracks). Norton and I had an anxious time belaying, and it began to be cold too as the sun had left us. Somervell made a very good show getting the men off – but I won't repeat my report. Time was pretty short as it was 4.30 when they began to come back, using Somervell's rope as a hand-rail. Naturally the chimney took some time. It was just dark when we got back to camp.

Norton has been quite right to bring us down for rest. It is no use sending men up the mountain unfit. The physique of the whole party has gone down sadly. The only chance now is to get fit and go for a simpler, quicker plan.

The only plump fit man is Geoffrey Bruce. Norton has made me responsible for choosing the parties of attack, himself first choosing me into the first party if I like. But I'm quite doubtful if I shall be fit enough. But again I wonder if the monsoon will give us a chance. I don't want to get caught, but our three-day scheme from the Chang La will give the monsoon a good chance. We shall be going up again the day after to-morrow. Six days to the top from this camp!

# PART 3
# OBSERVATIONS

# 1 PHYSIOLOGICAL DIFFICULTIES

BY MAJOR R.W.G. HINGSTON, IMS

The primary object of the Mount Everest Expedition was to reach the highest summit on the earth. Everything else was subordinate to this. Elaborate scientific investigations were impossible, and anything involving complicated apparatus was altogether out of the question. We had to content ourselves with simple experiments and with the records of the experiences of individual climbers. These, nevertheless, may prove of interest. They will give us some idea of the physiological difficulties involved in an ascent to so great a height.

*Alterations in Breathing.* – The most obvious of these is the difficulty in breathing. Owing to the gradual nature of our ascent this shortness of respiration was scarcely noticeable below 10,000 feet. It was definitely apparent above 14,000 feet, and above 19,000 feet the slightest exertion made breathing laboured and severe. When the body was at rest, even at extreme altitudes, the rate of breathing was apparently normal and as comfortable as at sea-level. But the very slightest exertion, such as the tying of a bootlace, the opening of a ration-box, the getting into a sleeping-bag, was associated with marked respiratory distress. The difficulties of the ascent were thus enormously increased. The breathing was quicker rather than deeper, but it was necessary to stop at frequent intervals and take a series of long deep breaths. This very quickly brought relief and made one ready for a further advance. Norton told me that, when he found himself dropping behind, his only chance of catching up the party was by taking a number of these deep long breaths. Somervell gives a record of his breathing at 27,000 feet. At that altitude he had to take seven, eight, or ten complete respirations for every single step forward. And even at that slow rate of progress he had to rest for a minute or two every twenty or thirty yards. At 28,000 feet Norton, in an hour's climb, ascended only about eighty feet. This was the highest point reached without the aid of oxygen. The strain at that altitude was certainly intense, but when we remember that the supply of oxygen is only about one-third of that available at sea-level, we are surprised that men can make these strenuous efforts, and still more that they can remain in comparative comfort when they sit down to rest.

The alteration in the rhythm of the breathing – commonly known as Cheyne-Stokes respiration – was frequently noticed during the Expedition. I heard one member of the party breathing in this way as low as 12,000 feet. Though as a rule it seldom occurs when awake, yet at the Base Camp I was conscious of this type of breathing before passing off to sleep. Illness at high altitudes markedly increases it. It was most pronounced in one member when suffering from fever at 15,000 feet, and still more so in a Gurkha when dying of cerebral hæmorrhage at 18,000 feet. The rapid breathing of cold dry air produces some important secondary effects. It causes inflammation of the respiratory passages. Every member suffered from sore throat, from hoarseness, or from loss of voice. Most had irritating coughs, but with little expectoration. Some of the porters developed severe bronchitis; one had a profusely ulcerated throat, another persistently coughed up blood. Dr Kellas was of opinion that the breathing was less laboured in a high wind. He thought that the wind might have the effect of packing the air into the lungs, also that it swept away the exhaled air and thus prevented it from being inhaled by the next breath. Our experiences did not agree with his. Mount Everest is noted for its heavy winds. They caused considerable obstruction to the breathing. A moderate breeze had a freshening effect, but a strong wind impeded progress, and there was a feeling of suffocation when facing powerful gusts.

I made some experiments on the respiration. The power of holding the breath is a simple test to which pilots are submitted in the Royal Air Force. The following table shows the diminution in this power at successive altitudes in the ascent. The first column is the most complete. Where at sea-level the breath was held for sixty-four seconds, at 21,000 feet it was held for only fourteen seconds.

| ALTITUDE IN FEET. | TIME BREATH HELD (IN SECS.). | | | | | | | | | |
|---|---|---|---|---|---|---|---|---|---|---|
| | R.W.H. | E.O.S. | B.B. | G.B. | E.F.N. | G.L.M. | J.V.H. | A.C.I. | T.H.S. | N.E.O. |
| Sea-level | 64 | — | 120 | — | — | — | 90 | 120 | — | — |
| 7,000 | 40 | 40 | 60 | 40 | 40 | 50 | 42 | 80 | 60 | 55 |
| 14,300 | 39 | 32 | 35 | 32 | 37 | 40 | — | 47 | 48 | — |
| 16,500 | 20 | 23 | 35 | 20 | 31 | — | 23 | 30 | 41 | 28 |
| 21,000 | 14 | 17 | — | 20 | — | — | 17 | — | — | — |

Another test used amongst airmen is the measurement of the expiratory force. This consists in blowing a column of mercury up a graduated glass tube. The height reached by the mercury is read off, and this gives a measure of the expiratory force. If the expiratory force is much below the average it suggests that the airman will be incapable of sustained effort. The following table gives the results of our experiments. It suggests that with increasing altitude the expiratory force tends to improve. Look again at the first column. At sea-level the expiratory force was 110 mm. Hg.; at 21,000 feet it was 150 mm. Hg.[1] The third, fourth, fifth, sixth, seventh, and eighth columns also show that an improvement has occurred.

| ALTITUDE IN FEET. | EXPIRATORY FORCE IN MM. OF Hg | | | | | | | | | |
|---|---|---|---|---|---|---|---|---|---|---|
| | R.W.H. | E.O.S. | B.B. | G.B. | E.F.N. | G.L.M. | J.V.H. | A.C.I. | T.H.S. | N.E.O. |
| Sea-level | 110 | — | — | — | — | — | — | — | — | — |
| 7,000 | 110 | 120 | 140 | 160 | 110 | 110 | 130 | 160 | 120 | 110 |
| 14,300 | 110 | 90 | 160 | 190 | 120 | 120 | — | 160 | 120 | — |
| 16,500 | 140 | 130 | 210 | 200 | 170 | — | 120 | 170 | 120 | 100 |
| 21,000 | 150 | 120 | — | 210 | — | — | 150 | — | — | — |

I did not anticipate this improvement in the expiratory force. But the test has little to do with the function of respiration. It is more an indication of physical fitness and muscular strength. And this tends to improve during an ascent, when the progress is slow enough to be accompanied with acclimatisation and before the wasting of high altitudes becomes marked. The march across Tibet made us tougher and harder. Hence the expiratory force improved. Mosso came to a similar conclusion in the Alps. He made his men perform exercises with dumb-bells, and was surprised to find that they did much more work at a height of 4,560 metres than when they performed the same exercises at Turin.

*Circulation.* – I pass to the changes in the circulation. Blueness of the face and lips, lividity of the nails, coldness of the extremities were the indications noticed of the impaired circulation at altitudes above 19,000 feet. Three of the members experienced giddiness. One noticed that it was immediately relieved by taking a deep breath. Once the extremities become cold at these high altitudes there is a great difficulty in regaining warmth, even in the interior of a sleeping-bag. The pulse is not markedly accelerated while at rest, but increases rapidly on the slightest exertion. Norton's normal pulse

---

1   [*Ed. note:* mm. Hg. = millimetres of mercury.]

is forty, and it was only sixty when he was resting at 27,600 feet. An intermittent pulse may develop at high altitudes. In one instance after crossing a
pass of only 14,000 feet the pulse missed four beats every minute without
causing any particular symptoms or distress. This irregularity of the pulse
seems to be a common feature. Mosso states that, when on Monte Rosa,
he noticed that nearly all the members of his party showed some signs of
irregularity of the heart. Hæmorrhages at high altitudes have often been
described, from the gums, the lips, the conjunctivae, the nose. Nothing of
the kind occurred amongst the members of our Expedition.

The following table shows the changes in the pulse of one individual at
successive altitudes above sea-level. The first column gives the pulse rate when
the person is at rest. There is no change except at the highest altitude, 21,000
feet. The second column shows the change that occurs when the person is
made to stand up. There is an increase in the pulse rate somewhat in proportion
to the altitude of the experiment. Column 3 shows the change after regulated
exercise. The exercise consisted in standing alternately on a chair and on the
ground five times in fifteen seconds. Again there is a marked increase in
the pulse rate, and this increase is greater the greater the altitude. The last
column gives the time in seconds that the pulse takes to return to normal.

PULSE RATE OF ONE INDIVIDUAL

| ALTITUDE IN FEET. | Pulse rate per minute, sitting. | Pulse rate per minute, standing. | Pulse rate per minute, after regulated exercise. | Time in seconds of return of pulse to normal. |
|---|---|---|---|---|
| Sea-level | 72 | 72 | 84 | 20 |
| 7,000 | 72 | 84 | 96 | 15 |
| 14,300 | 72 | 84 | 108 | 40 |
| 16,500 | 72 | 96 | 120 | 20 |
| 21,000 | 108 | 120 | 144 | 20 |

The blood pressure was taken with a sphygmomanometer in the manner
adopted by the Royal Air Force. The following is a table of results. There seems
to be no change in the blood pressure definitely associated with increase
in height.

PHYSIOLOGICAL DIFFICULTIES

BLOOD PRESSURE AT SUCCESSIVE ALTITUDES

| ALTITUDE IN FEET. | RWH | | EOS | | BB. | | GB | | EFN | | JVH | | GLM | | ACI | | THS | | NEO | |
|---|---|---|---|---|---|---|---|---|---|---|---|---|---|---|---|---|---|---|---|---|
| | Sys. | Dias. | Sys. | Dias. | Sys. | Dias. | Sys. | Dias. | Sys. | Dias. | Sys. | Dias. | Sys. | Dias. | Sys. | Dias. | Sys. | Dias. | Sys. | Dias. |
| Sea-level | 120 | 80 | — | — | — | — | — | — | — | — | — | — | — | — | — | — | — | — | — | — |
| 7,000 | 130 | 90 | 125 | 90 | 150 | 110 | 130 | 90 | 140 | 80 | 120 | 100 | 120 | 85 | 130 | 100 | 110 | 85 | 100 | 80 |
| 14,300 | 135 | 95 | 115 | 80 | 145 | 85 | 130 | 90 | 135 | 90 | — | — | 120 | 90 | 130 | 100 | 130 | 90 | — | — |
| 16,500 | 146 | 104 | 128 | 90 | 140 | 102 | 128 | 93 | 136 | 96 | 126 | 94 | 122 | 78 | 140 | 110 | 120 | 82 | 125 | 95 |
| 21,000 | 138 | 118 | 100 | 80 | — | — | 110 | 90 | — | — | 100 | 80 | — | — | — | — | — | — | — | — |

A well-known change that takes place during an ascent to high altitudes is the increase in the number of red corpuscles per unit volume of blood. The conditions on Mount Everest were too rough for these delicate determinations. But further west, on the Pamir plateau, I had previously made a series of blood counts up to 18,203 feet. The following table shows the results.

| DATE | ALTITUDE FEET. | CORPUSCLES PER CU. MM. |
|---|---|---|
| April 10 | 700 | 4,480,000 |
| May 12 | 4,390 | 5,240,000 |
| May 21 | 8,000 | 6,040,000 |
| May 28 | 10,000 | 6,624,000 |
| May 30 | 11,960 | 6,760,000 |
| June 1 | 12,400 | 6,800,000 |
| June 21 | 13,300 | 7,525,000 |
| June 23 | 15,600 | 7,840,000 |
| June 26 | 16,907 | 7,640,000 |
| July 27 | 18,203 | 8,320,000 |

There has been an increase in the number of red corpuscles from 4,480,000 at 700 feet to 8,320,000 at 18,203 feet. Another point of interest is that the people who live on the Central Asian plateau have a higher blood count than those at sea-level. The average blood count of the Sarikoli is 7,596,000, of the Kirghiz 7,920,000. The blood count of the European is about 5,000,000, but, on making an ascent to the Tibetan plateau, the corpuscles in his blood rapidly increase until they reach the number normal to the people who live permanently at those heights.

It is a matter of discussion amongst physiologists to what extent this increase in red blood corpuscles explains the adaptation to increasing heights. Professor Boycott has made an heroic suggestion. He points out that the capacity to increase red corpuscles can be increased as a result of practice.

Moreover, this practice can be given by bleeding. 'If you take an animal and take away one-third of its red corpuscles it will replace them in about twenty days; if you do it again in the same animal, it will grow the same number of red corpuscles at the end of six, seven or eight days; and again you can still further accelerate the process.' Presumably it would be similar with respect to man. That being the case, Professor Boycott suggests that the best preparation for the next expedition would be to have the party repeatedly bled.

*Muscular Power.* – Airmen describe great muscular weakness when flying at considerable altitudes. Even working a camera-shutter calls for enormous effort. We did not notice such pronounced effects, probably because our ascent was slow. But if inhalation is inadequate the legs soon become tired. It is not the tiredness of a prolonged walk, but more a heaviness and a lassitude which quickly disappears with a short rest.

The endurance test employed by the Royal Air Force is said to indicate the stability of the medullary centres and the capacity of the individual to resist fatigue. The test consists in blowing a column of mercury to a height of forty millimetres, and noting how long the person is able to sustain it at that height. The pulse is counted in periods of five seconds during the performance of the test. The following table gives the result of this test. Every column shows a diminution in the powers of endurance at each successive height. Take, for example, the first column. At sea-level the subject could sustain the mercury for forty-five seconds; at 21,000 feet for only fifteen seconds.

ENDURANCE TEST.

| ALTITUDE IN FEET. | TIME IN SECS. Hg MAINTAINED AT 40MM. | | | | | | | | | |
|---|---|---|---|---|---|---|---|---|---|---|
| | R.W.H. | E.O.S. | B.B. | G.B. | E.F.N. | G.L.M. | J.V.H. | A.C.I. | T.H.S. | N.E.O. |
| Sea-level | 45 | — | — | — | — | — | — | — | — | — |
| 7,000 | 35 | 30 | 60 | 50 | 20 | 60 | 35 | 45 | 50 | 50 |
| 14,300 | 30 | 30 | 25 | 40 | 25 | 35 | — | 45 | 25 | — |
| 16,500 | 23 | 23 | 23 | 15 | 23 | — | 17 | 25 | 22 | 20 |
| 21,000 | 15 | 15 | — | 15 | — | — | 10 | — | — | — |

The pulse rate was taken during the above test. Some of the results are given below. The first figure in each series shows the normal rate of the pulse during the five seconds before the test begins. This figure is separated from the following figures by a stroke. These following figures give the pulse rate during each successive period of five seconds throughout the performance of the test. Take, for example, the first line of figures in the first column, 6/7.8.9.9.8.7. The six is the pulse rate during the five seconds immediately before the test. The seven is the pulse rate during the first five seconds of the test. The remaining figures, 8.9.9.8.7, are the pulse rates during the successive periods of five seconds until the test ends. In this way we obtain the character of the pulse while the person is undergoing continuous strain.

PULSE RATE IN SECONDS DURING ENDURANCE TEST.

| ALTITUDE IN FEET. | E.O.S. | B.B. | G.B. | A.C.I. |
|---|---|---|---|---|
| 7,000 | 6/7.8.9.9.8.7. | 6/6.7.9.9.9.7.6.6.6.5. | 5/6.6.8.6.5.4.5.5.5. | 8/9.11.10.8.7.6.6.6.6. |
| 14,300 | 6/6.7.7.7.7.7. | 6/7.8.8.6.5. | 5/7.7.7.6.8.6.5.5. | 8/9.9.11.10.9.9.9.9.8 |
| 16,500 | 6/7.7.8.7. | 6/9.9.9.3. | 6/7.8.9. | 8/11.10.9.7.6. |
| 21,000 | 8/10.8.6. | — | 9/10.10.6. | — |

The chief point of interest in this experiment is the marked slowing of the pulse that takes place when the capacity of endurance is beginning to tell. At the commencement of the test the pulse first increases, but after a lapse of fifteen to twenty seconds it begins definitely to slow up. This slowing of the pulse is more marked at the higher altitudes. There is an extreme case in the lowest line of figures of column two. The 6/9.9.9.3 indicates that on the commencement of the experiment the pulse immediately rushed up from six to nine beats in the first five seconds, and after a lapse of fifteen seconds suddenly fell back from nine to three. This occurred at 16,500 feet. In the Royal Air Force instructions for the performance of this test it is stated that 'in case of marked physical inefficiency a characteristic response is for the pulse to jump up to a very quick rate during the second or third period of five seconds and then to fall away in rate to normal, or even below normal.' Thus it appears from this test that the cardiomotor mechanism of the vigorous man at a height of 16,000 feet closely resembles that of the physically inefficient person at sea-level.

*Special Senses.* – Changes in the function of the special senses have occasionally been noticed by mountaineers. They describe an impairment of vision, a diminution in hearing, alterations in the taste and smell. Most of our party noticed nothing in this respect, but two members were particularly emphatic in their loss of the sense of taste. One said that 'taste was distinctly affected,' that 'things seemed to have less taste, though there was no change in the character of the flavour.' He was unable to taste onions at 19,000 feet.

Another found food 'distinctly tasteless.' At 19,000 feet he could eat a slab of peppermint without strongly appreciating the flavour. Their sense of taste returned on descending to the Base Camp at 16,500 feet.

*Pain.* – The only kind of pain which we could attribute to high altitude was the occasional occurrence of a slight headache. Most of the members never experienced it, but some of us noticed it on first reaching the plateau, though, after a few days' acclimatisation, it completely disappeared. It usually commenced at the back of the neck, spread into a general mild headache, and disappeared after an hour's rest. Exercise, and particularly stooping, increased it. Lying down quickly brought relief. Our porters also suffered from headache. Many of them asked for headache tablets the first time we passed over into Tibet. Even the inhabitants of the plateau are not immune. It is common to see patches of plaster on their temples and black pigment smeared on their cheeks. These are remedies which they use to alleviate the headache caused by the altitude and wind.

*Gastro-intestinal Symptoms.* – Loss of appetite is a serious consequence of residence at great heights. Probably it is the cause of much of the wasting that occurs. There is much individual variation in this respect. Some of the climbers maintained that there was no loss of appetite. I found some dislike for food even at the Base Camp, though this disappeared on acclimatisation. Bruce thought that his appetite was unimpaired up to 21,000 feet. At 23,000 feet he found a disinclination for meat, though he still had an appetite for cereals and sweets. At 25,000 feet he lost all appetite for solid food, but could still take coffee, and to a less degree soup. Somervell at 27,000 feet found an absolute distaste for solids, though he enjoyed liquids and sweets and fruit. The general opinion seemed to be that sweet things were the most palatable and meat the least palatable above 19,000 feet. There was no suggestion of nausea or vomiting even at the highest altitudes reached.

Diarrhoea is not uncommon. It is usually of a transient nature and may be associated with much bile. Occasionally it may be more persistent, and refuse to yield to any treatment until a descent is made to moderate heights. Thirst is a far more important factor. It may be excessive at the end of a hard day, and, owing to the practical difficulties in obtaining water, may cause exhaustion of the climbers and failure of the climb. How best to relieve thirst at the high camps is a most important practical point. The craving for drink is not the result of perspiration, but of the loss of moisture in the respiratory passages from the excessive inhalation of cold dry air. This desiccation of the body at extreme altitudes may result in a great scantiness of urine. One of the climbers at 21,000 feet did not micturate for sixteen to eighteen hours; another on his descent from 28,000 feet did not do so for twenty-four hours.

*Mental Effects.* – High altitudes affect the operations of the mind. One member was confident of a dulling of the will power, a diminution in the strength of purpose, with less and less desire to reach the summit the farther he made the ascent. Somervell describes a lack of observance at and above 25,000 feet. Bruce records an enfeeblement of memory. He found an effort in recalling previous events. Above 23,000 feet his ideas became increasingly inaccurate. It was necessary for him to record them immediately as otherwise they would become forgotten or distorted. I think every one experienced some mental lassitude. Though the mind was clear, yet there was a disinclination for effort. It was far more pleasant to sit about than to do a job of work that required thought. We did not notice any peevishness or petulance, though I suspect that high altitudes would cause unsociability in a party less perfectly harmonious than ours. Though mental work is a burden at high altitudes, yet with an effort it can be done. One physiologist has said that sustained mental work is out of the question at anything over 10,000 feet. We certainly could not agree with this. Those who have read Norton's despatches to *The Times*, especially one dictated at Camp III, when he was burdened with anxiety and partially blind, will admit that this effort from 21,000 feet was not a bad intellectual performance. The main effect of altitude is a mental laziness which determination can overcome.

I made some mental tests on the members of the party. These tests were very simple. The first was a multiplication test. It consisted in multiplying the figures 123456789 by 7. The second was a division test, and consisted in dividing the same series of figures by 9. A record was made at successive altitudes of the time taken to do these sums. Probably these tests were far too simple. By an effort of concentration they could be easily done, and thus the effect of altitude was not properly shown. I give the results for what they are worth. They show no definite deterioration of mental activity. It will not please the members of the next expedition to hear that more complicated and worrying tests are required.

MULTIPLICATION TEST. SHOWING TIME IN SECONDS FOR COMPLETION OF SUM.

| ALTITUDE IN FEET | R.W.H. | B.B. | E.F.N. | G.L.M. | T.H.S. | E.O.S. | G.B. | J.V.H. | A.C.I. | N.E.O. |
|---|---|---|---|---|---|---|---|---|---|---|
| Sea-level | 20 | — | — | — | — | — | — | — | — | — |
| 7,000 | 25 | 25 | 27 | 13 | 40 | 43 | 40 | 35 | 25 | 80 |
| 14,300 | 25 | 24 | 19 | 15 | 28 | 43 | 25 | — | 28 | — |
| 16,500 | 18 | 23 | 28 | 17 | 40 | 35 | 35 | 55 | 35 | 30 |
| 21,000 | 17 | — | — | — | — | 35 | 27 | 40 | — | — |

DIVISION TEST. SHOWING TIME IN SECONDS FOR COMPLETION OF SUM.

| ALTITUDE IN FEET. | R.W.H. | B.B. | E.F.N. | G.L.M. | T.H.S. | E.O.S. | G.B. | J.V.H. | A.C.I. | N.E.O. |
|---|---|---|---|---|---|---|---|---|---|---|
| Sea-level | 30 | — | — | — | — | — | — | — | — | — |
| 7,000 | 20 | 20 | 30 | 10 | 25 | 55 | 15 | 35 | 15 | 45 |
| 14,300 | 28 | 20 | 13 | 23 | 20 | 45 | 17 | — | 17 | — |
| 16,500 | 13 | 27 | 23 | 17 | 40 | 38 | 23 | 43 | 20 | 50 |
| 21,000 | 15 | — | — | — | — | 40 | 13 | 59 | — | — |

The knee-jerks were examined at successive altitudes. In no case did they seem in any way affected by the height. Three of the party developed mild tremors: one a tremor of the eyelids at 14,000 feet, two a fine tremor of the fingers at 21,000 feet. This was an indication of nervous strain. It was a common sign of exhaustion and anxiety amongst those serving in the Great War.

*Sleep.* – To my mind insomnia was an unpleasant feature. But there were others who suffered from no lack of sleep except when they happened to be cold. Bruce on two nights slept for more than ten hours at 21,000 feet. He had a fair, but somewhat broken, night at 23,000 feet. He had about two hours' sleep at the beginning of the night, then a long period of sleeplessness, then a few more hours' sleep in the morning when at 25,000 feet. He always slept with his head raised, having learned the trick on the previous expedition. Somervell slept well at 25,000 feet and had two good spells of sleep at 27,000 feet. Norton, however, takes the record. He slept well and had an excellent night at 27,000 feet. A point about high-altitude sleeplessness is the fact that it is not associated with restlessness, nor does it cause weariness the next day. One lies awake, but does not toss about, nor is the sleep accompanied with irritable dreams.

*Glacier Lassitude.* – A distinct feature in the Mount Everest region is the very pronounced glacier lassitude which develops over tracts of ice. This was most marked on the Rongbuk Glacier, especially when passing through a trough in the ice at an altitude of about 20,000 feet. The trough was a remarkable feature, being girt on either side with walls of ice in many places hewn into fantastic pinnacles and ornamented with pyramidal spires. In this trough there was a peculiar sapping of energy, a weakness of the legs, and a disinclination to move. It was not a breathlessness due to exertion, but a loss of muscular power. There was a feeling of prostration. One seemed to drag oneself along, instead of going with the usual strength. A profuse sweating was not uncommon. It was something like the oppression experienced when marching through a hot moist jungle in the rains. The lassitude appeared immediately after stepping on to the glacier; it was as quickly relieved on again reaching rock or moraine. It was most noticeable in the absence of wind and in the middle of the day when the sun was strong. It was absent late at evening and in the early morning, and was less marked on cloudy days.

The cause of this lassitude is easily explained. The conditions for its development are a sheet of ice, a hot sun and a still air. The sun melts the superficial layer of the ice. The lowest stratum of the atmosphere becomes saturated with moisture, but does not rise owing to its being chilled by contact with the ice. Thus, when on the glacier, one is in a saturated atmosphere, and this, in conjunction with the high altitude, is sufficient to cause the unpleasant effects.

We did not notice that other atmospheric conditions had any special influence on these high-altitude symptoms. This was different from my experiences in the Western Himalaya. There, on two occasions, our party climbed the same peak to a height of 18,203 feet. During the first ascent the sky was clear, the air was free from moisture and our disability was slight. On the second occasion the conditions were different. The sky was dark, stormy weather was imminent, and the atmosphere felt heavy and damp. Our distress on this second occasion was acute. Every few paces found us gasping for breath, and we had repeatedly to make short halts. The same explanation applies to this as in the case of the glacier lassitude. On the second ascent the atmosphere was laden with moisture. The free evaporation of perspiration was checked, and, as a consequence, the high-altitude symptoms were increased.

*Individual Variation.* – The experiences of the party, as already detailed, indicate considerable individual variation with respect to oxygen want. It was obvious that some of us breathed more laboriously than others. One suffered from headache, another did not; one lost the sense of taste, another observed no such change; one was sleepless at comparatively low altitudes, another slept well at the highest camps. One member seemed particularly resistant to the lassitude that occurs over snow and ice. All were agreed that the Sherpa porters suffered, on an average, less than Europeans. Their power of carrying loads was extraordinary. They went with loads as fast as did the climbers without loads. It was not that they were muscularly more powerful than we. Probably their actual strength was less. It was their capacity to carry that was so much greater. This must be due to their permanent habitations being at altitudes of 12,000 to 14,000 feet, and to the fact that they habitually carry loads over passes of 16,000 and 18,000 feet.

*Oxygen.* – To what extent does the breathing of oxygen alleviate the symptoms already described? Theoretically we should expect an enormous benefit. We know of its great value in balloon ascents which could not be made to extreme altitudes unless oxygen was breathed. But our evidence on the subject is most unsatisfactory. The two climbers who could have told us most about it have perished on the mountain. Bruce used oxygen on his ascent to the North Col, that is between 21,000 and 23,000 feet. He noticed scarcely any benefit. Odell used it at the same altitude and considered that it gave no relief. Later he used it between 25,000 and 27,000 feet. There the oxygen seemed to relieve the breathing and diminish the tiredness of the legs. He thinks it may have helped to keep up the temperature. Its use produced an uncomfortable drying of the throat which necessitated frequent swallowing and expectoration. He abandoned the oxygen at 27,000 feet and descended easily without it. It is remarkable how little benefit was obtained from the oxygen compared with the experiences of the previous Expedition.

*Acclimatisation.* – I pass to the problem of acclimatisation. When we compare a rapid with a gradual ascent we see how powerful is this factor of adaptation to increasing heights. Haldane describes the condition of visitors after a rapid ascent of Pike's Peak to a height of only 14,100 feet: 'Many persons walked or rode up during the night to see the sunrise, especially on Sunday morning, and the scene in the restaurant and on the platform outside can only be likened to that on the deck or in the cabin of a cross-Channel steamer during rough weather.' Now the altitude at which this scene took place was about the same as that of the Tibetan plateau. But our ascent to the plateau was gradual, and, therefore, accompanied by acclimatisation. As a consequence we felt scarcely any distress. We were quite comfortable at a height where, if our ascent had been rapidly made, we should have been like the nauseated visitors on Pike's Peak.

But the contrast is more marked if we compare our progress with an air ascent. In the year 1875 Tissandier and his two companions made their famous ascent in a balloon from Paris. They were provided with oxygen, but were unable to make use of it. Tissandier fainted at 26,500 feet, and when he recovered consciousness the balloon was descending and his companions were dead. The balloon had reached an altitude of 27,950 feet. This was a rapid ascent with no acclimatisation. The result was death between 26,000 and 28,000 feet even when sitting quietly in a balloon. Compare this with a gradual attack on Mount Everest. Climbers without oxygen have ascended the mountain to 28,000 feet, somewhere about the same height where death occurred in the balloon. Yet at that altitude they were capable of strenuous effort; they showed no indication of fainting; they could sleep well at a slightly lower elevation, and were comparatively comfortable so long as they were at rest. The difference in the two ascents is due to acclimatisation, without which any attempt to reach the summit of Mount Everest would be altogether out of the question. The fact is that balloon ascents and experiments in air chambers are not at all comparable to the conditions of a prolonged climb.

A special point which the Expedition of last year taught us is that persons who have once experienced high altitudes will acclimatise very much more rapidly than those entering them for the first time. Those of our party who had been on two Expeditions were unanimous in the view that they suffered less on the second than on the first occasion. One said that his mind was much more active than it was in 1922, another that he reached Camp III with much less difficulty, another that he had not to breathe deeply at night as he found necessary on the previous Expedition. Also it was obvious that the new members of the party were distinctly more affected than the old. This is a point of practical importance. It means that, other things being equal, old hands will acclimatise more rapidly and be in a fitter state to climb the mountain than will be a party of fresh recruits. Even aviators have noticed the same thing. Although their ascents are so quick and short, yet they say that they get accustomed to the height. The body seems, as it were, to become trained by one experience, and, therefore, to make the necessary adjustments more easily on reaching high altitudes a second time.

In this connection we may recall those bleeding experiments already referred to in this chapter. The capacity of the animals to restore their red corpuscles became more rapid each time they were bled. Their powers of adaptation improved by experience. Their bodies, as a result of repeated deprivation, became trained to increased production. In acclimatisation we seem to have an analogous result. The climber, after long deprivation of oxygen, can adapt himself more rapidly on his next ascent.

To what height can acclimatisation continue? There seems to be no doubt of a steady improvement at 19,000 feet. Shebbeare spent over a month at that altitude in Camp II. At first he found the ascent to Camp III very laborious, but at the end of a month could do it with ease, and on the last day did it in the record time of 1 hour 55 minutes. Odell remained for ten days at 23,000 feet, and said that he certainly felt better as a result of this. Somervell believed that acclimatisation took place at 24,000 feet. But we must remember that while acclimatisation is in progress there may be physical deterioration at the same time. Though the body is becoming more accustomed to the altitude, yet simultaneously it is losing both in weight and strength. Dr Kellas puts the important question: 'Is it possible to become sufficiently acclimatised to altitudes of 24,000 feet to 26,000 feet to enable one to climb to over 29,000 feet?' I think that most of our party would reply in the affirmative. Two of them have already reached 28,000 feet aided by no other power beyond their own natural capacities for acclimatisation.

*After-effects.* – A note as to the after-effects consequent on residence at the high camps. The climbers were examined before we left the mountain. All of them showed signs of dilatation of the heart; in two it was decidedly marked. All were debilitated. All had wasted considerably, probably as much as 1½ to 2 stone. The porters too had lost much weight. Barcroft observed the same effect on his expedition to Peru. Loss of weight occurred in all the members of his party, the most marked being a decline from 155 to 131 pounds in twenty-seven days.

Those of the Expedition who had been badly frostbitten required treatment for weeks after we had left the mountain. Frostbite showed itself in two varieties: the moist form with large blisters full of fluid, and the dry gangrenous type. Snow-blindness also may need after-treatment. A point of interest was that Norton developed a severe attack of blindness when at high altitudes, though in the absence of snow. At 28,000 feet he was on bare rock. He thought it unnecessary to use his snow-glasses, and on the next day he was completely blind. The sun's rays in this thin air can cause a most acute attack of conjunctivitis even when reflected from bare dark rock.

Thus life on the mountain causes physical deterioration. Improvement followed on our return to the Base Camp with increase in appetite and better sleep. Finally we descended into the Rongshar Valley, where, at the pleasant altitude of 10,000 feet, all were quickly restored to health.

*Conclusion.* – A last word on the possibility of reaching the summit. In the year 1916, at an afternoon meeting of the Royal Geographical Society, Dr Kellas showed an interesting dissociation curve of Oxy-hæmoglobin in blood. On this curve he plotted the heights of some well-known mountains. From it he drew the following deductions. 'The curve,' he said, 'is very suggestive. It shows that the strain on the climber is nearly negligible up to 10,000 feet, and at about 15,000 feet becomes appreciable, but one must pass above 20,000 feet before the steepening of the curve indicates that the mountaineer will have to adapt himself carefully to his aerial environment. At 23,000 feet the curve is getting much steeper, and the climber will obviously be put on his mettle above 25,000 feet, for the curve then attains its steepest. Every 1,000 feet still higher must mean considerably increased difficulty, and the climber near the summit of Mount Everest will probably be on his last reserves in the way of acclimatisation and strength.' This deduction was made before the first assault on Mount Everest, and I think that we can now safely say that our practical experiences bear it out.

I think that climbers will reach the summit of Mount Everest even without the help of oxygen. Though the physiological difficulties are undoubtedly severe, yet they can be overcome. But the condition of the weather must be more favourable than last year. The climbers must be in perfect health and in first-rate training; they must be men of exceptional powers of endurance and their capacity for acclimatisation must be complete.

# 2 NATURAL HISTORY

## BY MAJOR R.W.G. HINGSTON, IMS

The collections brought back by the Mount Everest Expedition amount to over 10,000 specimens of animals and 500 specimens of plants. This material is now in the hands of specialists, and a detailed report on it will appear later in suitable scientific publications. All that I can attempt to do here is to touch briefly on some general observations, and, omitting as far as possible technical detail, to give a picture of animal existence at high altitudes on the plateau of Tibet.

*Protective Coloration at High Altitudes.* – The plateau of Tibet is a great desert at a height of about 14,000 feet. It is a broken desert, a Sahara elevated and crumpled into mountains, with characteristic features of its own. How forcibly do these physical features impress us! The vast empty spaces, the brown barren hills, the tracts of loose and crumbling sand, the cloudless skies, the penetrating light, the wide extremes of temperature, the scanty rainfall, the dry air, the fierce winds, the low thorny and monotonous vegetation: these are the most impressive features in this cold and elevated tract.

Our first acquaintance with the life of this plateau reveals one conspicuous fact. The majority of the animals are protectively coloured, as a rule some shade of buff or brown so as to resemble the plateau soil. Protective coloration is characteristic of deserts, and well known to occur in all low-lying wastes. It is interesting, therefore, to observe the same natural principle in this desert elevated to so great a height. On every side we meet with examples. Mammals, birds, reptiles, insects, all illustrate how important is protective coloration in the general scheme of high-altitude life.

I will mention some of the more striking illustrations. The mouse-hares (*Ochotona curzoniæ*) are common mammals of Tibet. They live in communities on the open plateau, establishing themselves usually on grassy patches, where they hibernate in burrows throughout the winter, and in summer come forth to collect food. They are delightful little creatures, about the size of a guinea-pig. Near Phari they live in immense colonies. The plain is there literally studded with their tunnels. On warm days they are busy and active, chewing at the grass, rooting in the soil, often peeping inquisitively from the entrance to their burrows, or scampering from hole to hole. We are attracted by their example of harmonisation, the pale grey colour of their fur blending well with the upland soil. This adaptation of colour must protect them from enemies, especially from the powerful birds of prey which circle over their exposed haunts. If we drop from the plateau into the main range, into those deep gorges stuffed with vegetation that lead to Sikkim and Nepal, we there find another kind of mouse-hare (*Ochotona sikimaria*). This is a darker coloured species, clothed in black and rusty hair. It lives on mountain slopes, in more gloomy surroundings, hiding as a rule beneath rocks and stones. Its coat is thus adapted to its special haunts, being conspicuously darker in colour than that of the pale species on the plateau of Tibet.

The marmots supply another example of harmonisation. We met with them in only a few places, usually near the summits of bare passes where they used to sit erect near the entrance to their burrows and utter loud whistling notes. Their colour blends well with these desolate surroundings, appearing as a kind of brownish yellow inconspicuous against the rock behind. The Tibetan hare is still another instance. This animal likes to haunt the stony mountains, especially those heaps of broken rock which have accumulated at the foot of the hills. It finds suitable hiding-places amongst the boulders, but in addition is so coloured that when it sits still it is lost to view amongst the broken stones.

Some of the larger mammals are protectively coloured. We frequently saw gazelle on the open plateau and noticed how their coats used to blend with the soil. It was the same with the wild sheep that haunted our Base Camp. Though of large size, yet they were comparatively inconspicuous against the hillsides. Our attention was sometimes first drawn to the herd by the clatter of falling stones which the animals displaced as they fed on the moraines.

The birds provide numerous examples of harmonisation. Mountain-finches are common high-altitude birds. We met with five kinds on our journey across the plateau. There was Blandford's mountain-finch, a fulvous-coloured bird, often seen near villages and in cultivated fields. Adams' mountain-finch was another species, a brown bird with a pretty white wing-patch. It used to visit our Everest Base Camp, and, when we left, was establishing its nest in a moraine. One commonly met with was the red-necked mountain-finch. This species also is brown in colour, with a white chin, a black moustache and a broad white band over the eye. It was a constant companion of the mouse-hares, living with them on the most friendly terms. Not unlike it was Mandelli's finch, though a bird of local distribution and thinly scattered. Occasionally we saw it entering the burrows of mouse-hares, at the bottom of which it undoubtedly breeds. Brandt's mountain-finch is somewhat different. It is darker in colour, especially in winter when the edges of the feathers get worn away. We saw it usually near villages and in cultivated fields. It was one of the most constant visitors of our Base Camp and used to like to haunt the high stony passes up to 17,000 feet. These five mountain-finches are fairly well protected by their plumage. They are dull, inconspicuous birds, coloured some shade of brown or fulvous and thus adapted to a life on these open plains.

Larks are amongst the commonest birds of the plateau. There was the Tibetan skylark, a bird almost identical with our species at home. We frequently met with it in the vicinity of villages, in cultivated fields or pasture areas, or following the plough in search of food. Sometimes we heard it singing high in the air after the manner of our English bird. The short-toed lark was still more common. It nested freely at these elevations, up to a height of 15,000 feet. Another kind was the large-billed calandra lark, a powerful, noisy bird which utters a loud call-note when in flight. It specially likes the marshy areas, where it hides its nest in an elevated tuft situated in the midst of the swamp. Like the finches, these larks frequent open places, and all are dull, sombre-coloured species which blend with their high-altitude haunts.

The Tibetan snow-cock is a good example of harmonisation. It is a large, powerfully built, red-legged partridge, ascending to high altitudes and feeding on the grass up to about 17,000 feet. Flocks used to congregate near the Rongbuk Glacier, searching the moraines or the high cliffs, and from the Base Camp we often heard their whistling notes ringing loudly across the gorge. These snow-cock blend well with the barren hills and are not easily seen amongst boulders and crags.

The Tibetan sand-grouse is another protectively coloured bird. It lives on the open stony plateau, where its pale fawn plumage blends with the ground. These sand-grouse congregate in considerable flocks. When in flight, they are noisy and conspicuous, showing their pale underparts and dark patches on their wings. But these colours disappear when the flock alights. Their wings fold so as to hide the black patches on the feathers, their pale underparts are concealed beneath them, and the birds look just like scattered stones.

The wall-creeper supplies an illustration from the cliffs. We met with it on the slaty hill of Shekar, also on the precipices above our Base Camp at a height of 18,000 feet. It creeps about on these high-altitude rocks searching for insects and spiders in the clefts. The plumage of its back is ashy grey, which blends well with the similarly coloured rocks. But the moment it takes to flight it becomes immediately conspicuous. Brilliant patches of crimson appear on its wings, also bright spots of white. Our attention is attracted to this flash of colour; then unexpectedly the bird alights, the crimson colour vanishes, the white spots disappear, and the bird again harmonises with the hill.

In the bed of the torrents we find another example. This is the ibis-bill, a high-altitude wader which lives on the layer of water-worn boulders strewn along the floor of the gorge. The colour of the ibis-bill is grey to ashy, very like that of the water-worn stones. On its breast, however, is a conspicuous gorget, but this the bird manages to conceal by its habit of crouching low. When alarmed, it remains stationary in the midst of the boulders, lowers its body so as to hide the colours on its breast, and is lost to view amongst the rounded stones. Its chicks are protected in the same way. The parent utters a loud cry to warn them of danger, and, on hearing it, they hide in the torrent bed.

The powerful birds of the plateau are not protectively coloured. They are well able to defend themselves and thus have no need of a special colour scheme. The raven is common around Tibetan villages, the steppe eagle soars over the colonies of mouse-hares, the kite comes down to take garbage from camps. These birds can have few if any serious enemies, and they are conspicuous from afar. So are the red-billed and yellow-billed choughs. Though these are less powerful birds, yet they are strong and pugnacious; also they keep together in flocks and seem well able to take care of themselves. Certain of the little birds are decidedly conspicuous, and in some cases we see the obvious reason why they do not require a protective scheme. The tree-sparrows and accentors may be quoted as examples. Their markings clearly do not serve to conceal them, but these birds keep near villages and amongst piles of stones where they can easily escape from birds of prey. It is those species which live on the open plateau that particularly require the protective scheme.

It has been said that the protectively coloured birds of the desert are made conspicuous by the shadows which they cast on the ground. The dark shadow patch attracts notice and is liable to direct attention to the bird. This may be so on an even desert where the sand is a smooth unbroken sheet. But it is not the case in these upland deserts. Here there are objects of every kind, stones and clods and dry tufts of grass. All these cast shadows when the sun is low. Consequently there is nothing specially attractive about the shadow cast by a bird.

Against what enemies have the small birds of the plateau to contend? I have frequently noted eagles circling round the hills. Buzzards investigate the mouse-hare communities. I have seen a falcon attacked by choughs. Probably the kestrels capture small birds, since they were fairly common on the plateau in April, when scarcely an insect of any kind could be found.

The lizards of the plateau are protectively coloured. They belong to the species *Phrynocephalus Theobaldi*. Small and active, they tunnel in the soil, constructing for themselves permanent habitations which open on the surface by a slit-like hole. On congenial days they come out from these burrows and sun themselves on the warm sand. Though all belong to the same species, yet these lizards vary much in coloration. Some are pale grey, others spotted with brown and yellow, still others with these markings arranged in bands. They all, however, blend well with the plateau and are thus protected from raptorial birds. A point of interest about these high-altitude lizards is the conspicuous colour of their under surface, which of course is ordinarily hidden from view. For this surface is almost pure white, but in the middle of the belly is a black patch, and there is a black mark near the end of the tail. We find the same peculiarity in certain lizards of the Sahara. It seems in some way related to desert conditions. But what is its purpose we are unable to explain.

The high-altitude spiders provide numerous examples of creatures coloured so as to resemble their haunts. Lycosids live near the Tibetan streams where they run over the sand and hide beneath stones. Their general colour is a pale brown marked with a delicate mottling and speckling that harmonises with the underlying sand. At higher altitudes on the moraines are other kinds which ascend to 17,000 feet. These are grey and brown like the particles of rock, an adaptation which may aid them in the capture of prey, but is probably of more service as a protection against wasps which pursue them at these desolate heights.

The moths of the highest altitudes are protectively coloured. These are little species resembling our *Anarta*. They haunted the moraines around our Base Camp, and even camps on the Rongbuk Glacier up to 18,000 feet. Seen from beneath they are very conspicuous, with black and white bands on the under surface of the wings. But this surface is concealed when the moth comes to rest by the pressing of its wings close against the stone. Only the upper surface is exposed to view, and this is mottled with delicate grey which blends with the granite rock.

We find a striking instance of protective colouring in the case of the grasshoppers. Unfortunately they cannot be properly identified since, owing to the early season of the year, those we found were mostly in the larval state.

Let us compare these larvæ with their selected haunts. One kind, the Central Asian migratory locust, was coloured a rich green, and we found it in patches of green grass at an altitude of 15,000 feet. Another kind, belonging to a new genus, was a resident of greater heights. In size it was minute, being immature and wingless, and it lived amongst boulders and decomposing grit on the moraines at 17,000 feet. Its scheme of colour was grey and black with delicate transverse bands across its thighs. This made it difficult to detect in its surroundings, since the pattern of colour closely resembled that of the granite flakes. At lower altitudes on the windswept sand we met with still another kind. This little species was brown in colour with markings of blue and rusty red. It harmonised well with its special haunts, for the sand was speckled with red and blue granules carried down from the neighbouring hills. A fourth kind was found on the water-worn pebbles along the bank of the Chiblung Chu. These pebbles were smooth and flat and composed mainly of bluish slate. The grasshopper that lived on them was the same shade of colour, a pale uniform slaty blue that harmonised well with the water-worn stones.

Thus we see how important is protective coloration in the struggle for existence at these great heights. It is in the vast and open tracts, the deserts, the snows, the elevated wastes, that we see this principle most lavishly illustrated. The reason for protection of this kind is clear. In the wilderness hiding-places are seldom available. There are no trees, no scrub, no profusion of grass in which the animals can conceal themselves when enemies approach. To avoid destruction they must seek evasion of some sort. Their only chance is to resemble their natural surroundings and escape by being passed unseen.

*Adaptation of Cold and Wind.* – It is interesting to observe how the animals at high altitudes adapt themselves to cold and wind. In winter the cold on the plateau is severe: at all times the range of temperature is considerable, often 50° in the twenty-four hours. We took temperatures at the Base Camp throughout the month of May. On the 27th there was a daily range of 53° Fahrenheit; on the 31st of 58° Fahrenheit. Tibet is notorious for its fierce winds. Near the Base Camp they had made their mark on the rocks. Deep grooves had been cut into the granite boulders. Their windward surface was so eroded that it looked like coral, while the leeward surface was ordinarily smooth. And this was all due to the persistent wind which poured through this narrow gorge. The animals which live on the surface soil must necessarily experience great extremes of temperature. Here are some records from the Base Camp taken on May 20 at a height of 16,500 feet:

|  | MAXIMUM IN 24 HOURS. | MINIMUM IN 24 HOURS. | DAILY RANGE OF TEMPERATURES. |
|---|---|---|---|
| Temperature of Sand. | 96 | 2 | 94 |
| Temperature of Air. | 55 | 11 | 44 |

It is probable that animals living on the sand, such as beetles, grasshoppers, spiders and others, will often have to endure a daily range of temperature of as much as 100 °F.

Many mammals at these high altitudes have thicker coats of hair, obviously to serve as a protection against cold. We see in this the herds of domesticated goats, delightful little animals, dwarfed in size, and provided with a thick hairy coat which hangs down like a kilt around their legs. Some of the Tibetan dogs are particularly well clothed, but I have seen better examples farther west on the upland plateau of the Pamir. They possess not only a coat of hair, but sometimes in addition a covering of wool. In spring this gives them a ragged appearance when large patches of the winter wool still cling to their hairy coats. Near Gautsa, at a height of 12,000 feet, I saw a herd of pigs in company with yaks. They seemed out of place at these elevations, and were covered in thick rusty-coloured hair quite different from the half-naked animals of the plains. The Tibetan hare has a dense coat, and it used to ascend as high as our Base Camp, to the moraines at 17,000 feet.

But the ordinary yak provides the best example. It is provided with a double garment. Next its skin is a layer of wool. Over this is a hairy coat which hangs down like a skirt from its huge body, especially around its legs. Its neck carries a strong mane, and behind it is provided with a bushy tail. This large tail is a most conspicuous feature. Its value at first sight is not very obvious, but becomes apparent when we see the animals grazing on a slope. For yaks, when feeding, turn their hind quarters to the wind. In this way they make use of their enormous tails, which sometimes reach almost to the ground. The tail supplies the animal with a kind of windscreen, while the hair from the belly that hangs around the legs increases the efficiency of this shield. The arrangement of the hair after the fashion of a skirt is probably of use when the animal is lying down. For the legs are then partially drawn up into the covering which may help to keep them warm.

The smaller mammals of the plateau are of the shelter-seeking kind. The Tibetan hare lives amongst broken rock. On the Pamir plateau it is said to have burrows of its own. The marmot, the vole and the mouse-hare all tunnel deep into the soil. The lizards also construct their own dens, of which the entrance is often sheltered by a tuft or stone.

The Tibetan wind commences to blow usually at about 10 a.m. At these altitudes the sun quickly warms the plateau. On a still morning, after a few hours of sunshine, the sand becomes warm to the touch. The low-lying air begins to shimmer: from the plateau visible currents ascend which spread into a pale mirage. This rapid heating of the plateau accounts for the strong winds. The warm air rises, and in order to fill the deficiency cold air pours down from the snowy range, often with tremendous force.

The birds that live on the open plateau are very discomfited by these diurnal gales. The mountain-finches, the ground-choughs, the larks and others seek shelter behind any available obstacle. For this reason we frequently find flocks of little birds collected on the leeward side of villages or behind chortens and stone walls. Many birds creep into more sheltered nooks. Tree-sparrows often hide in the holes of houses, choughs get under the lee of rocks, rose-finches nestle beneath ledges and stones. Those birds that live in company with mouse-hares roost in these animals' dens. The wind is injurious to their soft plumage. One of the most striking things about a collection from the plateau is the manner in which the feathers are dilapidated and worn.

It is interesting to note how all the birds face the wind when it blows at its full strength. This is essential for the little kinds that live on the open plains. If they stand across it they may be lifted off their feet. The larger birds also have to face the wind. Flocks of choughs like to feed on grassy areas, where they scatter about in individual pairs. As they probe the soil in these open tracts they all stand with their heads to the wind. The raven is a regular village scavenger. There it finds every kind of refuse, and we see it persistently facing the wind as it stalks about in search of food. Wind helps many birds in their aerial evolutions, and this is particularly noticeable in Tibet. The choughs ascend in clamorous flocks, floating and circling, rising higher and higher with only an occasional beat of the wing. It is wind that permits of these effortless movements. When the air is still they have to flap their wings. The lammergeier makes some use of it when breaking its food. It finds bones near villages, carries them aloft, then drops them until they smash to pieces on the ground. It employs the wind to aid its ascent, and, as it comes down on the broken fragments, it always heads the breeze. There are two common hovering birds of the plateau. We may often see the kestrel hanging stationary in the air watching for prey on the open plain. The Tibetan tern is a hoverer that makes its poise over a lake into which it plunges to seize a fish. The wind is a great help to these hovering evolutions.

They demand considerable muscular effort, particularly at an altitude where the rarefied atmosphere possesses only half its supporting power.

It is necessary for the birds of these windswept altitudes to find sheltered places in which to nest. We met with many examples on our march across the plateau. The choughs nest in holes on earthen cliffs up to 15,000 feet. The hoopoes seek the same kind of sheltered places. The tree-sparrows build in the village walls. We found the nest of the ground-chough at the bottom of a tunnel over four feet in depth; and the mountain-finches, as already mentioned, nest in mouse-hare burrows, where they are secure from both enemies and wind. The magpie builds an enormous nest, a much thicker and more bulky structure than that of our English bird. Those birds that build on the ground seek out suitable shelters. We found the shore-lark nesting behind a ridge of earth, the calandra lark in a tussock of grass, the short-toed lark in the lee of a vetch. This last bird in one instance showed an interesting modification. It had placed its nest under the shelter of a vetch, while at the opposite side it had built a little barrier, a low wall of pebbles about an inch in width, no doubt a protection against wind and sand.

The habits of certain Tibetan butterflies help them in their struggle with the strong wind. The species of *Parnassius* exemplify this. They are characteristic of these barren altitudes. We found them on the moraines in the vicinity of our Base Camp. They are insects of comparatively feeble flight and are easily carried along by a gale. Yet they love to haunt the wildest places, especially the passes up to 17,000 feet where the winds sweep furiously across the range. They escape being blown away by their peculiarities in habit. They are unwilling to fly except when the air is still. Moreover, when disturbed, they make only short flights, and when they settle they like to get into sheltered nooks. Their resting attitude is particularly advantageous. The moment they alight they spread their wings, then press them down close and tight to the ground so as to offer the least resistance to the air. Furthermore their wings are stiff and rigid and not likely to be torn when being battered by the wind. In this respect they are quite different from the more fragile butterflies that inhabit the valleys of the main range.

The swallowtail (*Papilio machaon*) and the tortoiseshell (*Vanessa cashmirensis*) were two other butterflies that ascended to our Base Camp at 16,500 feet. These kinds did not possess the habits of the *Parnassius*. But they happen to be strong and vigorous fliers, sufficiently swift and powerful on the wing to contend with the high-altitude winds. How different is this *Papilio* from the common forms of Sikkim, which, though larger and incomparably more beautiful in colour, yet float about high up in the gorges at the mercy of every breeze.

Certain moths at high altitudes behave like the *Parnassius* in their efforts to contend with the wind. There was a kind like an *Anarta* on the Rongbuk Glacier fully exposed to the Everest blast. Its haunts were the boulders that carpeted the ice, and it used to visit the highest alpine flowers. When the wind was strong it kept down amongst the rocks, shuffling between the boulders and fluttering through the crevices, instead of boldly taking to flight. When on the wing it was active in all its movements, making rapid skips from place to place, but seldom flying for more than a few yards without throwing itself again to the ground. Its resting attitude was like that of the *Parnassius*: wings outstretched and flattened against the rock so as to offer the least resistance to the wind.

A few diptera used to haunt the same high elevation up to 17,000 feet. In their actions they resembled the high-altitude moths. They liked keeping in amongst stones and rocks. When disturbed, they made only quick short flights, their actions being more like the leaps of a grasshopper than the ordinary movements of a fly. There was one kind, a Tachinid, which used to live amongst boulders along the banks of the plateau streams. It had a black hairy body, a spined abdomen, and fragile speckled wings. Now, this little fly seemed almost incapable of flight, so reluctant was it to take to the air in a wind. Its habit was to seek shelter beneath water-worn boulders, and, when these were upturned, it could be taken in the fingers, preferring capture to the risk of flight. Another kind, belonging to the genus *Gonia*, used to inhabit thorny scrub. It came out on sunny mornings when the air was calm. But its flights were short, only a few feet, as though it feared to trust itself to any distance in the air. When disturbed, it tried hard to remain within the scrub, flitting about from twig to twig, or coming to rest on the sand underneath. Thus it managed to evade the wind, partly by reason of its short flights and partly by keeping within the shelter of the thorn.

Hunting-wasps are common at high altitudes in Tibet. We found them in the tempestuous Rongbuk Valley, where they searched for spiders on the moraines. They work only in calm and sunshine. When the wind begins to blow they get down amongst the boulders, and, like the flies, they move in sudden leaps which prevent their being swept away. Humble bees also ascend to high altitudes. I saw one at a height of 21,000 feet. But these are strong insects of powerful flight, and pass boldly from flower to flower independent of any ordinary wind.

The *Pseudabris* beetles provide an interesting example of a method by which insects escape the wind. These beetles are conspicuous and brilliantly coloured with transverse bands of black and red. In places they congregate in great numbers, clustering on the vetches, also on the irises, where they feed on the young shoots and flowers. It is interesting to watch them when the wind blows hard. All the beetles let go their hold on the vegetation and throw themselves to the plateau soil. There they lie, all apparently dead. Each beetle is on its side, its head bent sharply at right angles to its body, its antennae turned down underneath it, its legs collected into a cluster of tags. They all lie motionless in this attitude of death, like a crowd of little corpses strewn over the ground. When the wind lessens we see them all revive. They run about the soil, return to the vegetation and resume their feeding on the vetch. We can stimulate this behaviour by blowing at them with the breath. They fall to the ground as in an ordinary wind, where, of course, they are far less exposed to danger, lying as if dead amongst the stones.

Thus we observe that the animals of high altitudes contend with the elements in many different ways. Some grow denser coats, others seek sheltered places, there is a great tendency to burrow in the soil. Certain butterflies and moths flatten themselves on the ground; many insects make only quick short flights; certain flies keep in amongst stones and bushes; certain beetles throw themselves for safety to the ground.

*Scarcity of Food at High Altitudes.* – Animals at high altitudes find considerable difficulty in contending with the scarcity of food. The domestic animals struggle hard for existence. It is wonderful to see a herd of yaks grazing on a hillside. The hill is brown and to all appearances barren. It shows not a trace of any green thing. Yet all the animals have their heads to the ground. They find a blade of grass in one spot; then, wandering on a yard or two, they happen to meet with another blade. In this way they gather a few mouthfuls, and manage to find sufficient food to maintain life during early spring. In summer, of course, they are better supplied. Grass shoots up during the quick short season. The yaks fatten, and the traveller is made aware of their improved condition by their capacity to carry loads. But in winter their struggle must be very acute. When snow is on the ground they dig through it to the vegetation. The Tibetans told me that they scraped up roots. I have seen them eating the fresh dung of a pony which happened to be better fed than themselves. The sheep find it difficult to maintain existence, especially in the early winter months when grass is beginning to appear. They have to work hard for each single mouthful. With their fore feet they dig into the soil, shuffle aside the superficial sand in order to get at the individual blades. The ponies may have to act in the same manner. When food was scarce, I have seen them cutting up the ground with their hoofs in order to get at the buried roots. Also they sometimes wade into the icy lakes, where they feed on the water-weed that grows up from underneath. The mules and donkeys will at times eat quantities of yak-dung, which does not seem to do them any special harm. But it is the mouse-hares that show the best example of husbandry. They store up quantities of seeds in their burrows to serve them as a winter supply of food.

*Change of Habit in Tibet.* – The peculiar environment of the Tibetan plateau has caused some of the high-altitude birds to change their customary habits of life. This is mainly due to the scarcity of vegetation. Tibet, as we have seen, is a broken desert. In winter the hills are utterly barren; in summer they support only a sparse growth. Such vegetation as exists has a desert appearance. We note the absence of trees, the thorniness of the plants, the short active season in which flowers rapidly bloom and as rapidly die away. Certainly in some spots up to a height of 14,000 feet we find occasional willows. But they are few and stunted, and, as a rule, are carefully tended by the people, who protect them within stone walls.

In such surroundings those birds which usually live in vegetation must of necessity find other haunts. Some of them have become exclusively village birds. Thus the tree sparrow has come to haunt human habitations. It is a common resident of every village, where it feeds in the streets and nests in the walls. The accentors also are village birds. On the plateau we met with two species, the robin accentor and the brown accentor. As a rule accentors frequent bushes and hedges. But on the plateau such haunts are seldom available. Hence these birds have come to occupy villages and to live near stone bridges and walls. The magpie is another good example. The Tibetan species is the same as our English bird which frequents trees and woods and cultivated fields. But the magpie of Tibet keeps mainly to houses. A colony had established itself near the village of Pangle. The birds lived on the roofs like jackdaws or house-crows, and used to ascend the precipitous cliffs which they shared with pigeons and choughs. This change of habit shows how pliable is animal instinct when necessity makes demand.

Certain birds in Tibet have lost their sense of fear. This is due to the absence of persecution. For the Buddhist religion forbids the taking of life, and this is strictly observed in Tibet. Thus many of the animals have become remarkably tame. The ruddy sheldrake and the bar-headed goose are in India amongst the most timid of birds, yet in Tibet they swim about the ponds near the villages almost as fearlessly as in a London park. Many birds haunt the Tibetan forts, especially ravens, lammergeiers, pigeons, and choughs. Of these the blue hill-pigeons (*Columba rupestris*) are remarkably tame. They enter villages freely, and used to feed in our Base Camp like the pigeons in a city street. But it is the wild sheep or burhel which provide the best example. Their timidity is known to every sportsman; wild sheep of all kinds are most difficult to approach. Yet in these barren altitudes they are remarkably tame. Herds used frequently to visit our Base Camp, feeding on the tussocks of dried grass that peeped out from amongst the stones. Sometimes they came within twenty yards of our tents, even when people were moving about in camp. Higher up on the mountain was a hermit's cell, and we were told that the sheep used to visit this sanctuary, where they took food out of the hermit's hands. Again we see how adaptable is animal instinct to the changes in surrounding life.

*Plateau Communities.* – A delightful feature in the life of the plateau is the manner in which certain birds and mammals live together in friendly company. This is most marked in the mouse-hare community. These little animals are markedly gregarious. Numbers collect in a common society and construct their tunnels on the same expanse of plain. With them associate different kinds of birds. Blandford's mountain-finch, Adams' mountain-finch, Mandelli's mountain-finch, the red-necked mountain-finch, Elwes' horned lark and the ground chough are the species most usually seen. All blend in colour with the plateau: as a rule they live in exposed places, the whole forming an instructive example of protectively coloured mammals and birds. The members of this family are remarkably tame, the birds living freely amongst the mouse-hares, finding fragments of food in the vicinity of their holes. Twenty or thirty mouse-hares may peer forth from their tunnels with mountain-finches hopping tamely around. The mouse-hares seem to take no notice of the finches: we never see a sign of any conflict; there is a perfect amity between the mammals and birds.

What is the object of this friendly association? I think it is all to the advantage of the birds, being a help to them in obtaining food. For these birds are seed-eating species. At these altitudes food is often scarce, but there are special attractions near the mouse-hares' holes. For these animals possess an instinctive forethought. The stress of conditions has driven them to husbandry. In summer they garner a supply of seeds; these they store in the bottom of their burrows, and devour them during the winter months. But where storage takes place there must certainly be some refuse. Little seeds will lie about in the vicinity of the burrows, and it is these waste fragments that attract the birds. It is probable that the birds also pillage the mouse-hares, for we frequently observed them entering the holes.

At greater altitudes, on the almost barren mountains, there is another community, a very simple one, but interesting because it occurs at so great a height. This is an association of choughs and wild sheep. The chough sits on the wild sheep's back, where it searches for insects in the animal's hair. The sheep seems pleased with the bird's attention and stands still while being explored. Thus engaged, they remain in one another's company and move slowly along the mountain slope. I have seen them on the cliffs above the Rongbuk Monastery as high as 17,000 feet. These wild sheep are amongst the mammals that reach the greatest altitudes, and choughs are probably the highest inhabitants of the earth. It is interesting to see these hardy creatures living such a sociable and friendly life.

*Hibernation.* – The summer at high altitudes is of short duration. Animal activity is therefore brief, lasting probably only about five months. In winter the cold is very severe, and most of the animals which cannot leave these elevations hibernate until spring returns. The mouse-hares sleep in the bottom of their burrows; so do the lizards in their narrow holes. When we reached the plateau early in April we found it almost destitute of animal life; there was not even an insect to be seen. Yet when we searched under the stones and dug into the superficial soil we found that in reality there was plenty of life. But every kind of creature was in a somnolent state. The ants were asleep in their subterranean galleries; under stones were beetles stiff and motionless, so torpid that they could scarcely move. We found centipedes rolled into motionless coils, spiders lying dormant in the interior of snail shells, caterpillars motionless and rigid, earwigs in a sluggish state with their antennæ thrust back along their sides. Insects were found in a state of hibernation up to a height of 18,000 feet. Many passed the winter in the larval stage. The ground beetles seemed habitually to hibernate in pairs. It was as if Nature had arranged their winter sleep in such a way that, when summer arrived, males and females should awake in suitable couples and be ready immediately to propagate their kind. In the galleries of the ants were eggs and larvæ, delicate forms of insect life to survive in this frozen soil. We some-times exposed numbers of dead insects, regular cemeteries underneath stones. It seemed as if many must have gone into hibernation and died in the severe cold.

A few experiments will prove the value of hibernation to the animals. On May 22 I made an artificial burrow at an altitude of 16,500 feet. The burrow was like the kind in which the mouse-hares hibernate. The follow-ing were the temperatures in the interior of this burrow one foot beneath the soil:

| HOUR OF DAY. | TEMPERATURE OF BURROW. | TEMPERATURE OF AIR. |
|---|---|---|
| 8 a.m. | 33 °F. | 34 °F. |
| Midday | 33 °F. | 48 °F. |
| 4 p.m. | 33 °F. | 42 °F. |
| 9 p.m. | 33 °F. | 29 °F. |

Thus from 8 a.m. to 9 p.m. the burrow remained at a uniform temperature. During the same period the temperature of the air varied through 19 °F. Thus the mouse-hares by hibernation gain great advantage. They escape extremes of temperature and find uniform conditions. And in winter they must gain it even still more when the soil is covered with snow.

The conditions under a stone are also favourable for hibernation. On May 21 I took a temperature record at 17,000 feet.

| | BENEATH STONE. | OF AIR. |
|---|---|---|
| Maximum Temp. in 24 Hours | 39 °F. | 56 °F. |
| Minimum Temp. in 24 Hours | 27 °F. | 12 °F. |

This shows a variation underneath a stone of 12 °F in twenty-four hours. During the same period the temperature of the air varied through 44 °F.

The following is a record at the same altitude two inches beneath the soil:

| | TWO INCHES BENEATH SOIL. | OF AIR. |
|---|---|---|
| Maximum Temp. in 24 Hours | 34 °F. | 59 °F. |
| Minimum Temp. in 24 Hours | 27 °F. | 23 °F. |

It shows that at two inches beneath the surface the temperature varied through only 7 °F, while that of the air during the same period ranged through 36 °F. Thus the smaller creatures likewise gain advantage by getting into the soil or underneath stones. The ants, the beetles, the caterpillars, the spiders find more uniform conditions for their winter sleep.

There were signs of animation towards the end of May at altitudes of 17,000 feet. Above the Base Camp on May 27 I found the first gentian in flower on the moraine; on the same day a tortoiseshell butterfly appeared; a few pale coloured moths began to skip about the debris; some immature grasshoppers were active on the stones and larvæ in the thawing pools. The beetles were definitely awakening, and came out occasionally from their retreats beneath the stones. Spiders are amongst the first to shake off this sleep; we may often see them crawling on the moist earth at the very edge of the retreating snows.

*Altitudes to which Animals Ascend.* – In the struggle for existence at great altitudes many animals are driven to extreme heights. It indicates how powerful is the vital force of this planet, how relentless is Nature in her efforts to populate every habitable corner of the earth. Let us consider the different groups of animals and the highest altitudes at which we found them.

First with respect to man. He struggles to exist wherever the earth provides the barest sustenance for life. The Tibetans plough the soil up to 15,000 feet, at which height they can glean a scanty harvest. Here men live in small stone villages, dirty, scanty, wind-swept habitations, almost the highest on the earth's surface. There is a monastery in the Rongbuk Valley at an altitude of 16,000 feet. Above the monastery is a dilapidated nunnery, and still higher at 17,000 feet is a cell in the mountain where a hermit has imprisoned himself for a term of years.

Certain mammals reach considerable elevations. Herds of burhel ascend to 17,000 feet. They work along the hillsides, displacing the boulders. At first sight there seems little to attract them at these altitudes; but even on these moraines there is a trace of vegetation, and the sheep here and there find a tuft of grass peeping out from amongst the stones. A few other mammals compete with the sheep in the altitudes to which they ascend. We saw marmots near the summit of the Pusi La at 16,500 feet. The Tibetan hare came as high as 17,000 feet, where it lived amongst the boulders close to our Base Camp. One day a little mouse-hare was seen in this camp sheltering underneath a stone. At 20,000 feet, in Camp II, Shebbeare noted tracks of a small mammal in the soft snow close to our tents. These had probably been made by a mouse-hare. At this altitude there was not a trace of vegetation, nothing on which a grass-eating mammal could exist. We think it likely that the animal was carried up in baggage rather than that it lived permanently at this height.

Birds in their migrations reach considerable altitudes; probably some of the smallest species cross the highest ranges on the earth. But there are many which populate this high-altitude plateau. They are true residents of these inhospitable regions: not like the migrants, mere travellers through the heights. On the plateau we noted fifty-six different kinds of birds at altitudes upwards of 14,000 feet. Mountain-finches were persistent visitors of our Base Camp. So was the brown accentor, more occasionally the wall-creeper, also ravens, lammergeiers, hill-pigeons, and choughs. Adams' mountain-finch and Guldenstadt's redstart nested at these heights. Many marsh-birds ascend as high as marshes exist. The bar-headed goose and the ruddy sheldrake collect in flocks on the Tibetan plateau at an altitude of 14,000 feet. The brown-headed gull and the Tibetan tern occupy the lakes and streams. The lesser sand-plover explores the brink of the rivers, and I have flushed snipe from an upland swamp at a height of 15,000 feet. It is the same with the birds of the torrents: they too send representatives as high as streams exist. The dipper goes as high as 16,000 feet, sometimes reaching the junction of the glacier with the stream. Guldenstadt's redstart ascends even farther; as a rule it is accustomed to cling closely to the torrents, but I have seen it as high as 18,000 feet on the ice near the foot of Everest.

Certain birds, in spite of wind and cold, followed up our camps to considerable heights. Camp I was inhabited by ravens and hill-pigeons, and the magnificent lammergeier used to soar above it at a height of over 20,000 feet. Camp II was a less attractive spot, and its only visitors were pigeons and choughs. Camp III was at 21,000 feet. There I saw choughs and a jungle-crow, also a rose-finch which seemed as if migrating across the range. Choughs were the only visitors to Camp IV at a height of 23,000 feet. But this is by no means their limit of altitude. Somervell saw choughs around the summit of Kharta Phu at 23,640 feet, and these same birds followed the climbers in their ascent to the immense altitude of 27,000 feet. There has hitherto been no record of living creatures from anything approaching such a height as this.

The fact is that animals will ascend the flanks of the mountains so far as their accustomed food supply is obtainable. We have already seen that this is the case with man, the Tibetans constructing their villages as high as they can till the soil. Animals are not deterred by physical inclemencies. They will brave the cold wind and the rarefied atmosphere provided that a suitable supply of food can be secured. This is the reason why the mammals reach the farthest limits of the vegetation, why the marsh birds ascend to the highest marshes, why the torrent birds reach the junction of torrents with glaciers. Were a camp established on the summit of Everest there is little doubt that it would be regularly visited by choughs.

Although reptiles and batrachians are susceptible to cold, yet examples of these groups occur on the plateau. I have already mentioned the lizard, *Phrynocephalus*, common at 14,000 feet. A few were seen on the Tinki La at 15,000 feet. The pools and marshes up to 15,000 feet contain frogs of the species *Rana pleskei*. We found no trace of the rare toad, *Cophophryne alticola*, taken on the plateau during the previous Expedition. Nor did I see any sign of snakes at these altitudes. In all likelihood their ascent is prevented by cold, for snakes have been observed at the hot springs in other parts of Tibet.

Beetles ascend to considerable altitudes. Those of the genus *Ascelosodis* are found under almost every stone in Tibet. In winter they lie stiff and torpid, but in spring they awaken and explore the soil. Click beetles were found at 15,000 feet sheltering underneath stones. Dung beetles are numerous after the break of the monsoon. In every pad of dung up to 16,000 feet, and beneath the carcass of every dead animal, we are certain to find examples of this group. Cockchafers were noticed at 15,000 feet. At night they came buzzing heavily through the air and often tumbled helplessly into the pools. Blue vetches clothe the plateau at 15,000 feet. In these we met with different kinds of ladybirds, one a bright red seven-spotted species like the kind so common on the Indian plains.

Colonies of ants are established in the soil up to 15,000 feet. They seem affected by the altitude and cold, being mere sluggish and impoverished communes quite different from the active ravagers of the plains. Bees and wasps ascend the mountains to a greater height than might have been believed. At 15,000 feet are noisy colonies of *Anthophora*. They make tunnels in the soil or in mud walls round which they gather in an active swarm. Humble bees are conspicuous on the open plateau. They occasionally visit the alpine flowers as high as 18,000 feet. I saw one near Camp III at 21,000 feet, far above the line of permanent snow. A rare little wasp occurs at 16,000 feet which is wont to work in clay. It attaches to the rocks a dome-shaped habitation which it fills with paralysed grubs. I found three kinds of hunting-wasps in the vicinity of the Base Camp as high as 17,000 feet. Their plan is to dig a tunnel in the soil and incarcerate their victims at the bottom of the shaft. For them life is a concentrated energy, since their work is confined to sunny days, when they bustle about with enthusiasm and zeal.

Butterflies ascend far up the mountains, where they are continually swept about by the wind. On the passes up to 17,000 feet we are certain to find different species of Apollo. One day I saw a tortoiseshell at 21,000 feet carried by the wind over Camp III. Companions of the butterflies, and ascending to the same altitudes, are certain day-flying moths. They follow up the alpine flowers to the farthest limit of the vegetation; and one of them, like the tortoiseshell butterfly, was seen swept by the wind to 21,000 feet.

It is strange to think that certain kinds of grasshoppers reach the highest limit of vegetable life. On the plateau they live in grass and on sand; but we found others at higher altitudes, immature forms of a new genus, that frequent the almost desolate moraines as high as 18,000 feet.

There are Diptera that ascend to equal elevations. Tachinids were common at the edge of a torrent at 17,000 feet. Robber flies (*Asilidae*) were seen at a similar height capturing small bees. Delicate Diptera resembling mosquitoes shelter under stones alongside the pools at 14,500 feet.

We met with different kinds of Hemiptera or bugs. Aphids were numerous at 15,000 feet, where they collected round the stems of the vetches and attracted colonies of ants. Another larger kind was found near the Rongbuk Glacier at a height of 16,500 feet.

Life exists in the streams and pools spread out over the plateau of Tibet. It is surprising to observe the numbers of fish, and one wonders how they can obtain food. In marshy places we are likely to find water-beetles crawling over the soft mud. At Lingka I dug them from beneath the ice at 14,500 feet. In the pools we find water-boatmen hovering beneath the surface, or shrimplike crustaceans skipping about; or at the bottom we may notice the larvæ of caddis-flies enclosed in their cases of weeds. In some places on the plateau there are hot springs which flow away in warm streams. We found one at a height of 15,000 feet teeming with pond life. I searched the high torrents near Camp III. Early in June they commence to thaw and go racing down the mountain under bridges of snow. But I could find no trace of any kind of life in these streams at 21,000 feet.

We found fragile Neuroptera at considerable altitudes. There were dragonflies in the marshes at 15,000 feet, slender Agrionids vividly adorned in black and turquoise blue. The pools and streams at 17,000 feet contained the larvæ of stone-flies, numbers of which sheltered underneath stones.

At high altitudes spiders are a conspicuous feature. Those that construct circular snares ascend to 15,000 feet. They lay their traps in the plateau gorse or any suitable kind of thorny scrub. The hunting kinds ascend to far greater altitudes, being common on the moraines near the site of our Base Camp. Solifugids occur up to 15,000 feet. They are smaller than those found in low-altitude deserts, but possess the same wandering habits by night. At great heights on the passes and moraines we meet with other unattractive kinds. Centipedes exist at 15,000 feet, and at 16,000 feet ticks shelter beneath stones.

Different kinds of molluscs live on the plateau. We found land shells under boulders at 14,600 feet. Some of the marshes teem with water shells, both univalves and bivalves being common up to 15,000 feet. We found no earthworms on the elevated plateau, but they occur up to 12,000 feet in the gorges of the main range. We found slugs in the Rongshar Valley at 16,000 feet; and in the icy streams at the same altitude numbers of little black planarians used to congregate beneath the stones.

Thus we see that many varied forms of life ascend the mountains to considerable heights. On Mount Everest we found traces of animal existence far above the last vegetable growth. The highest growing plant was seen near Camp I at 18,000 feet. Yet animals possessed permanent habitations as high as 22,000 feet. At this altitude we found little Attid spiders, immature, minute, black in colour. They lived amongst rocky debris, lurking in fissures and hiding beneath stones. I cannot think on what they feed at such a height where nothing exists but bare rock and ice. Other creatures may occasionally reach this altitude, such as bees, butterflies and moths. But these are only casual visitors carried by winds from their ordinary course. It seems to be the natural home of these spiders, which are therefore the highest permanent inhabitants of the earth.

We gain some impression of the struggle for existence from the manner in which animals secure a livelihood on tracts of snow and ice. Different kinds, as we have seen, force their way far above the line of permanent snow. At lower altitudes the ice supports animal existence. We found an interesting fauna on the Rongbuk Glacier at an altitude of 17,000 feet. The surface of this glacier was deeply fissured and in places covered with broken rock. It seemed at first sight utterly barren, yet some grass grew amongst the rocky fragments and patches of lichen appeared on the stones. Some animals lived even in this desolation. One day I saw wild sheep resting on the glacier surrounded by pinnacles of ice and stones. Certain birds used to frequent the icy tract. The snow-cock came down to it from the sides of the gorges. I saw Guldenstadt's redstart alighting on its pinnacles. Temminck's stint, while migrating through the gorge, halted near one of its icy pools. A tortoiseshell butterfly was sometimes seen on the glacier at 17,000 feet. A number of protectively coloured moths used to live on its surface moraine. Beetles and hunting-spiders found a shelter on it. It was the home of some minute flies. Between the pinnacles of ice were pools of water in which certain little animals managed to exist. These pools were beautifully blue in colour, and so cold that, after sweeping them with a net, the gauze remained frozen into a rigid bag. Yet in them we found the larvæ of both may-flies and stone-flies; in the debris at the brink were minute Hemiptera, and fragile Chironomids, delicate as mosquitoes, skated on the surface of the water.

These scattered notes tell us something of the struggle for life, how animals at high altitudes manage to compete with the cold, the wind, the scarcity of food. They indicate how intense is that vital force which compels existence at great elevations in one of the most inhospitable regions of the earth.

# 3 GEOLOGY AND GLACIOLOGY

## BY N.E. ODELL

I

GEOLOGY

In April, 1922, Dr Heron read to the Royal Geographical Society an admirable paper on the geological results of the first Expedition, that he accompanied as official geologist.[1] That paper gave an outline of his strenuous activities in the area lying to the north of Mount Everest, and his work was, as he himself has said, 'virtually a continuation to the westward of Sir Henry Hayden's pioneer investigations during the Tibet Expedition of 1903–4.' Heron's work was largely concerned with the sedimentary rocks that comprise the area to the north of the great belt of crystalline rocks developed along the main axis of the Himalaya. Time did not permit of his making more than brief flying visits, so to speak, to the crystalline zone, and he had hoped, on the next expedition, to study the crystalline area in detail. However in 1922, and again in 1924, political objections were raised to his accompanying the parties, and so the opportunity of much valuable work on the great problems of the uplift of the Himalayas, in a region hitherto inaccessible, had to be sacrificed to the tender feelings of the imaginative Tibetans. It is said that the Tibetans consider the hammering and chipping of rocks as detrimental to the equilibrium of the Spiritual and Material Worlds, since this little practice of geologists liberates devils from the former into the latter. Also they are said to consider the collecting of specimens as only undertaken for economic purposes, and therefore Dr Heron's specimens taken from the country must necessarily have been loads of rubies, garnets, or other precious stones, or even gold. In spite of their Buddhistic principles, however, the Tibetans appear to turn a blind eye to the wholesale slaughter involved in the collection this year of over 10,000 specimens by our ardent Natural Historian!

Consequently when I arrived at Darjeeling to join the last Expedition and it was incorrectly reported in the newspapers that the geologist to the Expedition had arrived, the Political Agent of Sikkim, Major Bailey, who has the Tibetan's cause so much at heart, at once wrote to General Bruce demanding

....................................

1   *G.J.* Vol. LIX, No. 6.

an explanation, since assurance had been given that no official geologist would accompany the Expedition. The explanation of course was simple: though a geologist by profession, I was merely a member of the climbing party and oxygen officer, although as a matter of fact the General did go as far as giving me the dubious appellation of 'oilman.' But it could hardly be expected that a geologist, however occupied with the numerous other duties appertaining to the Expedition, would keep his eyes closed to all the features of the landscape for the five months during which the Expedition lasted. And it is the results of those observations and a few of the conclusions drawn therefrom that I propose to describe. The paucity of the results I am only too well aware of, but preoccupation with the oxygen apparatus for use on the mountain, which necessitated continual work on it during the whole of the outward journey, as well as the time spent in the attempts on the summit, and all that this primary object of the Expedition involved, quite prevented my carrying out anything like the amount of detailed work I had hoped to do.

## GEOLOGY

*The Metamorphic Complex.* – I propose at the outset to skip over any observations I may have to record on the younger sedimentary rocks, of which the vast elevated plateau of Tibet is predominantly formed. I have scarcely anything to add to the work of Sir Henry Hayden and Dr Heron on these formations. My observations are principally confined to the crystalline and metamorphic zone of the main chain of the Himalayas, and their associated rocks, and may be considered as supplementary to those made by Dr Heron, more especially up to the northern border of the crystallines. I was able to penetrate well into this zone in two localities in particular, namely (1) that in the neighbourhood of Mount Everest itself, and (2) that of the Rongshar and Gaurisankar about forty miles to the west. But in neither case had I the opportunity of extending my investigations very far laterally, that is to say, east and west of these southward lines.

(1) *The Everest Region.* – In trekking southward from the town of Shekar Dzong *en route* to Everest the crystalline rocks first make their appearance in the valley of the Dzakar Chu at the point where the Gyachung Chu comes in from the west. The path to Rongbuk leads along on the true right bank of the Dzakar Chu, and apart from an interesting occurrence above the Chobu Monastery recorded by Heron, one first strikes the main mass of

the crystallines at the above river junction in a great cliff overlooking it on the eastern side. It is composed of dark horizontally banded biotite gneiss alternating with bands of light granite, though in the upper part of the cliff the latter is represented by pegmatite, and the whole appears to represent a large-scale example of *lit-par-lit* injection. The section showed a predominance of gneiss towards the top of the cliff. The gneiss itself shows an alternation of biotitic and felspathic bands, and this strongly foliated type is essentially non-porphyritic. The important question of the relation of this crystalline mass to the limestones that rest on it near the summit of the bluff will be dealt with later.

As one proceeds up the wide valley of the upper Dzakar Chu past the village of Rongbuk this same strikingly banded series continues on either side, often forming steep cliffs, especially on the east side of the valley, with inevitable talus slopes at their foot. Near Za-Rongbuk is a section close to the path showing clearly the biotite gneiss invaded and cut clean across by bands of pegmatite, indicating the younger age of the latter.

A far-flung head tributary of the Dzakar Chu enters the main valley from the east not far from the snout of the Rongbuk Glacier, and here in the gorge it has excavated I found a most interesting section through the banded gneiss and its associated rocks. Persisting in its horizontality for the most part, the former was again seen to be intimately mixed up with the light granite, which invaded it both along the planes of foliation and also right across them. This granite was pinkish in colour, contained tourmaline and garnet, and being poor in white mica frequently graded off into pegmatite. The biotite gneiss also was here notably garnetiferous. Isolated lenticles of the pegmatite within the gneiss were sometimes apparent, and that the whole had been reduced to a state of fluxion at some time in its history was evidenced by veinlets of the biotitic rock running off into the pegmatite. The gneiss on the whole had only local contortions, but at one point in the gorge a fault block had been turned through ninety degrees. Higher up in the gorge occurred a very coarse porphyritic granite or pegmatite with large phenocrysts of muscovite and tourmaline, often two or three inches across. Resting on the latter was a large mass of hard green variegated limestone, thoroughly crystalline, containing much epidote where the pegmatite had invaded it. The relation of these limestones to the overlying gneisses was unfortunately obscured by slopes of scree. In this gorge, which I tentatively dubbed the 'Hermit's Gorge' owing to the existence of a lama's retreat near its entrance, I was also interested to find pebbles of grey limestone, evidently washed down from the parent bed (Permo Trias) away to the east, but time did not admit of my ascertaining this.

Another locality that was examined in some detail was the steep face overlooking and to the north of Camp I by the snout of the East Rongbuk Glacier. Here was again found thoroughly metamorphosed and crystalline limestone resting on the schorl granite, which sent off apophyses into it. Above the limestone, which had perhaps an apparent thickness of about 100 feet, was the banded biotite gneiss associated with other metamorphic rocks appearing conformable upon the limestone, and looking more than ever like a bedded sedimentary series.

The same succession extends southward to the head of the East Rongbuk Glacier, giving the impression of a practically undisturbed stratified series. Near Camp III an exposure at the end of the eastern spur of Changtse showed the same metamorphic series, though without the limestone, garnetiferous biotite schist being predominant and the whole mass permeated with pegmatite. Southward across the *névé* basin of the East Rongbuk Glacier the series appears to continue in the lower part of the north-east ridge of Mount Everest itself, and the marked junction it makes with the overlying banded biotite gneiss is nowhere better seen perhaps than from Camp III, though bad weather and snow-covered rocks prevented my examining this junction in detail. A noted fault and anticlinal flexure of the beds is also seen from here.

The rocks of the North Col vary from dark, very fine-grained biotite gneisses to hornblende and tourmaline rocks, dipping northward at twenty-nine to thirty degrees. As one proceeds up the North Ridge of Everest the rocks change from the more silicious varieties found below to others decidedly calcareous in composition. At about 24,000 feet there was some slight evidence of an unconformable junction between the silicious and calcareous facies, but owing to the rolling of the beds and the general dip outwards (i.e. north) of approximately thirty degrees, the gradient of the ridge itself being here about thirty-five to forty degrees, together with the extensive screes, it was impossible to determine this precisely. It is of course this particular characteristic of the north face of Everest, namely, the outward sloping overlapping slabs with their numerous 'reversed scarp' faces, that makes the ascent so awkward, though not strictly difficult. The rocks moreover are not on the whole rotten since they have been considerably indurated.

I do not propose here to describe in detail all the petrographical types met with in the upper part of Everest, suffice it to say that they consist predominantly of dark calc gneisses, light limestones, and sandstones. Specimens brought back in 1922 by the high-climbing parties and examined by Dr Heron were diagnosed by him to be calc-silicate rocks for the most part, but unfortunately he was led badly astray in regard to one important zone. I refer to the light brown band of rock that extends so prominently from the north-east shoulder right along into the base of the final pyramid. Geologists should be the last people to depreciate assistance rendered by amateurs. Nevertheless the latter are apt to lead one astray in such matters as the exact localities at which material has been collected, and especially in regard to the predominance, or fortuitous occurrence, of any specimens collected. The party that reached the above light band of rock in 1922 brought back a specimen from it that Heron examined and found to be a schorl muscovite granite. I reached this belt of rock myself last year and found it to be undoubtedly formed of calcareous sandstone, which incidentally is at times micaceous. Now the whole metamorphic series of which Everest is composed is intruded by the light schorl granite and pegmatite, which breaks across the bedded rocks in conspicuous dykes and veins here and there, having come up through the subjacent biotite gneiss. This intrusive granitoid rock is very insignificant in amount relatively to the sediments, and occurs quite fortuitously. The simple explanation of the anomalous find of 1922 is that if it were definitely made at this light belt of rock at over 27,000 feet it was plucked from a chance occurrence of the granitoid rock within the sandstone. Consequently, I fear, the view expressed by Dr Heron that this supposed sill of hard granite is the main factor in preserving the prominent north-east shoulder, as well presumably as the main peak, is no longer valid. The final pyramid of the mountain is composed of a dark quartzose biotitic calc schist, very fine-grained and compact, which extends also some distance along the north-east shoulder as a cap rock to the above-mentioned sandstone, and this may in some degree be contributory to the pre-eminence of Everest. But, in my opinion, other and more cogent factors, causes predominantly tectonic, must be sought for a full explanation of this pre-eminence. The extra height of the final pyramid, however, would appear to be due to a fault of small throw bounding its eastern side, the line of which marks the pronounced couloir that was reached by Norton on the occasion of his record ascent.

Looking from high up on the north face of Everest, I had the opportunity in intervals of good weather – which when I was there were all too infrequent – to observe the continuation of the Everest sedimentary series northward in the North Peak (Changtse). The upper part of the latter is obviously composed of the Everest calcareous series, resting on the bedded biotite gneiss, profusely veined with the light pegmatites. The junction of the two series is most marked, owing to the colour difference, and is straight and regular. This is vividly shown in Somervell's wonderful photograph taken from 28,000 feet, where one is looking down the dip slope of the series. The true nature of this important junction it is difficult to tell, but it has the appearance of being a disconformable one, though one is apt to be deceived by the foliation as well as by the irregular veins and sills of pegmatite, which however are mostly confined to the dark gneiss below. The further extent of the upper calcareous series is seen in the upper parts of the higher peaks, such as Khartaphu to the north-east and probably Gya-chung Kang to the north-west, but the lower peaks are mostly of the lower biotite series, the prominence of many, no doubt, being partly due to their being fortified by the intrusive granites and pegmatites.

The marked extension almost horizontally of the west ridge of Everest itself is due similarly to its being composed of the more resistant biotite gneisses, the softer overlying calcareous rocks having been here eroded away.

In the region of the West Rongbuk Glacier, which was visited by Hazard for the purposes of extending the topographical survey, I understand there are representatives of most of the aforementioned metamorphic rocks, and these are in their expected positions relatively to one another.

(2) *The Rongshar Region.* – The Kyetrak Glacier, which flows northward between the lofty Cho Uyo and Cho Rapzang, occupies a valley which in its lower part is bordered by cliffs of the same series of banded biotite gneisses as exist in the Rongbuk Valley. Beneath these I found at several places the same metamorphosed sediments, in particular limestone, as obtained below the banded gneisses of the Rongbuk. These series were all well veined with pegmatites. In the neighbourhood of the Pusi La, that leads over into the Rongshar Valley at an altitude of just over 17,000 feet, I found unmistakable representatives of the upper Everest calc gneisses. These I first identified in the northern spurs of Pt. 18,620', which is a northern outlier of Cho Rapzang, and saw that they also extended all along the top of the range bordering the west side of the Kyetrak Glacier, both north and south of the Pusi La. I also found cliffs of limestone and calc-gneiss well over on the southern side of the pass. These were succeeded below, as was to be expected, by the banded biotite-gneiss series. In dropping down the upper part of the Rongshar, my notes

record a gradual change from the horizontally banded and foliated gneiss of the northern side of the range to the much more knotted and contorted gneiss that extended throughout the lower parts of the gorge. This latter gneiss was recognisable of course as the typical Himalayan 'Augen Gneiss' that forms the core of the whole extent of the range, and which has been so often described from numerous localities. It is almost unnecessary for me to repeat here that its truly intrusive character was long ago proved by the late Lieut. Gen. C.A. McMahon.[2] Both in texture and structure the contrast between this augen gneiss and the intensely foliated biotite gneiss could hardly be greater, though I cannot here go into the essential points of difference. The junction and relationship of the two in the upper Rongshar I was unable to determine with any precision, either owing to inaccessibility or the obstruction of talus and moraine, but it would certainly appear that the augen variety were the younger and intrusive facies. I might mention that Heron, from what he saw in the Kharta Valley and elsewhere, was obliged to leave the question of relationship undetermined. In the lower Rongshar the general dip of the augen gneiss appeared to be from twenty-five degrees to thirty degrees north, and this persisted right into Nepalese territory. Near Tasang, and lower down at Chupar, appeared schists, and other metamorphic rocks, including limestones – one more link, can we say, in the chain of evidence for an ancient sedimentary series, that may represent, as Hayden and others have supposed, a distant 'in-lier' of one or other of the Archean systems of the Indian Peninsula. Throughout the Rongshar region was again seen the typical schorl granite and its associated pegmatite, cutting across everything and exhibiting in places such extreme fluidity that parts of the gneiss into which it had been intruded were floated off during its injection.

Prof. Garwood, during his classic journey with Dr Freshfield round Kanchenjunga, was not able to find definite evidence that the pegmatites of that region were younger in age than the Himalayan gneiss, but thought that the former might be apophyses of the gneiss.[3] In the Rongshar, to the west, at any rate, the relation is unmistakable, that the pegmatites are the younger, though probably not by very much, since at places broad bands of pegmatite lie 'bedded' almost horizontally with the augen gneiss, and give the appearance of having been rolled out with the gneiss during movements subsequent to the latest intrusions.

......................................................................................................

2    *Records, Geol. Surv. of India*, Vol. XV (1882), p.44; Vol. XVI (1883), p.129; and *Geological Magazine*, Dec. III, Vol. 4 (1887), p.215.
3    Garwood in *Round Kanchenjunga*, D.W. Freshfield, p.292.

As to the structure of Gaurisankar itself I was never able to see it sufficiently clear of cloud or snow to be able to make out the nature of its upper part, but its lower rocks appeared to be of typical Himalayan ortho-gneiss much fortified with pegmatite dykes.

*Permo-Trias Limestones.* – Before attempting to base any conclusions upon the similar metamorphic suites of rocks of the two districts visited and described above, I propose to deal briefly with the series of limestones that Dr Heron found running along the southern border of the vast extent of Jurassic shales of the Tibetan plateau, and which are wedged in at places between these folded shales and the metamorphic rocks of the crystalline complex. These were found by Heron to be a uniform assemblage of unfossiliferous limestones with shaley partings, all fossils having been destroyed and now appearing supposedly as streaks of crystalline calcite. But in one locality a prolific fossil fauna of Productus and Spirifer was found indicating a probable Upper Permian age for the limestones. The Jurassic shales appeared to be lying conformably on these limestones. Now Hayden was of opinion, from his researches in the country to the east, that the Jurassic shales represent the upper part only of that system and are the equivalents of the Spiti shales, and that the lower (Lias) beds, as evidenced around Phari in particular, consist of various slates, quartzites, and limestones, the lowest of all being a brachiopod limestone, whose fauna indicated either Liassic or possibly Rhætic age.

Professor Garwood found an interesting crinoid limestone in Lhonak on the northern border of Sikkim, which in spite of earlier faunistic difficulties Hayden has shown to be very probably Jurassic: these difficulties, incidentally, were on account of its apparent equivalence to the crinoidal limestone found by Sir Joseph Hooker on the north-eastern border of Sikkim, and thought by him to contain nummulites and be therefore Tertiary in age.

But Hayden has shown the fallacy of this and the extreme probability of its also being Jurassic, and in particular Liassic. All these fossiliferous limestones along the northern border of Sikkim appear therefore to be coeval, and it is not until we get into the region of the Dzakar Chu to the west, where Heron found his Permian or Lower Trias limestone in a corresponding position with regard to the crystalline rocks, that difficulties of correlation arise. Briefly, it would appear that if the Upper Jurassic (Spiti) shales are resting upon the productus limestone then a large series of rocks, referred by Hayden to the Oolite and Lias stages, has been cut out, although Heron at this point says the shales seem to rest normally on the limestones. The point is of interest since to the west of the Dzakar Chu, and extending much farther west beyond the Lamna La, I found a large series of limestones overlapping on to the crystallines to the south and brought up against the shales on the northern side. These hard dark grey limestones, weathering reddish brown, were quite unfossiliferous and seamed throughout with calcite. Owing to their lithological resemblance and position, I took them at once to be the westward extension along the strike of Heron's Permo-Trias series, though in this locality he had mapped the occurrence of Jurassic only. Looking east across the Dzakar Chu one could make out by colour contrast their certain continuation into the area actually mapped as Permo-Trias. Now associated with these limestones near the Lamna La I found ferruginous quartzite, conglomerate, and the ever-ubiquitous shales, and it would seem that the association of these zones with the limestone would place the series on a par with Hayden's succession for the Jurassic in the Kampa and Phari regions, or at any rate with a good part of that succession. Certain beds of the succession at Lamna La seem to be missing, but there is considerable evidence of strike faulting which would explain this. While the limestone series here is so completely barren of fauna and calcitised and cannot be compared with the highly fossiliferous beds near Kampa, yet the character of the former may be entirely due to its proximity to the hard crystalline rocks and its alteration brought about by pressure against them, if not also by their igneous intrusives. At the same time it is equally possible that the same strike faulting and probable overthrusting, along the line of the Dzakar Chu and Lamna La, may have cut out some of the limestone and other zones of the Lower Jurassic, and have caused the Permo-Trias limestone, continued westward beyond the Lamna La, to be thrown against the Upper Jurassic shales. On two occasions, once by a flooded river and another time by a feeble pony, I was prevented from reaching Heron's type areas of the Permo-Trias limestone and so comparing their stratigraphical relationship and character with those of the limestones I found east and west of the Lamna La.

But whether this limestone be referred to the Permo-Trias or the Jurassic system, I noticed that it appeared to be strikingly unconformable to the banded biotite gneisses of the Metamorphic Complex on to which it transgressed. At the top of the cliff overlooking the confluence of the Dzakar Chu and the Gyachung Chu, mentioned earlier, it was seen that the limestone seemed to transgress the bedded biotite gneiss, but the flooded state of the river unfortunately prevented my crossing to it and ascertaining the true nature of the junction. It is quite possible, on the other hand, considering the overfolded character of the sedimentary beds to the north, that this is really the faulted junction of a thrust plane.

*Conclusions regarding Stratigraphy of Everest and Rongshar Regions.* – Some attempt will now be made to synthesise the information gleaned from the above localities and construct a stratigraphical picture of the whole region.

For many years controversy had raged around the true origin of the Himalayan Gneiss, the 'Central Gneiss' as it was once called, as to whether it were an intrusive igneous rock, or whether it represented an extreme stage in the metamorphism of ancient sediments, whether, in other words, it were an 'ortho-gneiss' or a 'para-gneiss' respectively. Reference has earlier been made to General McMahon's work in proving that it, or at any rate a large part of it, represents an ortho-gneiss. Mr R.D. Oldham has shown that it may be almost impossible to distinguish even microscopically the gneiss that was once a sediment from that truly an intrusive granite, and that field relations must be the chief factor in determination.

When I first reached the Everest region I took the banded biotite gneisses, so prevalent there, as unquestionably intrusive in character. It seemed to be only one more example of the great lateral extent to which intrusive rocks can travel in sills of nearly constant thickness. It seemed possible though that this might have been emphasised subsequently by overthrusting and rolling out of the beds upon one another as suggested by Heron. But my investigations, brief and incomplete as they were, have brought me more to the view that this particular series of banded biotite gneisses represents in actuality a highly metamorphosed series of sediments probably argillaceous and arenaceous in general character. Disregarding their strikingly bedded appearance, which is mainly due to the wholesale injection of pegmatite along foliation planes, their regular position between the upper and the lower calcareous series, throughout the Everest and Rongshar regions, and the absence of any evidence of apophyses running off into these series, seem to indicate with a fair amount of probability that they are of sedimentary origin. The difference between this biotitic felspathic gneiss, often garnetiferous, and the augen gneiss of the deeper core of the range has already been remarked. I could find no occurrence of the latter in the Rongbuk district, nor indeed on the northern side of the main range.

As to the upper calcareous series that forms the calc-gneisses and calc-schists of Everest, and also those of Kyetrak, they would appear to be the natural outlying extensions to the south of the so-called Permo-Trias limestone series, and their metamorphosed condition due to their being in the zone of maximum stress. If the upper calcareous series and the bedded gneissose series be definitely proved by future work in the region to be stages of a single sedimentary series, or separate ones not far removed in time, it may be possible, and their position suggests it, to link them up with Hayden's Dothak (Lilang) series of Phari, which has comparable lithological zones, though less metamorphosed.

The lower calcareous series, completely recrystallised to marbles, slates, schists, etc., that is only found beneath the bedded gneiss, would appear by its position and advanced state of alteration to be a much older series. Those exposures on the Tibetan side may conceivably be referred to Hayden's Khongbu Series of undoubted Pre-Jurassic and probably very much older Purana age, found also near Phari; while the lithologically similar assemblages found deep down in the Rongshar may be analogous to the Mallet's Daling Series of Sikkim or the Baxa Series of Southern Bhutan. But these are only suggestions, and much further work must be done before such correlations can be safely made.

I must mention that in my reading of the structure of this region I have endeavoured to avoid the invocation of elaborate movements or even of extensive overthrusting. Overfolding and complicated dislocations without doubt there are in the area of the younger and more yielding Tibetan sediments, but on the northern borders of the main range the more compact and indurated rocks are strikingly free from much appearance of lateral thrust. I sought in vain for real evidence of an overthrust, and only at the junction of the Liassic (or Permo-Trias) limestone with the banded gneisses in the Dzakar Chu, already cited, was I able to recognise such a possibility. The complicated nappes and decken movements of the Alps do not appear to have afflicted the Eastern Himalaya – at any rate as yet, and it is better I think to postulate rational, rather than irrational, quantities to elucidate problems on first acquaintance with a region.

But if evidence of lateral thrusting is meagre, it is not at all the case with vertical movements. On all hands throughout the small portion of the Tibetan side of the Central Himalaya I traversed there is plain evidence of great vertical uplift. Chomulhari raises its head nearly 9,000 feet abruptly from the Tibetan plain. Almost more impressive still is the great gneissose wall of Kanchenjhao and Chomoyumo in the north of Sikkim rising vertically out of the sediments of the Kampa plain. Many observers have of course seen ample signs of special elevatory forces, other than mere folding or intrusion alone, to give such prominence to this great sector of the Earth's crust, and it seems more than probable that the supremacy of Everest itself, since we now know it to be in greater part of soluble calcareous rocks, must be largely due to vertical uplift in the past that may be continuing at the present time. It is not outside the bounds of possibility that the next climbing party may have a few more feet to go to reach the top!

*The Kampa System and Jurassic Shales.* – As mentioned earlier I have very little to say in regard to the rocks of the Tibetan plateau, which date roughly from Jurassic to Eocene. The hurried outward and return journeys prevented more than passing observations, and these were mostly confirmatory of Heron's much more detailed work. The absence of the latter in India (I had only the opportunity of seeing him for half an hour in Edinburgh before he returned from leave last autumn), and our consequent inability to compare notes, may detract somewhat from the value of the following short remarks on the above rocks, and modification may later be necessary.

On the return journey via Tingri I made an abortive attempt to reach the Permo-Trias area to the north and north-east of the sacred Lapche Kang Range. The pony that carried me paid far too much attention for my liking to her foal that accompanied us, and too little to the business in hand, and always tried to bite me whenever I suggested that we must be getting along; and indeed she was so far uninterested in the local geology as to once run right away, and I only caught her after a long chase by the dangling reins tripping her! In consequence I eventually only reached the neighbourhood of Kura at the south-western extremity of the vast Tingri plain. Coming from Sharto, south-south-west of Tingri, one skirted along the spur to the west that submerges itself at Shar in the alluvium of the plain. This seemed to be formed of dark sandy limestone weathering reddish, and it had a very slight northern dip. The hill against which Kura stood was of the same sandy limestone, dipping north, and forming with another outcrop across the valley, dipping south by west at sixty-five degrees, an isoclinal anticline. No fossils could be found, but the writer knows of no arenaceous limestone of this character except within the Kampa System. Farther south-west along the ridge, against this limestone anticline was faulted an anticline of dark shales with the steep limb to the north, and then followed a rusty limestone the beds of which curved round to vertical, where they in turn were faulted against the steep limb of the shales. Subsequent folds revealed successively white calcareous sandstone, dark calcite-veined limestone and reddish quartzite, that seemed to abut against the crystalline metamorphies without the intervention, as far as could be seen, of the Jurassic shales. The above sequence of folds could be roughly traced across the valley to the east in the shoulder running north to Shar as already mentioned. Now the hill behind Kura, as well as much of the rising ground beyond to the west, has been mapped in 1921 as alluvium, and this without doubt is a mistake. More important is the mapping of the sandy limestone at Shar as Jurassic, when it would appear, unless Heron found fossil evidence to the contrary, that this represents one of the typically similar limestones of the Kampa System. It would certainly seem that in these folded rocks at Shar and at Kura, as well as farther west, we have at least some representatives of the Kampa Series. The ill representation of the Jurassic shales, if the above shale beds are in fact these at all, may be explained by the close folding and evident reverse faulting that has cut out no doubt a considerable proportion of known zones. The prevailing pressure from the north would seem here to have brought the Kampa beds right up against the Metamorphies, or otherwise regarded to have entrapped synclinally a Kampa out-lier within the older folded Jurassic rocks.

*Lapche Kang (Munkri) Range and Gyankar Range.* – The above-described locality, south-west of Tingri Dzong, is of considerable interest on account of its being at the north-eastern extremity of the great Lapche Kang Range, which, like the similar and parallel Gyankar Range eighty miles to the east, raises its jagged crest in a direction roughly transverse to that of the general trend of the Himalayan ranges. To the writer the existence and strike of these two ranges is highly significant, and they appear to have had a marked effect upon the river systems of the country, particularly in the case of the Gyankar Range. The latter was investigated by Dr Heron in 1921, more especially in regard to the remarkable gorges through which the Yaru Chu and Arun make their way. The Gyankar and Lapche Kang Ranges are evidently not due to a transverse system of folding, but to intrusions of granitic rock along these lines. Their relation to the geological structure and drainage of the region, apart from the direction they take across the strike of the main ranges, suggests that they have undoubtedly arisen subsequent to the latter. This assumption at any rate would help to explain the extraordinary deflection of the Yaru Chu east of Nyönne Ri and Sanghar Ri, which possibly had its continuity with the lower Arun interrupted by the range rising faster than the river could keep open its channel across this area, the formation in consequence of a lake, and final outlet through the Rongme Gorge, to the north – a similar chain of processes that I believe Mr C.C. Fox has suggested for the remarkable lower gorge at Yö Ri.[4] Dr Heron has mentioned that at Yö Ri the river plunges into a gorge of hard gneiss, but I should like to have the actual formation here confirmed. If, as I suppose, both these ranges mark intrusions late in the scheme of events, then it is of interest to know whether they are not of the later granitoid rocks, i.e. the schorl granite, or the two-mica granite of the Northern Range that Heron found in a good many localities, or even, with some slight possibility, the hornblende granite that Hayden mapped in the neighbourhood of the Tsangpo. The concentration of intrusions of the two-mica granite in the Northern Range, particularly on the prolongation northward of the two lines of ranges, rather suggests that the latter may be genetically connected with them. Heron's reference to the rock at Yö Ri being gneissose may be on account of local foliation at the time of its intrusion.

## II

## GLACIOLOGY

The Everest Massif has all the characteristics of a mountain region in an advanced state of glacial erosion and corrosion, whether we attribute the greater cause to the mechanical action of glaciers or to frost action. The long 'through' glaciers, whose heads and tributaries have eaten their way back into the innermost recesses of the mountains to form innumerable cirques and corries, delimited by sinuous ridges and steep arêtes, all point to a state of nearly mature glacial denudation. But though the present length of the glaciers on the northern side of the range is considerable – the Rongbuk Glacier is about eleven miles – yet it is nothing compared with their former extent. On all hands it is evident that the glaciers of this region are shrinking back into the recesses where they have their birth. And this does not appear to be sea- sonal variation alone, but in common with so many other glaciated regions of the world at the present time, a secular movement in a retrograde direction.

Take, for example, the valley of the Dzakar Chu. This long U-shaped valley bears all the signs, even in its lower parts, of having been sculptured directly

---

4   *G.J.*, Vol. LIX, No. 6, p.433.

and indirectly by glacial action, and banks of moraine attest to its former occupation by ice. In its upper parts above the Base Camp are conspicuous three systems of moraine shelves extending along the valley sides one above the other. They are especially noticeable on the west side, though the uppermost shelf at the foot of the crags is discontinuous owing to its being broken across at places by drainage from the corries. These morainic terraces far above the level of the present lateral moraines of the Rongbuk Glacier can be said to correspond to periods of stagnation in the gradual retreat of the once enormously vaster glacier, since the maximum ice flood of the Glacial Cycle. That the Rongbuk Glacier has halted at times in its retreat is also borne out in an interesting way by the large mounds of terminal moraine that it has dumped at intervals in the bed of the valley, the greater segregations being separated by areas relatively clear and level. Our Base Camp was situated on one such collection of mounds, and for nearly three-quarters of a mile ahead of this was an even plain, levelled no doubt to some extent by the outwash from the glacier, right up to the present moraine-covered snout. Other evidence of progressive retreat is to be found at the termination of the East Rongbuk Glacier, which has shrunk back nearly a mile from its former confluence with the main Rongbuk Glacier.

Evidence of three separate periods of glacial extension has been discovered by Oldham in Kashmir, and similar oscillations have been observed by Huntingdon in the Pangong valley of Ladak, but it would be altogether premature at this juncture to suggest correlation between these and the movements of the Everest glaciers so far to the east.

*Conditions at the North Col.* – In the mind of the writer a particular and somewhat peculiar local case of this wholesale waning of glaciation is to be seen at the North Col: between the peak of Everest and Changtse. Here is a col at 23,000 feet piled up in the most impressive and weirdest way with gigantic blocks of ice – their sides clean cut for the most part, seeming to be the disrupted fragments of a much greater mass of ice that once capped the col. The eastern slopes of the col, up which lay our regular route, consisted of hard *névé* at an average angle of about thirty-five degrees, broken at intervals by 'schrunds and ice facets. The western face towards the West Rongbuk Glacier is mostly of steep ice-slopes. Now in this high country with such evident signs on all sides of slight precipitation, and probably increasingly so, it is extremely difficult to see how the present snowfall is sufficient to give this enormous accumulation of ice on the eastern side and maintain it constant in such vast amount and in such a position. And if that were so, it seems incompatible indeed with the occurrence of the great disrupted blocks of well-consolidated *névé*, on the top of the col, which under normal conditions of annual precipitation would be speedily submerged and formed into a regular and continuous cornice. Colonel Norton, on the other hand, considers that the present snowfall, concentrated on convergent lines into the funnel that the North Col forms, is probably sufficient to explain the amount of the ice present, though he admits the difficulty in this view of explaining the well-consolidated cut-up blocks at the top. In my opinion this great ice mass in all probability represents the lingering remains of a once greater amount that may have been more un-interruptedly continuous with the East Rongbuk Glacier when the latter at an earlier period filled its basin to a higher level: in other words it may be described as a relic of the past – a mass of 'fossil *névé*.'

*Motion of the Glaciers.* – The northern side of the Great Himalaya is a region that exists in, and is subjected to, a set of physical conditions unique probably in the world, and the effects of these conditions on its glaciers are correspondingly great. Low mean annual temperature, extreme dryness, great altitude, together with a tropical sun, must be expected to produce marked results, quite different from other effects in glaciated regions of more temperate climate and of other latitudes. In many of the phenomena I was reminded of the Arctic, the glaciers of Spitzbergen in certain respects exhibiting comparable features. Owing to low mean temperature the ice of these Everest glaciers must be proportionately low in temperature, and this will mean that it has a correspondingly higher degree of rigidity or viscosity, whatever may be our views as to the ultimate structure of glacier ice in general and its mode of flow. Mostly the ice is of a very coarse texture, the granules being on the whole about the size of walnuts, a condition in which they simulate arctic glaciers more than they do alpine. On account of the rigidity of the ice the motion of the glaciers will be slow. Somervell and I endeavoured to estimate the rate of flow of the East Rongbuk Glacier by the motion of one of the pinnacles well out in the ice stream. In ten days we found it had only moved about two and a half feet, equivalent to three inches per day. Such observations as have been made on the motion of Himalayan glaciers on the southern side and at the north-western end of the range have given a diurnal motion of three to five inches at the side, and eight to twelve inches in the middle.[5] Though our observation was

PLATE 55
Hingston, the expedition doctor and naturalist, who had a passion for insects, captured in affectionate caricature by Norton, probably early in the expedition.

Head of Burhel
feeding
within 25ˣ
of Base Camp
Cook House
16 5/24.

Kyang &
gazelle
on Tingri Plains
5 7/24.

PLATE 56 (↑)
Pencil sketches by Norton of burhel (wild sheep) at Everest Base Camp. *See pages 207, 218–219 and 221.*

PLATE 57 (↓)
Kiang (wild horses) and gazelle sketched by Norton on the plains near Tingri. *See pages 135–136 and 207.*

PLATE 59

Watercolour by Norton of meconopsis or blue poppy at Chagun La on the return journey between Kampa Dzong and Phari. *See page 143.*

PLATE 58

Watercolour by Norton of irises at the campsite at Tropdé in the Rongshar Valley and primulas nearby. *See page 128.*

PLATE 60

Ice formations in the East Rongbuk Glacier. *See pages 52–53.*

PLATE 61

Ice pinnacles in the 'trough' in the East Rongbuk Glacier between Camps II and III. *See pages 52 and 246–249.*

PLATE 62
Pumori from the West Rongbuk Glacier. *See page 118.*

PLATE 63

Looking northward from about 28,000 feet on the north face of Everest down towards the North Col and the North Peak (Changtse), showing the continuation of the same geological strata as on Everest (see page 232), with the East Rongbuk Glacier behind. Photographed by Somervell during his summit attempt with Norton on 4 June 1924. See page 89.

## MOUNT EVEREST EXPEDITION

## EQUIPMENT.

The following notes on equipment for the 1924 Expedition are circulated as a guide, and to ensure all members being properly equipped. Those items marked with a * are essential and of standardized pattern, supplied by the firms named, who are giving trade discount prices to the Expedition.    All members not already in possession of them (or of some-thing very similar) should order them.    Items so marked will be paid for by the Committee and, with the exception of the suit cases, packed and despatched en bloc by the firms supplying them; members should therefore arranged to have theirs marked with their names or initials.

### WINDPROOF CLOTHING.

"Shackleton" outfit consisting of

Smock *

Overalls * (it is essential to tuck the smock into something; if windproof knickers will admit of this, overalls could be dis-pensed with; but the coat probably prevents this being done.    The overalls should be fitted long and strapped round ankles.

Helmet * unless an R.A.F. or similar helmet is taken.

Mits *

The above outfit only weighs 2 lbs. and can be carried as an extra over

(a) ordinary tweed,    or

(b) windproof knickerbocker suit - knickers of this can be lined with very light woollen material (a suit of this sort supplied to Major Norton was a great success last year).

Messrs. Burberry,
Haymarket.
(ask for Mr. Pink)

Captain Finch last year wore an eider down quilted balloon cloth coat on the march, in camp and at high altitudes; it was light and  exceedingly warm and he found it a complete success.

An old tweed coat and knickers are useful for the march, base camp,etc; some liked a pair of trousers. Shorts are very good for Sikkim and the return march through Tibet.

SOCKS AND STOCKINGS to taste; the Expedition will provide 2 or 3 pairs of thick skiing socks per member as a reserve.
Some prefer goats hair, some jaegar, some lambs wool. For high altitudes at least 2 pairs must be worn, not

1.

PLATE 64
The first page of a note on equipment which was sent to expedition members by the Mount Everest Committee before the end of 1923. Its recommendations drew on the experience of previous expeditions both to Everest and to the Antarctic.

*(Tom Longstaff)*

E V E R E S T.

1.     ACCLIMATISATION.

Last year all members of the party went very badly
over 17,000 ft. (or higher) passes going west;  on the return
journey however - even after losing stones in weight and being
much pulled down - all made nothing of these altitudes.

Three months or less at over 13,000 had acclimatised
everyone to a considerable extent.    To take every advantage of
this process it is suggested that the climbing party leave
Darjeeling as soon after March 15th as possible, and spend a
fortnight at the dak bungalows of GAUTSA (12,000 odd) and PHARI  ?
(13,000 odd) and up to 16,000 on the surrounding hills.

Every little helps and this may acclimatise to altitude
under conditions sufficiently comfortable to prevent staleness.

*It will cut more fig.*
*My Waniorko doto.*
*GAUTSA*

2.     PRELIMINARY RECONNAISSANCES.

Two are suggested;-

(a) To find if a route via the main Rongbuk Glacier and up the
    western slopes of the North Col is possible.
    The advantages of this would be;-
    (i) It might eliminate the dangers apparently inseparable
        from the Eastern approach whenever the snow conditions
        become bad.
    (ii) It might cut out one day's march to the North Col.
    Its disadvantages would be;-
    (i) It approaches the Col from the windy side.
    (ii) The actual climb may be nearer 3000 than 2000 ft.
    It is probably worth trying.    Finch and Longstaff both
    believe in it. *Worth examination.*

(b) If (a) is impracticable a reconnaissance by last year's route
    to find the best route this year from No. III to No. IV Camps
    and on to the North Col.

    To avoid wasting time No. I Camp could be made the first
    stage by either route and stores could be collected at No. I
    Camp while the reconnaissance (a) is being carried out, the party
    for (b) meeting them at No. I on their return, and going straight
    on of (a) no good.

*Yes*

    Each party should consist of one member of last year's
    party and two of the new members.    All four of the latter would
    thus be tested up to 23,000.

    It is calculated (see para. 8) that, assuming the Base
    Camp is reached by May 1st, reconnaissance (b) could be completed
    by 13th May, as was done last year.

PLATE 65
Before Christmas 1923 Norton sent a preliminary discussion document outlining possible climbing strategies
to General Bruce, George Mallory and Tom Longstaff (the medical officer on the 1922 expedition) *(see page 30)*.
He began with thoughts on acclimatisation and a possible route to the North Col from the head of the main
Rongbuk Glacier. This copy shows Longstaff's pencil annotations on the first page.

## Herschel House,
### Cambridge.

(2). It must be remembered that the head of the Rongbuk Glacier is only 19000 ft; there are very big crevasses for the 1st 1500 or 2000 ft on this side; & as the way would be more complicated it would accordingly be longer. It is very unlikely from the general shape of the west side, which is more of a funnel that a less dangerous way could be found there. Bullock who saw it better than I in 1921 had no doubt that the east side was better & Strutt who saw it only from above in 1922 believed we had come the best way to the North Col. Three camps below the N. Col would certainly be necessary & Camp III, presumably from 2000 to 2500 ft below the col, & a big supply camp, would necessarily be on snow & almost certainly without water. The porterage for a reconnaissance on this side would be considerable & I don't think it worth the risk of wasting so much *time & effort* for anything so unlikely to be of value. Every effort should be made to speed up operations up to the N. Col following the certain way we know.

(3). Acclimatisation :— My belief is that men fit to climb the
i. mountain without oxygen will continue acclimatising at 23000 ft. The most expert scientific opinion (Barcroft) states a belief that it would pay us, ceteris paribus, to spend about 5 nights at 25000 ft before going on. As an ideal aim I should say anyone before attempting the summit should spend 1 week at 21000 & an additional 3 nights or at least 2 at 23000. The plan of having the non-oxygen attempt first would scarcely allow of this — better that if men are to use oxygen they should be too little acclimatised before oxygen attempts.

ii. I think it much more likely that those who have tried will oxygen provided they have been properly fed, will be able to try again than those of a non-oxygen party. This again points

*Surely not — Reaction —*

---

PLATE 66

Mallory's response to Norton's discussion document *(previous image)* begins with his reasons for rejecting an approach to the North Col from the main Rongbuk Glacier, which he had examined at first hand during the 1921 reconnaissance expedition. He continues with his thoughts on acclimatisation – some of which Norton, in his pencil comment at the bottom left-hand corner, disagreed with. See page 30.

## Everest.

The following is the result of circulating a previous paper to Gen. Bruce, Longstaff + Mallory + of their comments.

Bullock's photographs of the N. Col from the W. + Mallory's opinion make it evident that it is not worth the time + effort to reconnoitre that route.

Acclimatisation at GAUTLA will hardly be possible as the majority of the climbers only arrive at DARJEELING about March 18th.

The mountain may be tackled by any one of four methods or by a series of attempts combining two or more of these.

A  Using oxygen + sleeping thrice above 23000.

B  Using oxygen + sleeping once only above 23000.

C.  Without oxygen + sleeping thrice above 23000.

D.  Without oxygen + sleeping once only above 23000.

Appendix I goes into the bandobast for A in detail.

It entails about 6 or 8 working days after the No IV camp has been established + fully stocked with oxygen to establish a camp + oxygen dump at No VI (about 27000).

20 porters will have been to No V followed by 8 to No V + then to No VI. + unless these parties are to be unaccompanied by a climber some 4 or 5 climbers out of a possible 8 will have probably shot their bolt.

Further it assumes that porters can carry loads from 25000 to 27000 + return. In other words the whole resources of the expedition will have been expended to give a party of 2 or 3 climbers one dash for the top.

An accident to man or instrument, the break down of a climber, impossible weather conditions (the odds are probably on this) or an unexpected climbing obstacle probably mean failure for the year.

In addition the achievement would be a triumph of organisation + of the Sherpa, who, without oxygen, carries loads to 27000, but the climber who does the last 2000 without oxygen cuts a poor figure.

-- P R O G R A M M E --

| Date | Mallory & Irvine | Odell | Hazard | Norton & Somervell | Bruce | Beetham | Noel | Porters. | Loads. |
|---|---|---|---|---|---|---|---|---|---|
| 5 | To 3 and stay. | To 3 and stay. | To 3 and stay. | | | | | Party A (20 men) to 3 & stay. | 20 to 3  20 |
| 6 | Rest | Rest | Rest | | | | | Party A rest and make camp. Party B (20 men) to 3 & return to 2. | 20 to 3  16 |
| 7 | Reconnais-sance | Establish camp 4. | Establish camp 4. | | | | | Party A to 2 and back ... Party B rest at 2. | 20 to 3  12 |
| 8 | Rest | Go down | Go down | To 3 | | | | A rest,B to 3. Porters re-assembled into 3 groups:-W(12 men).V & X (14 men each) V stay 3,W & X to 2. | 20 to 3 |
| 9 | Rest | Rest | Rest | To 3 | | | | W to 3 & stay,X to 3 & return 2,V rest 3 M.B. All tents available. | 28 to 3 |
| 10 | 1st.Escort to 4 & stay | Rest | Rest | Rest | | | | V to 4 & stay,W rest 3,X rest 2. 4 porters tents go up,10 remain. | 12 to 4 |
| 11 | To 3 | 2nd.Escort to 4 & stay | Rest | Rest | | To 3. | | V rest 4W to 4 & return,X to 3 & stay. 4 loads. | 14 to 4  4 / 3 to 7 |
| 12 | Rest | Establish camp 5. | 3rd.Escort to 4 & stay. | Establish camp 5. | | Rest | | V to 5,W rest 3,X to 4 & return. | 13 to 5 / 14 to 4 |
| 13 | 4th.Escort to 4 & stay | Go down | Go down | Rest 4. | Go down | Rest | 5th.Escort to 4 & stay. | V to 2 & exit.W to 4 & stay,X rest 3. | 14 to 4 |
| 14 | Rest 4. | | | Rest 4. | 5th.Escort to 4 & stay. | 5th.Escort to 4 & stay | | remaining loads to 4. | |
| 15 | Rest 4. | | To 3 (?) | To 5 | In support | In support | In support | V to 5 & stay,X return to 4 or 3. | Previously 12 now to 7. |
| 16 | To 6. | | | To 7 | In support | In support | In support | W to 7 (8 men) & return. X 4 men to 5 & return 3,10 men to 6 & return 4. | 6 to 7 & return / 8 to 6 & 4 to 5 |
| 17 | To summit | | | To summit | In support | In support | In support | | |
| 18 | | | | | | | | | |
| 19 | | | | | | | | | |
| 20 | | | | | | | | | |
| 21 | | | | | | | | | |

PLATE 68

Norton and Mallory continued to discuss climbing strategies in the early months of 1924 and during the journey out from Darjeeling. On 17 April they finally agreed a plan *(see pages 35, 38, 171–173)*. A programme detailing the movements of porters and climbers right up to the summit was then worked out and typed up before they reached Base Camp. On Norton's copy the first two days have been ticked off as completed. His annotations for 7 May followed by a blank eloquently convey the confusion caused by the blizzard on the East Rongbuk Glacier and the subsequent abandonment of the plan *(see page 56)*.

OUR PICTURE PUZZLE PAGE

Who is this?
What is he reading?
How long has he been here?

TIMES LITERARY SUPPT

PLATE 69
Postmarks on the envelope of a letter from Sir Francis Younghusband (see plates 47–48) evoke the extended line of communications between London and Everest. The official postal services carried the mail as far as Phari, from where it was carried by local couriers across Tibet. On the back of the envelope Norton has sketched a climber.

PLATE 70
The post from England made possible one of the most unlikely pictures from the expedition: Odell reading The Times Literary Supplement at 17,000 feet on the Pusi La. See pages 127 and 134.

Shebbeare .    "It was grand to see that mountain horseman ride."

Mah Jong

PLATE 71 (↑)
Pencil sketch by Norton of Shebbeare, the transport officer, on horseback. Shebbeare seldom rode *(see page 36)*, hence the quotation from 'The Man from Snowy River' by Andrew Barton 'Banjo' Peterson.

PLATE 72 (↓)
Pencil sketches by Norton of two of the horses used by the expedition members on the trek across Tibet.

PLATE 73 (↑)
Pencil sketches by Norton of three of the pack animals on which the expedition relied for transporting their stores across Tibet. Also a faint rear view of a Tibetan woman.

PLATE 74 (↓)
Sketches by Norton of some of the local people encountered on the expedition.

PLATE 75
Tibetans at Tingri. *See pages 137–138.*

an isolated one in the lower part of the glacier and but roughly undertaken, it seems to indicate a relatively slow rate of movement for these glaciers, such as would be expected. But though the velocity be low it must not be supposed that the erosion of their beds by the glaciers will be correspondingly less, for the extra rigidity of the ice will hold stones in the base of the glaciers with increased firmness and abrade the bottom with greater force. The gigantic moraines of these Everest glaciers are evidence enough of the destruction wrought mechanically by the motion of the glaciers, apart from that brought about by the agency of frost action.

*Length and Minimum Altitude of Glaciers.* – The present lengths of the glaciers of the Everest region compare fairly favourably with those of other parts of the Himalaya, and are only notably exceeded by the immense 'longitudinal' ice streams of the Karakorum. The Rongbuk Glacier system has a greatest length of about twelve miles and the snout is at an altitude of nearly 16,500 feet; while the Kyetrak Glacier is nearly eleven miles in length and descends to about 15,400 feet. These are the two principal mapped glaciers on the northern side of the main axis, and typify the 'transverse' glacier, that is one flowing down a valley at right angles to the range. Elsewhere in the Himalaya the latter never attain the size of the longitudinal type, which occupy troughs between the ranges. The only mapped representative of the longitudinal variety is the Kangshung Glacier on the northern side of the Makalu Group, which has an approximate length of twelve miles and whose snout is at 14,600 feet above sea-level. As an eastward-flowing glacier it is comparable to the Zemu Glacier of the Kanchenjunga Group, which, however, has a length of sixteen miles and descends to 13,900 feet. That none of these figures for the minimum altitude reached by the glaciers is as low as those of the north-western end of the range is probably chiefly on account of the lower latitude, though other factors of local situation, supply, and gradient, must always be taken into account. The glaciers of Kumaon and Lahoul have a lower limit of 12,000 feet, while those of Kashmir descend to about 8,000 feet in some cases.[6]

*Wastage Effects.* – In spite of the low mean annual temperature from which this region suffers, its situation in such a low latitude (Everest is twenty-eight degrees north) causes it to experience the effects of a very hot sun.

5   D.N. Wadia, *The Geology of India*, p.15.
6   D.N. Wadia, *The Geology of India*, p.14.

On the North Col, at 23,000 feet, on more than one occasion when I took temperatures at midday, the air temperature was 29 °F, whilst the sun temperature at the same time was 105°. In such a degree of heat with a high-pitched sun the melting effects on the glaciers and snow-fields are immense, though actually the visible melting is surprisingly little, the high evaporation under such low atmospheric pressure causing the solid forms of water to pass direct into vapour without the intermediate liquid state. High up on the face of Everest this is strikingly the case, and a considerable snowfall will in spring and summer have evaporated into thin air in a few hours without any visible melting. Consequently, and fortunately, 'verglas' does not exist. On the glaciers the same condition holds in less degree, and it is only in their lower parts that streams of any size develop, and then not in our experience till the end of May. The intense ablation of the glacier surfaces gives rise, amongst other things, under these conditions to the remarkable ice pinnacles to be shortly described. And in spite of this ablation, and in contrast to the dirt-strewn glaciers of the north-western end of the Himalaya, these in the east and on the north side of the range are relatively clean. The Kangshung Glacier, however, on the southern side of the main axis shows in the photographs taken in 1921 a decidedly dirty surface due to mud or moraine. This may be owing to the even greater ablation that goes on on the warmer southern side; at the time these photographs were taken the monsoon was actually in progress. On the other hand it might be suggested that this effect is partly due to the deposition of dust borne on the prevailing winds from the plains of India, as has been claimed for the dirty state of the ice of the north-western glaciers, but since the prevailing winds at Everest appear to be westerly this can hardly be maintained. In Spitzbergen, after a period of great ablation and thaw, I have seen the glaciers appear quite black, and in that remote region dust deposition cannot obtain; on examination the incorporated dirt has proved to be highly comminuted mud derived from the rocks over which, or between which, the glaciers pass, which is concentrated by the action of thaw and ablation. The state of the Kangshung Glacier is, nevertheless, most probably brought about by the greater temperature variation of this south side, increased frost action, and consequent extra rock-waste from the surrounding cliffs, and from the south-east face of Everest in particular, where the inward dip of the beds lays them open to special attack.

On the East Rongbuk Glacier were some rather beautiful examples of the so-called 'cryoconite holes' or 'dust wells,' in which small particles of morainic material had melted their way down into the surface of the ice, as is so often to be seen on arctic glaciers especially. Here, with the high altitude sun, the small stones and particles had melted their way very deeply down, and the well becoming filled with water during a warm period it had later crystallised in a radial manner, and given the effect of round flowerlike forms of clear ice within the surface of the glacier. The typical honeycombed ice of the arctic was, however, not noted to any extent.

A striking example of the effects of a tropical sun is the way in which eastward and westward flowing glaciers frequently have their southern sides melted back into steep ice cliffs, a case in point being the tributary to the East Rongbuk at Camp II, though others on the eastern flank of the latter were equally affected: this action is aided by reradiation of heat from rock-walls enclosing the glacier.

An important factor in promoting ablation is the high wind, and we had no better example of its force than near the Base Camp. Here reinforced by sand, and impinging on blocks of granite situated in gaps between moraine heaps, it was sufficient, blowing through these funnel-like gaps, to have grooved the blocks on their windward southern faces to a depth of an inch or more – long incisions across them independent of their mineral character and cutting across crystals of felspar and tourmaline alike. The sand-blast had been sufficiently intensive to have done its work since these morainic blocks were dropped by the glacier now not much more than half a mile away.

A melting effect, which, unfortunately, I never had the opportunity to examine close at hand, is the conspicuous flutings on many of the peaks, particularly on their northern faces. The Lingtren Group of peaks at the junction of the main Rongbuk and West Rongbuk Glaciers are notable examples of this. Many travellers have no doubt considered such flutings elsewhere to be merely the result of a scoring and gouging of the face by falling cornices and avalanches, and the writer must admit that he had formerly rather subscribed to this view. But it is evident in numerous instances that the sharp ridges and arêtes above these fluted faces do not, nor ever have, supported sufficient snow or ice to gouge out by their fall such deep incisions. I could only conclude, from rather distant observation, that the flutings and ribs, which often extend in pronounced degree right up to the crests which support them, must be caused by a differential melting effect of the rays of the hot sun inclined obliquely to the face on which they act; though here again melting and consequent fluxion in the ordinary sense, owing to the high altitude and quick evaporation, is non-existent. I am not aware that the phenomenon is known, at any rate in such pronounced form, outside the Himalayan range, though it may possibly be seen in other high ranges of the tropics.

*The Trough.* – This interesting and possibly unique feature that provided a natural causeway for nearly two miles of the way up and down the East Rongbuk Glacier between Camps II and III, will ever be remembered as a fairy scene, of the greatest beauty and highest artistry, by those privileged to use it as a highway to the precincts of the throne of the Great Goddess – Chomolungma. Imagine a corridor up to fifty feet deep and 100 feet wide with steep sides buttressed and pillared with fretted ice of exquisite tints of blue and white and green, and paved at intervals with ice-covering of charming glacial lakelets, out of the surface of which were growing here and there clusters of ice-pinnacles, themselves sculptured into an infinity of forms. It was through scenery of this description that our way lay – exhilarating in the extreme, except at the hot hours of the day in late May and June, when the close stagnant air within the depression of the Trough was apt to produce a certain lassitude and disregard for its remarkable beauty!

The Trough, as a depression running longitudinally down the East Rongbuk Glacier, may be said to commence somewhere about the 20,000 feet contour of Major Wheeler's one-inch map, and it continues uninterruptedly as far as the moraine-strewn lower end of the glacier. On first acquaintance I was at a loss to account for this remarkable feature. In early May the winter snow was still forming a practically continuous covering over the upper half of the East Rongbuk Glacier, and it was in consequence impossible to make any examination of the nature of the ice in the neighbourhood of the first pronounced depression. I noticed, however, that the snow seemed to be concealing a notable amount of ridging of the ice near the commencement of the Trough proper. It was not till later, when the new snow had evaporated sufficiently to reveal the underlying ice, that it was apparent that the latter exhibited plain evidence of severe stress. Here on the prolongation of the line of the Trough was a beautiful development of Forbes' 'Ribbon or Vein Structure' – clear blue bands of ice alternating with granular and more opaque air-filled varieties, the whole running parallel with the direction of motion of the glacier. It will be remembered that Forbes, who first described this 'ribbon structure' during his classical researches on Alpine glaciers, showed it clearly to be a structure set up in ice in consequence of great compression and shear; in fact, it is precisely comparable to the foliation of rocks under like conditions of stress. Without following Forbes *in extenso* in his ideas of the true plastic character of ice and the consequent viscous flow of glaciers, developed partly around his discovery of the 'ribbon structure,' the writer has from his own observations in the Alps, Spitzbergen, and the Himalayas seen sufficient evidence to satisfy him that this banded 'ribbon structure' in ice, usually seen vertically disposed, though by no means always so, is definitely and chiefly brought about by intense compression, such as at the junction of two convergent ice streams, and is not to be confused, as some glacialists have done, with the bedded structure of glacier ice due to seasonal ablation and deposition, or concentration of silt in layers within the ice.

That the ice above the Trough was undergoing severe stress was apparent not only from its foliation, but also from the faults – 'flaws' or 'tear-faults' – that had been extensively developed in this area, indicating that the ice was endeavouring to adjust itself to exterior forces; and where dislocation did not bring relief a ridging up of the ice was prevalent, as referred to above. At the commencement of the Trough itself the foliation bands seemed to have reached their greatest development, actual fusion of the ice taking place from the heat engendered by the compression, accompanied by simultaneous evaporation of the fused ice. And on this line of fused ice the depression of the Trough seemed to have developed, its walls displaying the banded structure in decided, though less pronounced, degree, and standing somewhat in relief above the general surface, on account, no doubt, of adjustment to stress. Now the distance of the line of the Trough from the true left side of the glacier is about 400 yards, and coincident with it seems to be the medial moraine from the north-east shoulder of Everest, carried englacially, for patches of moraine appear at intervals in the bed of the upper part of the Trough. Below the 19,750 feet contour it converges with the moraine coming from the north spur of Pt. 22,090, and this material largely carpets the continuation of the depression down the left centre of the lower glacier. The weathered walls of this lower part showed marked traces of the longitudinal banding due to their earlier foliation.

The Trough seems to be a line of special stress between the two ice streams, the one made up of the tributaries from the North Col and eastern slopes of Pt. 22,090 of Changtse, and the other the main mass of the glacier to the east, and its formation would appear to be due to the compression of the smaller western ice streams by this main eastern mass, especially in the narrow constriction between Pt. 22,090 and the opposite side (western spur of Khartaphu), through which the whole of the glacier must pass. A glance at the map will show clearly the bottle-neck character of this outlet and how at the critical point an extra tributary from the western slopes of Khartaphu adds its quota of ice to the already constricted mass. And it is just here that the conditions of stress above referred to are met with, and the Trough develops. The constriction appears to set up forces of compression and shear that along the line of englacial moraine from the north-east shoulder reaches its maximum, the upper layers of ice being fused and the lower layers only retaining their necessary viscosity or rigidity on account of their solid morainic content.

It may be objected that if, as postulated above, the ice is definitely fusing under compression, it should appear in the liquid state along the line of greatest stress and perhaps even be present as a stream of water flowing down the Trough. Actually the latter showed no signs of earlier or later water erosion, nor was there present in it a stream of water until late May, and then only in its lower part after its junction with the moraine from Pt. 22,090 above referred to. On theoretical grounds, even if partial melting took place with the development of interstitial or interfoliate water along the line of greatest compression, such water as was liberated at the surface would tend to be quickly evaporated under the prevailing conditions of aridity and low pressure. Whilst in the light of Mr C.S. Wright's researches on Antarctic ice and his conception of ice structure on the line of the quantum theory (to use his own words) 'the development of heat by pressure should not bring about melting, but the resulting energy cause an increase in the number of mobile ('vapour') molecules which merely have a tendency to diffuse to points (within each individual crystal) less favoured in this respect.'[7] And it must be noted that 'this diffusion does not require a free surface for its operation.' In this view, presumably, the line of the Trough, owing to the operation of exceptional outside forces, should have an increased mobility; and it may be this which helps to produce a drag and cause the system of faultings above its commencement, already referred to.

The Trough therefore in my opinion would appear to be a permanent feature of the East Rongbuk Glacier: permanent, that is to say, under the present conditions of glaciation. That the explanation given above is probably not the whole story of its origin, I am quite prepared to admit, for though my conclusions as to its formation were formed on the spot, they were

..................................
7   G.J., March, 1925, p.212.

made somewhat hurriedly in the little time available. And, moreover, it was more and more impressed upon one during one's short stay that the unique glacial conditions of this region are deserving of years of special study to fully understand all.

*Ice Pinnacles.* – Connected with the phenomenon of the Trough was the perhaps even more striking one of the gigantic ice pinnacles, that have lent themselves so well to photography. They had their best and largest development in the lower part of the Trough, though their birth was traceable to the walls of the upper portion. As these walls became weathered and melted back differentially during the bodily progress of the Trough down the glacier, buttresses and spurs make their appearance, and tend eventually in proportion as the processes of ablation and thaw increase in the lower reaches of the glacier to become detached and stand in isolated masses. And an important factor, which promotes undoubtedly their tapering and spired form, is that of the high-altitude sun of these latitudes, which during the middle hours of the summer day can shine down on them from a position within comparatively few degrees of the zenith and so produce a nearly equal melting effect on every side. The slight inclination of the sun to the southward does, however, produce a marked steepness on all their southern sides.

In a similar way in different parts of the glaciers was to be seen the incipience of pinnacles from smaller ice cliffs than those of the Trough, the process being frequently started by morainic material (like small glacier-tables) protecting the ice column beneath them from the steep rays of the sun, and when the protecting cap fell off, the pinnacle assuming a sharp conical or pyramidal form. A similar genetic process can be ascribed to the pinnacles of the main Rongbuk Glacier and others, the principal necessary conditions being a preliminary splitting of the glacier surface into cliffs of whatever size and steep solar rays to act upon them. The phenomenon of 'nieves penitentes,' first described from the Andes, is undoubtedly equivalent in its genesis to that of these enormously larger pinnacles, conditions of latitude, etc., being similar; in fact, typical examples of normal nieves penitentes were to be seen on the Everest glaciers.

*Earth Pillars.* – Fine examples of these were to be seen on the steep slopes of old moraine above the end of the main Rongbuk Glacier. Some of them were twenty feet or more in height, although the capping stones, essential especially to the earlier stages of their growth, were in most cases missing.

Their continuance in spite of this loss is only another indication of the diminished precipitation of the region.

*Polygonal Surface Markings.* – I was particularly interested to come across examples of these frost-jointing forms, since they are confined almost entirely to the circumpolar regions. I cannot here go into the question of the mechanism of their formation, suffice it to say that Mr J.S. Huxley and the writer, from investigations in Spitzbergen, have already described the role of frost-action as being the primary genetic process.[8] A climate that is fairly dry, and has for a portion of the year at least a temperature alternating repeatedly on either side of the freezing-point, is productive of the best results. Hence the rare occurrence of the phenomenon in low latitudes, unless other factors such as altitude come in. The present examples were seen at an altitude of about 17,000 feet on an old upper moraine terrace of the main Rongbuk Glacier on its eastern side. They were mostly stone polygons about four feet across, with a network of secondary fissure polygons within the former. The stone borders were composed chiefly of slaty material, as is so frequently the case in the Arctic, and on excavation these were found to be quite superficial, extending down only two or three inches into the mud. No 'tjaele,' or frozen soil, could be found beneath. In order to get some indication of the forces acting, and if possible to confirm our earlier views as to these, I displaced some of the stones from the borders, but in the short interval of observation – about a month – no movement was discernible, though much drying out of the ground had taken place. Besides these compound 'stone-fissure polygons,' there were to be seen systems of the simple fissure polygons, quite small in size, and with appearances of relatively recent formation, giving the impression in this case of desiccation rather than repeated frost-action.

*Former Extent of Regional Glaciation.* – With such clear evidence in the Everest region of a once greater extent of the glaciers, let us endeavour now to form a picture of the state of affairs when the maximum phase of the Glacial Cycle was operative. Reference has been made to the former much greater bulk of the Rongbuk Glacier. But I think without doubt the most amazing cases we saw of the once enormously greater expansion of these Tibetan glaciers was west of the Lamna La, where huge moraines bordered the valleys debouching from the south on to the plains. And perhaps the

--------------------

8   G.J., March, 1924.

wide valley, in whose upper reaches lies the Kyetrak Glacier, was most impressive of all in this respect. Here immense morainic ramparts towered nearly 200 feet on either side above the wide alluvial valley, and extended to the Tingri plain, a distance of fifteen miles or more from the present snout of the Kyetrak Glacier. Hence in all probability the present site of Tingri was once engulfed by ice. Now throughout our march from Sikkim by way of the valleys of the Chiblung Chu and Phung Chu was plain evidence in the systems of terraces along the hillsides of former extensive flooding of these valleys. In so far as I was able to investigate, these terraces in scarcely any cases indicated fluviatile action alone, and there can be no doubt that such accumulations of material as are to be found on the Linga Plain, and in particular the typical boulder clay in the gap west of Kyishong, represent fluvio-glacial, if not direct glacial deposits. In the hilly tract of country around the Ruli La, and particularly in a valley north of Dra, were to be seen terraces and cliffs of boulder clay, in places tunnelled out in a curious manner and presumably connoting the work of glacial streams during the local wane of the ice.

It is unnecessary to multiply these illustrations. Nevertheless, I must refer to the case of a peculiar find on the Pusi La at the head of the Rongshar Valley. Here Beetham brought to me a rounded clay pebble, split on one side and exposing the whorls of an ammonite cast: a specimen of indubitable Jurassic origin. As already mentioned the rocks found *in situ* in this district are entirely of the pre-Jurassic Metamorphic Series, and there are but three possible explanations of the occurrence of this Jurassic specimen on the Pusi La. Either it represents an ice-borne erratic that had been carried something like twenty miles from the nearest Jurassic outcrops to the north and dropped on this pass of 17,000 feet under conditions which must imply an ice flood sufficient to overflow the lowest cols of the present divide of the main range and reverse the northward flow of many existing glaciers; or it was carried to the top of the pass and deposited there by some wily Tibetan in order to involve the inevitable foreign traveller in scientific difficulties and wranglings; or alternatively it was dropped accidentally (we must hope so in view of the last statement!) by Dr Heron, when he crossed this same pass in 1921 with Colonel Howard Bury, on the assumption that an unfortunate hole in his pocket let slip such a specimen that must have been collected many miles away in the Jurassic zone! Personally, I incline towards the first alternative, though the difficulties resulting in its adoption are very considerable. I could find no unequivocal evidence of other erratic material on the Pusi La, and the rounded character of the surface features may have been caused by sub-aerial action other than glacial.

Now if we consider, in the light of such morainic evidence as remains, what the effect on the country of the maximum phase of the Glacial Cycle must have meant, we must conclude that the ice completely blocked most of the valleys, and in fact that in many instances the ice streams were linked up on this north side of the main chain. Whether during the maximum stage the ice floods were ever sufficient to form a more or less continuous sheet, of the nature of what in the Arctic has been called 'Highland Ice,' is questionable; more morainic or other evidence must be found, apart from the solitary Pusi La specimen, before such a thesis can be confidently maintained. But if such were the case, the range lying to the north and forming the southern boundary of the Tsangpo watershed – the Trans-Himalayan Range – would have at any rate its passes overrun by the ice; and under similar conditions one can only assume that considerable portions of the Tibetan plateau to the north would be in like manner engulfed.[9] It is difficult to resist this inference when one considers such a highly elevated tract as Southern Tibet subjected to the frigid conditions known to have obtained elsewhere. At the same time the question must be borne in mind whether during the European Glacial Epoch the then precipitation was sufficient to accumulate the amount of ice suggested above – at any rate in the plains of Central and Southern Tibet. Dr Hedin has assured me that he found no certain evidence from glacial deposits of an ice sheet as far south as the Trans-Himalayan Ranges. But for all that one must conceive of a great accumulation of ice in between the latter and the Great Himalayan Range, during the Glacial Epoch, for there is no reason to suppose that the general trend of monsoonic precipitation was much different then than now; and if, as the stratigraphical and structural evidence earlier cited rather suggests, the Great Range has become progressively elevated since Pleistocene times, due, possibly, to relief of its ice load or some other isostatic adjustment, its once less formidable barrier may have allowed of even greater precipitation on the northern side than at the present time. But whether regionally this were the case or not, the local maximum ice mass in the Tingri and Kyetrak districts would have to be sufficient not merely to raise the present surface of the Kyetrak Glacier by over 1,000 feet – an inconsiderable amount taking into account

....................................................................................................

9    This was the name given by Sven Hedin. It is doubtful if Godwin Austen's 'Ladak Range' is continuous
      with this, or that its name can be legitimately, and even tentatively, applied to it, *vide* Burrard and Hayden,
      *Geography and Geology of the Himalaya Mountains and Tibet*, Pt. II, p.92.

the subsequent erosion of its bed – but by such an amount more as would give a trend to the mass southward over the Pusi La and other passes, in order to carry the Jurassic specimen, and any other similar material, to its position on the former from the nearest parent outcrops to the north. Such an ice mass surging over the lower cols of the Great Range would send its glaciers far down on the southern side of it, much below the limits reached by the present representatives. Although I could find no unmistakable evidence in the Rongshar of the presence of a glacier below 14,000 feet, I feel decidedly that more extensive search than I was able to make, pent up as one was in what is most probably a profoundly 'overdeepened' gorge, would reveal at least as low moraines as those found by Professor Garwood in the Lachen Valley of Sikkim at 8,790 feet: certainly at Trintang (12,000 feet) in the Rongshar could be seen a shelf on the valley side very suggestive of earlier glacier formation. And in regard to the suggestion that the Tibetan plateau may at one time have had such an accumulation of ice that it overflowed the present water parting, Dr Blanford long ago showed that there was distinct evidence of such having occurred at the head of the Lachen Valley, a dictum in which Professor Garwood was inclined to concur.[10] Although without further extensive work it may perhaps be premature to suppose, as the writer has sometimes ventured, that the great transverse gorges of the Himalayan axis may have been largely due to the work of glaciers descending from a Tibetan Ice Cap, or from a Highland Ice Mass as postulated above, yet we may consider that when the upper Arun basin was occupied with the ice it must have held during the Glacial Epoch this mass and its concomitant moraines must have had a considerable effect, especially during its wane, upon the natural trend of the drainage and very conceivably been the determining factor in the astounding course taken by the River Arun at Yö Ri and in its upper reaches of the Yaru Chu. All these fascinating problems can only be solved if and when political restrictions cease, and further work can be done amongst the innermost recesses of this important and little known portion of the Great Himalayan Chain.

10   *Round Kanchenjunga*, p.299.

# 4 PHOTOGRAPHY

## BY BENTLEY BEETHAM

Although Noel was the official photographer to the Expedition, his time was so fully taken up with cinema work that most of the still photography had to be done by other members of the party. Noel was absolutely indefatigable in his efforts to record every phase of the daily life and of the achievements of the Expedition. He was usually off ahead of the main party in the morning and was the last to arrive in camp in the evening. At some carefully chosen view-point *en route* we would find him waiting for us, with his elaborate apparatus trained upon the track all ready to film the long cavalcade as it went by. How successful were his efforts most of us have already seen in the beauty of the photography of 'The Epic of Everest.'

But 'movie' photography, however valuable it may be, is essentially for the few and they specialists. The bulk and weight of the equipment would alone prohibit any expedition allowing ordinary members from indulging in this branch of the art. Noel's outfit entailed a separate bandobast of mules and men as well as its own interpreter. It must not be forgotten, however, that this same bandobast included in it a dark-room and a general photographic equipment, which Noel placed unreservedly at the disposal of all members. Indeed the dark-room was probably used more by others than by himself, since the cinema film was all despatched for development to a laboratory specially built and equipped for the purpose in Darjeeling, only trial scraps being developed in Tibet.

Concerning the rest of us, it may be said at once that our photographic outfit was most essentially of the tourist description – a battery of nine hand-cameras amongst ten men! These ranged in size from a spacious post-card down to the vanishing point in the VPK's. These latter are probably ideal for photography high up on the mountains, where every ounce of weight and every mechanical detail, bother, or intricacy, are of importance, and it may be mentioned that it was with such an instrument that Somervell, on two successive Expeditions, took his wonderful pictures above 25,000 feet.

It is then for the ordinary members of a future party that these brief notes are primarily intended.

Two general methods of procedure are open: (a) to develop *en route* as one goes along whenever opportunity offers, and (b) to send or take everything back to Darjeeling undeveloped. There are obvious advantages in each method. Probably the ideal is a combination of the two – develop a few (and these as far as possible duplicates of others left for after-treatment) at every convenient halt, and take the rest, the bulk of the work, back for careful development in a proper dark-room. Such a plan would give three advantages. It would provide a constant check on one's exposures, detect at once any light leakage or other flaw in the instrument, should such be brought about in transit, while at the same time it would ensure that the bulk of the negatives were not needlessly impaired by mechanical damage – abrasions, pinholes, dust specks, etc., those banes of future enlargement and slide-making.

The actinic value of the light we found most difficult to judge until we were settled down at Base Camp. It may be worth recording that, generally speaking, we were all inclined to under-expose in tropical Sikkim and to over-expose in arctic Tibet. Moreover this was just as noticeable in the work of those who used an actinometer as in that of those who didn't. Another point of interest was that the time that had to be allowed in time development was inconsistent with that given in the tables. Even if the solution was heated to the standard temperature, the time required was still about double the normal. Somervell believed in a factor of x4, and often doubled the strength of his solution.

At first none of us, not even Noel, could get negatives of character, with any sparkle in them; our best efforts were but dull records. Every one was using films, rolled or cut, but had we been working with glass plates, their imperishable nature would, at this period, have ensured a permanent trail being laid by which later parties might have traced our course across Tibet. Once on the plateau the conditions for the taking of photographic records are excellent, though hardly pleasant. For instantaneous work the incessant icy wind is only a personal discomfort, it is immaterial to the result, while the atmosphere is of truly extraordinary clarity. This very clearness, this lack of 'atmosphere,' is a great difficulty in any attempt to make a pleasing picture of the Tibetan landscape, until after the advent of the monsoon. Distance is annihilated; range succeeds range without a suggestion of the spaces in between, spaces that are occupied by arid stony plains of unwonted uniformity and flatness. It might perhaps be inferred from this sketch of its landscape that Tibet is an ugly land. I do not think it is so, but its beauty, its charm is that of colour rather than of form, and as such is better portrayed by the painter than by the photographer. He can alter the perspective to show what he knows to be there: photography is bound to optical exactitude.

But though on the plateau the conditions obtaining in spring are with this exception favourable for the actual taking of the photograph, the after-treatment of the negatives is often somewhat of a nightmare. By means of keeping up friendly relations with the cook it is usually possible to obtain warm water for the actual development fixation, which may thus be made tolerable enough. I have had films frozen in their rack within the tank, but this danger, once realised, can, of course, easily be guarded against, and it is only when the negatives are ready to come out of the fixing bath that the trouble begins. In the general course of events it will be night when this part of the work is being done, and the temperature may be very low. A little stream which was still running in the evening may be solid in the morning, and films left therein to wash overnight will be frozen to the bottom beneath a block of ice. We were caught this way near the Bahman Dopté on the way up. Sometimes the camp is beside a shallow lake and a hole may easily be broken in the thin evening's ice, and the racks lowered carefully so as not to stir up the muddy bottom. They are then in stagnant water, however, and will require a succession of movements at intervals to ensure their proper washing. A fresh lid of ice forms over the hole after each movement, and when one has broken this and thrust the arm down into the icy water to grope about for the racks a few times, one is, perhaps, inclined to be unduly optimistic about the rapidity of this washing process. As a matter of fact the washing was usually done in the developing tanks, coolies bringing canvas bucketfuls of water from the drinking supply. This worked quite satisfactorily, though slopping about with water during a Tibetan night was never popular with either porters or sahibs.

As soon as the negative is washed the real difficulty presents itself – that of drying it. If it is hung up in the tent, it promptly freezes, and the drying process ceases. Not only so, but as the ice crystals form within the film, they disarrange its particles and no amount of subsequent thawing or rewashing ever removes the imprint of the iceflowers. I tried putting the tank of washed films beside me in my sleeping-bag and hanging them up to dry in the morning as soon as the sun had warmed the tent above the freezing-point. But, quite apart from the tank proving a very cold bed-fellow, it always happened that either the camp had to be struck before they were dry, or a sudden dust-devil sprang up in response to the increasing warmth of the day and covered them with sand. As a last resource we threaded as many as fifty to sixty on cotton as soon as they were washed and suspended them in rows in the apex of Noel's double-walled tent. Then we brought in great glowing trays of smouldering yak-dung and set these on the floor so that the heat might rise and circulate about the films and prevent them from freezing. Besides the heat the fumes and smoke rose also, and we coughed and blinked and laughed. Noel complained that he had to sleep in the tent; we complained that he was the only man to have a fire in his bedroom. Generally this method of drying the films worked well, though occasionally, despite the early heat, a few were found frosted in the morning.

A good supply of methylated spirit would obviate all this trouble and save countless little blemishes. Later, at Base Camp, we got a bottleful from Hingston's store, and it proved a very great boon.

As to camera equipment, nothing of a special character is really necessary. If only one camera is taken then I suppose it must undoubtedly be of the 'hand' variety, though I, who learned photography behind a tripod, often longed for a good old-fashioned field camera with its rigid stand, focussing screen and dark slides. But it must be admitted that the occasions when such an instrument would be used were few and rather specialised, being chiefly in relation to technical work. Good colour photography would be very valuable, alike for scenery and for natural history work.

A highly concentrated developing solution like Rodinal would often be very welcome in preference to powders or tablets which require to be dissolved. At least one batch of what would otherwise have been valuable negatives was ruined through commencing development in the tank before solution had been fully effected. Time and patience are both apt to be getting rather short before one is able to attend to this work while on the march.

For use in an emergency, a little of one of the patent hypo eliminators would be a comfort, as would a vessel for carrying a working quantity of acid hypo in solution.

Finally, it must be remembered that all apparatus will be subjected to very rough usage on occasions, and one should be provided with the knowledge and materials necessary to carry out minor repairs *en route* – there is no Kodak agency in Tibet.

# 5 ON THE USE OF OXYGEN

## BY N.E. ODELL

The results of the Second Expedition to Mount Everest in 1922 went to show that two schools of thought prevailed from the experiences of the high-climbing parties. The one maintained that oxygen was not only desirable but necessary if a party were going to reach an altitude much greater than that made by the climbers who essayed to attain the summit without its use that year. It went further and said that 'on any further attempt upon Everest oxygen will form a most important part of the climber's equipment.'[1] The other school of thought held that 'the chances of climbing the mountain are probably greater if oxygen be not used,'[2] since the oxygen prevents the degree of acclimatisation in the individual that should be acquired, and in the event of its failure endangers the party's return. Also 'it were better to prepare for a number of attempts each by a small but acclimatised party, rather than to stake all on one or two highly organised endeavours, in which oxygen, and a large number of coolies, are used.'

In addition there were certain members who adopted a middle view and said that the case was not proven, and provided the apparatus could be lightened, and that the organisation would allow of sufficient porters being available to carry up supplies, benefit would no doubt accrue from its use: at any rate oxygen should be available in case of need.

The first school was championed by Finch, who with G. Bruce reached an altitude of about 27,235 feet, using oxygen continuously from a little above 21,000 feet. His view is that owing to the sapping of one's reserves of strength at altitudes above that at which true acclimatisation takes place, namely what he adjudges to be between 21,000 and 23,000 feet, it is obligatory to avoid more than a single camp above the North Col (23,000 feet), and so reduce one's time at these great heights to a minimum, and to make from this high camp the final dash to the summit. And judging by the achievements of the two parties, the one with oxygen and the other without it, he thinks that the former not merely showed that it could be done, but also would have been successful if it had been favoured by better weather conditions. But Finch is careful to say that a necessary part of this programme for the

---

1    *The Assault on Mount Everest,* 1922, p.257.
2    *Ibid.,* p.304

continuous use of oxygen would be the carrying up of supplies of oxygen, to a height about 1,000 feet above that at which he would propose pitching the highest camp (26,500 feet), by a corps of porters specially detailed for the work. And this in itself, as is known from later experience, will be by no means easy of achievement.

The second school of thought, claiming the merits of the disuse of oxygen, had for its advocate Somervell, who with Mallory and Norton reached in 1922 an altitude approximating to 27,000 feet. Apart from his own great powers of endurance, and performance on the mountain, Somervell's opinion as a physiologist could not be disregarded, and his studied views touching the important factor of acclimatisation gave a very special interest to the controversy. And into this controversy were thrust all the varying and often opposite views of the many eminent physiologists, whose evidence was derived from, or their opinion founded on, either mountain ascents to moderate altitudes, balloonists' and aviators' ascents, or experiments in laboratory pressure-chambers.

Consequently the Third Expedition started with opinions more or less divided as to the efficacy of an artificial supply of oxygen for the high-climbing parties. The Mount Everest Committee had however decided, in view of the inconclusive character of the results of 1922, again to equip the outgoing expedition. The writer was placed in charge of this oxygen equipment, though his absence in Persia the winter previous to the expedition prevented his taking any part in the supervision of its preparation at home. It is unnecessary to repeat the description of the breathing apparatus sent out, since in design it is nearly identical with that already fully described by Mr Unna in the *Alpine Journal*, vol. XXXIV, and by Captain Finch in the *Assault on Mount Everest*, 1922, Chapter IX. Certain modifications had nevertheless been deemed advisable, especially in the cylinder containers, which were of a new make with increased capacity. But though economies in weight had been effected in certain features, the total weight of the new outfit had not been reduced, which complete with full supply of oxygen amounted to thirty-two to thirty-three pounds. During the course of the trek across Tibet defects were found in the breathing sets, and working under the greatest difficulties of climate as well as lack of an anything like adequate workshop, Irvine managed to rebuild the breathing apparatus to a modified design, the saving in weight involved being about five pounds. Without his wonderful mechanical ingenuity we might well have been without a serviceable outfit: and serviceable the outfits as re-created by Irvine undoubtedly were, though it must be admitted that perhaps not all the party had complete confidence in them considering the amount of fresh work that we had had to put in to get over a host of difficulties that ought never to have occurred.

And now as to our own observations and opinions regarding the use of oxygen at extreme altitudes. It is not my purpose here to discuss more of the controversial physiological aspects of the subject than bear immediately on the problem of its future use and advisability at extreme mountain altitudes, and the exigencies of space will oblige my being brief.

From what has been said earlier it will have been seen that the attempts on the summit, aided by oxygen, were reduced last year to one – the last fatal one, and the merits of the oxygen in this case we shall never know. It has been explained also, more especially by Norton, that the extremely bad weather conditions and the consequent shortage of available porters had precluded the transportation of oxygen supplies sufficiently far up the line to admit of an oxygen attempt earlier. This emphatically was the main reason, though a secondary one, as mentioned above, may have been that not the entire party had complete faith in the resurrected apparatus. But if we had had at the outset the serviceable apparatus we expected, and conditions had allowed of oxygen supplies being carried to the North Col at an earlier stage in the proceedings – an event which would at the same time, probably have prevented our proving as we did what acclimatisation could accomplish – then there is no doubt that oxygen would have been in evidence in earlier attempts. It must not be thought therefore that as a party we were prejudiced against oxygen.

I must mention that as the result of a trial climb with the apparatus on a hill near Shekar Dzong on the outward journey, at that early stage I myself began to realise that oxygen might not do for every one all that had been claimed for it: Mallory, Irvine and Somervell were with me, and we all seemed to do as well without it, both climbing on steepish crag, where of course the bulky apparatus was a great inconvenience, and on easier ground near the summit where we went fairly fast. This, it is to be noted, was at an altitude of only 15,000 feet, and we had had nearly three weeks already in Tibet to get acclimatised to this particular altitude.

After our first repulse from Camp III by blizzards, on our return there Geoffrey Bruce and I used oxygen on an attempt to reach the North Col under very bad conditions of snow. On that occasion I was feeling somewhat unfit, but thought that the oxygen would give the necessary bracing needed: instead it gave so little effect and the apparatus proved such an irksome load that I was glad to hand the outfit over to a porter to carry. Bruce could similarly derive no benefit from it, and this was the more remarkable since he had used it to such apparent advantage when accompanying Finch in 1922. At this time we had been living at altitudes up to and over 21,000 feet for nearly three weeks, with visits to 22,000 to 23,000 feet, and so must necessarily have undergone a considerable degree of acclimatisation.

Later in the campaign, when I was in charge of Camp IV on the North Col and lived there for eleven days, not sleeping below 23,000 feet save once, I had the truth, as well as the value, of acclimatisation fully brought home to me. It is unnecessary to reiterate the details of my climbs from this camp to over 27,000 feet, except to mention again that on my second ascent to that altitude I used oxygen from Camp V at 25,000 feet, but at rather over 26,000 feet I felt I was deriving so little benefit from it that I turned it off and did not use the gas again. I had been using a relatively small quantity only, rather more than one litre per minute, but before switching it off I gave myself a full two litres or more per minute, and really the only advantage I seemed to gain from it, was a more or less imagined slight relief of fatigue in my legs.[3] But when I had reached Camp VI and dumped the apparatus, and set off again on my search for the missing party, I felt able to progress altogether better than when I had been breathing oxygen, a contributory factor to this being, no doubt, that I was without the bulk and awkwardness of the apparatus. On the descent of the mountain I was so far unaffected by the altitude as to be able to go from Camp VI to V in about one hour, and from the latter to Camp IV in about thirty minutes, partly glissading near the North Col.

I only venture to give these results and figures to show how real is the capacity for acclimatisation to these extreme altitudes, and there seems no reason at all to suppose that this important physiological capability, other things being equal, should not be possible at an altitude equivalent to that of the top of Mount Everest, and perhaps considerably more. I say other things being equal, though realising this is scarcely likely at any time to be the case, temperature especially altering for the worse, that is of course decreasing, as one gets higher; in addition chemical changes and reactions of the blood become more acute. But our evidence has shown us emphatically that one can live and feel fit for an indefinite period at 23,000 feet, and an altitude below this can no longer be considered, as Finch has maintained, the upper level of true acclimatisation.[4] Somervell considers that acclimatisation may

3   Prof. Dreyer, of Oxford, had suggested a supply of 2.4 litres per minute for the highest parts of the mountain: A.J., XXXIV, No. 224, p.242.
4   He considers this critical altitude to be somewhere between 21,000 and 23,000 feet. The Assault, p.257.

take place at 24,000 feet, but in the present state of our knowledge I think no upper limit can be given. If this acclimatisation is as real as we seem to have found it to be, then the advantage of carrying a heavy and bulky supply of oxygen is very dubious. It is important to remember in Finch's case that he has accustomed himself during his Alpine career to carry very heavy loads, and this alone must be very contributory to his ability to be at ease with a heavy oxygen apparatus. But the main point, without doubt, is that he derived the benefit he did from the oxygen on account of his not being acclimatised. He and Geoffrey Bruce had come straight up from the Base Camp and been but five days at Camp III before starting their high climb.

It is very evident, I think, that no adequate degree of acclimatisation for the ascent of the mountain can be acquired unless the climber has the opportunity of living for not less than the bare minimum (for most people) of a week at the highest possible camp, and of making excursions higher on the mountain prior to the main attack. This 'acclimatisation camp' cannot be higher than the North Col, owing to the exposure and lack of all shelter, even if a suitable spot could be found above on the mountain. The dis-advantage of the North Col is the fact that the camp here must be pitched on snow, though under all but the worst conditions this need not rule it out. Camp III has the advantage of being on rock and of being accessible in almost any weather. But our experiences on this last expedition showed us that if this latter camp is to be rendered habitable without detriment to the personnel under as severe conditions again, then something more weather-proof than the tents we had will be necessary. It might be possible to have a light hut, that could be carried up in handy sections and quickly erected on the spot, as suggested by Captain Noel. If as many of the party as possible could be housed at such a camp, and at the North Col as well if conditions permitted, then with the necessary excursions higher for the purpose of carrying stores and establishing camps, such a degree of acclimatisation would be acquired in two or three weeks' time as would fit physiologically a much larger proportion of climbers for reaching the top.

It is not a question of whether or not the top of the mountain can be reached without oxygen, but what, considering all the circumstances of the case, is the way most likely to succeed, and which is to the greatest extent within the powers of the average climber. In our opinion the individual's inherent capacity for acclimatisation is likely to serve him better than doubt-ful adventitious aids. From the point of high Himalayan mountaineering generally it is certainly desirable in the interests of economy that the private explorer or mountaineer should know that his expeditions need not be burdened with the additional expense of oxygen apparatus, even though he aspire to attain the highest summits: he must merely so lay his plans that his party may acclimatise itself to as high an altitude as possible before making its ultimate attempts. But for any future expedition that will go out to make sure of the world's highest summit this consideration of economy in the matter of equipment, such as oxygen, should not count. Nor should the authority responsible pay too much heed to the dictates of those physiologists who would like to make the climbers subjects of experimentation in the ultimate reactionary effects of the human system to an exceptional environment. In the interests of science as well as mountaineering it were better that separate parties were sent out to attain these distinct objects! Moreover, should any attempt be made to carry out the threat of our ardent, though ever jocular, Medical Officer of the last expedition to extend his experiments to 'more complicated and worrying tests,' then it were far preferable that he should recruit and conduct his own selected squad of patient subjects through their tortures, than amuse himself by adding to the already adequate troubles of the climbers that of a feeling that they must exert, if not well-nigh contort, themselves to attain some standard of 'physiological respectability,' without which they dare not set foot on Everest! Fortunately the performances of some poor humans at great altitudes were better than the artificial tests indicated they ought to be! And in this connection it must not be forgotten that any data for physiological capability derived from experiments in laboratory pressure-chambers or elsewhere are unreliable when applied to the mountaineer, since they leave out entirely the important factor of acclimatisation: in other words, the individual's adaptation to his environment in relation to time.

In spite of our findings of last year, and although I maintain that acclimatisation to an altitude of not more than 23,000 feet would enable an average suitable individual to reach 29,000 feet unaided, yet in the present state of our knowledge I am not prepared to say that a future expedition to Everest may dispense with oxygen entirely. What I wish to emphasise is that the oxygen outfits used heretofore are much too heavy, and their weight quite obviates any advantage that might be derived from them. This weight was chiefly on account of the large amount of gas carried, sufficient for nearly twelve hours. We are now having designed an entirely new and lightened apparatus, that with a less, though, in the light of our later experience, quite adequate, supply of gas will, we hope, be not more than about eleven to twelve pounds in weight. If members of a future party are prevented for some reason or other from acquiring the requisite degree of acclimatisation, which it should be their purpose to attain, such a lightened form of apparatus would be available, if only for the final dash from some high camp to the summit, or alternatively merely as an emergency measure, if found beneficial.

It is true that we are really not yet in a position to judge as to whether oxygen is the best stimulant for use at high altitudes. In use we found it had a drying and irritating effect upon the throat! It might be mentioned that Captain Spelterini, from his vast and varied balloon experience at high altitudes, maintained that oxygen was not desirable, was liable to upset the functions of the system, and was too much of a specific. His remedy for debilitation at exaggerated altitudes was light alcohol in effervescence – champagne! It might well be thought desirable and preferable that the Medical Officer's 'experimental squad,' suggested earlier, be experimented upon with the latter versus oxygen, rather than run risks with the climbers on Everest! But in the meanwhile, until some new evidence is forthcoming as to the real nature of debilitation at high altitudes, and how properly it should be met and countered, it were far preferable in my opinion that the future Everest aspirant should mainly depend on his own inherent capacity to adapt himself to the conditions encountered, and thereby keep himself well within his powers, than resort to any artificial means that in the event of their failure may be the cause of his collapse.

# 6 THE ORGANISATION OF THE EXPEDITION

(NOTES MADE BY THE MEMBERS OF THE EXPEDITION DURING THE RETURN JOURNEY)

## A PRELIMINARY ORGANISATION, JOURNEY AND MARCH BY LIEUT. COLONEL E.F. NORTON, DSO

1. *Preliminary.* – The leader of the Expedition should have the last word in selection of the party – he has to live and work with them. The plan of campaign should if possible be settled in England before sailing. The reason for this is that both the scale of porters' equipment and the packing of sahibs' food for high camps largely depend on the plan. The difficulty is the possible absence – say in India – of some prominent member of the climbing party whose views must be consulted. This is only one more reason for starting preparations many months before the party sails: the views of such a climber can then be obtained by letter. At the worst the plan can be settled in Darjeeling before marching; conditions on the Tibetan plateau in April are not the most favourable for reconciling conflicting points of view.

The president of the Equipment Committee should be a prominent member of the party, who has been on a previous expedition; he need not do detailed work himself, but must supervise all departments, obviate gaps and keep everybody up to time. He should have all equipment (including oxygen) completely ready three or four months before shipment – only thus can everything be properly 'vetted' and criticised. For last two Expeditions some of the equipment has always been very late.

2. *Voyage.* – On the voyage out I would urge every one to study either Nepali or Tibetan – or else polish up Hindustani. The importance of every one being able to talk to porters cannot be exaggerated. A vocabulary of 200 words can easily be acquired in a month, and this alone will go a long way. I also suggest all climbers learn Morse signalling for intercommunication at high camps.

3. *Darjeeling.* – The leader and at least one transport officer should be in Darjeeling a full month before the Expedition starts. A local agent is required; he can advertise the Expedition beforehand and have a large number of porters, etc., ready for inspection. He may buy stores of grain, etc., required for porters' food. He is invaluable to procure locally the hundred and one

minor articles wanted at the last minute. After the Expedition has started he pays family allotments, and in the event of native personnel being sent home early for discharge he pays them off.

Railway concessions probably procurable: EIR half-price personnel and stores. DHR free goods vans Darjeeling to Kalimpong Road.[1]

Mr Stephen has always most generously given free accommodation at the Mount Everest Hotel, Darjeeling, as well as Grand Hotel, Calcutta. Write to Deputy-Commissioner, Darjeeling, for permission to use all Dak bungalows in Sikkim, and to Political Officer, Gangtok, for any beyond Jelap La. Mule transport for both advance and accompanying transport – agents: – Darjeeling: J.F. Madan & Co.; Kalimpong: R.B. Mintri & Co. – both are reliable, if expensive.

4. *On the March.* – Comfort is essential if climbers are to start work really fit. A remarkable improvement can be effected in this respect by consulting previous experience. It is for consideration whether it will pay to cut out Phari and the exposed Donka La route, sending climbers anyhow via Gangtok to Kampa Dzong. The march across the Tibetan plateau should be very leisurely, both to avoid fatigue and to give time for acclimatisation: halt for a day at least every three or four days – preferably at transport stages. Consequently a start should be made from Darjeeling timed to reach the Base Camp by this method not later than May 1.

Every one should have a good pony of his own bought in Darjeeling, or through Mr John Macdonald in Yatung. This is expensive compared to hiring, but essential to comfort. Discourage climbers from walking too much on outward march. They must take their own saddlery, including grooming kit, horse-rug, good nose-bag, clippers, shoeing outfit, stable head-collar, head-rope, etc. They should also have a reliable head syce who can shoe. The condition of the ponies must be continually watched and all ponies inspected at least once during May and June, while they are at Tashi Dzom or Chödzong, and scale of feeding adjusted if necessary.

The mess-tent used in 1924 was invaluable, and exactly what is required both for march and Base Camp; Whymper tents ditto – one per sahib and one spare. Meade tents are excellent, twenty-three in 1924 were ample. Light Meade tents ditto, six ample. Suitable porters' tents may be got from Cawnpore. Mess-tables should be of 1924 pattern, with a spare set of shorter

--------

1   [*Ed. note:* EIR – East India Railway, DHR – Darjeeling-Himalayan Railway.]

legs for two of these tables, for use at Camp III, sitting on boxes. Four Kran-zow clockwork lamps used in 1924 were a complete success. Each member must bring his own chair – mess should supply two spare.

Water must be boiled in Sikkim. Three Expeditions have now suffered from dysentery, probably picked up in Sikkim below 7,000 feet. This is Medical Officer's department, but leader should see to it. In Tibet a pair of mule 'pakhals' will often enable good water to be fetched from a distance. A good pair of mess mules are needed for taking on mess-tent daily.

As regards Dzongpens, etc., the leader of the Expedition should take a moderately respectable coat or suit, and so eat no shame when interviewing Tibetan officials. Presents for these should be carefully selected: hats – not too cheap; scarves are not appreciated; camp chairs, etc., are; as also wrist-watches, good electric torches, thermos flasks, snow goggles, etc. In the treatment of Dzongpens and other Tibetans, anyone who knows the East has not much to learn. The interpreter will explain etiquette as regards presents, 'khaddars,' etc. It should be remembered that the Expedition are guests in a friendly country, and a troublesome Dzongpen cannot be treated quite as cavalierly as, say, an obstructive Tehsildar in India. He is fifth highest official in Tibet. At the same time it pays to be firm over prices of transport, etc.; always think of possible subsequent Expeditions, leave a good impress-ion, but do not spoil the market.

Keep good discipline among the porters or they will play hell on the return journey. Be careful how you send an inferior gang of porters home in advance for discharge, or they will cause trouble ahead of you all the way home. Transport drivers cannot be trusted, thieving has increased a lot: must watch this. Cases of theft, etc., must be dealt with through the local authorities, not direct. Otherwise these transport drivers are good fellows, and respond readily to a cheery word. They are frightfully slow and ineffi-cient, but wonders can be done by turning on Tibetan-speaking porters to ginger them up. For specially long marches it will pay to summon 'Gyembos' overnight, and insist on a 7 a.m. start – it *can* be done. Finally, a friend at court at Lhasa to whom reports can be made is invaluable (e.g. General Dzasa Laden La in 1924). On the march there is much work to be done. Oxygen apparatus keeps one or two men busy every halt or short march. Practise porters with ice axe and rope. Except for this keep all ice axes packed – do not distribute them to porters or they will be broken. Continual check-ing of stores essential. Practise Morse signalling, chits to Gurkha NCOs, etc.; communiqués to write; mess secretary generally a busy man.

Dak (post) gave great trouble in 1924. Continually pilfered. Suggest leaving our own men at Phari, Khamba, Tinki, and Shekar – only safe way. The Press is very slippery ground. Must be very careful to have the clearest possible understanding with any paper which has monopoly before leaving England. Settle number, length and scope of wires required. Relay runners exclusively for Press communiqués were used in 1924 and did excellent work. The bandobast was run by Mr John Macdonald. *The Times* paid £200 for it.

A well-stocked book box is worth a lot. Take a little trouble over it. Start with a nucleus of twenty real good volumes, compiling the list with care. Then add the private books of members who can spare the books they have read. The Expedition should stock soap, tooth-powder, toothbrushes, a spare sponge or two, writing-paper and envelopes, stamps, pencils, glue, elastic bands, pins, etc., as people are always running out.

5. *Base Camp.* – Should be a happy home for returning climbers and porters. Study comfort, feeding, sanitation. No necessity for leader to be there once camp and routine are satisfactorily established, but there must be one sahib there always, as the money is too big a responsibility for anyone else; dealings with outside world are few, but may be important. All routine work is done through the Dzongpen's agent (see Personnel Notes). Sahib at Base Camp must keep a careful watch on stores, as this is a period of great leakage. Some good system should be devised by which one sahib may hand over to another. Arrange to have whole Expedition blessed by Rongbuk Lama – preferably *en route* to the Base Camp. This has a good moral effect.

6. *Tibetan Government Permit.* – It is suggested that a clause should be added in future to the effect that Dzongpens are to make it their duty to see that postal arrangements run smoothly and efficiently.

Both in the 1922 and 1924 permits they are told to supply transport at 'current rates.' This appears to be meaningless – there being no such thing in Tibet. Experience this year has shown that an average fair rate per riding pony or pack animal (yaks, donkeys, zoes, etc.) is four tankas a day. If some such rate could be definitely specified in any future permit there would be a great saving of time, and probably money too. Finally, when application is being made to the Indian Government for the permit, the exact districts in Tibet through which the Expedition expects to travel should be stated. This year Tingri was not included (Rongshar being in this district). The difficulty was, however, got over by obtaining letters of recommendation from the Dzongpen of Shekar.

## B LOCAL PERSONNEL
## BY CAPTAIN J.G. BRUCE

1. *Personnel of the Expedition.* – This includes Interpreter, Sirdar, Gurkha Quartermaster, Gurkha NCOs, cooks, bootmaker, syces, storeman, mess servants, porters, and locally enlisted coolies.

The selection of these men is of primary importance, since once Darjeeling is left there will be no chance to change anybody.

*Interpreter* must be well educated, presentable in appearance, and above all thoroughly acquainted with the etiquette and customs of the Tibetan 'gentry.' Should in addition be a good all-round man, accustomed to travel and ready to turn his hand to any job.

*Sirdar.* Strictly speaking, is the headman of the porters, but we found it infinitely preferable to deal with the latter direct, or through the Gurkha NCOs. A sirdar such as Gyalgen is worth anything as general utility man, is excellent with transport, can be relied upon to conduct a party of sahibs across Tibet on the return journey, and acts as reserve interpreter when occasion arises.

*Gurkha Quartermaster.* This year we had nobody who quite filled the part. It is suggested for any future expedition that a well-educated and senior Quartermaster-Sergeant from a Gurkha battalion be employed, who will, from the start, take charge of all stores. He will not go beyond the Base Camp, and will at any time be able to give accurate information as to the whereabouts of any article of stores or equipment. The chief characteristic of the Gurkha is his absolute honesty, which admirably fits him for this post.

*Gurkha NCOs* should be selected more with a view to taking charge of Camps I, II and III, than as actual climbers. They should be able to read and write simple Hindustani in Roman characters, so that climbers may communicate with them by this means if required. They must be self-reliant, and capable of taking charge of parties of men unaided.

*Cooks.* Must be able and willing to function up to Camp III. Should be Sherpa, Bhotia, or Lepcha – i.e. Tibetan-speaking – otherwise will have difficulty in getting what they want and in dealing with local vendors. Four cooks are necessary, one at the Base Camp, and one at each intermediate camp.

*Bootmaker.* So far this post has not been satisfactorily filled. A good practical boot-repairer is what is required: he must know how to put alpine nails into boats, and be capable of doing sail-maker's work. Must be fit and strong.

*Private servants* are not necessary. If brought, must be of one of the local races. Indian servants will only be a nuisance in Tibet. Private servants like

Shebbeare's Tippoo are worth their weight in gold, and are a great asset in the mess.

*Porters.* Their selection forms one of the most difficult problems the leader of the Expedition has to solve. Our experience goes to prove that the light, well-proportioned, clean-bred man is the one to take. All carrying porters should be either Sherpas or Bhotias. The Civil Surgeon at Darjeeling will always help with medical examination of all prospective starters. Old hands should only be employed a second time if their record and conduct on the previous occasion were outstandingly good. A few old hands are desirable for obvious reasons, but should be very carefully chosen. Otherwise new keen men are infinitely preferable, and are less likely to play the 'old soldier.'

*Syces.* Mostly drawn from the ranks of the porters. On reaching the Base Camp all except two or three selected syces remain for work on the glacier, while the latter take over the ponies and go down to some neighbouring village until operations are over. These selected syces should be really good men with horses, as they will have all the ponies and mules on their hands for six weeks. They should have a working knowledge of cold shoeing.

*Rates of Pay, etc.* See the records of this year's Expedition for exact amounts. An advance of one month's pay is advisable before leaving Darjeeling, as many men will want to make provision for their families. After that it is asking for trouble to give out any money except the daily ration allowance.

*Family Allotments.* The agent of the Expedition in Darjeeling is shown the individuals to whom allotments are to be paid, and the amounts. The bank is authorised to pay a fixed lump sum to the agent every month for this purpose. This system of family allotments is very popular and much appreciated by all.

2. *Clothing and Equipment.* – Tents for travelling across Tibet are best obtained from Elgin Mills, Cawnpore. They should be light, windproof, and easy to pitch. It is unlikely that porters' tents will fetch a reasonable price on return to India. They will be black with smoke (all cooking being done inside the tent), and however well-made are sure to be considerably torn. It is therefore best to get tents that are calculated to last for just the period of the Expedition and no more.

*Blanket and Sleeping-Sacks.* Patterns as supplied this year were good. Every man in the Expedition should be issued with one blanket either in Kalimpong or Phari. This goes with him *everywhere* up to and including Camp II. A reserve dump of twenty blankets should be maintained at

Camp II. There should be a total of forty eiderdown sleeping-bags for use in Camp III and above. Only twenty were supplied this year, and were not nearly sufficient.

*Jerkins, Leather.* Of very doubtful value – the main drawback being that they have no sleeves. A suggested substitute is a Willesden canvas smock, which would be windproof and light, and would do away with the necessity of the upper portion of the high-altitude overalls as supplied this year.

*Jerseys and Shirts.* Satisfactory, but there should be one per man throughout, and five per cent, spare.

*Boots.* Size 9, five pairs; size 8, ten pairs; size 7, fifty-five pairs. Sizes correct, but they should be made on Gurkha last (most important).

*Puttees, Breeches, Mufflers.* All satisfactory; scale should be as for jerseys above.

*Socks.* Army pattern can be obtained in India. Should be on the scale of five per man who carried loads on the glacier. In addition there should be a reserve of some thicker type of sock, which can be worn over the Army socks at Camp III. These would only be issued to men going high.

*Woollen Gloves* as supplied were much too thin, and wore badly. They should have light leather palms, and be very thick. A large proportion of spares are necessary.

*Windproof Smocks and Trousers (for High Altitude).* See Jerkins, above, ¾ trouser portion also necessary, and should be of stout Willesden canvas.

*Goggles.* Pattern good, and 200 pairs correct amount.

*Crampons.* Only twenty pairs were supplied – not nearly enough (fifty pairs required). They must be much stronger, like the climbers' pattern. The bindings were good, but not enough of them were sent out.

*Sheepskin Gloves.* Good, but double the number necessary (i.e. forty).

*Climbing Boots (High Altitude).* Size 7, ten pairs; size 8, six pairs; size 9, four pairs. Boots excellent. These figures should be doubled. Allow for extra socks.

*Cooking Utensils, Mugs, etc.,* are easily obtained in Darjeeling.

3. *Darjeeling to the Base Camp.* – For this period the porters should be divided up as required to look after the sahibs (two or three each), as syces, and as a permanent mess squad for pitching and striking the mess-tent, etc. It is not advisable to give them loads, except light articles such as cameras, lamps, etc. This is the time to nourish them and get them into first-class condition before they reach the Base Camp. The ration allowance of six annas per diem should be enough as far as Rongbuk, but close supervision is necessary to

ensure that the money is spent on good food, and not on inferior liquor. Occasionally a free extra issue of meat should be made. Daily sick parade under one of the Gurkha NCOs is very important, otherwise men will neglect small ailments which can be put right at once if nipped in the bud. The officer in charge of the personnel should visit the men's tents every evening after the march, preferably when they are feeding. He can then see to the quality of the food, and the health and comfort of them all at the same time. When opportunity offers, instruction in the use of alpine rope and ice axe is advisable.

On the march Gurkha NCOs are best utilised in turn for (a) going ahead with the mess-tent, and seeing it properly pitched in a good place; (b) marching with the money boxes, and handing them over to the sahib responsible for them at the other end; (c) remaining on the old camp site until all baggage has been loaded up, marching behind the last animal of the convoy, looking out for looting by Tibetans on the road, and reporting to one of the transport officers all correct or otherwise on arrival in the new camp. It is suggested that riding ponies be hired locally for fifty per cent NCOs, fifty per cent cooks and servants helping in the mess, and for any sick men. The Interpreter and Sirdar will probably have their own ponies.

4. *Arrival at Base Camp to End of Operations.* – From the time the Expedition reaches Rongbuk the whole personnel should be given free rations and the ration allowance stopped, until the beginning of the return journey. All porters are now pooled, irrespective of what work they have been doing on the march across Tibet, and made up into parties for work on the glacier and on the mountain. It is most important that an adequate reserve of really good men should be formed, and not employed in the initial stages of establishing high camps. Then, as was the case this year, if reverses are met with, and the main portion of the porters become somewhat disheartened, this fresh and staunch party can be called up, and will in all probability by their presence restore the *moral* of the rest.

As regards making Porter NCOs – the experiment of this year is well worth repeating, but it will not be advisable to make the appointments at too early a date. I would suggest that they be made on arrival at the base, and that, in making up the parties of which these Porter NCOs will have to take charge, the latter should be allowed to say whether they are satisfied with the men detailed to them or not.

This year Camps I and II were established entirely by local labour under the supervision of the Gurkha NCOs. This method is thoroughly to be recommended, as it saves the climbers and regular porters from much hard work of a kind that does not improve condition. These local men are obtained through the good offices of the Shekar Dzongpen. The Dzongpen details a 'Chonzay', or steward, to accompany the Expedition from Shekar and to work with it as a kind of agent as long as is necessary. On the last few marches to Rongbuk this Chonzay recruits any able-bodied villagers he can and pays them from the date they actually join us. The agreement this year was that they should carry loads up to, but no farther than, Camp II, find their own food and bedding, and receive four tankas per diem. They seemed to jump at these conditions, with the result that on arrival at the base we had 151 local coolies ready to start for Camp I on the next day. In three days both Camp I and Camp II were fully established, and the coolies dismissed. It was an unexpectedly rapid performance, which may well be repeated another time. These local people must, of course, be treated with every consideration, and now and again be given a good 'blow out' free of charge. Judicious distribution of 'bakshish' and a few cigarettes also helps to keep them going.

The Gurkha NCOs should now be in permanent charge of Camps I and II, and a cook sent to each to cater for climbers passing through. These NCOs must be made responsible for everything that goes on in their camps. Their chief duties are: Despatching convoys with note stating exactly what is in them, receiving convoys from other camps, and checking loads on arrival; demanding stores and rations to keep their own camps fully stocked well before any commodity runs out (unless heavily lectured about this, they will leave it until too late); seeing to the comfort and welfare of any porters or local coolies; personally issuing rations to them; keeping the camp and vicinity clean and tidy. It is advisable that climbers should practise writing messages for these NCOs (Hindustani or Khaskura in Roman characters) and seeing whether they are understood on the march across Tibet and at the Base Camp – later on much may depend on such a message being correctly interpreted. At Camps III and IV, whenever these camps are occupied, there will almost certainly be sahibs present. At Camp III, at any rate, either a Gurkha or a Porter NCO should be placed in charge of all porters' rations and equipment, and should be changed as seldom as possible. All men sleeping at Camp III or above should be provided with an eiderdown sleeping-bag. These bags should be kept in the various camps as camp equipment, and moved up and down as little as possible. They are on no account to be looked upon as individual property.

This year it was decided to burn yak-dung ('shing') up to and including Camp II. Supplies of shing were arranged for through the aforementioned

Chonzay. To keep each camp fully supplied with this commodity is no easy task – this falls to the lot of the sahib in charge of the Base Camp. At Camp III and above Primus stoves or Meta come into use. In each party of porters one cook and one understudy must receive thorough instruction in both these methods of cooking. When on the move the cook should be given the lightest load, and both he and the other members of his party must understand that he is responsible for producing their food at the other end.

For this year's Expedition porters' rations were arranged for as follows: We brought from Darjeeling and put into the Base Camp sixty maunds[2] rice, twenty-seven maunds ata, seven maunds ghoor, two maunds dhal, also chillies, dharria, cloves and tumeric; sixteen pounds tea, cigarettes. A daily scale was worked out for each camp, and NCOs instructed to adhere rigidly to it. The results were very satisfactory. The scale shown below was calculated for twenty days' complete occupation of Camps I to IV by forty men.

| | | |
|---|---|---|
| GUR | 4 oz. × 800 | 200 lb. |
| CHAMFA AND BISCUIT | 24 oz. × 800 | 1,200 lb. |
| SOUP | 4 oz. × 800 | 200 lb. |
| TEA | 2 oz. × 800 | 100 lb. |
| SALT | ½ oz. × 800 | 25 lb. |
| JAM | 4 oz. × 800 | 200 lb. |
| MILK | 4 oz. × 800 | 200 lb. |

N.B. – Meat should be procured from the base through the Chonzay, and sent up the line every four or five days. Meat for higher camps should be cooked in Camp I to economise fuel. Tibetan butter is much appreciated by the men and can be got with the meat. Rice may be substituted for chamfa at Camp I, but it is no use sending it higher on account of its taking so long to cook.

The following is an average table of timings for laden porters under favourable conditions:

| STAGE. | UP. | DOWN. |
|---|---|---|
| Base to I | 3 hrs. | 1 hr. 45 mins |
| I to II | 4 hrs. | 4¼ hrs. |
| II to III | 3 hrs. 45 mins | |

5. *The Return Journey.* – There will presumably be some members of the climbing party who want to get home quickly after the mountain is finished with.

...............................................
2   One maund equals eighty pounds.

Others will probably recuperate for a short time at moderate altitudes before beginning the journey home. It is suggested that only those porters who have done really well on the mountain should be kept with this second party. All the rest should be sent off to Darjeeling at the first opportunity to be paid off by the agent there. The Sirdar should accompany this party, and be placed in charge of the porters, as the Gurkha NCOs will most probably be with the second party. The payment of ration allowance recommences from Rongbuk. On the return journey porters should be made to carry moderate loads – it tends to keep them out of mischief.

6. *Language Difficulties.* – These are great, but are by no means insuperable. Every climber coming to join an Expedition should make himself acquainted with a stock of useful phrases in either Hindustani or Nepalese. He should know the name of every man in the Expedition – it is the first step towards creating an understanding between the sahibs and the porters. In the high camps it is the definite duty of one of the climbers to see to the porters' feeding and welfare generally. This is most important, for these men are tremendously dependent upon their sahibs, particularly on the mountain, and failure to visit their tents and enquire after their well-being will almost certainly result in loss of *moral*, and even in their refusing to go on the next morning. Although on the march across Tibet all these points are seen to by one special officer, it is very essential that all climbers should actively interest themselves in the porters from the start – later the success or otherwise of any climbing party may hinge upon the manner in which the climbers handle their men.

7. *Drink.* – Both on the march out and on the homeward journey drink is the chief vice to guard against. It can be reduced to a minimum, by making no cash payments to the men beyond their daily ration allowance of six annas, and by punishing really heavily the first offenders. When these men get drunk they almost invariably fight with the local inhabitants, and in this way are apt to bring a bad name to the Expedition.

After the first two Expeditions much was said about the honesty of the porters and the Tibetans. They are not so honest that they will not steal or pilfer store boxes, or even sahibs' kit, if there is a reasonable chance of not being found out. This year there was a regrettably large amount of stores and equipment pilfered by our own porters in the glacier camps. Occasional surprise kit inspections are the only way to check this disgraceful behaviour, followed by very heavy punishment for offenders.

## C NOTES ON OFFICE AND MONEY IN TIBET
## BY CAPTAIN J.G. BRUCE

One box the size of a suit-case should be sufficient for all stationery. A few file covers are useful to keep the correspondence on various subjects separate.

A portable typewriter is almost an essential. Remington & Co. have very kindly presented each of the previous Expeditions with a portable machine.

Money is best carried in strong wooden boxes, preferably tin-lined to keep Treasury notes dry, similar in shape and size to the S.A. ammunition box. Four to six will be required according to the amount of hard cash taken. This year we started with Rs.18,000, but found it was not enough and had to have another Rs.6,000 sent up to Shekarjong by Mr John Macdonald. For a future Expedition similar to this year's Rs.23,000 to Rs.25,000 should be taken from Darjeeling, mostly notes – about Rs.500 in silver should suffice. The British Trade Agent at Yatung will arrange for exchanging Tibetan for Indian money. He should be given a fortnight's notice. Between Rs.12,000 and Rs.15,000 worth of Tibetan currency will be required. Indian currency is accepted in Phari, and limited amounts can be exchanged by Nepalese traders in Shekar and Tengri. At the Base Camp Tibetan money is a necessity, and in all out-of-the-way places. As in India, it is very desirable that all payments should be made by, or in the presence of, a sahib. Detailed receipts for amounts paid to Dzongpens for transport, post, etc., should be obtained on the outward journey in case they try to raise the prices against the Expedition on the way home. They are also a useful record for future occasions.

On the march the money-boxes and office are best safeguarded by one or more of the Gurkha NCOs. In camp they should be quite safe in a sahib's tent.

## D MEDICAL NOTES
## BY MAJOR R.W.G. HINGSTON, IMS

1. *Congo Chest.* – Eminently suitable and satisfactory. Suggest the following changes: Omission of one container ergotin, essence ginger, phenacetin (two in chest). Replace the above by additional container of pot. chloras., quin. bihydrochlor., ipecac. with squill.

2. *Case of Surgical Instruments.* – Suitable as supplied.

3. *In addition to above the following equipment is required:*
   (1)   Tabloid first-aid box
   (2)   Snow goggles, 3 pairs
   (3)   Chloroform, 10 ounces
   (4)   Bandages, assorted, 1 gross
   (5)   Castor oil, 8 ounces
   (6)   Magnes. sulph., 4 pounds
   (7)   Rubber tubing, 1 yard
   (8)   Adhesive plaster, assorted, 6 reels
   (9)   Mustard leaves, 12
   (10) Cyanide gauze, 2 pounds
   (11) Boric acid, 8 tins
   (12) Hot-water bottles, 2
   (13) Quin. hydrochlor. gr. 5, 4 bottles (100 tablets in each)
   (14) Aspirin gr. 5, 12 bottles (25 tablets in each)
   (15) Calomel 1 gr., 4 bottles (25 tablets in each)
   (16) Caffeine, 2 bottles (25 tablets in each)
   (17) Mercuric potass. iod., 1 bottle (25 tablets)
   (18) Tabs. cathartic co., 200
   (19) Pil. lead and opium, 200
   (20) Tabs. ipecac., 100
   (21) Pil. ipecac. and squill, 400
   (22) Castor oil, 4 bottles
   (23) Kruschen salts, 2 bottles
   (24) Surgeons' needles, assorted
   (25) Gut ligatures, 1 packet
   (26) Silk ligatures, 1 packet
   (27) Plaster of Paris bandages, 6

(28) Cotton wool, 6 rolls, 1 pound each
(29) Plain lint, 3 rolls, 1 pound each
(30) Gutta-percha fillings for teeth, 1 small box
(31) Santonian pills 1 gr., 50
(32) Man carrier, 3
(33) Lanoline, 6 pots
(34) Vaseline, 6 pots.
(35) Gletshersalbe, 24 tins
(36) Oiled silk, 8 ounces
(37) Rowntree's eucalyptus jujubes, 3 dozen tins
(38) Tinc. iodine, 6 pounds

4. *The following stores sent out with 1924 Expedition not required:*
(1)   Sechehaye pomade
(2)   Milton
(3)   Valentine's meat juice
(4)   Dr Shaw's food
(5)   Case of oxygen-administering apparatus
(6)   Water-steriliser tablets
(7)   Essence of garlic
(8)   Allenbury's diet
(9)   Rucksack
(10) Anusan suppositories

5. *The following should be taken for possible medical use:*
Brand's essence, 4 tins
Cornflower, 4 tins
Bovril, 6 tins
Essence of chicken, 12 tins
Essence of beef, 12 tins
Brandy, 4 bottles
Champagne, 2 bottles

6. *Suitable Equipment for High Camps.* – This should be collected and packed in England. The equipment should be packed in separate boxes marked: 'Medical Camp I,' 'Medical Camp II,' 'Medical Camp III,' 'Medical Camp IV.'

*For 'Medical Camp I':*

Tabl. sod. salicylas gr. 5, 50

Tabl. Dover's powder gr. 5, 50

Tabl. lead and opium gr. 4, 50

Tabl. quin. hydrochlor. gr. 5, 50

Tabl. aspirin gr. 5, 100

Tabl. pot. chloras gr. 5, 100

Tabl. calomel gr. 2, 25

Tabl. soda mint, 50

Tabl. ipecac. and squill gr. 4, 50

Tabl. caffeine gr. 5, 50

Eucalyptus jujubes, 4 tins

Tabl. boric acid gr. 10, 100

Bandages assorted, 12

Lint, 8 ounces

Gauze, 8 ounces

Oiled silk, 1 yard

Plaster, 2", 1 reel

Scissors, 1

Dressing forceps, 1

Scalpel, 1


*For 'Medical Camp II' and 'Medical Camp III', as for Camp I*


*For 'Medical Camp IV':*

Tabl. Dover's powder gr. 5, 25

Tabl. lead and opium gr. 4, 25

Tabl. quin. hydrochlor. gr. 5, 25

Tabl. aspirin gr. 5, 50

Tabl. calomel gr. 2, 25

Tabl. caffeine gr. 5, 50

Bandages, 6

Lint, 4 ounces

Gauze, 4 ounces

Plaster, 2", 1 reel

7. *Notes on the Duties of MO –*

(a) *At Darjeeling.* Preliminary inspection of porters. If official MO not present, the Civil Surgeon should be asked to do this. Porters should be vaccinated, and given suitable treatment for hook-worm.

(b) *On the March.* MO should request Commander of Expedition to appoint NCO in charge of sick parade! The NCO should collect all sick porters one hour after arrival of party in camp and parade them for inspection by MO. Sanitation of camps needs little attention while on the march, since camps are evacuated daily. The quality of the water must, however, be carefully watched. Dysentery is the most dangerous infectious disease likely to be encountered. On no account should unboiled water be taken by any of the British members of the party, unless it comes direct from the snow, glacier or spring without any possibility of contamination. Chemical disinfectants of water are not so satisfactory as boiling.

(c) *At the Base Camp.* The MO is likely to spend some weeks at the Base Camp. He may be employed for general administrative duties there. The sanitation of the Base Camp requires supervision. This is difficult owing to the presence of Tibetans and of porters who are unused to disciplinary measures. Latrines must be established, and steps taken to see that they are used.

(d) *During the Climb.* The place for the MO is Camp III. He should be there before the climbers are likely to return. Two man-carriers and suitable medical equipment should be available in camp. MO should be prepared to accompany sick climbers to the Base Camp.

## E  HIGH CAMPS
## BY T.H. SOMERVELL

1. *Positions of Camps.* – Camps I and II were both in satisfactory positions, and none better or more suitable are likely to be found. In future Expeditions there will probably be someone who was on the 1922 or 1924 Expeditions; failing that, the camp sites will be marked, probably, by the remains of walls and 'sangars.'

Camp III is rather exposed to wind, which in 1924 rendered us very un-comfortable. There is a less exposed place half a mile farther on, almost at the upper limit of the stony moraine on the true left bank of the East Rongbuk Glacier. But a camp here would be very far from Camp II, making a very fatiguing journey for loaded men at this stage; if Camp III be placed at the higher site, a dump for stores (in itself an undesirable thing, inviting theft) would seem to be essential half-way between Camps II and III.

2. *Functions and Size of Camps.* – No. I is a stopping-place only. Whymper tents for four sahibs, and sangars (square shelters of stones about three feet high, that can be roofed in with flies from Whymper tents) or tents for twenty to thirty porters, should be ample accommodation.

No. II is an important camp for porters while the higher camps are being equipped. Whymper tents for four sahibs, and sangars or tents for forty porters were required in 1924.

No. III should contain ten sahibs and twenty to thirty porters. It is the base of operations for the climbing, and often both sahibs and porters have to stay there for a few days or weeks. It must, therefore, be made as comfortable as possible, the sites of tents being well levelled, and walls protecting from the winds being built if necessary. A mess-tent should be provided, and the comfort of both sahibs and porters studied in all possible arrangements: on this will largely depend fitness, and therefore possibility of success.

The tents used in 1924 at this camp were Meade tents, of two sizes: the larger held two sahibs, or at a pinch three; the smaller held three porters. In 1922, No. III Camp had a supply of water all the time it was used. In 1924, no water was available until about May 20, and snow had to be melted. Allow for this possibility in calculating the allowance of fuel. All cooking at this camp is done with Primus stoves.

3. *Fuel.* – Nos. I and II Camps can be supplied with shing, largely carried by Tibetan coolies. It should be insisted on that no other fuel be used at these camps; Primus or other stoves should therefore not be issued below Camp III, except in emergency, and unauthorised use of Meta or liquid fuel should be severely dealt with early.

At No. III Camp, in 1924, only Primus stoves were used, and no other kind; if this is done again, no Meta should be allowed to be used, except in emergency, apart from the small pieces (unnecessary) used for the starting of Primus stoves.

At No. IV Camp, both Primus and Meta stoves were found to be desirable.

At Nos. V and VI Camps, Meta fuel alone is used.

Unna or other cookers for Meta fuel should therefore not be issued below No. IV Camp; if the pans from them are issued at No. III, account should be kept in case they are required for the higher camps.

4. *Bedding.* – No definite rules can be given, but as a guide it may be mentioned that in 1924 the bedding was arranged as follows:

No. I. Two beds in camp. If more are required they must accompany sahibs.

No. II. As No. I.

No. III. All the rest of the bedding should be taken to this camp during its establishment. Much is required higher up, and any not so required will increase the comfort of the camp, a most desirable thing.

No. IV. The beds in 1924 consisted of sleeping-bag, mattress, valise, and carrying-bag. To lighten loads up the steep ascent to this camp it is best to take only the absolute essentials. This is a matter of taste, but personally I am for the sleeping-bag and mattress alone.

Nos. V and VI. To these camps sleeping-bags alone should be taken, on the scale of two per sahib. One can then be used as a mattress, and is always available as an emergency bag in case plans go wrong and someone extra turns up.

For distribution of porters' sleeping-bags see page 270. One per man must be taken to Camps V and VI.

5. *Ice Axes.* – These should not be unpacked until the Base Camp be reached, or they will be broken by being used for digging, prising up stones, etc. When they are issued, it should be at the rate of one per porter; they should

be issued personally to individual porters, who will then be more likely to take care of them.

6. *Crampons.* – These are useful, and in May 1924 were indispensable between Camps II and III, and desirable from III to IV. They are useless higher. They should be issued personally to porters. Plenty of spare bindings must be taken. In 1924 many crampons were broken; stronger ones are essential, and spares should be taken.

7. *Rope.* – When a track is once established rope is not always an essential. On the first journey from Camps II to III and III to IV, rope must be taken, as there are numerous crevasses. But most of these are small or obvious, and afterwards the rope may be dispensed with, but only at the discretion of an experienced sahib. After fresh snow the rope should again be used, until a track is again made. In every ascent from III to IV porters should be roped, unless a really efficient system of fixed ropes is established. The pitons used in 1922 and 1924 were very satisfactory for this purpose, and in many cases porters were allowed down from the North Col unescorted, so complete was the system of fixed ropes. (About 700 feet of fixed ropes were used.)

8. *Other High-Altitude Equipment.* – Goggles must always be worn by all ranks, even on stones or rock, above Camp I. One or two spares should be taken by every party on the glacier.

*Hats.* Soft hats are sufficient for most people as a protection against sunstroke, but anyone who is not sure of himself should wear a topi.

*Grease.* Gletschersalbe before, and lanoline after, exposure to the sun, are found to give the best results as preventatives of sunburn.

Beards are desirable for the same purpose, if obtainable, during the trek across Tibet. Gloves should be worn on the glaciers, or the hands may get badly blistered by the sun.

*Rope Ladder.* This was not taken in 1924, but one 70 feet long had to be made; 120 feet or so of light ladder might be taken. The steep ice cliffs of the North Col are safer than the avalanchy slopes.

*Ladder Bridge (rigid).* The one taken in 1924 was not used, and with luck may be still on the glacier in 1930. It was intended for the crossing of impassable crevasses on the North Col, but there were none.

9. *Scientific Instruments.* – Temperature observations to be of value should be taken simultaneously at various heights. Each camp should therefore have a set of thermometers, and definite times should be fixed upon at which anyone who happens to be at any camp should take observations. Each camp should therefore have a notebook, kept in a definite place, in which such records are to be made, together with particulars of all movements of parties to or from the camp, weather reports, and other observations which may be deemed desirable or pleasing to scientists. Such are records of barometer, katathermometer, etc., badly kept in 1924.

10. *Food.* – At Camps I, II, and III the food is much the same as on the march or at the Base Camp, with this exception, that 'made' dishes are almost impracticable, and the heating of tinned foods constitutes the chief part of the cooking that is done. Usually one's appetite up to Camp III is fairly good, and not very different from what it is at the Base Camp, though heavy meals are undesirable and usually unappetising. Food such as meat (fresh) and scones made at the base and sent up to the higher camps is always welcome. Of tinned foods, variety is important, as far as the tins will allow of it.

Above Camp III, there are two differences:

(1)   Cooking, which is done by sahibs, must be very simple, and economical in fuel if possible.

(2)   Appetite is altered, e.g. meat is not desired except in very small quantities, though it should be eaten as a duty, even if it has ceased to be a source of pleasure.

Suitable foods for these highest camps are:

> Bully beef, tongue, sardines.
> Pemmican, tea; cocoa, café-au-lait in tins (especially the last).
> Biscuits – mixed, ginger-nuts, Plasmon, and Parmena.
> Jam – a variety in small tins.
> Sweets, especially butterscotch and peppermint.
> Force and Grape-nuts, spaghetti in tins, cheese.
> Crystallised fruits, ginger, and French or Elvas plums.

Apart from these, no varieties of food will be found necessary, or (for the matter of that) appetising.

In 1924 there were no cooks above Camp III, but it might be possible to have one at Camp IV, though not higher up than that.

11. *Thermos Flasks.* – These were not found to be essential at or below Camp III. Their uses are twofold above this place:

(1) For storing heated drinks at night, when cooking is inevitable, for use in the early morning when cooking is an avoidable hardship.

(2) For use during the ascent. As a matter of fact, in 1924, the only flask we took with us was forgotten, while we were climbing.

About twelve large and eight small flasks are sufficient for all high camps.


## THE WORKING OF HIGH CAMPS

Tibetan coolies can be hired to do most of the carrying as far as Camp II, both of equipment and of provisions; they will also be able, if a few be kept on throughout the period of climbing, to keep Camps I and II stocked with shing.

Beyond these camps, the Himalayan members of the Expedition have to do all the carrying. Loads for Camp III should not be more than forty pounds. They should be sorted at the base or at Camp II, in order of priority, and go up in this order. A list of all stores required above Camp II must therefore be made, and any deviation from it may have serious results.

Porters at Camp II, of which, during the establishment of Camp III, there should be a large number – say forty – will be able to carry to Camp III and return to II the same day. They should rest all the following day, thus carrying on alternate days. Camp II must therefore be able to accommodate forty porters.

Crampons and rope are desirable above Camp II, as already mentioned. The route from Camp II to Camp III, for a mile or so, is very intricate, as it involves the passage of complicated seracs. The first party must therefore be guided by a sahib with plenty of glacier experience. The route varies considerably from year to year. There is, however, no difficulty when once the route is found, and porters may be allowed unescorted on the glacier, at the discretion of a sahib.

Above Camp III, conditions are very different. The slope of the ice and snow leading to the North Col is considerable, and in places dangerous from avalanche. It is desirable that a party of experienced sahibs make the first journey to the North Col, finding the safest rather than the easiest route, and cutting good steps where necessary; for the Sherpa porter is not an expert mountaineer, especially on ice or snow. The first party should take with them several hundred feet of rope, and some wooden pitons, fixing the ropes in any place where difficulty or danger from avalanche is likely to be met. In this connection the liability of Himalayan snow to avalanche must be remembered; an alpine standard is no use, and caused the loss of seven lives in 1922.

Once the track is established, porters may possibly be allowed on it without a sahib; in 1922 this was done, while in 1924 sahibs accompanied every party going up and most going down. European judgment must decide these points.

Camp IV was in both years pitched on a snow-ledge about fifty feet below the top of the col, on its eastern side. Parties to equip this camp should not consist of more than ten men or so. They can return to Camp III the same day if desired. The question as to whether anyone should sleep on the North Col before the actual climbing operations begin depends on plans for acclimatisation, etc., but on no account should porters be allowed to sleep there without a sahib. They are very superstitious, and may be badly scared.

*Arrangements of Porters above Camp III.* – In 1924 the porters were divided into three parties, each of twelve to fifteen men, and each under an NCO selected from their number. Their duties alternated – e.g. of parties V, W, and X, V carried loads from Camp II to III, W rested at III, X carried from III to IV and return ... on the next day V and X rested while W carried loads from III to IV, and so on, a rest day alternating with a working day in every case. Some arrangement similar to this is advisable.

The equipment of Camp IV, including as it does all the loads for Camps V and VI, necessitates the earmarking and supervision of every single load, whether of equipment or of food, for the three Camps IV, V, and VI. The loads must go up in their proper order, and the whole business must be made to fit in with the plans for the attack on the mountain. Otherwise some essential for a high camp may be missing when wanted at Camp IV.

In 1924 the original plan of campaign was found to be impracticable owing to bad weather. So a shortened and lightened form had to be adopted, a description of which will probably be of service, together with some of the details of our movements and equipment. It must be remembered, however, that this plan is not ideal, but was forced upon us by long delay owing to bad conditions, and represents an attempt to make the maximum 'push' in the minimum time.

*Movements of Climbing Party.* – Day 1. Two sahibs and eight porters go to 25,000 or 25,500 feet, and take with them:

> Three Light Meade tents,
> Eight Sahibs' sleeping-bags,
> Four porters' ditto,
> Food, cookers, and Meta fuel for two days at least.

They pitch two of the tents, one for sahibs, one for porters, and keep four of the porters, sending the remainder back to Camp IV, a journey they will easily manage unescorted. Enough food is cooked for the evening meal, and all liquids required for the morrow are heated and put into thermos flasks.

Day 2. The two sahibs and four porters, or as many as are fit – at least three are required – go on carrying:

> One Light Meade tent,
> Sahibs' sleeping-bags,
> Food, cookers, and Meta fuel for at least twenty-four hours.

In 1924 the next and highest camp was made at 26,700 feet; but it were better if possible to get to 27,200 feet, just under the north-east shoulder of the mountain, before pitching the tent. As soon as this is done, all four porters should return to Camp IV, which they can do in about three hours; for all this to be done in a day it is of course desirable that an early start be made. The rate of progress from 25,000 to 27,000 feet is very slow; eight hours is not bad time. The sahibs cook and eat their food, as at the lower camp, however difficult both processes may seem, and sleep if they can. An early start *must* be made on Day 3, when it is hoped they will ascend the mountain, and descend to Camp VI. Arrived there they will be able to see if they have sufficient energy and time to get to Camp IV. In case these two nights should have to be spent at Camp VI, the provision of food taken up on the previous day must be ample to allow for this eventuality.

*Movements of the Supporting Party.* – In 1922 the first attempt on Everest was made without support, and much discomfort and risk from lack of food and drink resulted. In 1924, therefore, it was arranged that every attempt should be supported by sahibs ready to give help in emergency, and food and drink on the return of the climbers.

Day 1. The party of two sahibs must be at the North Col.

Day 2. They should go to Camp V, with their own food. They will of course find four sleeping-bags and a cooker at Camp V.

They stay the night at Camp V.

Day 3. If this party is merely in support, they should stay at the level of Camp V, in a place where they have the maximum field of vision of the mountain. They should look out for any signals, and in general try to gauge the progress of the climbers above. Their subsequent action, whether as escort down to Camp IV, or of preparing a meal in advance at either Camp V or IV, must depend on circumstances, of course.

If the supporting party is also prepared to attempt the climb in event of the first party not being successful, they must on Day 3 go up with a day's provisions and fuel to Camp VI. In this way they are an ideal support in case of accident or sickness, as they are more on the spot than in the alternative case; if the first party are quite fit, but unsuccessful, they (Party 1) can probably get to a lower camp, leaving Party 2 to try to attain the summit on Day 4. Party 2 will have fortified the other party meanwhile by a meal. In any case they should have some thermoses ready on Day 3 for the support of their friends and themselves.

The question as to whether the supporting party should take porters with them to Camp V depends on whether they think they can carry their food and fuel. This, besides wraps, is all they will have to carry.

*Signals.* – In case of accident, illness, etc., the best signal that the high party can give as an urgent appeal for assistance is probably a magnesium flare. This can be obtained and made to burn for a minute. If the supporters see it at Camp VI or anywhere else they understand that they must at all costs go to the assistance of those above them at the earliest possible opportunity.

A telephone between Camps III and IV is ideal; failing that, Morse signalling with lamps, or flags, at a stated hour or hours each day (say 8 a.m., 2 p.m., and 8 p.m.) known to those at both camps, is the best substitute.

In 1924 a very simple and limited code was devised, signals being given by means of blankets put out on the snow in certain easily visible arrangements.

*Food at High Camps.* – Food for sahibs has already been dealt with. Enough should be taken by both or all parties for a possible extra night. If the first party are well supplied with porters, it were probably better that they should take enough food up to both Camps V and VI to support both parties; the second party will then only have to carry their warm wraps, and will certainly be able to dispense with porters.

Food for Porters: Chamfa in small amount, reinforced by such things as meat and vegetable ration, bully beef, jam, cheese, biscuits, tinned milk: all these latter from the sahibs' food-boxes. Rice is no good up high; it cannot be boiled except with great expenditure of fuel.

*Fuel at High Camps.* – For each camp above Camp III, five to ten packets (fifty to 100 tablets) of the round variety of Meta fuel are sufficient for two whole days for two sahibs. In 1924 we used about twenty tablets at each camp for supper and breakfast. The porters will want a similar amount at Camp V.

## F OXYGEN APPARATUS, ETC
## BY N.E. ODELL

The main points suggested for future apparatus to enable it to be used with the maximum advantage and the minimum encumbrance to the climber are as follows:

Total weight of apparatus must be reduced; a maximum of twenty pounds, and preferably fifteen pounds, if possible. This will necessitate reduction in the weight of the cylinders as well as that of the instruments, and possible modification of the breathing apparatus. If reduction in weight necessitates reduction in size of the cylinders, it may be possible to make up for this by increasing the charging pressure: the latter may mean employing an alloy steel of greater tensile strength than the 'Vibrax' steel used in the 1924 cylinders. The weight of three charged cylinders alone amounted to about twenty-five pounds, giving a total oxygen content (at 120 atmospheres) of about 1,605 litres. In the writer's opinion this is a more than ample margin of gas to be carried at a time, since at a consumption of as much as two litres per minute – a rate found to be by no means necessary, even at 27,000 feet – that amount would sustain the user for a period of at least twelve hours. If adequate arrangements are made to provide dumps of reserve cylinders on the mountain, it should not be necessary for each climber to carry more than two cylinders of the existing capacity. Not merely are three cylinders of the present dimensions cumbersome, but their weight in addition seriously interferes with the climber's balance, even on the comparatively easy rocks of Mount Everest.

With regard to the breathing apparatus, the many faulty parts and leaky joints found to exist in every set sent out in 1924 led to our building up the parts afresh and modifying the system of supporting them. An attempt was made to do away with the rigid arm supporting the instruments, that passed over the left shoulder, since it proved to be a considerable encumbrance. Instead, the instruments – i.e. flow-meter alone – was connected up with the rubber tubing conveying the gas from the cylinders to the mouthpiece, which passed under the right arm. It was suspended from the coat in front in a visible and comfortable position. The pressure gauge was connected close to the mouths of the cylinders on the back, and the rate of flow regulated by a needle-valve close beside it, accessible to the right hand. In this way the total weight was reduced considerably, and the only hampering of movement was caused by the lower ends of the cylinders, which were in the way when going down steep rocks facing outwards. This arrangement avoids a long length of high-pressure tubing, but the gauge can only be read by someone else at the wearer's back, an obvious disadvantage. It was necessarily an improvised arrangement, but an apparatus designed somewhat on these principles should have considerable advantage in weight and convenience over the older and heavier pattern.

But it is earnestly hoped that a far lighter and handier apparatus may be evolved in the near future, preferably employing oxygen in the liquid state. If such could be designed in conjunction with a suitably light power plant for the production of liquid oxygen near the mountain, the problem of respiration on Everest and other high summits would seem to be near approaching a solution.

*Cookers.* – What was known to the 1924 Expedition as the Unna cooker – manufactured under Mr Unna's direction by Messrs The Meta Co., in Switzerland – proved at high altitudes to give the best results. Its especial advantage was that it could be used with 'Meta' as fuel as well as in conjunction with Primus stoves. But it still should have two saucepans that nest into one another, instead of the single one provided. For this arrangement was the chief convenience in the similar stove of less general utility which was designed by Dr Longstaff for this Expedition. Since the heating capacity of a saucepan is directly proportional to the area of the bottom which is exposed to the flame, it would be advisable to have the pans of slightly greater diameter in proportion to their height. Saucepans of rather larger capacity than three litres could with advantage be provided, so long as the weight and bulk be not unduly increased; the total weight, with accessories, of the 1924 Unna cookers was about 3 ¼ pounds only.

The Duralumin stand provided was of special advantage from the point of view of safety, when the stove was used in the confinement of a tent, often standing on a sleeping-bag.

About fifteen such cookers of the above pattern should be ample.

*Primus Stoves.* – The large collapsible pattern of these stoves were found to be most satisfactory, and ample spares and accessories were provided and were found most necessary. In order to obtain sufficient pressure on pumping at high altitudes, it is essential that the clearance space in the pump chamber be reduced to a minimum, or filled in altogether with a washer on the pump rod. The latter is probably preferable. There need be little fear of danger from bursting of the container by excessive pumping, since all containers are tested to eighty pounds per square inch or more.

The silent type of burner is essential: all others, even those which were specially designed for high altitudes – of the 'roarer' pattern – were found to be quite unreliable.

A dozen of these stoves in all should be sufficient.

*Fuel.* – The fuel used in 1924 consisted chiefly of one part of petrol to two of paraffin. A half-and-half mixture of the two was also tried, and in Primus stoves was found to give equally satisfactory results; this was as far as the altitude of the North Col, 23,000 feet.

It is desirable that mixtures of these fuels, purchased in India, be made up in tins and sealed before the start of the Expedition, the tins being packed in sealed cases for the high camps. But since paraffin alone is required for use in lamps during the march across Tibet, it is preferable that only, say, seventy-five per cent of the mixture required be actually made up beforehand, so that any surplus of paraffin left over after the climbing is done may be available for the mess lamps.

*Meta.* – This solid fuel was satisfactory in every way, and was used with very good results in all camps above 23,000 feet, where it was the only fuel used. No trouble was experienced in igniting it, nor did it seem to fall off in calorific value in the very dry atmosphere in which it was used – a possibility cited by the manufacturers. Little use was made of the small Meta sticks intended for starting Primus stoves, this being done usually by means of their own liquid fuel.

*Issuing of fuel* should always be under the supervision of a sahib, who should have the tins of it in full view of his tent, and should see that every precaution is taken to husband it.

## G TRANSPORT
## BY E O SHEBBEARE

*Food Cases.* – This year the cases varied slightly in size and shape, according to their contents, so that each should weigh just forty pounds. This is convenient and should be repeated in any future expedition.

The contents of each case (with a few exceptions) were all of one kind. This involved the opening and repacking of numerous cases at Kalimpong to make up the high-altitude boxes, as well as on the road to supply the mess. Frequently several cases of the same commodity were opened because the one originally broached could not readily be found when wanted. Thus the transport officer had in his charge a mixture of opened and unopened cases.

Anyone armed with a screwdriver could open any case.

Padlock cotters, by which any case could be locked up, were supplied with every fourth one, but, as was inevitable to avoid hopeless confusion, all keys were of one pattern. No real security therefore resulted from this precaution.

I am of the opinion that any scheme involving the opening and reclosing of cases which are then returned to the general store pile makes pilfering easy.

The scheme suggested for the future is to have the cases packed in three different ways in London, namely: (1) Marching cases for the journeys across Tibet, (2) high-altitude cases, and (3) reserve cases. In (1) and (2) each case would contain a sufficient ration of all kinds of food for a given number of 'men-days.' In (3) each case would contain one commodity only as at present to be used to supplement deficiencies in (1) and (2).

Variety in diet will be achieved by the scheme suggested in the mess secretaries' note: that of having A, B, C cases.

'Marching cases' will be issued to the mess secretary as required. Each will contain a printed list of its contents from which he can strike off the stores as expended. In the event of an excess of any kind of food it can either be put into the expense boxes or, as one kind is sure to predominate throughout, given away. The cost of carrying unnecessary stores is greater than their value. In the event of a deficiency the party can either go without the particular kind of food until the next case is opened, or the deficiency made up from the 'reserve cases.' This latter course would only be followed on the outward march in exceptional cases. 'Reserve cases' so broached would not be kept with the unopened ceases, but put under the charge of the Quartermaster.

The forty-pound cases will all be strapped together in pairs on the march by means of one of the several makes of sealing hoop-iron or wire now on the market. This strapping should be put on lengthways as well as breadth-ways. The transport officer will keep a reserve of strapping and sealing apparatus at hand as it may be necessary to separate the loads into forty-pound ones in case of weak transport or difficult fords.

Transport drivers are accustomed to build sangars out of the cases during the march. This is, I think, unavoidable in windy weather. There is no objection to this practice provided only un-broached cases are used.

Cases should be numbered on all sides, but especially on the recessed ends as was done on the 1922 Expedition. This was not done this year, and the omission led to much unnecessary man-handling.

*Store-Book.* – The store-book supplied by the packers was useful for finding out in which case a given article could be found, but it did not work in the other direction, that is as a means of finding out what a case of given number contained. It was necessary, therefore, to prepare a serial list in Kalimpong. This should have been done by the packers as was done in 1922. The serial list is sent as a sample of what is required, but could be improved upon.

*Payment of Transport.* – It is customary in Tibet to pay for transport in advance to the Dzongpen through whom it is obtained, and not to pay the drivers direct. The Dzongpens have, however, on rare occasions been willing to allow a slightly lower rate in consideration of baksheesh paid to the drivers later, and this system has worked well.

*On the March.* – At each stage where transport is changed it is necessary for the transport officer to remain behind to see that all loads are cleared and to insist on sufficient animals being produced. When there is no change of animals it is sufficient if an NCO sees the last of the transport off. On all marches one NCO goes ahead with the mess-tent, the remaining NCOs accompanying the treasure chest. They should have six or seven porters with them in the event of any attempt at robbery on the way.

*Mules and Ponies.* – Unless any other member of the Expedition better fitted by his knowledge of horsemastership undertakes the care of the mess mules and Expedition ponies, this work will devolve on the transport officer.

*Calcutta to Phari.* – Although it is probably best for all members of the Expedition to collect in Darjeeling, nothing beyond what they actually require for their short stay there should be taken. Everything else – personal baggage and Expedition equipment of all sorts – should be booked direct from Calcutta to Kalimpong Road station.

All baggage, stores and equipment must now be divided into two categories: (a) the portion that will not be required until Phari or later; and

(b) the portion actually wanted on the march from Kalimpong to Phari, or Kampa Dzong, if the climbers go via Gangtok and Lachen.

This is where the contractors mentioned on page 266 come in. The contractor now takes over from the transport officer (who should be living in Kalimpong for this part of his work) all equipment, etc., in category (b), and despatches what he takes over in his own time to Phari, the latest date by which these consignments must arrive being fixed in the contract.

Category (a), equipment, etc., is collected by the transport officer in Kalimpong, and is ready to accompany the members of the Expedition by whatever route they march.

## H  THE MESS
## BY BENTLEY BEETHAM

Experience in 1924 has shown that stores will be stolen on the march, in camp, and especially at dumps, whenever opportunity offers – the Tibetan's good name for honesty is gone: stores must be safeguarded as much as possible. This may be done best by having as few boxes opened and in use at a time as possible. Once a case is broached its contents are in danger.

No doubt in future the special cases for high camps will all be sent ready packed from London instead of being made up in Tibet; this will save an immense amount of case-opening later. It would also be a great convenience to both the mess secretary and the transport officer if boxes containing a complete supply of food for so many days were put up in London for use on the march. These should be numbered A1, A2, A3 – B1, B2, B3 – C1, C2, C3, etc. The contents of all A cases would be alike, but different from those in B, C, or D. They would be used in the order, A1, B1, C1, D1; A2, B2, etc. By this method constant repetition of the same food (the chief source of grousing and lack of appetite in the mess) would be avoided. The number of 'expense boxes' required by the mess would be greatly reduced. One would be used for sundries, cooking materials, etc. Into a second would be emptied the contents of one of the lettered cases as issued. Two or three others only would be required to hold a reserve of general foods with which to use up the remnants of the lettered cases; as even with the nicest calculation it is impossible to ensure that the various items would be consumed simultaneously.

*Water.* – Too much attention can hardly be given to this. In each of the three Expeditions members have suffered from dysentery, generally contracted before the Tibetan boundary was crossed. Native cooks are utterly indifferent to the quality of water – the nearest is that which they use. Unless its source is obviously uncontaminated it should only be drunk after boiling, as tea, etc. This precaution is useless if milk is allowed to be made with unboiled water.

Contrary to Alpine tradition the muddy, turbid water of glacial streams apparently may be used without irritation to the lining of the stomach. A 'clean' drink is often the most difficult thing for the mess to provide, and one has a longing, almost a craving, for fresh water. It is suggested that a future expedition take a couple of pakhals or collapsible chaghals, and that these be filled whenever a good spring is passed.

Champagne is certainly not worth its weight: a little whisky or port may be. A couple of Sparklet syphons would be good. Lemonade powders, etc., are excellent.

*Sugar, Milk, Jam, and Tea.* – These are the things which disappear most rapidly; their consumption should be specially watched.

*Candles, Matches, Toilet Paper, Soap (Toilet and Washing).* – All these should be readily accessible in camp.

*Potatoes.* – Potatoes may be bought from July onwards in Tibet and obtained from Solah Khombu in Nepal from the middle of May. They form a very valuable addition to the dietary.

*Fresh Supplies.* – The buying of eggs, fowls and sheep whenever opportunity offers is to be encouraged. In many places where the killing of animals is prohibited they may be purchased alive – their subsequent history is not enquired into.

The cook's method is to kill immediately before cooking. Meat will keep weeks in Tibet, and is the better for hanging.

*Local Wild Products.* – In the warm valleys a good cook knows excellent substitutes for spinach (nettles and other plants); many fungi, though inferior to the English mushroom, help the stew; young bamboo shoots are delicious cooked with cheese.

*Light.* – The four Kranzow lamps taken in 1924 proved ideal. Paraffin, however, is a constant source of danger in the cook-house. The slightest taste may ruin a meal. Paraffiny fingers will taint the whole canteen. Moreover, unless a strict check is kept on the oil it is sure to be used for fire-lighting.

*Shing.* – The payments for shing (yak-dung) may be represented as being relatively enormous – as much as seven maunds (a quarter of a ton) has been put down for one day's consumption! In the latter part of the 1924 Expedition a fixed rate of two rupees a day was allowed where shing had to be bought, and though this is obviously excessive, contentment in the cook-house was thus cheaply purchased. The strictest honesty in the East demands a hidden commission on every purchase, the percentage of which is liable to grow at an alarming rate if not checked. Bow to the inevitable, countenance what you deem to be reasonable, but prune early with a firm pencil anything excessive. Do not attempt to argue, simply prune. Fire-stoves and a large black yak's-hair tent to serve as a kitchen can usually be hired at the camping ground for about ten annas; failing this, two Whymper flies may serve.

*Mess-Tent.* – This should be sent off as early as possible before breakfast every morning, being carried by the mess mules, which are quite distinct from the general transport. The tables are left. Breakfast in the open may be chilly in April at 16,000 feet, but comfort is less required at the beginning of the day than at the end after a long march. Moreover, the mornings are usually sunny.

Immediately after breakfast the rest of the mess equipment should be got away, the cook leading on a pony with tiffin complete, so that a meal may be actually ready on the arrival of the sahibs. Nothing is more trying than a long wait for food at the end of a trek. If the day's march is long, pocket tiffin will be required *en route* (best take it always): suitable provision should be made for this – potted fish and meats in small tins, ships' or similar biscuits, chocolate, dried fruits, etc. *Note.* – Any one kind of chocolate soon palls; a variety would cost no more and occupy the same space – plain, nut, milk, nut-milk, Bitro, vanilla, coffee, etc.

*Base Camp.* – Catering here should be on a generous scale. Climatic conditions are tending to debilitate the climbers; the mess should try to counteract this. Parties and individuals coming down from high altitudes should find every possible comfort at the base.

The best cook should be retained here. While the actual climbing is in progress nearly all the personnel will be in the various high camps, and the work at the base will be correspondingly light. The cook's time may then be most profitably employed in making fresh scones, sausage-rolls, etc., and in cooking potatoes, supplies of which may be sent up the line daily, where they are much appreciated, little cooking other than the warming up of tinned food being possible in the high camps.

*Mess Servants.* – Only mess servants should be allowed in the cook-house – hangers-on are a constant source of leakage.

The cook should present to the mess secretary every night (a) a list of the stores used during the day, (b) an account of any petty expenses incurred. For the latter it is convenient to give the cook an advance of say fifty rupees at a time.

The canteen should be carefully checked some days previous to arrival at Darjeeling, and again there.

# INDEX

*pl. or pls. denotes plate number*

physiological problems
  acclimatisation at altitude 155–156, 159, 202–204
  after-effects 204–205
  alterations in breathing 191–193
  circulation 193–196
  coughs and sore throat 61, 70, 86, 88, 187
  dysentery 28, 35, 171, 172, 267
  gastro-intestinal symptoms 198–199
  glacial lassitude 184–185, 201
  mental effects 199–200
  muscular power 196–197
  oxygen use debate 154–155, 158–159, 202
  pain 198
  palatable food 155, 159
  sleep 200
  special senses 197–198
  sunburn 168
  sustainable pace 153–154
  tummy upsets 168
porters
  Camp IV and onwards discussed 74–75
  Camp IV, porter rescue 70–74
  camp organisation (1924) 56–57, 176–177, pl.24
  carrying abilities 49, 141, 202
  climber admiration 28, 46, 148–149
  climbing abilities caution 66, 153
  drink and theft 19, 268, 275, 295
  duties and terms of work 45–46
  effective organisation 153, 157, 267–268, 271–272
  final redistribution 119, 274–275
  high camp organisation 281–283, 288
  high camp working 285–288
  injuries and sickness 55, 56, 70, 85–86, 100, 185
  language difficulties 120–121, 265, 275
  low morale, Camp II to III 51–52, 53, 55, 180–182
  physical limits reached 83–84, 107
  recruitment 15, 33, 48, 265–256, 269–270
  religious beliefs 149
  sociable supervision 39–40, 48
  summit attempt 98–99, pl.44
  'Tigers', Camp V ascent 77–78, 81, 83–84, 85–86
Puchung Chu 140–141
Pugh, Griffith ix
Pusi La 127, 134–135, 232, 251

## R

Rawlinson, Henry, Lord 13
Rongbuk 42, 50, 228
Rongbuk Glacier
  Camp I 47
  Camp II to III in cold winds 50–53, 179–181
  Camp III, poor conditions 53–56
  camp organisation 45–50, 176, pl.25
  geology 230, 232
  glacial features 240–241, 243, 246–250, pls.60–61
  Gurkha led surveys 50
Rongbuk Monastery 41–42, 56, 57–58, 123–124, 149
Rongbuk Valley 41–42, 119–120, 122–123, 177
Rongli-Chu 19, 164, pl.3
Rongshar Valley 118, 127, 251
Royal Geographical Society 3

## S

Scott, Doug ix–xi
Semchumbi 81, 85, 86–87
Shamsherpun, Lance-Naik 34, 47, 56, 57
Sharto 136, pl.15
Shebbeare, Edward
  acclimatisation 204
  ascent discussions 52, 74–75, 76
  Mallory's opinion of 163, 165
  personal qualities 15
  transport supervision 27, 33, 80, 114, 118–119, 142, 292–294, pl.71
  venture into Nepal 131, 132
Shekar Dzong 37–38, 139–140
sherpas 6, 7, 15, 19, 33, 48, 49–50
Sichu 125–126, pl.10
Sikkim 19–20
Somervell, Howard
  acclimatisation x, 4–5, 204, 261–262
  appetite changes 198
  ascent discussions 30, 174
  Camp III ascent 50, 52
  Camp IV ascent 67–68
  Camp IV, porter rescue 70–74, 187
  Camp V and VI ascents 81–87
  descent to Base Camp 93, 98
  experienced mountaineer 16–17
  Gaurisankar sighting 133–134
  high camp organisation 281–285

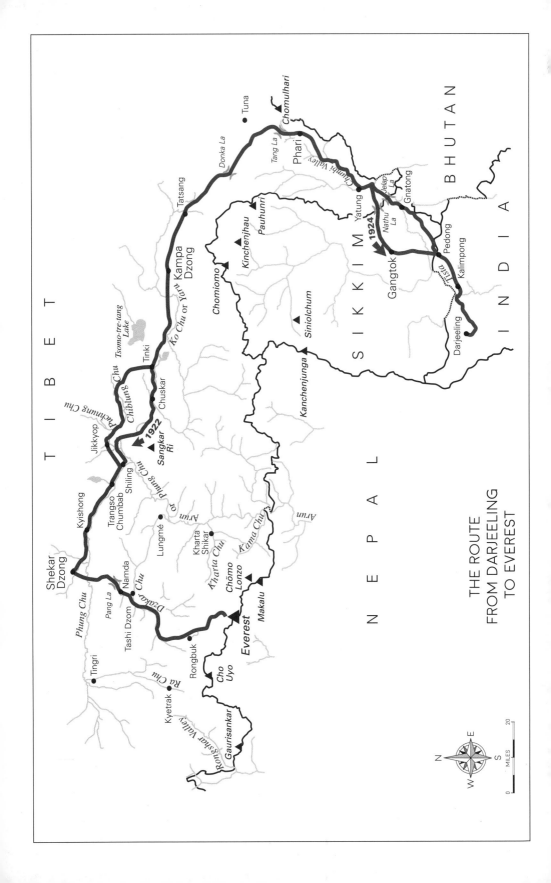

THE ROUTE
FROM DARJEELING
TO EVEREST